McNae's Essential Law for Journalists

McNae's essential law for journalists

Twenty-first Edition

Mark Hanna Mike Dodd

OXFORD UNIVERSITY PRESS

OXFORD
UNIVERSITY PRESS

Great Clarendon Street, Oxford, OX2 6DP,
United Kingdom

Oxford University Press is a department of the University of Oxford. It furthers the University's objective of excellence in research, scholarship, and education by publishing worldwide. Oxford is a registered trade mark of Oxford University Press in the UK and in certain other countries

Impression: 1

British Library Cataloguing in Publication Data

Data available

Library of Congress Cataloging in Publication Data

Data available

ISBN 978–0–19–960869–0

Printed in Great Britain by
Ashford Colour Press Ltd, Gosport, Hampshire

To my wife Linda, my son Rory, my father Michael and my mother Mary

M.H.

For my wife, Sarah, and sons, William and Robert, without whom this would not have been possible

M.P.D.

Preface

The closure of the *News of the World*, Britain's biggest-selling Sunday newspaper, in 2011 came about as a result of further disclosures about the phone-hacking activities of some of its former staff. The newspaper closed although most of its journalists were not accused of any responsibility for the hacking scandal. In this respect, the majority paid with their jobs for the 'sins' of a few. As we explain in chapter 2 and on this book's website, www.mcnaes.com, those revelations led to the Government establishing an inquiry, chaired by Lord Justice Leveson, with a brief to examine the culture, practices and ethics of the press.

As this, the twenty-first edition of *McNae* entered its production process, the Leveson inquiry had started work. Its recommendations are expected to seek to change what Lord Justice Leveson sees as wrong in the culture of the UK media, and, presumably, how it is regulated, or regulates itself. The hacking scandal itself has already led to additional emphasis from media organisations' managements on the need for journalists, including freelancers, to meet ethical and regulatory standards when news-gathering.

To reflect this, the structural innovations in this edition of *McNae* include separate chapters (2 and 3) to introduce the standards in the Editors' Code of Practice and the Ofcom Broadcasting Code more fully and earlier in the book than in previous editions. Honouring these standards is the hallmark of good journalism, but it is also important – particularly at a time when journalistic practices are under such close scrutiny – that in many circumstances they also reflect and reinforce the law. This structural change also reflects the decision of the National Council for the Training of Journalists (NCTJ) to extend its law exams to include the Ofcom code.

Other changes will be apparent to regular users of the book. For example, we have covered new law, recent cases and changes in journalistic practice – such as the new opportunities to 'tweet' reports of court cases. We also record, in chapter 18, how the increasingly online nature of modern journalism has led, since the previous edition, to the first case of contempt of court arising from website publication by media organisations.

This edition follows the practice in the twentieth edition of using the term 'media organisations' to encompass the publishers of newspapers, magazines and websites, and broadcasters. The term is not wholly satisfactory, especially where the point being made also applies to freelance journalists or to any individual 'blogger' or 'tweeter', but we felt it remains the most practical option to reflect the technological convergence in how journalism is published.

The amount of law affecting UK journalism continues to grow, and we are using mcnaes.com to provide content for which there was no space in the book. For example, mcnaes.com supplements the explanation in chapter 13 of the complex law governing reporting of family courts. The site will also be used for updates, such as on legislation arising from the Government's review of defamation law.

We are keen to hear what you think of this edition and of the mcnaes.com site. We particularly hope that both project the fact that journalism remains an exciting, varied career, that most of its practitioners pride themselves on being ethical and law-abiding, and that they can and do 'make a difference', not least in their watchdog role of exposing wrongdoing and reporting on and analysing the workings of society. It is worth noting that the extent of phone-hacking by some journalists, or private investigators working for them, was revealed to the public by other journalists, not by the original police investigation.

If you wish to contact us, our email addresses are given below.

This book covers the law in England, Wales and Northern Ireland which it is essential for journalists to know. A chapter on mcnaes.com provides an introduction to Scottish law most relevant to journalists.

Acknowledgements

As authors we are grateful to the NCTJ's chief executive Joanne Butcher, its media law examinations board and NCTJ staff for support and suggestions as we wrote this edition. We owe a great debt to Olivia Rowland who was publishing manager at the Higher Education Department of Oxford University Press for her ideas, guidance and patience.

We also owe thanks to the following people who helped us by making suggestions for content, including those who read drafts of chapters or responded to our queries when we sought to draw on their expertise: Amanda Ball, the NCTJ's chief examiner, a senior lecturer at Nottingham Trent University; Peter Berry, broadcast journalist and journalism educator; Sarah Dave, news editor of the *Reading Post*; Jackie Errigo, chief examiner of the NCTJ media law examinations board, a senior lecturer at Brighton University; Gary Hudson, a senior lecturer at Staffordshire University; Marie Kinsey, chair of the Broadcast Journalism Training Council, a senior university teacher at Sheffield University; Keith Mathieson, a partner at Reynolds Porter Chamberlain; Heather Rogers QC, of Doughty Street Chambers; Richard Royle, a senior lecturer at the University of Central Lancashire; Kevin Steele, the senior legal trainer at the BBC College of Journalism; Hugh Tomlinson QC, of Matrix Chambers; Simon Westrop, Head of Legal, Newsquest Media Group.

We are grateful too that Tom Welsh and Walter Greenwood, who were authors of *McNae* for more than 30 years, and David Banks, co-author of the nineteenth and twentieth editions, agreed to act as honorary consultants for this edition, and that Walter kindly took the lead in writing its chapter 37 on Northern Ireland law.

We also thank the Judicial College for permitting use of diagram material, the Press Standards Board of Finance (Pressbof) for permitting reproduction of the Editors' Code of Practice and Ofcom for allowing us to cite extracts from its Broadcasting Code.

We owe thanks too to our employers – in Mark's case, the Department of Journalism Studies, Sheffield University, and in Mike's the Press Association – for their support and encouragement.

The main body of the text of this edition was completed in early October 2011, but it was possible to add some late news until January 2012.

Mark Hanna, chair of the NCTJ media law examinations board
Email: *M.Hanna@sheffield.ac.uk*
Mike Dodd, Legal Editor, Press Association
Email: m_dodd@msn.com

This book bears the name of its first author, the late Leonard McNae, who was Editor of the Press Association's Special Reporting Service. Its first edition was published in 1954.

Summary Contents

Detailed Contents

On www.mcnaes.com

Late News

Journalists can 'tweet', email or text reports from courts without permission

Journalists who want to use 'live, text-based communications' to report court cases no longer need to ask the court's permission.

In December 2011 the Lord Chief Justice, Lord Judge, issued new guidance on journalists using internet-connected laptops or mobile phones in courts to email or text court reports, or to post them directly on the internet, including on Twitter.

Interim guidance issued in 2010, and an amendment in October 2011 to Rule 16.9 of the Criminal Procedure Rules (see chapter 11) had specified that anyone wanting to use such devices would in each case need to apply for the court's permission. Rule 16.9 also said anyone wanting to apply should give advance notice to each party in the case and to any other person the court specified.

But in his new guidance Lord Judge said that journalists and legal commentators no longer needed to apply for permission, though members of the public should do so.

The guidance says: 'It is presumed that a representative of the media or a legal commentator using live, text-based communications from court does not pose a danger of interference to the proper administration of justice in the individual case. This is because the most obvious purpose of permitting the use of live, text-based communications would be to enable the media to produce fair and accurate reports of the proceedings. As such, a representative of the media or a legal commentator who wishes to use live, text-based communications from court may do so without making an application to the court.'

The guidance, which applies to 'court proceedings which are open to the public and to those parts of the proceedings which are not subject to reporting restrictions' adds that 'an unobtrusive, hand held, silent piece of modern equipment for the purposes of simultaneous reporting of proceedings to the outside world as they unfold in court is generally unlikely to interfere with the proper administration of justice.'

But it also makes clear that a court can decide to forbid 'at any time' all use of such devices. It also stresses that photography in court is still forbidden, saying: 'Any equipment which has photographic capability must not have that function activated.'

The full text of the guidance is at: www.judiciary.gov.uk/Resources/JCO/Documents/Guidance/ltbe-guidance-dec-2011.pdf.

As he handed down his guidance to reporters, Lord Judge said: 'Twitter as much as you like from today' (*Media Lawyer,* December 14, 2011).

Televising of Crown court trials will be limited to judges' duties

Justice Secretary Ken Clarke told the House of Commons that his proposals to allow filming of Crown court cases would not lead to footage of defendants making 'a theatrical display in the witness box'. He said: 'We are talking about judgments and what is said as part of his official duties by the judge, and at this stage I am not contemplating going any further' (*Hansard,* column 650, December 13, 2011). See chapter 11 for further detail of these proposals.

Abolition of committal hearings for either-way cases

Mr Clarke announced in December 2011 that committal hearings for ***either-way*** cases are to be phased out, to make the justice system more efficient (*Hansard,* column 55WS, December 8). If a magistrates court decides an either-way case is too serious for ***summary*** trial, or the defendant wants a jury trial, it will be 'sent for trial' to a Crown court as indictable-only cases already are, without magistrates considering whether there is a prima facie case. See chapter 7 for detail of committal hearings and the sending procedure.

The reform is to be achieved by bringing into force Schedule 3 of the Criminal Justice Act 2003. The new system is due to be introduced in some regions in April 2012, and subject to a satisfactory assessment, will be rolled out in all regions over the next year.

Although earlier changes in the law meant that it became rarer for evidence to be aired at committal hearings, their abolition will further reduce the media's opportunity to hear courtroom references to evidence in a newsworthy case before it reaches Crown court, and thus glean knowledge of the background to a case.

Mr Clarke did not mention amendment to reporting restrictions for preliminary hearings at magistrates courts.

But contemporaneous media reports of such hearings will normally remain restricted. Schedule 3 of the 2003 Act contains provision to insert a new section 52A into the Crime and Disorder Act 1998, creating a set of reporting restrictions similar to those in section 8 of the Magistrates' Courts Act 1980. Section 52A will repeal the older restrictions, which were designed for the committal procedure being phased out. See chapter 7 for detail of committal hearings and section 8 of the 1980 Act. Section 52A covers 'allocation' (that is, mode of trial) hearings and 'sending for trial' hearings in magistrates courts, whether the latter concern either-way or indictable-only cases. It also covers any preliminary hearing which occurs before these stages.

The section 52A restrictions will only allow reporting of:

- the name of the court, and the name(s) of the magistrate(s);

- the name, age, home address and occupation of the accused;
- in the case of an accused charged with a 'serious or complex' fraud, any 'relevant business' information' – see below;
- the offence or offences, or a summary of them;
- the names of counsel and solicitors engaged in the proceedings;
- where the proceedings are adjourned, the date and place to which they are adjourned;
- arrangements as to bail;
- whether legal aid is granted.

Under section 52A, if a sole defendant asks for these restrictions to be lifted the magistrates court will decide whether to do this (whereas under the 1980 Act the making of the request has automatically led to its restrictions being lifted). Under section 52A the court also will have power 'of its own motion' to lift these section 52A restrictions, even if no such request is made by a defendant.

If any defendant objects to the restrictions being lifted, the court must decide if it is in the interests of justice to lift them. Even if the restrictions are lifted, reporting of any argument in court about that decision is not allowed until the conclusion of all proceedings in the case (for example, the conclusion of a Crown court trial). The restrictions, if they have not been lifted before then, automatically expire at that conclusion.

The 'relevant business information' which the media can report from preliminary hearings at magistrates courts, when the section 52A restrictions are in force, will be the same as that which can be reported from Crown court hearings for such charges to be dismissed. See chapter 8. Schedule 3 of the 2003 Act also contains provision to abolish the 'transfer' procedure used in magistrates courts for serious fraud cases and other types of case involving alleged offences against children. This procedure is outlined in chapter 7. When the schedule is in force, these types of case will also be 'sent for trial' to Crown court, a procedure similar to transfer.

Teachers given anonymity

Proposals to give lifelong anonymity to teachers accused of committing criminal offences against children at their schools became law in November 2011 when the Education Act 2011 received the Royal Assent.

The reform will make teachers the first group of people in British legal history to have automatic anonymity when they are accused of a criminal offence.

The anonymity ends if the teacher is charged with an offence, or a court agrees to an application that anonymity should be lifted in the interests of justice.

The anonymity also ends if the Education Secretary publishes information about the person who is the subject of the allegation, in connection with an investigation or decision relating to the allegation, or if the General Teaching Council for Wales publishes information about the individual in connection with an investigation, hearing or decision on the allegation. The individual teacher may waive his or her anonymity, by giving written consent to be identified. But the consent is not valid if it is proved that there was unreasonable interference with his/her peace or comfort to obtain it.

The anonymity provisions are in the Act's section 13, which will amend part of the Education Act 2002. When this section is brought into force it will be unlawful to identify a teacher who has been accused of assaulting or sexually abusing a child at his or her school if that teacher has not been charged with a criminal offence – even if the accusation is referred to in public, for example at an Employment Tribunal hearing at which the teacher claims unfair dismissal. It is not clear when section 13 will come into force – section 82(5) states: 'Before making an order bringing section 13 into force, the Secretary of State must consult the Welsh Ministers.' Publication of anything which identifies a teacher who is alleged to have committed an offence against a pupil at his or her school is punishable on summary conviction by a fine of up to £5,000.

But it is a defence for anyone accused of publishing such information to show that at the time he or she was not aware, and did not suspect or have reason to suspect, that the publication included the information in question, or that he or she was not aware, and did not suspect or have reason to suspect that the allegation had been made.

PCC criticises failure to retain contemporaneous notes from inquest

The Press Complaints Commission has stressed that contemporaneous notes need to be retained as evidence for the accuracy of reporting.

It ruled that *The Citizen*, Gloucester, breached clause 1 (Accuracy) of the Editors' Code of Practice when reporting an inquest into a man's suicide. The man's mother complained about the coverage. The PCC said the newspaper was unable to corroborate most of the information which was challenged, because the reporter's notes were transcribed directly on to a computer without retaining the originals.

The PCC said errors about the mother's personal details, together with the newspaper's inability to corroborate a quote attributed to her, represented a lack of 'sufficient care', but the newspaper had already offered a sufficient form of remedial action by offering to publish a correction. PCC Director Stephen Abell said: 'The Commission has made clear the lesson it expects the industry to take from this important adjudication: the need to retain contemporaneous notes as evidence for the accuracy of reporting' (*Ms Denise Brown v The Citizen (Gloucester)*, adjudication and PCC press release published October 13, 2011). Chapter 2 explains the PCC's role.

Changes to Editors' Code

The preamble to the Editors' Code of Practice was changed on January 1, 2012 to 'require editors who breach the Code to publish the PCC's critical adjudication in full and with due prominence agreed with the PCC's director'.

Another change, which came into effect on the same date, amended the Code's public interest section to 'require editors who claim a breach of the Code was in the public interest to show not only that they had good reason to believe the public interest would be served, but how and with whom that was established at the time.'

Paul Dacre, editor of the *Daily Mail* and editor-in-chief of Associated Newspapers, who chairs the Editors' Code Committee, said the changes were designed to ensure that the normal good practice followed in most newspaper offices in most cases became enshrined in the Code itself. 'The public interest amendment underwrites the need for editors and senior executives to give proper consideration before they consciously decide to breach the code – something that should never be done lightly. They should be ready to demonstrate they have observed this process. Most do it already. This measure should be a safeguard, not a burden' (*Media Lawyer*, December 20, 2011). Chapter 2 explains the Code.

Ofcom closes Press TV

Ofcom revoked the licence of Iranian News Channel Press TV, which broadcast in the UK. The regulator found that it was apparent that 'editorial control of the channel' rested with Press TV International (based in Tehran) which, it said, breached broadcasting rules stating that the licence holder must have general control of programming.

The decision to revoke the licence, made on January 20, 2012, came after Ofcom had fined Press TV £100,000 for having broadcast an interview with a journalist who was being held in an Iranian prison. Ofcom said the interview was 'obtained under duress'. It also said Press TV had 'indicated it is unwilling and unable to pay' the fine.

Ofcom rules woman's privacy was not breached

Ofcom ruled that the Channel 5 programme *Police Interceptors*, which featured the work of a police unit in Sheffield, did not breach the privacy of a woman filmed when she answered her door while wearing a dressing gown. Police wanted to trace a couple who failed to pay a taxi fare. The woman was not involved in that incident, but was filmed when police knocked at several houses at around midnight. Her face was obscured in the programme, she was not named and no street address was given. But the programme specified the district and her voice could be heard as she told police she lived alone. She told Ofcom she did not know she had been filmed.

Ofcom's adjudication said her identity would have been discernable to people who knew her, but noted that the programme's measures to limit infringement of her privacy included obscuring her house number and car registration plate. It did not uphold her complaint, ruling that the public interest in showing the challenges faced by police officers was significant, and that in the case's particular circumstances the broadcaster's right to freedom to impart information outweighed her expectation of privacy Complaint by Ms G. *Ofcom Broadcast Bulletin*, No. 196,

December 19, 2011). Chapter 27 explains the Ofcom Broadcasting Code's protection of privacy.

Claimants to employment tribunals may be charged fees

The Government is consulting on plans for employment tribunals to charge claimants up to £2,350 if their case goes to a hearing. The level of fee would depend on the level of award sought. Under the plans, employment tribunals would have power to order the unsuccessful party to reimburse fees paid by the successful party. This would change the current position in which employment tribunals rarely award costs against either party. Chapter 17 explains employment tribunals.

Freedom of Information Act covers three more bodies

The Freedom of Information Act has been extended to cover the Association of Chief Police Officers (ACPO), the Universities and Colleges Admission Service (UCAS) and the Financial Ombudsman Service, so the media and public can now make FoI requests to these. The Ministry of Justice is also consulting other bodies about including them in the Act's scope (Ministry of Justice press release, November 1, 2011). Chapter 30 explains the Act.

FOI Act covers private emails

The Information Commissioner's Office has confirmed that non-governmental email addresses, as well as text messages, are covered by the Freedom of Information Act (FOI), meaning that Government Ministers and officials can be ordered to hand over emails sent from their private accounts if they contain details about Government business.

The move follows concerns about the way in which requests for information were handled at Michael Gove's education department and allegations that messages containing sensitive information were being kept away from the department's own civil servants as well as the public.

Information Commissioner Christopher Graham said: 'It should not come as a surprise to public authorities to have the clarification that information held in private email accounts can be subject to Freedom of Information law if it relates to official business. This has always been the case – the Act covers all recorded information in any form.'

The Information Commissioner's Office (ICO) issued guidance which he said had two key aims – to give public authorities an authoritative steer on the factors that should be considered before deciding whether a search of private email accounts was necessary when responding to a request under the Act, and second to set out the procedures that should generally be in place to respond to requests (*Media Lawyer*, December 16, 2011).

Brady wins right for his mental health tribunal to be in public

A mental health tribunal hearing about Moors murderer Ian Brady will be held in public, a judge has ruled. Brady had applied for the hearing to be in public. Judge Atherton said the date of the tribunal hearing and appropriate arrangements were being determined and would be published as soon as possible. But he added: 'The fact of this decision should be published. The tribunal also ordered that the reasons for the decision must not be made public' (*Media Lawyer*, December 9, 2011). Chapter 17 explains mental health review tribunals. It is very rare for their hearings to be held in public.

Justice Secretary rejects need for public interest defence in Bribery Act 2010

The Justice Secretary has rejected suggestions that the Bribery Act should contain a public interest defence.

The Act, which came into force in July 2011, introduced a corporate offence of failure to prevent bribery, and made it a specific criminal offence to give, promise or offer a bribe. Kenneth Clarke's comment came after he was told at the Society of Editors' Conference in November 2011 by *The Sun*'s managing editor Richard Caseby that the newspaper technically breached the Act when it helped to secure the first conviction under the new legislation. The conviction was of a court clerk who took bribes to avoid putting details of traffic summonses on a court database, meaning alleged offenders avoided prosecution. The clerk was prosecuted after being exposed by a *Sun* 'sting'. Mr Caseby told Mr Clarke that the sting involved making a payment to the corrupt clerk, and so technically breached the Act. Mr Caseby said the current laws left his reporters and his newspaper open to prosecution, and called for a public interest defence. But Mr Clarke ruled the idea out, saying the Director of Public Prosecutions (DPP) would simply dismiss any cases in which a prosecution was not in the public interest (*Media Lawyer*, November 14 and 18, 2011).

Misconduct offence cited in police probe

In January 2012 the Metropolitan police arrested four current or former senior journalists of *The Sun* newspaper and a serving police officer as part of an investigation into payments allegedly made to police officers. The four were arrested on suspicion of corruption under the Prevention of Corruption Act 1906, aiding and abetting misconduct in a public office and conspiracy in relation to both offences, police said.

The common law offence of misconduct in a public office involves a 'public officer' wilfully neglecting to perform his/her duty and/or wifully misconducting himself/herself to such a degree as to amount to an abuse of the public's trust in the office holder, and without reasonable excuse or justification. As chapter 34 explains, the 'aiding and abetting' charge was used in 2008 against journalist Sally Murrer, who was cleared.

McNae's at a glance

McNae's Essential Law for Journalists contains a range of features to help you find the information you need quickly – in class and on the job. This short guide outlines these features and how they can help you.

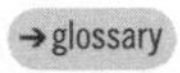

Glossary terms are highlighted in the text and defined in the glossary at the back of the book and on www.mcnaes.com.

Use the cross-references to find related information elsewhere in the book.

Case studies appear throughout the text to provide context and examples of how the law has been applied and of adjudications by the Press Complaints Commission and Ofcom.

Advice from the authors on applying media law on the job, and reminders about relevant content elsewhere in the book.

The website that accompanies this book, www.mcnaes.com, contains additional chapters and information on a range of key topics, advice from the authors, updates and testing resources.

Useful website addresses lead to more information.

Plus

Chapter summaries introduce each chapter and outline the content – and why it matters to a journalist.

Each chapter features a recap of essential points ideal for revision and as an at-a-glance reminder.

www.mcnaes.com

This edition of *McNae's Essential Law for Journalists* is accompanied by a free-to-use website – www.mcnaes.com – that features extra resources for both students and journalists.

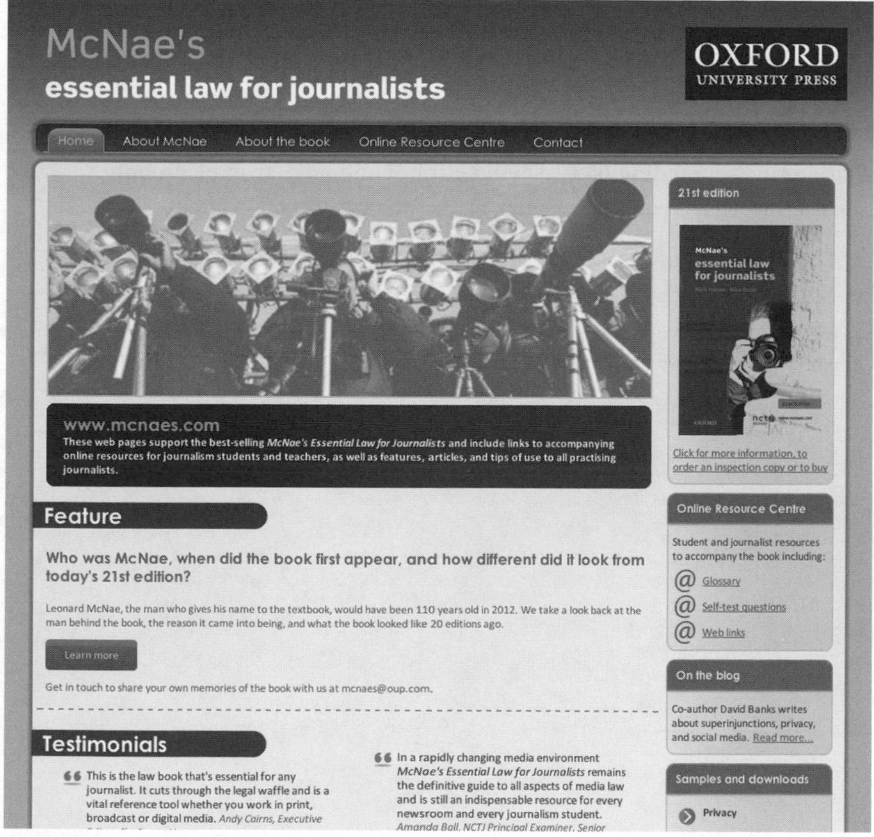

Updates

Visit www.mcnaes.com to find out about changes in media law and regulation that have happened since this book was published.

Online-only chapters

Access extra online chapters on the Official Secrets Act, Scottish media law, family law and the incitement of hatred.

Additional information

The authors have provided additional commentary and resources on a range of topics, including media coverage before trial, reporting on juveniles, challenging the courts and privacy.

Self-test questions

Test your knowledge and get feedback with chapter-related questions.

Glossary

For easy reference, www.mcnaes.com contains the glossary of legal terms used regularly in the book.

Extra resources

Writing tips – including how to avoid clichés and advice on commonly confused words – from the experts at Oxford University Press.

Part 1

The landscape of law, ethics and regulation

1

Introduction

Chapter summary

The UK media enjoy freedoms which are the envy of journalists in oppressed societies. Nevertheless, the UK has more laws affecting journalism than is the case in some other democracies, and so a sound, thorough knowledge of legal matters is especially important for UK journalists, particularly in their role as 'watchdogs' acting on the public's behalf. This chapter explains how the UK's laws are made, and how the European Convention on Human Rights helps safeguard freedom of expression. It also outlines the distinction between criminal and civil law, and between solicitors and barristers.

Free but with restrictions

Although the United Kingdom has a 'free press' in comparison to the authoritarian censorship which stifles liberty in some other nations, the description must be qualified because of the many and growing restrictions on what can be published. This book shows the many laws affecting journalism, including an increasing number of **statutes**.

The importance of freedom of expression, and the journalist's position as a public watchdog, ensuring a properly informed populace in a democratic society, has been stressed by both the UK courts and the European Court of Human Rights in Strasbourg.

The senior law lord, Lord Bingham, said in the House of Lords in 2000:

> In a modern, developed society it is only a small minority of citizens who can participate directly in the discussions and decisions which shape the public life of that society. The majority can participate only indirectly, by exercising their

rights as citizens to vote, express their opinions, make representations to the authorities, form pressure groups and so on. But the majority cannot participate in the public life of their society in these ways if they are not alerted to and informed about matters which call or may call for consideration and action. It is very largely through the media, including of course the press, that they will be so alerted and informed. The proper functioning of a modern participatory democracy requires that the media be free, active, professional and enquiring (*McCartan Turkington Breen v Times Newspapers Ltd* [2001] 2 AC 277). ”

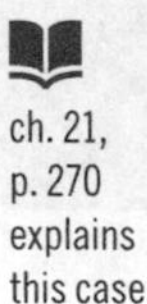
ch. 21, p. 270 explains this case

It is the journalist's job to help safeguard freedom of expression and a free media, by reporting accurately and ensuring that people are properly informed about what is being done in their name by those who claim to govern them. It is also the job of journalists to safeguard the principle of an independent judiciary by reporting what is going on in the courts, which apply the laws intended to safeguard the interests of all.

To do all this journalists need to know the law – where it comes from, what it says and what it allows them to do or stops them from doing.

The UK has a vibrant and wide-ranging media – newspapers, magazines, radio stations and television channels and of course the ever-growing worldwide communications system which is the internet, with the myriad text and audio-visual sites it offers – and the law applies to all of them. Many are also subject to regulatory systems. This book explains how reporting restrictions, libel and privacy laws limit what can be published – and the financial consequences of mistakes or recklessness in journalism. But it also emphasises the freedoms which exist to publish and investigate. Only by knowing what is and is not possible, and what may or may not be done, can journalists, broadcasters, website operators and those who work with them keep the freedoms and variety of platforms they have now, campaign for greater freedom, and ensure that their work is not curtailed by some foolish but expensive error.

Increasingly, journalists' ethics are under scrutiny. The observance of ethical codes should be an integral part of how journalists operate, to help produce respected, fair journalism but also to preserve freedoms. The risk is that if some journalists do not respect these media codes, new and punitive laws will be created in an attempt to curb malpractices, and that such laws, if too wide in scope, may hinder the work of all journalists.

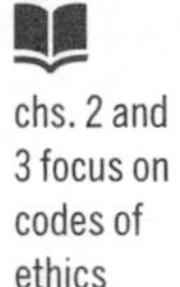
chs. 2 and 3 focus on codes of ethics

Sources of law

The main sources of the law have traditionally been custom, precedent and statute.

Custom

When the English legal system began to take shape in the Middle Ages, royal judges were appointed to administer the 'law and custom of the realm'. This developed into the **common law**.

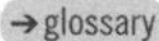
→glossary

Precedent

As judges applied the common law to the cases before them, their decisions were recorded by lawyers. This process continues. Records of leading cases give the facts considered by a court, and the reasons for its decision. The UK has a hierarchy of courts, so a decision made by a lower court can be challenged by appeal to a higher court. The decisions made by the higher courts – precedents – are then binding on all lower courts, thus shaping their future rulings. Precedents evolve and develop the common law.

Figure 1 is a diagram of the hierarchy of the courts in England and Wales. The nature and role of these courts is explained further in later chapters.

See ch. 37 on Northern Ireland and see www.mcnaes.com for an outline of the Scottish court system.

A Supreme Court judgment binds all UK courts, apart from – in most respects – Scottish criminal courts. The Supreme Court Justices can refuse to follow their earlier decisions, which otherwise can only be overturned or reversed by legislation.

Below the Supreme Court, the Court of Appeal's decisions bind the High Court and the lower courts, and High Court decisions bind all lower courts.

Statutes and statutory instruments

Common law can be modified or replaced by statutes – Acts of Parliament, which are primary legislation. But UK governments have made increasing use of secondary legislation known as statutory instruments. Parliament frequently uses Acts to enshrine broad principles in legislation, but delegates the detailed framing of the new law to the departmental Minister concerned, who sets out its detail in statutory instruments in the form of regulations or rules. Statutory instruments must be approved by Parliament.

European regulations and directives

As the UK is part of the European Union, EU treaties and other EU law are part of UK law. The EU's Council and its Parliament agree regulations and directives which are binding on member states as part of the EU's *raison d'être* of encouraging trade between member states by harmonising laws throughout its area. EU Regulations apply in the form in which they are drawn up, but member states decide how directives should be implemented, through their own legislation.

The European Court of Justice, based in Luxembourg, clarifies – for the national courts of EU member states – interpretation of EU legislation. It can, for example, rule on allegations that a member state has infringed EU law to gain advantage in trade, and penalise a state for such infringement. This court is not to be confused with the European Court of Human Rights.

Figure 1 Hierarchy of the courts.

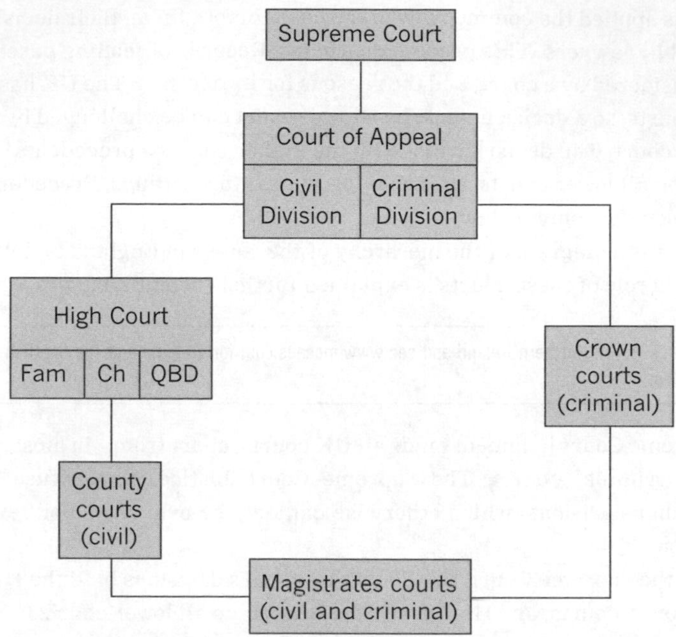

Fam = Family (civil); Ch = Chancery; QBD = Queen's Bench (civil and criminal). See chs. 8, 11 and 12.

The European Convention on Human Rights

The repression by and genocide of Nazi Germany in the Second World War prompted West European nations to create the Council of Europe to promote individual freedom, political liberty and the rule of law. The Council's work led to the European Convention for the Protection of Human Rights and Fundamental Freedoms – usually referred to as the European Convention on Human Rights – which sets out rights which must be protected by signatory states, and to the foundation of the European Court of Human Rights (ECtHR), which sits in Strasbourg. Among the rights the Convention guarantees are the right to respect for privacy and family life and the right to freedom of expression. Forty-seven nations have adopted the Convention, and any of their citizens can take a case to the Strasbourg court to argue that a signatory nation has failed to protect them from, or to sufficiently compensate them for, a breach of a Convention right. The Convention has very wide application, because a nation will be held to have breached a right if its legal system fails to stop or offer an adequate remedy for a violation of an individual's rights by a private body or individual as well as by a state authority or body.

The Human Rights Act 1998

The Human Rights Act 1998, which came into force on 2 October 2000, puts the Convention into UK law, greatly increasing its influence on UK courts. Individuals can require any UK court to consider their rights under the Convention in the context of any case.

The Act requires any UK court determining a question in connection with a Convention right to take account of the ECtHR's decisions. It also says that new UK legislation must be compatible with Convention rights, and old and new legislation must be construed so far as possible to conform with them.

It is unlawful for UK public authorities to act in any way that is incompatible with Convention rights.

Convention rights

Adopting the Convention directly into UK law has required judges to consider systematically Convention rights, and these rights conflict with each other in many cases.

For journalists, the most important part of the Convention is Article 10, which says in part: 'Everyone has the right to freedom of expression. This right shall include freedom to hold opinions and to receive and impart information and ideas without interference by public authority.'

Article 10 makes clear that restrictions on this right have to be justified, necessary in a democratic society and 'prescribed by law'.

Journalists wanting to exercise their rights under Article 10 may find themselves facing a claim under Article 8, which protects the right to respect for privacy and family life, and could be used by someone seeking an injunction to stop publication of a story about his or her personal life, or seeking damages if the material has already been published.

Weighing competing rights

The methodology a court should use to decide in any particular case whether one Convention right should prevail over another was detailed in *Re S (A Child) (Identification: Restrictions on Publication)* [2004] UKHL 47. In that House of Lords judgment, Lord Steyn said:

> "First, neither article has as such precedence over the other. Secondly, where the values under the two articles are in conflict, an intense focus on the comparative importance of the specific rights being claimed in the individual case is necessary. Thirdly, the justifications for interfering with or restricting each right must be taken into account. Finally, the proportionality test must be applied to each. For convenience I will call this the ultimate balancing test."

Lord Steyn was emphasising that the particular circumstances of each case must be intensely considered to decide which Convention right – and therefore which party to the argument – prevails in each matter to be decided.

www.mcnaes.com ch. 13 has more detail of the *Re S* judgment

In some judgments relevant to the media, Article 2 (the right to life) and Article 3 (the right against degrading treatment, including torture) are cited and, by their very nature, can have great weight – for example, if it is argued with justification that someone's name or address must not be published to protect them from violent criminals or vigilantes.

Articles 2 ,3, 8 and 10 are set out in Appendix 1, pp. 427–428.

Divisions of the law

There are two main divisions of the law – criminal and civil.

Criminal law deals with offences which harm the whole community and thus are considered to be offences against the sovereign. A Crown court case in which John Smith is accused of an offences is listed as R v Smith. 'R' stands for Regina (the Queen) or Rex (the King), depending on who is reigning at the time, and 'v' for 'versus'.

A lawyer talking about this case would generally refer to it as 'The Queen (or the King) against Smith'.

See chs. 4–10 for more detail on criminal law.

Civil law concerns disputes between individuals and organisations, and includes the redress of **torts** – that is, wrongs suffered. Medical negligence, defamation and breach of copyright are all torts. A case in which Mary Brown sues John Smith will be known in writing as Brown versus Smith. Lawyers will speak of the case as 'Brown *and* Smith' (our italics).

In practice, the two divisions overlap – many acts or omissions are offences for which an individual may be prosecuted and punished as well as being 'wrongs' for which an injured party may recover compensation. For example, a road accident may lead to a motorist being prosecuted for dangerous driving, and being sued by someone injured in the crash.

There are differences in terminology between civil and criminal law cases. In criminal courts a defendant is prosecuted, pleads guilty or not guilty, and will be acquitted or convicted, and if convicted, fined or jailed. In civil courts a claimant sues a defendant or respondent, who admits or denies liability, and is found either not liable or liable, and, if liable, ordered to pay damages.

Civil courts also resolve disputes between couples such as divorce actions.

Chs. 12 and 13 explain the civil courts.

The legal profession

Lawyers are either solicitors or barristers.

By tradition and practice, solicitors deal directly with the client – a defendant in a criminal case or someone seeking advice or representation in a civil case. Solicitors advise, prepare the client's case and take advice, when necessary, from a barrister specialising in a particular area of the law. Solicitors may represent their clients in court, and solicitor-advocates may appear in the higher courts.

Barristers are known, singly or collectively, as '**counsel**'. Barristers wear a wig and gown in the higher courts, the Crown courts and county courts, but not in magistrates courts. Barristers who have been practising for at least ten years may apply to the Lord Chancellor for appointment as a Queen's Counsel, and, if successful, use the letters QC after their names.

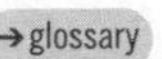

D High offices in law

The constitutional position in the UK and other democracies is that the nation's 'executive' (the government) is separate from the judiciary (the judges), to help ensure that the judiciary is independent of political influence, and that the government is subject to the rule of law, just as other organisations and citizens are.

The head of the judiciary is the Lord Chief Justice.

The UK Government is advised on law by the Attorney General, which is a political role, with some holders being of Cabinet rank. The Attorney General also has a role in prosecutions, in that he/she approves the instigation of, and may personally conduct in court, prosecutions in certain important types of cases. These include, as chapter 18 explains, proceedings against media organisations for contempt of court.

Recap of major points

- The media are the eyes and ears of the general public, and free media are an essential element in maintaining parliamentary democracy.
- The European Convention on Human Rights has codified fundamental freedoms, including that of freedom of expression.
- Sources of UK law include custom, precedent, statutes and statutory instruments, and European Union regulations.
- The two main divisions of the law are criminal law and civil law, and journalists need to use correctly the legal terms appropriate for the type of case they are reporting.

Useful Websites

www.parliament.uk/about/how/laws/
UK Parliament – 'Making Laws'

www.echr.coe.int/echr/
European Court of Human Rights: the 'Basic Texts' link leads to the Convention

www.judiciary.gov.uk/
Judiciary of England and Wales – information on judges and the courts system

www.lawsociety.org.uk/becomingasolicitor/careerinlaw/difference.law/
Law Society information on solicitors and barristers

www.barcouncil.org.uk/about/whatbarristersdo/
Bar Council site – 'What barristers do'

www.attorneygeneral.gov.uk/
Attorney General's Office

2

The Editors' Code of Practice

Chapter summary

People aggrieved by what newspapers or magazines and their websites publish about them, or by how journalists have treated them can ask the industry's complaints body to intervene or adjudicate. As this book went to press, this body was the Press Complaints Commission – PCC – which was created by the industry to self-regulate and raise journalistic standards by administering the Editors' Code of Practice. An official inquiry into press ethics launched in 2011 could lead to radical reform or even replacement of the PCC. But a reformed PCC or any new organisation created to handle complaints against the press is likely to use the Editors' Code of Practice or something similar. This chapter introduces and outlines the code.

Introduction

There are no state controls in the UK on who can own or run newspapers, magazines, their online versions or any kind of website, except those relating to some anti-monopoly laws on corporate mergers. Anyone with the resources can launch a new publication. These liberties help keep the UK's media relatively free from state influence. Newspapers, magazines and websites are free to be partisan about social issues, and can support a political party. Editors, subject to their proprietors' wishes, may use leader columns, news stories and features to campaign on any issue – for example, environmental law or tax reform, or against the closure of a local hospital. They and their journalists can also publish, subject to the restraints of libel and other laws, their own fierce criticisms of those in the news, or anyone else. The lack of any requirement for these media sectors to be impartial contrasts with the position of the broadcasting industry, as the next chapter explains.

But newspaper and magazine owners recognise that irresponsible journalism could lead Parliament to introduce some statutory system of regulation, specify standards of accuracy, fairness, and so on, or even establish an official tribunal to hear complaints against publications, impose financial penalties or compel editors to publish corrections or replies.

The newspaper and magazine industry created the PCC to keep the threat of statutory regulation at bay. It helps the industry regulate the conduct of journalists and editors, and operates a free and relatively fast service for people with complaints against newspapers, magazines, their websites and 'online-only' publications (mainly online magazines).

see also p. 19, 'The PCC's future' and the Book List on p. 443

The PCC, launched in 1991, replaced the Press Council, a self-regulatory body which became discredited because it was slow, ineffective – a criticism now levelled at the PCC – and was not respected by all editors.

The PCC's structure and role

The PCC's chair and the majority of its 17 Commissioners are 'lay' people – not from media backgrounds – which gives them some independence from the industry. The other Commissioners are serving editors. The Commissioners oversee its secretariat and adjudicate on complaints. The cost of running the PCC – £1.83 million in 2010 – is met by an annual voluntary levy on the industry which is collected by the Press Standards Board of Finance, PressBof. But not all newspapers and magazines have consistently supported the PCC: in January 2011 Richard Desmond's Northern and Shell group withdrew, taking *OK!* magazine and the *Daily* and *Sunday Express*, *Scottish Daily* and *Sunday Express*, the *Daily Star* and *Daily Star Sunday* from the PCC's remit, after saying it was no longer willing to pay the voluntary levy.

see 'The Evolving Code of Practice' in Useful Websites

The PCC oversees the ethical standards detailed in the Editors' Code of Practice, which is outlined below. Editors must prove they have complied with the code, both in letter and spirit. The code is drawn up by the Editors' Code of Practice Committee, which comprises 13 editors from national, regional and local newspapers, and magazines, and periodically reviews and updates or amends its scope and wording.

An aggrieved person or organisation must complain first to the relevant editor, and can contact the PCC if he or she is still dissatisfied.

In many cases, the PCC has ruled that a complaint was not justified or that an editor's response, such as a private or published apology or an offer to publish a correction, was enough to resolve an issue. It also negotiates resolutions to problems, and often intervenes before material is published – for example, in cases in which people wish the press to leave them alone.

In 2010 the PCC received more than 7,000 written complaints. Of these, 899 fell outside its remit – for example, complaints about poor taste. Complainants dropped 2,774. In 2010, the PCC judged 750 complaints to have merit and raise a likely breach of the code. In these cases it upheld the complaint in a written ruling, which the editor involved then published, or ruled that the editor's response was a sufficient remedy. In 18 cases it published formal rulings – adjudications – censuring titles which breached the code and failed to remedy the breach, or committed breaches so serious they could not be remedied. It has also published adjudications in other cases which significantly illustrate its interpretation of the code.

The PCC cannot force editors to publish adjudications. But no editor has failed to do so, not least because, broadly speaking, they and publishers support the PCC system. Critics have argued that because the PCC has no power to impose a financial penalty, it is too weak to be effective. But the PCC and many editors say it has force because editors are shamed when they publish adverse rulings. The PCC has said that adherence to the code is a contractual obligation for editors of publications supporting its system, and for many journalists working for them.

The scope of the Editors' Code

The Editors' Code – reproduced in full in Appendix 2 of this book – has 16 clauses setting out ethical standards on: accuracy, opportunity for people to reply to inaccuracies, privacy, harassment, intrusion into grief and shock, excessive detail in covering suicides, the welfare of children who become the subject of journalism, anonymity for children in sex cases as well as all victims of sexual assault, making inquiries at hospitals, crime reporting, and secret filming and recording and using subterfuge or misrepresentation.

Appendix 2 is on pp. 429–433

It also bans the use of pejorative material which discriminates on grounds of race, religion, sexual orientation, gender or disability, sets standards for honesty in financial journalism, requires the protection of confidential sources, bans payments to witnesses in active criminal cases or to people who might become witnesses in trials, and bans press payments to criminals or their associates.

In this book most of the code's clauses are featured with case studies in relevant chapters – for example, clause 3 (Privacy) is featured in chapters 26 and 27. Chapter 27 also covers clause 6 on children's welfare. This book's index entry for the Editors' Code lists pages featuring each clause. This chapter deals with some clauses of wide application and some relevant to comparatively rare practices or specialist work in journalism.

((•)) see Useful Websites, below, for the Codebook and PCC site

The Editors' Codebook, produced by the Editors' Code of Practice Committee, offers guidance on the code and PCC rulings. Also, it is useful to browse the PCC's online archive of cases.

Neither the code nor the PCC deal with issues of taste and decency. The industry says that as these are subjective matters rulings on them could compromise freedom of expression.

! Remember

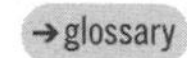
Breaching the Editors' Code is not a criminal offence or a civil **tort**. But observing its requirements is ethical conduct and can help journalists avoid legal problems. Judges ruling on claims of media intrusion into privacy must consider relevant codes.

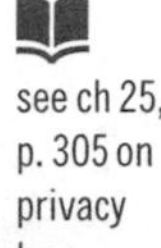
see ch 25, p. 305 on privacy law

Public interest exceptions in the Editors' Code

Some clauses or sub-clauses in the code are marked with an asterisk, which indicates that breaches of these parts can be justified if an editor can demonstrate that what was done was 'in the public interest'.

The code adds 'the public interest' includes, but is not confined to:

- detecting or exposing crime or serious impropriety;
- protecting public health and safety;
- preventing the public from being misled by an action or statement of an individual or organisation.

The code says editors seeking to rely on public interest exceptions must 'demonstrate fully that they reasonably believed that publication, or journalistic activity undertaken with a view to publication, would be in the public interest and how, and with whom, that was established at the time.'

The code adds: 'There is a public interest in freedom of expression itself'.

An adjudication, even in these categories of stories, is also likely to consider whether what was done in research and what was published was 'proportionate' – that is, not excessive.

The code makes clear that when a story involves children under 16, editors seeking to justify breach of a relevant clause 'must demonstrate an *exceptional* public interest to override the normally paramount interest of the child'.

Accuracy and opportunity to reply

Clause 1 of the code says: 'The Press must take care not to publish inaccurate, misleading or distorted information, including pictures'. A 'significant' inaccuracy, misleading statement or distortion must be corrected promptly, and any correction or apology must be given 'due prominence'. The press can be partisan but must 'distinguish clearly between comment, conjecture and fact'.

Clause 2 says: 'A fair opportunity for reply to inaccuracies must be given when reasonably called for'.

Each year the majority – usually nearly 90 per cent – of complaints to the PCC allege breaches of clauses 1 and/or 2. Neither clause is subject to the public interest exception – there is no public interest in inaccuracy.

Case study

In 2010 the PCC upheld a complaint of inaccuracy against the *Daily Star* over a front-page report that a Rochdale shopping centre had installed 'Muslim-only squat-hole loos' on which the local council had wasted 'YOUR money'. The PCC said the toilets were not paid for by the local council and could not be described as 'Muslim only'. It was particularly concerned at the newspaper's lack of care in its presentation of the story (*Adam Sheppard v Daily Star*, adjudication issued September 27, 2010).

Coverage of suicides

Research has found that news of suicides may prompt others to take their own lives in the same way. To minimise this risk, clause 5 of the code says reports of suicides should avoid giving excessive detail about the method used. The PCC ruled that a report of an inquest into a suicide breached the clause because it named the anti-depressant pills used and said how many were missing from the packet (*A Woman v The News (Portsmouth)*, adjudication issued January 28, 2010).

Deception (subterfuge and misrepresentation)

Clause 10 of the code says:

> “ i) The press must not seek to obtain or publish material acquired by using hidden cameras or clandestine listening devices; or by intercepting private or mobile telephone calls, messages or emails; or by the unauthorised removal of documents or photographs; or by accessing digitally held private information without consent.
>
> ii) Engaging in misrepresentation or subterfuge, including by agents or intermediaries, can generally be justified only in the public interest and then only when the material cannot be obtained by other means. ”

ch. 28 explains data protection law

It makes clear that journalists should normally be open and transparent when seeking information or comment, making clear from the outset to anyone unfamiliar with them that they are journalists.

It also means that normally photography or filming must be done openly, and that eavesdropping by using 'bugs' or audio-recording by hidden microphones will breach the code because the activity is 'clandestine'. Irrespective of the code, using hidden cameras or microphones could be a breach of privacy law, as chapters 26 and 27 explain. In most circumstances hacking into computers for private information will breach the code and the law.

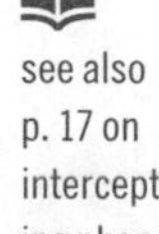

see also p. 17 on intercepting phone calls

But clause 10 is subject to the public interest exceptions, so that if the story or journalistic activity is justified by a sufficient public interest, a journalist posing as someone else or using other kinds of subterfuge, including hidden cameras or microphones, is not breaching the code. Such deception is common in investigative journalism. But the code says such tactics and methods should only be used when an open approach would not work, even when a public interest exception applies.

Case study

In 2009 the PCC rejected a complaint by the mother of murderer Levi Bellfield after a *Daily Mirror* reporter used subterfuge to interview him in prison by phone. Bellfield had already been convicted of murdering two young women, and his relatives helped arrange the interview after the reporter falsely offered to help his appeal. The reporter's true objective was to ask Bellfield about events relevant to a third murder of which he was suspected – that of schoolgirl Milly Dowler. The PCC said the reporter had not misrepresented his identity and when interviewing Bellfield had obtained significant and new information about Milly's murder. The subterfuge was fully justified by this objective (*Mrs Jean Bellfield v Daily Mirror*, adjudication issued July 23, 2009 and *Press Gazette*, August 2011). In 2011 Bellfield was convicted of Milly's murder.

'Fishing expeditions'

The PCC has made clear in adjudications that it will not condone subterfuge or misrepresentation, or infringement of privacy, in 'fishing expeditions' – including using hidden cameras or recording devices. A 'fishing expedition' is an investigation launched without sufficient, **prima facie** grounds to justify such methods. An editor who authorises their use needs to be able to demonstrate there is a specific allegation serious enough to justify them – for example, that the investigation's target was committing crime, guilty of serious impropriety, misleading the public or putting people's health or safety at risk. An editor will also need to be able to demonstrate that using these methods was proportionate and necessary.

→glossary

Case Study

In 2011 the PCC upheld a complaint by the Liberal Democrats about a *Daily Telegraph* undercover investigation in which reporters posed as constituents to talk to Lib Dem Ministers during constituency surgeries, secretly recording the comments. The object was to gather evidence that the Ministers were misleading the public by making official statements in support of the Lib Dem–Conservative coalition government while privately expressing views at odds with coalition policies. The PCC said the reporters' misrepresentations breached clause 10. The *Telegraph* did not appear to have had, before launching the investigation, any specific information that the targeted Ministers had expressed such views, it said. The PCC added that what information the newspaper did have in advance was not sufficient to warrant the undercover taping of the MPs as they did their constituency work, even though the newspaper had pointed out that during the surgeries most of them had voiced opinions about the coalition which were at odds with their public positions (*Liberal Democrat Party v the Daily Telegraph*, adjudication issued May 10, 2011).

Recording phone calls

Journalists, particularly those involved in investigations, may decide to record their own telephone calls, for example when they are interviewing the target of their inquiries. The recording may be needed as proof if the subject sues for libel over what is published. In the UK it is legal for one party in a phone conversation to record it, even if the other is unaware this is being done.

The PCC has made it clear that journalists who record calls they make or legitimately receive are not regarded as using a clandestine recording device under clause 10, even if they do not tell the other person the call is being recorded (*Messrs Lewis Silkin on behalf of Mrs Isobel Stone*, Report 49, 2000), so do not require a 'public interest' exception to justify this conduct.

But a journalist who fails to declare in such a call that he/she is a journalist may breach the code's ban on subterfuge and misrepresentation, unless the 'public interest' criterion applies and it seems reasonable to conclude there is no other way to obtain the information.

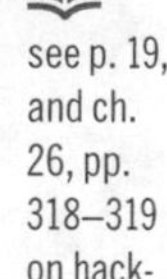

see p. 19, and ch. 26, pp. 318–319 on hacking and interception

But *intercepting* a phone call – using external technology to hack directly or 'tap' into a phone system to listen to or record other people's conversations or messages – in most circumstances would breach the code and be illegal, as demonstrated by the scandal which closed the *News of the World* in July 2011.

Discriminatory material

Clause 12 of the code bans publication of pejorative material which discriminates on grounds of race, religion, sexual orientation, gender, disability or physical or mental illness. References to an individual's race, religion, sexual orientation, illness or disability must be genuinely relevant to the story.

Case study

In 2010 the PCC ruled that reviewer A.A. Gill's reference to TV journalist Clare Balding as 'a dyke on a bike' in a *Sunday Times* article on her programme 'Britain by Bike' breached clause 12. It said Gill's use of the word 'dyke' – whether or not it was intended to be humorous – was pejorative, demeaning and gratuitous, and the newspaper should have apologised at the first possible opportunity (*Clare Balding v the Sunday Times*, adjudication September 17, 2010).

Financial journalism

((•)) see also Useful Websites, below for PCC guidance on financial journalism

Clause 13 of the code seeks to prevent journalists making personal profit by anticipating movements in share prices, on the basis of information leaked to them by business contacts or embargoed. It says journalists 'must not use for their own profit financial information they receive in advance of its general publication, nor should they pass such information to others.' It also bans journalists from dealing in shares or securities about which they have recently written, or intend to write, as what they publish might affect market prices, and it would be unethical for them to take financial advantage of this power. It says journalists must tell their editors about shares or securities in which they or close relatives have a significant financial interest.

Payments to witnesses in criminal trials

When covering high-profile stories, a media organisation may pay people, including the victims of notorious crimes, for the exclusive right to publish their accounts of events. In the case of crime victims or other witnesses, those accounts would be more than the evidence they can give in court, which would not have exclusive value. An account could include, for example, descriptions not limited by court rules on evidence. Clause 15 of the code aims to prevent these 'chequebook journalism' deals interfering with the process of justice. The risk of contempt of court which can arise from these deals, or from a reporter interviewing anyone due to testify in a trial, is explained in chapter 18.

The first part of clause 15 says: 'No payment or offer of payment to a witness – or any person who may reasonably be expected to be called as a witness – should be made in any case once proceedings are active as defined by the Contempt of Court Act 1981.' The ban applies until a case ceases to be active or the suspect pleads guilty.

The second part says that:

> “where proceedings are not yet active but are likely and foreseeable, editors must not make or offer payment to any person who may reasonably be expected to be called as a witness, unless the information concerned ought demonstrably to be published in the public interest and there is an over-riding need to make or promise payment for this to be done; and all reasonable steps have been taken to ensure no financial dealings influence the evidence those witnesses give. In no circumstances should such payment be conditional on the outcome of a trial.”

It says a payment or an offer of payment made to a person who is later called to testify in proceedings must be disclosed to the prosecution and defence.

Payments to criminals

Clause 16 of the code says: 'Payment or offers of payment for stories, pictures or information, which seek to exploit a particular crime or to glorify or glamorise crime in general, must not be made directly or via agents to convicted or confessed criminals or to their associates – who may include family, friends and colleagues.' This recognises that the public, particularly crime victims, are likely to condemn a deal under which criminals or those close to them profit from tales of wrongdoing. But the clause also recognises that press payment to a criminal may be justified by the code's public interest exceptions.

The PCC's future

The biggest press scandal in recent years has been that of journalists, or colluding private detectives, secretly and illegally 'hacking' into people's mobile phones to hear their private messages.

See www.mcnaes.com ch. 2 for a full account of this scandal, which in 2011 closed the *News of the World* newspaper: 'The scandal of phone-hacking and payments to police'.

In July 2011 the scandal, and the police's apparent failure to investigate fully when it first came to light, led Prime Minister David Cameron to announce an official inquiry into 'the culture, practices, and ethics of the press', including the relationships between national newspapers and politicians, and the press and police. A senior judge, Lord Justice Leveson, was chosen to lead the inquiry. Its terms of reference include making, within 12 months, recommendations 'for a new more effective policy and regulatory regime which supports the integrity and freedom of the press, the plurality of the media, and its independence, including from Government, while encouraging the highest ethical and professional standards.'

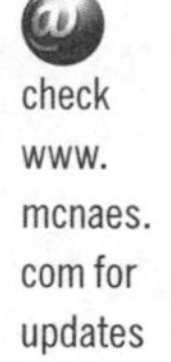

check www. mcnaes. com for updates

These recommendations seem highly likely to lead to radical reform or replacement of the PCC, which had already been widely criticised for failing to recognise or properly investigate the extent of hacking.

Recap of major points

- The Editors' Code of Practice sets standards for journalists working for newspapers, magazines and free-standing editorial websites.
- It has clauses to uphold accuracy and to protect people's privacy.
- The code permits undercover reporting, but only if justified by special, 'public interest' factors.
- The Press Complaints Commission, which adjudicates complaints against editors and journalists in these media sectors, requires editors to publish adverse adjudications.
- The PCC is likely to be reformed or replaced as a result of the official inquiry into press ethics.

((•)) Useful Websites

www.pcc.org.uk/
PCC home page

www.pcc.org.uk/cop/practice.html/
The Editors' Code of Practice

www.pcc.org.uk/cop/evolving.html/
The Evolving Code of Practice

www.editorscode.org.uk/
Editors' Committee and Editors' Codebook

www.pcc.org.uk/advice/editorials-detail.html?article=NDIwMA==/
PCC guidance on the reporting of mental health issues

www.pcc.org.uk/advice/editorials-detail.html?article=OTM=/
PCC guidance on best practice in financial journalism

www.pcc.org.uk/about/whoswho/pressbof.html/
About the Press Standards Board of Finance

http://mediastandardstrust.org/projects/press-self-regulation/a-more-accountable-press/
The Media Standards Trust, which has proposed reform of the PCC

www.number10.gov.uk/news/leveson-inquiry-panel-terms-of-reference/
The terms of reference of the Leveson inquiry into press ethics and regulation

www.publications.parliament.uk/pa/cm200910/cmselect/cmcumeds/362/36202.htm
House of Commons Culture, Media and Sport Committee – 2010 report on press standards, privacy and libel

www.pcc.org.uk/news/index.html?article=NjMyNA==/
PCC response in 2010 to the above report

3

Broadcast regulation

Chapter summary

Journalism broadcast on television and radio in the UK is regulated by **statute**. The Office of Communications (Ofcom), the independent regulator, adjudicates on complaints against broadcast journalists. Ofcom's code of rules says commercial broadcast organisations must be impartial when covering politics and social issues, and must be accurate, treat people fairly, respect privacy and avoid causing harm and offence. Ofcom can impose substantial fines for breaches of the code. The BBC is also required to be impartial and ethical. It is subject to the Ofcom code in some respects, but also has a system of self-regulation involving the BBC Trust.

→glossary

Introduction

In the UK commercial broadcasters – those funded by advertising revenue – are regulated in terms of ownership and journalistic output. As the previous chapter explains, newspapers, magazines and online-only publishers are free to be politically partisan. But broadcast organisations and their journalists must, when reporting news, be impartial about politics and social issues, though they are free to cover them in depth. The regulatory system also requires broadcasters to observe 'due accuracy' in news, and other ethical norms. The regulator, Ofcom, can levy substantial fines on any broadcast organisation which seriously breaches journalistic standards.

Why regulate broadcasters?

Historically, broadcast media have been seen as having particular potential to influence, offend or harm their audiences. The emotional impact of moving images and sound can be greater than that of printed text and still pictures, and the ability of television and radio to air material instantaneously means they have great potential to provoke immediate public disorder or violence.

A further rationale is that television is seen as having great potential – because moving images and sound can often portray intimate or harrowing experiences more vividly than photographs or text – to intrude into privacy, or to harm children because it can project unsuitable portrayals of sex or violence or other disturbing material directly into their homes.

Politicians also decided that broadcasting must be regulated because for decades transmission was only possible on analogue wavelengths. These are relatively scarce, so a regulator was needed to decide who could broadcast, and on which frequency. The consensus was that the regulator should specify requirements for quality in programmes and diversity in output to make best use of scarce wavelengths.

These rationales for regulating broadcast media have lost some force as technological advances mean newspapers, magazines and other publishers can 'broadcast' audio-visual material on websites, so this power is no longer exclusive to TV and radio. Digital transmission also allows many more channels, giving the public greater freedom to choose what is worth watching or listening to.

There is also an argument that regulating broadcast journalism is a socially beneficial counterbalance to the unregulated politically partisan journalism of newspapers, magazines and online-only publishers, although it could also be said that regulation means broadcast journalism tends to have less 'bite' and impact than newspapers.

Ofcom – its role and sanctions

Commercial broadcasters cannot transmit without a licence from Ofcom, which began operating in 2003, replacing previous regulatory bodies. It is structurally independent of the Government, although Ministers appoint members of its main board. Ofcom, which for 2011/12 had a budget of £115.8 million, is funded mainly by licence fees paid by broadcasters, other charges it imposes, and Government funds. It has a range of duties, including regulating phone services. The Communications Act 2003 gives Ofcom roles which include ensuring the existence of a wide range of TV and radio services of high quality and wide appeal, and maintaining plurality in broadcasting. When deciding on applications for national, regional or local broadcast licences, it considers what programming is being proposed and whether the applicant is 'fit and proper'. Ofcom monitors whether TV and radio service providers comply with the conditions of their licences – for instance, by meeting a 'public service' obligation to provide news. Licences are granted for set durations, for example 12 years, and can be renewed.

The 2003 Act and the Broadcasting Act 1996 require Ofcom to draw up standards for programme content. These are detailed in the Ofcom Broadcasting Code. Anyone aggrieved by a programme's content or by how they were treated when it was made can – as long as the programme has been broadcast – complain to

Ofcom, which assesses complaints against those standards. Ofcom does not regulate all aspects of the BBC's output. Web content, even on sites run by broadcasters, is not subject to the code as it is not classed by law as broadcast material.

If Ofcom upholds a complaint it can direct that a programme should not be repeated, or that the broadcaster must air a correction or a statement of its findings in a specified form.

It can impose a fine if it considers breach of the code serious or reckless. If breaches by a broadcaster are persistent, it can shorten or suspend the broadcaster's licence and in the worst cases, revoke it – that is, close the station. The Independent Television Commission, an Ofcom predecessor, used this power in 1999 to close Med TV, a satellite station which broadcast across Europe to Kurdish people. The ITC said that Med TV repeatedly failed to report the conflict between Kurdish separatists and Turkey impartially, favoured Kurdish groups and 'transmitted material likely to encourage or incite' crime or disorder.

Ofcom cannot shorten, suspend or revoke the licences of the BBC, S4C or Channel 4 – they are public service broadcasters. But it can fine the BBC or S4C up to £250,000 for a code breach. For other broadcasters, the maximum fine is £250,000 or 5 per cent of the broadcaster's 'qualifying revenue'. In 2008 Ofcom fined ITV plc a total of £5,675,000 for multiple breaches which involved the misleading of viewers in phone-in competitions.

see Late News section for Press TV fine

Case study

The highest regulatory fine imposed for unethical broadcast journalism is £2 million paid by Central Independent Television, part of the ITV network, after a 1998 Independent Television Commission ruling that scenes in *The Connection* – a documentary which claimed to show a new heroin smuggling route from Colombia to the UK – were fabricated. The ITC said this was 'a wholesale breach' of the trust viewers placed in programme makers. *The Connection* had won awards before its authenticity was questioned in an investigation published by *The Guardian* newspaper, which led to the ITC's findings (ITC press release and *The Guardian*, December 18, 1998).

The scope of the Ofcom code

The Ofcom Broadcasting Code has rules on protecting under-18s (section 1); avoiding harm and offence (section 2); covering crime (section 3); covering religion (section 4); due impartiality and due accuracy and undue prominence of views and opinions (section 5); covering elections and referendums (section 6); fairness (section 7); protecting privacy (section 8); commercial references in television programming (section 9); and commercial communications in radio programming (section 10).

see Useful Websites, below, for the code's full text

With appendices and index, the code runs to 134 pages and covers all broadcast output, including drama and entertainment programmes.

Protecting the under-18s in the audience

see also p. 26, Imitation of harmful behaviour

Section 1 of the code says: 'Material that might seriously impair the physical, mental or moral development of people under 18 must not be broadcast' (rule 1.1). Broadcasters must take all reasonable steps to protect those under 18 (rule 1.2), it says, adding: 'Children must also be protected by appropriate scheduling from material that is unsuitable for them' (rule 1.3). 'Children' here means those under 15.

The TV watershed

Rule 1.4 says television broadcasters must observe the 9pm 'watershed' marking the transition for free-to-air TV channels between the times of day – from 5.30am to 9pm – when children are most likely to be watching, and later slots for which the audience is assumed to be more adult. Material unsuitable for children must not, in general, be broadcast pre-watershed, and the transition to post-watershed material must not be unduly abrupt (rule 1.6).

For pre-watershed broadcasts clear information should, if appropriate, be given about content which might distress children (rule 1.7). For example, news anchors can warn if footage about to be shown portrays violence. Violence or its after-effects must be 'appropriately limited' in pre-watershed broadcasts, and be justified by context (rule 1.11).

Rules also limit the pre-watershed televising of offensive language (rules 1.14–1.16), and portrayal or discussion of sexual behaviour (rule 1.20).

Times when children are likely to be listening to radio

The term 'watershed' is not used for radio. But the code says radio broadcasters must have particular regard to what is aired when 'children are particularly likely to be listening' (rules 1.5–1.6). Rules on content involving violence, offensive language, sexual material, and so on apply to radio at such times – for example, breakfast time.

Protecting children involved in programmes

Ofcom code rule 1.28 says broadcasters must take due care over 'the physical and emotional welfare and the dignity' of children under 18 who take part or are otherwise involved in programmes, irrespective of any consent they, their parents or guardians give. Rule 1.29 says they must not be caused unnecessary distress or anxiety.

Other elements of the code's protection of children are dealt with elsewhere in this book.

See p. 30 on informed consent; ch. 10, p. 111 on children in sex offence cases; see ch. 27, p. 329 on privacy.

See also www.mcnaes.com ch. 4 on children and teenagers involved in pre-trial investigations into crime.

Harm and offence

Section 2 of the Ofcom code says in rule 2.1 that 'generally accepted standards' must be applied to the content of television and radio broadcasts to protect the public from the inclusion of harmful or offensive material. Material which may cause offence includes pictures or sounds of distress, humiliation or violation of human dignity; offensive language; violence; sex; and treatment or language which discriminates on grounds of, for example, age, disability, gender, race, beliefs or sexual orientation. Material likely to cause offence must be justified by context, and appropriate information should be broadcast where it would help avoid or minimise offence (rule 2.3). Section 2 says context includes the programme's editorial content, the time of the broadcast and the likely size, composition and expectation of the potential audience.

Case study

In 2006 Ofcom ruled that the GMTV channel breached rule 2.3 in the way it showed CCTV images of an unprovoked knife attack by three men on two students, one of whom – Daniel Pollen – was killed. Police released the footage, with the students' families' permission, after a murder trial. Ofcom said the violent images were already being seen on screen by the time the newsreader completed an introductory sentence, and the tone of the introduction did not convey any sense of warning about the shocking images broadcast. Also, the wording left the impression that viewers were watching the actual murder when in fact the images ended just before the fatal blow. Ofcom said this casual use of exceptionally violent material added to the potential for causing offence to viewers (*Ofcom Broadcast Bulletin*, No. 68, September 4, 2006).

The code says demonstrations of exorcism, the occult, the paranormal, divination or related practices which purport to be real (as opposed to entertainment) must be treated with due objectivity and, if they are for entertainment, this must be made clear (rules 2.6 and 2.7).

There is also a general rule (2.2) that factual programmes or items or portrayals of factual matters must not materially mislead the audience (though accuracy in news output is regulated under the code's section 5, see p. 27).

Imitation of harmful behaviour

Programmes should not include material which, taking into account the context, condones or glamorises violent, dangerous or seriously anti-social behaviour and is likely to encourage others to copy it (rule 2.4). Violence, verbal or physical, which children can easily imitate in a harmful or dangerous manner, or easily imitable dangerous behaviour of any kind, or portrayals of it, must not, without editorial justification, be broadcast pre-watershed on television, or on radio when children are particularly likely to be listening (rules 1.12 and 1.13).

Methods of suicide and self-harm must not be included in programmes except when justified editorially and by context, to avoid people imitating them (rule 2.5).

For the rationale of the rule on reporting suicide methods, see ch. 2, p. 15 on similar provision in the Editors' Code of Practice.

Photosensitive epilepsy

Broadcasters must take precautions to avoid harm to viewers who have photosensitive epilepsy (rule 2.12), who can be affected by broadcasts of flashing lights, including news footage of photographers using flash equipment.

Crime

Section 3 of the code says material likely to encourage or incite the commission of crime or to lead to disorder must not be included in television or radio services (rule 3.1). Descriptions or demonstrations of criminal techniques which contain essential details which could enable the commission of crime must not be broadcast unless editorially justified (rule 3.2).

Broadcasters must use their best endeavours not to broadcast material which could endanger lives or prejudice the success of attempts to deal with a hijack or kidnapping (rule 3.6).

! Remember

Police dealing with kidnaps may ask news media to observe a temporary news 'blackout' to help preserve the victim's life. Also, coverage of anti-terrorist or hostage recovery operations should not include broadcasts of live material which might alert the terrorists to armed police or special forces launching a rescue operation.

see p. 31 for the Ofcom code's public interest exceptions

Payments to criminals

Section 3 forbids making any payment or promise of payment, directly or indirectly, to 'convicted or confessed criminals' for a programme contribution by the criminal relating to his/her crime, unless doing so is in the public interest (rule 3.3). As with similar provision in the Editor's Code of Practice, this is to avoid distressing victims of crime and outraging the public.

Payments to witnesses

Section 3 also prohibits broadcasters making or offering payments to witnesses in active criminal cases, or to anyone who might reasonably be expected to be called as a witness, though they can be paid expenses (rule 3.4). If a criminal case is not active, but is likely and foreseeable, payment should not be made to anyone who might reasonably be expected to be a witness unless there is a clear public interest. Any payment should be disclosed to the defence and prosecution if the person becomes a witness (rule 3.5).

see ch. 18 on contempt law and active cases

These rules are to ensure broadcasters do not jeopardise the administration of justice or commit contempt of court.

Religion

Section 4 of the Ofcom code says the views and beliefs of those belonging to a particular religion or religious denomination must not be subject to abusive treatment. Rule 4.7 says religious programmes containing claims that a living person (or group) has special powers or abilities must treat such claims with due objectivity. They must not be broadcast when significant numbers of children may be expected to be watching or listening.

Due impartiality and due accuracy

Section 5 of the Ofcom code sets out impartiality and accuracy requirements for broadcasters other than the BBC, which has its own regulatory requirements on these matters.

see p. 34 on the BBC

Rule 5.1 says: 'News, in whatever form, must be reported with due accuracy and presented with due impartiality'.

Section 5 says impartiality means not favouring one side over another, and that the qualification 'due' means adequate or appropriate to the programme's subject and nature. 'So "due impartiality" does not mean an equal division of time has to be given to every view, or that every argument and every facet of every argument has to be represented. The approach to due impartiality may vary according to the nature of the subject, the type of programme and channel, the likely expectation of the audience as to content, and the extent to which the content and approach is signalled to the audience.'

Politicians may not be used as newsreaders, interviewers or reporters in any news programme unless, exceptionally, this is editorially justified and the individual's political allegiance is made clear to the audience (rule 5.3).

Owners of broadcast organisations may not use them to project their own views on 'matters of political or industrial controversy and matters relating to current public policy'. The code offers a general definition of such matters in this section.

Rules 5.5 to 5.12 require the providers of television programme services, teletext services, national radio and national digital sound programme services to preserve due impartiality on such matters in their output. This may be achieved over a series of programmes 'taken as a whole' rather than in a single programme.

The code seeks to ensure the presentation of a diversity of opinion in respect of major political and industrial controversy and major matters of current public policy, saying 'an appropriately wide range of significant views must be included and given due weight in each programme or in clearly linked and timely programmes' (rule 5.12).

Case study

In 2008 Ofcom ruled that Channel 4 breached impartiality requirements in part of *The Great Global Warming Swindle*, a programme challenging the mainstream scientific view that human activity is the major cause of climate change. When the programme referred to policies espoused by Western nations – that industrial production must be restrained worldwide to limit global warming – the narration suggested that a consequence of these policies was a lack of electricity in many parts of the developing world, and resultant higher rates of mortality and respiratory disease. Ofcom said the programme had not presented an appropriately wide range of significant views on these policies (*Ofcom Broadcast Bulletin*, No. 114, July 21, 2008).

The code says that any personal interest of a reporter or presenter which would call the due impartiality of the programme into question must be made clear to the audience (rule 5.8).

'Personal view' and 'authored' programmes

Rule 5.9 says: 'Presenters and reporters (with the exception of news presenters and reporters in news programmes), presenters of "personal view" or "authored" programmes or items, and chairs of discussion programmes may express their own views on matters of political or industrial controversy or matters relating to current public policy. But alternative viewpoints must be adequately represented either in the programme, or in a series, taken as a whole. Presenters must not use the advantage of regular appearances to promote their views in a way which compromises the requirement for due impartiality. Presenter phone-ins must encourage and must not exclude alternative views.'

'Personal view' programmes are defined as those presenting a particular view or perspective. These could involve a person who is a member of a lobby group and is campaigning on a subject expressing highly partial views, or 'the considered "authored" opinion of a journalist, commentator or academic, with expertise or a specialism in an area which enables her or him to express opinions which are not necessarily mainstream.' The code says a personal view or authored programme or item must be clearly signalled as such at the outset (rule 5.10).

Accuracy considerations

Ofcom guidance says that the clarification of the term 'due' in respect of impartiality, mentioned above, also applies to the accuracy requirement. Significant mistakes in news should normally be acknowledged and corrected on air quickly, with corrections appropriately scheduled (rule 5.2). Views and facts must not be misrepresented (rule 5.7).

see Useful Websites below for this guidance

! Remember

A journalist who, to produce a dramatic effect, edits news or documentary footage or an audio recording in a way which, when it is broadcast, misrepresents a sequence of events would breach the code. The code would also be breached if a broadcaster stages and airs a reconstruction of a news event while failing to make clear to the audience that it was not the real event.

Undue prominence of views and opinions

Rule 5.13, which applies to local radio services and local digital sound programme services, including those at community level, says their broadcasters 'should not give undue prominence to the views and opinions of particular persons or bodies on matters of political or industrial controversy and matters relating to current public policy' in programming when 'taken as a whole', by which it means programming 'dealing with the same or related issues within an appropriate period'.

Section 5 defines 'undue prominence of views and opinions' as a significant imbalance of views.

Section 6 of the Ofcom code sets out specific requirements for broadcasters to maintain impartiality during election and referendum periods and restricts use of exit polls – see ch. 32 of this book.

Fairness

Section 7 of the Ofcom code sets out general principles on how programme makers should treat people or organisations participating or featured in programmes.

Rule 7.1 says 'Broadcasters must avoid unjust or unfair treatment of individuals or organisations in programmes'.

The section details 'Practices to be followed'. If a failure to follow a practice results in unjust or unfair treatment this will be a breach of the code.

Practice 7.2 says broadcasters and programme makers should be fair in dealings with potential contributors to programmes unless, exceptionally, doing otherwise is justified.

Informed consent

Practice 7.3 says people or organisations who agree to take part in programmes should do so on the basis of 'informed consent', which requires that a person invited to contribute to a programme should (unless the subject matter is trivial or their participation minor) normally be told:

- its nature and purpose, and what it is about, and be given a clear explanation of why they were asked to contribute and when and where it is likely to be broadcast;
- the kind of contribution they are expected to make – live, pre-recorded, interview, discussion, edited, unedited, etc.;
- the areas of questioning and, wherever possible, the nature of other likely contributions.

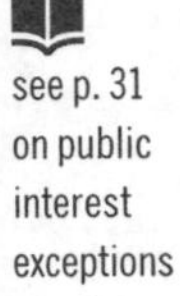

see p. 31 on public interest exceptions

The code adds that the public interest may justify withholding all or some of this information.

Case study

In 2007 Ofcom ruled that the makers of a programme *The Toughest Seaside Resorts in Britain*, featuring Saltcoats, Ayrshire, shown on Sky One, treated North Ayrshire Council and councillor Peter McNamara unfairly. It said the makers did not provide adequate information about the programme's likely nature when dealing with the council and Mr McNamara, who was interviewed. In an initial letter the programme's associate producer told the council the intention was 'to celebrate "the best of British"', without indicating the programme's full title. Ofcom said the featured local residents – one was shown wielding a knife and displaying fight scars – would inevitably have left viewers with an extremely negative impression of the resort. The programme also suggested that the resort's beach and seawater was polluted, although it had won an environmental award. Ofcom said the programme was likely to have misled the audience into forming an unduly negative impression of Saltcoats (*Ofcom Broadcast Bulletin*, No. 82, April 10, 2007).

The code says that guarantees given to contributors, for example relating to the content of a programme, confidentiality or anonymity should normally be honoured (practice 7.7).

See ch. 34 for cases in which journalists ethically kept secret the identities of their sources.

Informed consent in the case of children

If a contributor is under 16, a parent or guardian's consent should normally be obtained. Those under 16 should not be asked for views on matters likely to be beyond their capacity to answer properly without such consent (practice 7.4).

Getting and airing the other side of the story

Practice 7.11 says that if a programme alleges wrongdoing or incompetence or makes other significant allegations, those concerned should normally be given an appropriate and timely opportunity to respond. Where a person approached to contribute to a programme chooses to make no comment or refuses to appear, the broadcast should make this clear – and give their explanation if it would be unfair not to do so (practice 7.12).

Public interest exceptions

Ofcom accepts that programme makers may be justified in breaching some of the code's provisions 'in the public interest'. It uses the term 'warranted' to indicate when there must be a public interest, or some other exceptional justification, to merit breaching the usual rules.

Section 8 says that examples of public interest include:

- revealing or detecting crime;
- protecting public health or safety;
- exposing misleading claims made by individuals or organisations; or
- disclosing incompetence that affects the public.

 There are similar public interest exceptions in the Editors' Code of Practice, see ch. 2, p. 14.

Deception and misrepresentation

The Ofcom code says in practice 7.14 that

> broadcasters or programme makers should not normally obtain or seek information, audio, pictures or an agreement to contribute through misrepresentation or deception.

But the code adds that it may be warranted to use material gained by such tactics if it is in the public interest and the material cannot reasonably be obtained by other means.

A journalist who lies about the nature of a programme in order to trick a criminal into taking part will not breach the code's fairness rule if the programme's purpose is to expose sufficiently serious offences. Similarly, giving a false reason to a public institution when seeking consent to film its activities will not be a breach if the public interest is sufficient, such as exposing incompetence affecting the public. The public interest can justify journalists misrepresenting themselves, for example by posing as members of another profession or an uninformed citizen. But in all such instances, if a complaint is made, Ofcom will consider whether what was done was proportionate (not excessive) and whether there was any other way the material could reasonably have been obtained.

Secret filming and recording – deception

The Ofcom code says in practice 7.14 that 'surreptitious' – secret or undercover – filming or recording is a type of deception. Under the code, material gained in this way should not normally be broadcast unless the person filmed or recorded consents.

Surreptitious filming or recording includes using long lenses or recording devices, and leaving an unattended camera or recording device on private property without the full and informed consent of the occupiers, or deliberately continuing a recording when the other party thinks it has ended (section 8).

But practice 7.14 says that it may be warranted to use, without consent, film or audio gained surreptitiously, if it is in the public interest and the material could not have reasonably been obtained by other means.

Practice 7.14 adds that if an individual or organisation filmed or recorded surreptitiously is not identifiable in the programme as broadcast, their consent to be included in it is not required (though their right to privacy would need to be taken into account).

Secret filming and recording – intrusion into privacy

Surreptitious filming or recording can violate privacy, for example by recording private conversations without consent, even if the person is not identified in, or the conversations included in, what is broadcast.

Section 8 of the code, which deals with protecting privacy, says any infringement of privacy in programmes, or in connection with obtaining material included in programmes, must, unless broadcast with consent, be warranted by the public interest or some other exceptional reason (rule 8.1 and practice 8.5). Ofcom will deem a failure by programme makers to observe any of the 'practices to be followed' in section 8 as breaching the code if it leads to an unwarranted infringement of privacy.

Practices 8.13 and 8.14 say surreptitious filming or recording should only be done when warranted and that normally it will only be warranted if:

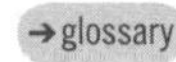

- there is **prima facie** evidence of a story in the public interest; and
- reasonable grounds to suspect that further material evidence could be obtained; and
- it is necessary to the programme's credibility and authenticity.

for explanation of 'fishing expeditions' see ch. 2, p. 16

The requirement for prima facie evidence is to prevent arbitrary 'fishing expeditions'.

Ofcom guidance says broadcasters should take care not to infringe the privacy of bystanders who may be caught inadvertently in the recording – for example, it may be necessary to obscure the identities of those recorded incidentally.

Recording phone conversations

Practice 8.12 of the Ofcom code says broadcasters can record telephone calls if they have, from the outset of the call, identified themselves, explained to the other person the call's purpose and that it is being recorded for possible broadcast (if that is the case) unless it is warranted not to identify themselves or give such explanation. 'Warranted' means that failing to tell the person that the call is being recorded for broadcast, failing to explain its purpose or broadcasting a recording of it without consent can be justified if the journalism is 'in the public interest'.

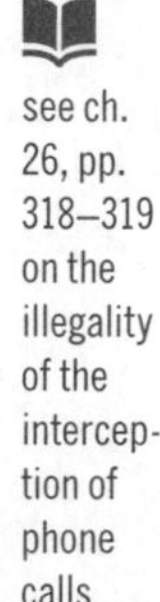
see ch. 26, pp. 318–319 on the illegality of the interception of phone calls

Ofcom might class recording a phone call without the other person's knowledge as a surreptitious recording, and therefore – if the intention is to broadcast it – practices 7.14 and 8.13 apply. But Ofcom guidance states that it is acceptable for journalists to record their own calls for note-taking purposes.

Privacy in general

Section 8 of the Ofcom code includes general provisions for protecting people's privacy in relation to journalists openly filming or audio-recording. These are explained in chapter 27 of this book, which also explains the code's use of the term 'legitimate expectation of privacy' and its restrictions on 'doorstepping'.

Practice 8.2 says the location of a person's home or family should not be disclosed without permission, unless it is warranted.

Financial journalism

Appendix 4 of the code sets out 'binding guidance' on how commercial broadcasters must operate to comply with legislation prohibiting financial promotions and setting standards for investment recommendations. For example, people working on programmes who make an investment recommendation must disclose any financial interest they have that 'may reasonably be expected to impair the objectivity of that recommendation'.

Other parts of the Ofcom code

Parts of the code regulate commercial references in television programming (section 9) and commercial communications in radio programming (section 10). These sections have overarching rules to ensure there is a distinction between editorial and advertising content, and set out specific principles of editorial independence as regards television. News and current affairs programmes on television must not be sponsored (rule 9.15). No commercial reference is permitted in or around radio news bulletins (rule 10.2). There are also rules on the broadcasting of charity appeals. With the exception of relevant 'product placement' rules for television, these sections do not apply to BBC services funded by the TV licence fee as they do not carry advertising.

The BBC

The BBC, the biggest broadcasting organisation in the world, has eight national TV channels plus regional programming, ten national radio stations, 40 local radio stations, plus its website.

The legal bases for the BBC's existence are its Royal Charter and the Agreement with Parliament, which are renewed every ten years. The Agreement specifies that the BBC must do all it can to ensure that controversial subjects are treated with due accuracy and due impartiality in all relevant output. These aspects of its output, including its journalism, are regulated by the BBC Trust, the BBC's governing body. This means that complaints about inaccuracy or lack of impartiality in BBC output cannot be considered by Ofcom, only by the BBC itself. Also, Ofcom does not regulate the BBC's online output or its World Service.

The BBC has an Editorial Complaints Unit. Complainants unhappy with its decisions can appeal to the Trust, which publishes its appeal findings online.

In other respects – for example, if it is alleged that material broadcast was unfair or offensive – Ofcom regulates the BBC, which is therefore subject to relevant parts of the Ofcom code. So, while the BBC will consider complaints about all such matters, complainants can contact Ofcom directly, either initially or if they are dissatisfied with the corporation's response.

see Useful Websites below

The BBC's Editorial Guidelines set out standards for its journalism, including undercover investigations. The BBC's online College of Journalism, which helps train its journalists in law and ethics, is accessible to everyone.

Recap of major points

- Broadcast journalism is regulated by the Office of Communications (Ofcom).
- Broadcast organisations must comply with the Ofcom Broadcasting Code, which requires them to avoid harm and offence, to be fair and to protect people's privacy.
- Ofcom considers complaints against broadcasters, and has a statutory power to compel them to air its adjudications.
- It can fine them for the worst transgressions of the code, and can close a commercial broadcaster which persistently or recklessly flouts the code.
- There must be 'due accuracy' and 'due impartiality' in all broadcast news.

- The BBC is not regulated by Ofcom as regards accuracy and impartiality. The BBC Trust is the ultimate adjudicator on complaints against the BBC in these respects.

((•)) Useful Websites

www.ofcom.org.uk/about/what-is-ofcom/
What is Ofcom?

www.ofcom.org.uk/about/how-ofcom-is-run/
How Ofcom is run

http://stakeholders.ofcom.org.uk/broadcasting/broadcast-codes/broadcast-code/
The Ofcom Broadcasting Code

http://stakeholders.ofcom.org.uk/broadcasting/guidance/programme-guidance/bguidance/
Ofcom's guidance on the code

www.bbc.co.uk/aboutthebbc/
About the BBC

www.bbc.co.uk/historyofthebbc/index.shtml
History of the BBC

www.bbc.co.uk/guidelines/editorialguidelines/
BBC Editorial Guidelines

www.bbc.co.uk/guidelines/editorialguidelines/news/news-2011-09-13/
BBC revised guidance on investigations and secret recording

www.bbc.co.uk/journalism/
BBC College of Journalism

www.bbc.co.uk/complaints/
BBC complaints system

www.bbc.co.uk/bbctrust/index.shtml
BBC Trust

www.parliament.uk/documents/lords-committees/communications/BBCgovernance/BBCgov.pdf/
The Government's 2011 response to a proposal that Ofcom should regulate the BBC on impartiality and accuracy.

www.cpbf.org.uk/
Campaign for Press and Broadcasting Freedom

Part 2

Crime, courts and tribunals

4

Crime: media coverage prior to any court case

Chapter summary

This chapter explains how police investigations are driven by the standard of proof needed to convict someone of a crime. Reporters should understand police powers to arrest and to detain. There is a strong public interest in the media reporting on crime and how police investigate it. But the media need to be wary of contempt of court law, made 'active' when a crime suspect is arrested and in other circumstances. There can also be libel risks if media reports identify a suspect before he/she is charged.

Standard of proof in criminal law

Those accused of crime enjoy 'the presumption of innocence'. This legal principle means that if they are charged with a criminal offence the law does not require them to prove themselves innocent. The onus is on the prosecutor to prove guilt 'beyond reasonable doubt', the standard of proof necessary in law for a conviction. Police and other agencies which investigate crime need clear evidence to meet this standard.

Arrests

Police have wide powers of arrest. Under the Serious Organised Crime and Police Act 2005 a police officer can arrest a person who has committed, or is committing, an offence (however minor), or is about to commit one, or anyone for whom there are reasonable grounds to suspect of a crime. But the officer must also have reasonable grounds for believing the arrest is necessary to achieve one of the purposes specified in the Act – for example, that the arrest is necessary to allow 'prompt and effective investigation' of a crime, or to stop a person from obstructing the highway. Police can use 'reasonable force' to make an arrest. An arrest automatically makes the case 'active' under the Contempt of Court Act 1981, affecting what can be published about it.

! Remember

The 1981 Act, explained in chapter 18, safeguards the fairness of trials. That chapter explains what types of material, if published about an active case, can breach the Act. A breach is a contempt offence, for which a media organisation can be heavily fined.

Police questioning of suspects

A person under arrest is usually taken to a police station. A suspect who goes to a police station voluntarily may be arrested there. Police sometimes tell the media that someone is 'helping with inquiries'.

Journalists should check whether the suspect is helping police voluntarily or is under arrest, because newsrooms need to know if the case is 'active'. If it *is* 'active', contempt law affects what can be published.

Limits to detention by police, prior to any charge

To protect civil liberties, no one should normally be held under arrest for more than 24 hours, and if they have not been charged within that period they must be released. This period runs from the time of arrest or from the time the suspect was brought into the police station, depending on circumstances. A police superintendent can authorise that someone suspected of an **indictable offence** be detained for a further 12 hours. If police apply to a magistrates court it can authorise the person's detention for another 36 hours. If a further application is made, the court cannot extend this detention beyond a maximum period of 96 hours – that is, 96 hours since detention began. People suspected of terrorism can be detained longer without charge. The Protection of Freedoms Bill contains provision to reduce this period from 28 days to 14 days for those suspected of terrorism.

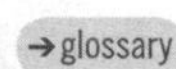

False imprisonment

If an arrested person later decides to sue the police for damages, alleging 'false arrest' or 'false imprisonment', he or she must prove that the police grounds for detention were unreasonable.

www.mcnaes.com ch. 4 explains the *habeas corpus* procedure in which the police and other official agencies can be required to justify to the High Court why a person is being detained.

Ch. 36 explains that photo-journalists covering tense incidents may be threatened with arrest.

The Crown Prosecution Service

Most prosecutions are the responsibility of the Crown Prosecution Service (CPS), a government department. It has local bases serving each of the 43 police areas in England and Wales. The head of the CPS is the Director of Public Prosecutions. It is independent of the police, but has the duty to advise and direct them in all investigations, except those relating to the most minor crimes. The CPS decides, in all major cases involving police investigation, whether a suspect should be prosecuted, and if so, what the charge(s) should be.

- A charge is a formal accusation, giving the alleged offender basic details of the crime allegedly committed, including the name of any alleged victim. It means the case will be prosecuted, and so go to court.

((•)) see Useful Websites, below, for the CPS site

Usually a suspect is charged at a police station. He/she should be given the charge in written form, but may already have been charged orally, before that document was ready. The charge makes the case 'active' under the Contempt of Court Act 1981, if not active already because of an arrest.

The case ceases to be 'active' if an arrested person is released without charge, unless he/she is released on **police bail** because police want more time to complete investigations. A suspect on such bail must return to a police station at a specified date. Then the suspect may be charged, or be released without charge.

→glossary

The www.mcnaes.com chapter on Scotland provides an outline of the prosecution system in Scotland.

Decisions on whether to prosecute

When considering whether a suspect should be prosecuted, CPS lawyers assess if there is 'a realistic prospect of conviction'. If the case passes that test, they consider if it is in the public interest to prosecute. In almost all serious cases, consideration of the public interest leads to a decision to prosecute.

Limits to detention by police, after any charge

Once a person has been charged police questioning of him/her must stop, except in limited circumstances. The person, if under arrest, must by law be brought before a magistrates court on the day he/she was charged or the following day, except for Sundays, Christmas Day or Good Friday. Alternatively, after being charged, the person may be released and given police bail to attend the court.

In cases arising from police investigations, lawyers employed by the CPS conduct the prosecution in the courts, apart from in some minor cases in which the police prosecute.

Other prosecution agencies in the public sector

Various other governmental agencies investigate and prosecute offences. For example: local authorities can investigate and prosecute property landlords for breach of tenants' rights; the Serious Fraud Office, a government department, investigates and prosecutes serious and/or complex fraud.

Laying or presenting of information; summonses; requisitions

The decision whether to prosecute may be taken quickly – for example, soon after an arrest, or the decision may not be taken for months if this time is needed to gather evidence. A prosecution can then begin either with a charge, or by the 'laying of information' before a magistrate. In the latter procedure, an allegation that a crime has been committed is made orally or in writing to a magistrate. He/she will, without at that stage full consideration of evidence, issue a summons to be served on the alleged perpetrator.

- A summons is a formal document, issued by a magistrates court, setting out one or more crime allegations in similar detail to a charge. It requires attendance at court on a specified date to respond to the allegation(s).

The summons makes the case active under the Contempt of Court Act 1981, as chapter 18 explains.

The Criminal Justice Act 2003 is replacing, for some public prosecutors including those of the CPS, the 'laying of information' with a streamlined procedure called 'written charge and requisition' in which a written charge is issued by the prosecuting agency to the accused person. The requisition served with it is formal notification of the date for him/her to turn up at the magistrates court. The service of the charge makes a case 'active' under the 1981 Act.

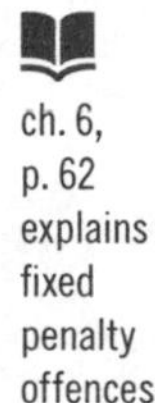

ch. 6, p. 62 explains fixed penalty offences

Summonses and requisitions are used routinely for minor offences involving 'fixed penalty'.

Arrest warrants

- An arrest warrant is a formal document in which a magistrate empowers any police officer to arrest the suspect wherever he/she is located in the UK, to be brought to the magistrates court.

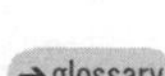

→glossary

Magistrates can issue an arrest warrant if sworn, written information is laid before them that a person has committed an indictable offence, or any **summary** offence punishable by imprisonment, or in any case in which the person's address is not sufficiently established for a requisition or summons to be served. The indictable and summary categories are explained in the next chapter.

Arrest warrants can also be used for a suspect 'on the run'. When an arrest warrant is issued, its terms may allow a person, after being arrested and having completed formalities at the police station, to be released on **bail** to attend the magistrates court at a future date.

→glossary

The issue of an arrest warrant makes the case 'active' under the 1981 Act, if it is not already active because of an oral charge, a summons or service of a written charge.

'Private prosecutions'

Any citizen can, by the laying of information before a magistrate, start a prosecution seeking to prove that the individual accused is guilty of a specified crime. The police and the CPS may be aware of the allegation, but have concluded there is no or insufficient evidence. This capacity for any citizen to start a 'private prosecution' is seen as a fundamental right to counterbalance any inertia or partiality by police or other official agencies. But a magistrate can refuse to issue a summons if the allegation is deemed frivolous. A private prosecution may quickly become unsustainable because, for example, an individual citizen lacks the investigatory powers given in law to police. The CPS can take over the conduct of a 'private prosecution', and therefore also withdraw the case. The Attorney General can also stop private prosecutions.

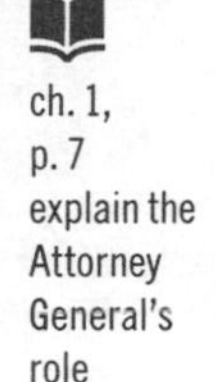

ch. 1, p. 7 explain the Attorney General's role

The Royal Society for the Prevention of Cruelty to Animals regularly conducts successful 'private prosecutions' for cruelty to or neglect of animals.

The risk of libel in media identification of crime suspects

The media may discover that someone is being investigated by the police or another agency – for example, that the person is under arrest. If a media report publishes the suspect's name, or other detail identifying him/her in this context, that person could successfully sue the publisher for libel if the investigation does not lead to a prosecution. Publishing a statement that someone is under investigation, even when this is factually correct, is defamatory because it creates an inference that the person may be guilty.

chs. 19 and 20 explain libel dangers

Case study

In 2011 Bristol landlord Chris Jefferies won 'very substantial' settlements in libel actions against eight national newspapers for articles published after one of his tenants, the architect Joanna Yeates, was found dead. Mr Jefferies had been arrested at one stage by police but was later released. The newspapers published defamatory material about him. But then another man was charged with murdering Joanna. Louis Charalambous, Mr Jefferies' solicitor, said of the libellous coverage: 'Christopher Jefferies is the latest victim of the regular witch hunts and character assassination conducted by the worst elements of the British tabloid media' (*Media Lawyer*, July 29, 2011).

As chapter 18 explains, what was published about Mr Jefferies also led to two newspapers being convicted of contempt of court.

If a spokesperson for a governmental agency, for example the police, CPS or a local council, officially releases to the media the name of a person under investigation/arrest, then the media can safely publish it, protected by the libel defence of qualified privilege if its requirements are met. Chapter 21 explains this.

In reality, when reporting high-profile investigations, especially if a celebrity or public figure is a suspect, media organisations may choose, within the fierce competition to break news, to publish the suspect's name before it is known if he/she will be charged and without any qualified privilege. The media may decide that the person is unlikely to launch a libel action because, for example, a celebrity or politician may not wish to alienate the media or stir up more publicity. Or the media may take the risk of naming the person because police leaks indicate that a charge is sure to follow. If the person is charged, a libel action over pre-charge publicity becomes less likely, because any damage this caused to the person's reputation will usually be dwarfed by, or indistinguishable from, damage caused by reports of the consequent court case, which the media can safely publish.

ACPO guidelines on police naming of suspects and victims

Guidelines issued to police forces in 2010 by the Association of Chief Police Officers (ACPO) state that generally police do not give to the media the name of a person under investigation prior to any charge but that some details – for example, that the person is 'a 27-year-old Brighton man' – may be released, and that some forces will confirm the name of such a person if put to them by the media.

These guidelines state that most forces will, if a person is charged, tell the media his/her name, age and occupation and may, unless there is an operational reason not to, give his/her home address, plus detail of the charge and forthcoming court appearance. The guidelines add that forces will generally confirm investigations into companies.

((•)) see Useful Websites, below, for the ACPO guidelines

The guidelines warn that police usually consider the names of witnesses and crime victims to be confidential, but that dead crime victims will usually be identified to the media after immediate relatives are informed.

Pre-charge anonymity for teachers

Section 13 of the Education Act 2011 will, when put into force, ban the media from identifying any teacher alleged to have committed a criminal offence against a pupil at the teacher's school, unless the teacher is charged. The section says: 'No matter relating to the person is to be included in any publication if it is likely to lead members of the public to identify the person as the teacher who is the subject of the allegation.' The ban is automatic and indefinite, and therefore bestows life-long anonymity if there is no charge. It lapses automatically if there is a charge. Also, a court can make an order to remove the anonymity 'in the interests of justice', or the teacher can waive the anonymity. Section 13 was a response to teachers' groups complaining of false allegations made by pupils. But it is controversial, because no other profession has such pre-charge anonymity.

see Late News section

See mcnaes.com ch. 4 for law banning the disclosure of the identities of police informants, including 'investigation anonymity orders'; ethical considerations when journalists accompany police 'raids' to arrest or search; what the PCC and Ofcom say about the media identifying juveniles involved in pre-trial investigations.

Recap of major points

- When covering crime stories, there are contempt of court dangers for the media, because an arrest, an oral charge, service of a written charge or the issue of a summons or an arrest warrant makes a case 'active' under the Contempt of Court Act 1981.
- When covering crime stories, there could well be libel risks if a suggestion is published, prior to any charge, that a suspect is guilty of a crime.
- But if the police or another governmental agency, in an official statement, identifies a person as a suspect, it is safe to report the statement.
- Some police informants are protected by anonymity orders.

((•)) Useful Websites

www.cps.gov.uk/
Crown Prosecution Service

www.cps.gov.uk/about/principles.html
Code for Crown Prosecutors

www.acpo.presscentre.com/content/default.aspx?NewsAreaID=19/
Association of Chief Police Officers (ACPO) Communication Advisory Group – Guidance 2010

5

Crimes: categories and definitions

Chapter summary

All criminal cases begin in the magistrates courts. The most serious cases – for example, charges of murder, rape or robbery – progress to a Crown court. Journalists must know the different categories of crime to understand when reporting restrictions affect what can be published in court stories. Also, journalists need to know the legal definitions of some crimes to avoid libel problems when referring to offences.

Categories of criminal offence

Criminal charges – and therefore the offences they allege – are grouped into three categories: indictable-only, either-way and summary.

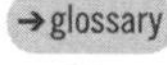

(1) ***Indictable-only offences*** are the most serious crimes, punishable by the longest prison terms – for example, murder, rape, robbery. Such a case is processed initially by a magistrates court, but cannot be dealt with there because the maximum jail sentence which magistrates can impose (six months) would be too lenient for a defendant convicted of a serious offence. So, indictable-only cases progress quickly to a Crown court, as explained in chapter 7. If the defendant admits the charge there, or a jury finds him/her guilty, the judge will sentence. The term 'indictable-only' derives from 'the indictment', the document used at a Crown court to record the charge(s).

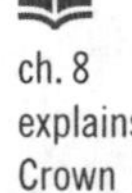

ch. 8 explains Crown courts

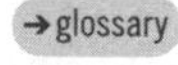

(2) ***Either-way offences*** include theft, sexual assault and assault causing grievous bodily harm. This type of charge can be dealt with either at a Crown court or by magistrates, hence the term 'either-way'. For this category, magistrates may – after hearing an outline of the case – decide it is so serious that only a Crown court can deal with it. As chapter 7 explains, if the

magistrates decide they *can* deal with the case, the defendant may nevertheless exercise his/her legal right, which exists for either-way offences, to opt for trial by jury at a Crown court. Either-way offences are regarded as being less serious than indictable-only offences, but nevertheless include distressing, harmful crimes.

! Remember

Confusingly, indictable-only and either-way charges are sometimes referred to collectively as 'indictable' charges, because both categories share the possibility of jury trial at a Crown court. But, as stated above, magistrates can decide to deal with an either-way case in their **summary proceedings** that is, as if it were a **summary offence.** →glossary

(3) ***Summary offences*** These are comparatively minor offences, and include common assault, drunkenness and speeding offences. Summary charges are dealt with in magistrates courts, except in some cases in which a defendant faces both summary and either-way or indictable charges arising from the same event, in which instance a Crown court may deal with all of them. But people charged with a summary offence have no right for it to be tried by jury. So, 'summary proceedings' means 'proceedings in a magistrates court', with the term 'summary' indicating the relative speed of this process.

Defining criminality

There are two elements in most crimes:

- an act which is potentially criminal – which lawyers refer to as the *actus reus* (which is pronounced, in lawyers' Latin, 'actus reeus'); and
- a guilty mind – referred to as the *mens rea* ('menz reeah'), which means that such an act was carried out, or planned or attempted, with guilty intent – that the perpetrator knew he/she was acting, or intending to act, in a way which is morally wrong.

The general principle is that a prosecutor has to prove both elements. In the crime of murder, the *actus reus* is that of unlawfully killing someone, and the *mens rea* is that the act was done with 'malice aforethought'. If there is no such **malice**, a killing may be a lesser crime – for example, manslaughter. →glossary

Strict liability

Some offences are of **strict liability.** Strict liability, when it applies in law, removes or strictly limits any legal defences to the charge. Strict liability means

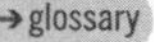

that a motorist who exceeds the speed limit commits an offence, even if he/she did not realise how fast he/she was driving. A motorist who drives with too much alcohol in his/her blood commits an offence, even if he/she did not intend to breach the alcohol limit. Strict liability can be seen as a practical, societal solution to deter dangerous or anti-social conduct for which, in many cases, it would be impossible to prove that *mens rea* – a guilty mind – existed.

ch. 18, p. 215 explains this strict liability contempt offence

Journalists need to understand this concept, not least because some criminal offences arising from publishing material are of strict liability, meaning it is not a defence to say 'Sorry, I didn't intend to...' – for example, if matter is published which breaches the Contempt of Court Act 1981.

Definitions of crimes

chs. 19–20 explain libel

A victim of theft may tell friends he/she has been 'robbed'. If a journalist makes this colloquial error when reporting a court case he/she seems foolish and – worse – the error could lead to a libel action. If a defendant is guilty of a minor theft, but is wrongly reported as guilty of robbery, the mistake suggests to the public that he/she committed a much worse crime, in that a robbery – because it involves violence or threatened violence – is generally regarded as worse than a theft.

The crime definitions listed below are simplified. For fuller definitions, see the Crown Prosecution Service's Legal Guidance section, listed below under Useful Websites.

Crimes against people

Murder The unlawful killing of a human being, 'with malice aforethought' – that is, the intention was to kill or cause grievous bodily harm. An adult convicted of murder must be sentenced to life imprisonment. Indictable-only.

Manslaughter The unlawful killing of another person, but without malice aforethought. Manslaughter can be a charge in its own right. Alternatively, a jury in a murder trial, if it finds the defendant not guilty of murder, can in some circumstances convict him/her of manslaughter as an alternative. Indictable-only.

Corporate manslaughter An offence for which the senior managers of an organisation, including a company, a government department or a police force, can be convicted if it causes a person's death in the circumstance of a gross breach of a duty of care owed to that person, if the way in which its activities were managed or organised by its senior management was a substantial element in that breach. Indictable-only.

Causing or allowing the death of a child or vulnerable adult An offence introduced in 2004 to close a legal loophole through which, for example, a couple whose child died because of physical abuse could escape justice by blaming each other, making it difficult to prove which of them was the killer. This offence enables both to be prosecuted. Indictable-only.

Infanticide The killing of an infant under 12 months old by its mother, when her mind is disturbed as a result of the birth. Indictable-only.

Assault, common assault, battery, assault by beating The way these offences evolved in **case law** led their definitions to overlap. 'Assault' and 'common assault' can mean an unlawful infliction of force/violence, or a hostile act – for example, a threatening gesture – which causes another person to fear that immediate violence will occur. Journalists should not assume that an assault charge necessarily alleges that a physical attack occurred. A push can be a common assault. Either type of act must be proved as intentional or reckless. Battery can also be expressed as a charge of 'assault by beating'. One of these four charges tends to be used if no, or only transient or trifling, bodily injury is allegedly caused. They are summary, unless there are allegedly racial or religious motives in the assault, in which event they are either-way.

→glossary

Assault occasioning actual bodily harm (ABH) An assault – that is, a threat and/or attack, see above – which caused harm more than transient and trifling. Either-way.

Wounding or inflicting grievous bodily harm (GBH) These charges are in section 20 of the Offences Against the Person Act 1861, and overlap in their definitions. It must be proved that the perpetrator intended or foresaw causing some harm, and – depending on which charge the prosecutor chooses – that the harm caused was a wound or grievous (that is, serious) harm which was not or not only a wound. Either charge, in full form, includes the term 'malicious' – for example, 'malicious wounding'. A 'wound' is the slicing-through or breakage of skin, and can be a mere cut. But a wounding charge tends to be used only if the wound is serious. A GBH charge tends to be used, for example, if the harm includes broken bone, or led to substantial loss of blood, and/or extended medical treatment and/or permanent disfigurement and/or permanent disability. These charges are either-way.

Wounding 'with intent'/inflicting grievous bodily harm 'with intent' Under section 18 of the 1861 Act, the wounding or GBH is deemed to have been 'with intent' if there is intent to cause GBH or to resist 'lawful apprehension'. Such a charge is indictable-only. It carries a maximum penalty of life imprisonment.

Rape Indictable-only. See definitions of sexual offences in chapter 10, which also explains that victims of these offences must have anonymity in media reports.

Crimes against property or involving gain

Theft Dishonest appropriation of property belonging to another with the intention of permanently depriving the other of it (Theft Act 1968). Either-way. The act of theft is stealing. Do not refer to the offence as robbery.

Robbery Theft by force (that is, violence), or by threat of force. Indictable-only.

Handling Dishonestly receiving goods, knowing or believing them to be stolen; or dishonestly helping in the retention, removal, disposal or sale of such goods. Either-way.

Burglary Entering a building as a trespasser, and then:

- stealing or attempting to steal from it; or
- inflicting or attempting to inflict grievous bodily harm to anyone in it; or
- making a trespassing entry to a building with:
  - intent to steal; or
  - intent to inflict GBH; or
  - intent to do unlawful damage.

Generally, burglary is an either-way charge, though in some circumstances it is indictable-only.

Aggravated burglary Burglary while armed with a firearm, imitation firearm or any other weapon or explosive. Indictable-only.

Fraud Under the Fraud Act 2006, there are now general offences of fraud, defined as conduct 'with a view to gain or with intent to cause loss or expose to a risk of loss' involving either:

- a dishonest making of a false representation (for example, using a credit card dishonestly, or using a false identity to open a bank account); or
- a dishonest failure to disclose information when under a legal duty to disclose (for example, failure when applying for health insurance to disclose a heart condition);
- dishonest abuse of a position (for example, an employee swindling money from his/her employer).

The Act also includes a fraud offence of obtaining services dishonestly. Fraud charges, such as obtaining property or services by deception, created by earlier legislation, survive transitionally, their use dependent on when the alleged offences occurred. These statutory fraud offences are either-way, but if deemed to be of sufficient 'seriousness or complexity', are treated procedurally as indictable-only in transfer procedure, explained in chapter 7. Conspiracy to defraud is indictable-only.

Blackmail Making an unwarranted demand with menaces with a view to gain. This offence could be a threat to reveal to others an embarrassing secret, or embarrassing photos, unless money is paid. But it could be another type of extortion – for example, a threat to a supermarket company that goods on its shelves will be contaminated unless money is paid. Indictable-only.

Taking a vehicle without authority – sometimes referred to as TWOC (taking without owner's consent). It can cover conduct known as 'twocking' or 'joy-riding' in which perpetrators abandon a car after using it. This offence does not involve an intention to deprive the owner permanently of the vehicle, and so should not be described as theft. Summary.

Aggravated vehicle taking When a vehicle has been taken (as above) and, because of how it was driven, someone is injured or the vehicle or other property is damaged. Either-way.

Motoring crimes

Driving under the influence of drink or drugs Driving a motor vehicle despite the ability to do so being thus impaired. Summary.

Driving with excess alcohol When alcohol in the driver's body exceeds the prescribed limit; that is, 80 milligrammes of alcohol in 100 millilitres of blood, 35 microgrammes of alcohol in 100 millilitres of breath or 107 milligrammes of alcohol in 100 millilitres of urine. Summary.

Causing death by careless driving when under the influence of drink or drugs The driver must be unfit to drive through drink or drugs; or must have consumed excess alcohol or failed to provide a specimen. Indictable-only.

! Remember

It may not be fair or accurate (and therefore could be a libel problem) to describe a driver with more than the prescribed limit of alcohol as 'drunk'. He/she may be only marginally over the limit. It is safe to use the term 'drunk' if and as it is expressed in evidence or if – in the case of a convicted defendant – the evidence clearly supports this.

Other noteworthy crimes

Perjury Knowingly giving false evidence after taking an oath as a witness to tell the truth in court, or in an **affidavit**, or to a tribunal. Indictable-only.

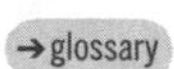

Perverting the course of justice Concealing evidence, or giving false information to the police. Indictable-only.

Wasting police time A lesser offence than the two above. It is committed by a person knowingly making a false report that a crime has occurred or falsely claiming to have information material to an investigation. Summary.

Kerb-crawling The colloquial term for the offence, usually committed by men in streets frequented by prostitutes, of 'soliciting' (which, in this context, means seeking the services of a prostitute) from a motor vehicle in such a manner as to cause annoyance to the person approached (who may be a local resident, not a prostitute) or to others in the neighbourhood. Summary.

Though it is not an offence to be a prostitute, it is an offence for a prostitute to loiter in a public place, or to 'solicit' there (which means, in this context, to offer sex in return for money).

➡ Recap of major points

- There are three main categories of criminal offences:
  - indictable-only, which can only be dealt with by a Crown court;
  - either-way, dealt with by a Crown court or a magistrates court – see chapter 7;
  - summary – almost all such cases are dealt with by magistrates.
- If an offence is of 'strict liability', the defendant can be convicted even if he/she had no clear 'intent' to do wrong.
- If a media organisation fails to report an offence or charge accurately, it may be successfully sued for libel by the defendant.

((•)) Useful Websites

www.cps.gov.uk/legal/
Crown Prosecution Service, 'Legal Guidance', which explains offences

6

Magistrates courts: summary cases

Chapter summary

Magistrates courts deal with about 95 per cent of all criminal cases, and send or commit the rest – the most serious – to Crown courts. Hearings in which magistrates try or sentence defendants are known as summary proceedings. This chapter sets out the offences they can deal with, which include burglaries, sexual assault and dangerous driving, and who they can convict. It also explains what bail is, and details the automatic reporting bans which restrict what the media can publish from pre-trial hearings at magistrates courts.

Who are magistrates?

The role of magistrates originates in the twelfth century. They still use the ancient title of 'justice of the peace'. Almost all are volunteers and part time – that is, lay magistrates. Recruitment tries to ensure that magistrates are from a range of social backgrounds. There are around 30,000 lay magistrates. They are trained and paid expenses. There were more than 300 magistrates court houses in England and Wales, although in 2010 the Ministry of Justice announced that 93 would be closed to cut costs.

If lay magistrates try a criminal case, there must be at least two of them. A trial in a magistrates court is known as a summary trial. The term 'summary' reflects the fact that magistrates dispense quick and relatively informal justice, suitable for cases they deal with, whereas the higher courts, with more serious and complex cases, have slower processes.

see www.mcnaes.com ch. 6: 'More about magistrates'

One magistrate is sufficient for some court duties. When a court hearing has more than one magistrate, one acts as chair and announces decisions. Magistrates are advised on law by a justices' clerk or by one of his/her staff of qualified lawyers, who sits in front of them in court.

District judges

As well as lay magistrates, there are about 130 professional magistrates (that is, they get a wage) known as district judges, appointed after at least seven years' experience as a lawyer. Most are in city districts with high caseloads. A district judge used to be officially known as a stipendiary magistrate (from the Latin term stipend, meaning a wage) and is still sometimes called, in slang, 'the stipe'. A district judge tries cases on his/her own. For convenience, this book refers to 'magistrates' (that is, plural) sitting in court, because two or three lay magistrates sit in many hearings.

The taking of pleas

→glossary

Defendants facing **summary** charges are asked, during their first or a subsequent appearance in the magistrates court, how they plead. If they plead guilty to a charge, this means they are convicted of it. Sentencing usually takes place at a later date, to allow time for a background report on the defendant to be prepared.

ch. 5 explains categories of charges

If a defendant pleads not guilty to a summary charge, a very minor offence may be tried there and then. But in most instances a contested case will be adjourned for summary trial. When it is first adjourned, the magistrates must decide, unless the charge is a minor one, whether to grant **bail**.

→glossary
→glossary
→glossary

Defendants who deny **either-way** charges can ask magistrates to try them. This **mode of trial** procedure is outlined in the next chapter, which explains how a denied either-way charge is tried at a Crown court if the defendant wishes, or if magistrates decide it is too serious for them to try.

Bail

Bail is the system by which a court grants a defendant his/her liberty until the case's next hearing.

The court may impose conditions – for example, that the defendant should live at his/her home address.

The Bail Act 1976 has a general rule that a defendant must be granted bail unless:

- the court is satisfied there are substantial grounds for believing that if bail is granted
  - he/she will abscond, or
  - commit another offence, or
  - obstruct the course of justice (for example, by interfering with witnesses);
- the court decides the defendant should be kept in prison for his/her own protection (for instance, if the alleged crime has so angered the local community that a mob may attack him/her);

- the defendant is alleged to have committed an offence when he/she was on bail granted in an earlier case;
- the defendant is already serving a jail sentence; or
- there is insufficient information to decide on bail.

A court must give reasons for refusing bail.

A defendant charged with murder can only be given bail by a Crown court judge.

Evidence and previous convictions aired

When deciding on bail, the court is told of any relevant previous conviction(s) the defendant has, and some details of prosecution evidence about the charge(s) faced.

A defence lawyer arguing for bail may outline defence evidence.

Surety

In some cases, a court will insist that the defendant has a surety before bail is granted.

A surety is someone, for example a relative or friend of the defendant, who guarantees the defendant will 'surrender' to bail – that is, turn up at court as required. The surety agrees to forfeit a sum of money, fixed by the court, if the defendant absconds.

If the defendant absconds, a surety can be jailed if he/she does not pay that sum.

Failure to surrender

If a defendant fails to surrender to bail, that is a criminal offence, and will probably result in the court issuing an arrest warrant for him/her, authorising police to arrest and bring him/her to court.

Appeals

If bail is refused by magistrates the defendant can apply to a judge at Crown court for bail. The prosecution, if the alleged offence is one punishable by jail, can, by appealing to a Crown court judge, challenge a magistrates court's decision to grant bail.

Reporting restrictions for pre-trial hearings

When a denied charge is heading for a summary trial, magistrates may hold at least one pre-trial hearing to rule on any dispute between prosecution and defence on admissibility of evidence or points of law, and to decide on bail.

→glossary Section 8C of the Magistrates' Courts Act 1980 has **automatic** restrictions which limit contemporaneous reporting of these pre-trial hearings.

The restrictions are intended to prevent the risk of prejudice should a case originally due to be tried by magistrates end up being tried by a Crown court jury. Parliament anticipated that, because of changes to integrate the courts system, a case – even if a magistrates court had started preparing to try it – could end up being tried at a Crown court with a 'related' either-way or indictable-only case. Also, a magistrates court could initially agree to try an either-way case but later in a pre-trial hearing decide that a Crown court should try it. The rationale would be that the alleged offence was more serious than it first appeared, and magistrates felt their powers of punishment would be inadequate if they convicted the defendant.

The type of material aired in a pre-trial hearing which could, if published contemporaneously by the media, subsequently prejudice a jury's verdict at Crown court is outlined in the next chapter, but it includes evidence which magistrates in a pre-trial hearing rule to be inadmissible. Jurors are regarded as susceptible to prejudicial material. These pre-trial reporting restrictions prevent people who become jurors from reading or hearing about suspect evidence which, having been ruled inadmissible, they should not be aware of during the trial.

The scope of the section 8C reporting restrictions

The section 8C reporting restrictions automatically apply for cases at magistrates courts in which a defendant pleads not guilty.

They ban publication of:

- any rulings by magistrates in pre-trial hearings on admissibility of evidence and points of law, and any order made in them to discharge or vary such a ruling;
- the proceedings, in those hearings, concerning applications for such rulings and for such orders, including legal argument and discussion about whether such a ruling or order should be made.

The Act defines a pre-trial hearing as any proceeding which occurs after a defendant has pleaded not guilty but before magistrates start hearing prosecution evidence at the trial. So section 8C could cover most of a defendant's first appearance at court, as well as any other pre-trial hearing, but does not prevent contemporaneous reporting of the plea.

While the restrictions are in force, the media can only report seven categories of information from the pre-trial proceedings. These are (in simplified form):

- the name of the court and the magistrates' names;
- the names, ages, home addresses and occupations of the defendant(s) and witnesses;
- the charge(s) in full or summarised;

- the names of solicitors and barristers in the proceedings;
- if the case is adjourned, the date and place to which it is adjourned;
- arrangements as to bail;
- whether legal aid was granted.

It is also safe to publish that reporting restrictions are in force, because this is not prejudicial.

The effect of the restrictions is to ban publication of any reference to evidence, except as it is encapsulated in the wording of the charge(s).

As regards 'arrangements as to bail', it will be safe to report, unless the court orders otherwise, whether bail was granted or refused, and, if it was granted, any bail conditions and **surety** arrangement.

But the media should *not* report in most instances why the prosecution opposed bail or reasons the magistrates gave for refusing it – because that information could be prejudicial.

ch. 7, pp. 65–66 explains this risk of prejudice

It would be safe to report that someone was remanded in custody for their own protection, because it was feared, for example, that their life would be at risk if they were to be released.

The home addresses which may be published are those current when the report is published and former addresses which were current during events which gave rise to the charge(s).

! Remember

If a report refers to a defendant's former address or includes a picture or footage of it, it should make clear that he/she no longer lives there. Failing to do so could cause the current occupants to sue for libel because people might think them linked to the court case.

The section 8C restriction on publishing pre-trial argument and rulings about evidence and points of law is apparently a 'belt and braces' approach, since its limitation of reports to the seven categories cited above has the same effect.

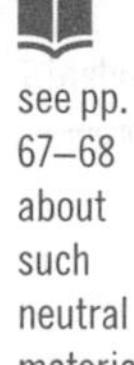
see pp. 67–68 about such neutral material

A media report of a pre-trial hearing can safely include neutral (that is, non-prejudicial) descriptions of the court scene and neutral background information.

When do the section 8C restrictions cease to apply?

The magistrates can lift the section 8C reporting restrictions, wholly or in part, to allow the media to publish contemporaneously fuller reports of these pre-trial applications, and of any ruling or order made in them.

If any defendant objects, the court can lift them only if satisfied that doing so is in the interests of justice. If there are objections, they and any representations made to the court about them (that is, argument in court about whether the restrictions should be lifted) cannot be reported until the 'disposal' of the case, even if restrictions are lifted earlier in other respects.

The section 8C restrictions automatically lapse when the case is 'disposed of', which the Act says is when all defendants in the case are acquitted or convicted of all charges in the case, or if it is dismissed by the court (for example, because of insufficient evidence, see below), or the prosecutor decides not to proceed with it.

So, at the end of the trial, a media organisation could publish a report of evidence ruled inadmissible some weeks or months previously in a pre-trial hearing, or of any ruling made in it.

Liability for breach of the section 8C restrictions

A proprietor, editor or publisher can be prosecuted for breach of these restrictions. The maximum fine is currently £5,000.

Procedure in summary trials

A trial at a magistrates court can usually be reported fully as it occurs. No restrictions under the 1980 Act apply, but could apply under other law, explained in chapters 9, 10 and 11.

The usual procedure at summary trials is:

- The prosecutor makes an opening speech, describing the alleged crime.
- Witnesses testify, after swearing an oath or affirming that their evidence is true.
- Prosecution witnesses are called first. Each is asked questions by the prosecutor to elicit their evidence-in-chief (that is, evidence given during questioning by the side which called them). The defence can cross-examine them. The prosecution may then re-examine them.
- When prosecution evidence ends, the defence may submit, for any or all charges faced, that there is no case to answer – that is, that the prosecution cannot meet the standard of proof required.
- If the magistrates agree with this submission, they will dismiss the charge. Otherwise, or if there is no such submission, the trial continues.
- Defence witnesses are then called. These may include the defendant, though he/she cannot be compelled to testify.
- Defence witnesses are questioned to elicit their evidence in-chief. They can be cross-examined by the prosecutor, and then re-examined by the defence.
- When the court has heard all witnesses, the defence may address the court in a closing speech, arguing how facts and law should be interpreted. Either side can address the court twice in total, in opening or closing speeches. The defence has the right to make the last speech.
- If the magistrates feel a charge is not proved, they will acquit the defendant.
- If they find him/her guilty on any charge, he/she is convicted of it.

ch. 4, p. 39 explains the standard of proof

The magistrates will then sentence the defendant, or adjourn to sentence at a later date.

! Remember

There is a national protocol agreed by the Crown Prosecution Service on what prosecution material can be released to the media to help coverage of cases – see pp. 160–161.

Hostile witnesses and leading questions

Normally, to ensure witnesses tell of events in their own words, leading questions are not allowed to be put to them when they give evidence-in-chief, but:

- a witness who refuses to testify or retracts a statement made to investigators can be ruled by the court to be 'a hostile witness' – that is, someone who *can* be asked leading questions by the side which calls him/her.
- A leading question is one which suggests what answer is expected. 'Did anything happen after that?' is not a leading question, but 'Did you then see a man with a knife?' is.

A defendant's 'bad character'

As a general rule, prosecutors in trials cannot refer to a defendant's previous conviction(s) because – to comply with the principle of the presumption of innocence – the focus is on evidence for the charge(s) being tried, not any past crime.

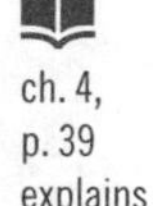

ch. 4, p. 39 explains this principle

But evidence of previous misconduct (which includes crimes and other reprehensible behaviour) can be introduced to correct a false impression given by the defendant, or as evidence that he/she follows a distinctive method when committing offences of the kind with which he/she is charged, or if the defendant's evidence has attacked another person's character.

Sentencing by magistrates

In sentencing hearings for an admitted charge, the prosecution gives magistrates details of the crime. If there is dispute about the facts of an admitted offence the magistrates must accept the defence version unless the prosecution proves its version in a **Newton hearing**. →glossary

Otherwise, defendants who admit an offence and those convicted at trial are sentenced in the same way:

If the crime inflicted suffering on a victim, the court will consider any written statement the victim provides. Before sentence is passed, the defendant's lawyer can make a speech of **mitigation**, citing any extenuating circumstances while asking for leniency. →glossary

A defendant may also ask for other offences to be 'taken into consideration'.

Offences to be 'taken into consideration' – which should not be confused with previous convictions – are crimes which the defendant admits although he/she has not been charged with them.

The defendant brings these crimes to the court's attention to be sentenced for them as well as for the charged offence(s). By admitting uncharged crimes – for example, burglaries – the defendant removes the possibility of being prosecuted for them in the future, giving them the opportunity of a fresh start.

Magistrates may also consider a 'pre-sentence report' about the defendant's background, prepared by a probation officer.

((•)) see Useful Websites, below, for details of the probation service

Jail sentences

Magistrates can jail a defendant for up to six months for a single offence, and for up to 12 months for more than one offence if they decide that jail terms should run consecutively, depending on penalties specified for an offence.

- *Consecutive sentences* are two or more jail terms ordered by the court to run one after the other, imposed when the defendant is convicted of more than one crime. If a sentence of six months is made consecutive to one of three months, the defendant is sentenced overall to nine months.
- *Concurrent sentences* are those where the defendant is sentenced overall only for the length of the longest sentence imposed. In the above example, this would be six months.

Courts can give a suspended sentence to a defendant deserving leniency.

- If a defendant is given a suspended sentence, he/she does not have to go to jail unless he/she commits a further offence, for which a jail sentence could be imposed, during the period for which the sentence is suspended.

A jail term of six months can be suspended for two years. If the defendant commits no other offence punishable by jail in that time, the suspended sentence lapses.

If a jail sentence is suspended, reports must make this clear.

see ch. 21 for libel considerations in court reporting

! Remember

A report which inaccurately portrays a suspended sentence as an immediate jail term could create a libel problem. In some circumstances, the defendant could sue for the inference that the crime was worse than it was.

Committal for sentence

Magistrates who convict a defendant of an either-way charge can committed him/ her for **sentence** to the Crown court if they believe, because of what they are told

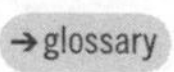

of the case, and/or about any previous conviction(s), that their punishment powers are insufficient. A Crown court judge can impose longer jail terms.

Fines

Broadly speaking, the maximum fine which magistrates can impose is £5,000. Most fines are much lower, although an employer can be fined up to £20,000 for health and safety breaches. Failure to pay a fine could lead to a jail sentence.

Other types of sentences

- A community order – this means the court orders a defendant to obey one or more requirements, which could include:
  - unpaid work in the community under a probation officer's direction;
  - a curfew, with a requirement that the defendant wears an electronic 'tag' to monitor whether he/she obeys it;
  - receiving treatment for drug or alcohol dependency;
  - going to an attendance centre for a specified number of hours for group sessions to reflect on his/her misbehaviour.
- A conditional discharge – this means that the court has not immediately imposed or specified punishment, but states that if the defendant commits any other offence within a period laid down by the court, for example, a year – he/she is liable to be punished for the first offence as well as for the subsequent conviction.
- An absolute discharge – this means that the court feels that no punishment, other than the fact of the conviction, is necessary.

! Remember

Absolute and conditional discharges, which follow convictions, must not be confused with a 'discharge' in a committal hearing, a term signifying that evidence was insufficient for a charge to be tried.

ch. 7 explains committal hearings

A court can order a defendant to pay compensation to a crime victim. It can also defer a decision on sentence to a specified date within six months of the conviction, to assess the defendant's conduct in that period – for example, to see if he/she actually fulfils a requirement of reparation.

Binding over and restraining orders

Since the fourteenth century, courts have had power to 'bind over' a person 'to keep the peace'. This can be used to resolve, without trial, minor allegations of assault, threatening behaviour or public disorder, in that the prosecution may drop a charge if the defendant agrees to be 'bound over'. A binding over can also follow a conviction, and a witness can also be bound over, if, for example, he/she seems to have been involved in a fracas. When binding over, the court specifies a sum of money which the person must pay if he/she breaches the peace – for example, by violent or threatening conduct – within a period specified by the court. The order is a preventative, civil law measure, not a punishment, and is *not* a conviction, and so should not be reported as such.

A court may impose a restraining order on a defendant, even one acquitted at trial, to protect another person – for example, an ex-partner – from harassment. The order may ban the defendant from any contact with that person.

Section 70 committal

Magistrates can make an order under section 70 of the Proceeds of Crime Act 2002 committing the case of a convicted defendant to a Crown court hearing to assess what money or property he/she has gained from crime and, if there are such proceeds, to make a confiscation order. No automatic reporting restrictions apply to this type of committal hearing.

Many cases dealt with by post

Magistrates courts also deal with minor, 'fixed penalty' offences such as speeding. A defendant does not need to appear at court if he/she, having received written notice of the charge, returns a form admitting guilt and pays the standard fine.

Appeal routes from magistrates courts

The defence and prosecution may contest a ruling by magistrates by appealing to the High Court on a point of law, by means of the 'case stated' procedure. In other

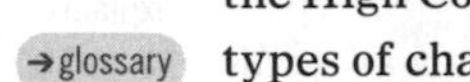

types of challenge, the defence can ask the High Court for a **judicial review**.

A defendant appealing against a conviction by magistrates or the severity of the sentence imposed appeals to a Crown court.

These High Court and Crown court roles are explained in chapter 8.

Recap of major points

- Trials and sentencing at magistrates courts are known as summary proceedings.
- Automatic reporting restrictions, under section 8C of the Magistrates' Courts Act, limit what the media can report from pre-trial hearings.

- But trials at a magistrates court can usually be reported fully and contemporaneously.
- A magistrates court can jail a convicted defendant for up to six months for one offence, and for up to 12 months for two or more offences.

((•)) Useful Websites

www.direct.gov.uk/en/CrimeJusticeAndTheLaw/Goingtocourt/DG_196034/
Government information about magistrates courts

www.magistrates-association.org.uk/
Magistrates Association

www.justice.gov.uk/guidance/prison-probation-and-rehabilitation/before-after-release/probation/htm
Ministry of Justice information on probation

7

Magistrates courts: the most serious criminal cases

Chapter summary

Those charged with the most serious crimes – such as murder and robbery – make their first court appearance in a magistrates court, usually having been held since arrest in police and court cells. Journalists may be on the court's press bench. This chapter sets out the automatic reporting restrictions that are in force in these preliminary hearings, to safeguard the defendant's right to fair trial by jury, because the case is bound for the Crown court. It is illegal for the media to breach the restrictions, but some newsworthy facts can be reported immediately from the magistrates court. The restrictions apply too in preliminary hearings for either-way charges, such as sexual assault. Magistrates try some either-way cases.

Indictable-only charges – 'sending for trial'

Defendants charged with the most serious crimes cannot be tried by magistrates. These cases are, as chapter 4 explains, **indictable-only**. They have an initial phase in the magistrates court, where procedural decisions may be made, but are quickly 'sent for trial' to a Crown court where, if the defendant denies the offence, a jury trial will take place.

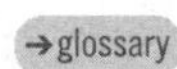

So, when a defendant on an indictable-only charge appears in a magistrates court, this is a preliminary hearing. Yet it will be of great news interest if the crime is locally or nationally notorious. For most indictable-only cases magistrates can decide on bail. But only a Crown court judge can decide on bail if the charge is murder (when it is exceptional for bail to be given).

bail is explained in ch. 6, pp. 54–55

→glossary

The formality of **sending for trial** may occur when the defendant first appears before magistrates.

Section 8 automatic reporting restrictions

Automatic reporting restrictions tightly limit what the media can publish contemporaneously from any preliminary hearing at a magistrates court if the case has potential for jury trial. Currently these restrictions are in section 8 of the Magistrates' Courts Act 1980 (the 1980 Act) and their scope is set out below. Unless lifted, they cover all indictable-only cases processed at these courts, and some **either-way** cases. They prevent media reports of these hearings revealing details which could create a risk of prejudice to jury trials.

→glossary

The concern is that people who read or hear what the media publish from preliminary hearings may include some who months later will be summoned to Crown court to be jurors in these cases. Justice demands they try it only on the evidence presented at those trials, and not be influenced by what they remember from pre-trial coverage. Section 8 is apparently due to be replaced by new, similar law. See this book's Late News section.

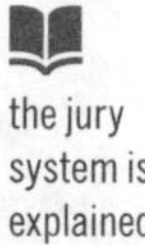

the jury system is explained in ch. 8

Types of prejudicial matter

The section 8 restrictions are designed to prevent publication from preliminary hearings of:

- any reference to evidence in the case, apart from what is encapsulated in the wording of charge(s);
- any previous conviction(s) the defendant has;
- any other material with potential to create prejudice.

Evidence Some evidence may be detailed in a preliminary hearing – for example, magistrates may need to hear it to assess the risk of a defendant offending if given bail. But some evidence related to them by a prosecution or defence lawyer may not figure later if there is a jury trial. The Crown court judge may have ruled some evidence is so unreliable that it is inadmissible. For example, evidence that a defendant confessed to the crime could be ruled inadmissible if the judge accepts the confession was made under duress. Yet if the media, when covering a preliminary hearing, could immediately report such evidence, a juror could remember reading about that 'confession' and not understand that it was discredited. That recollection could contaminate the jury's consideration of the case, and a defendant could be wrongly convicted.

Previous convictions Generally, in accordance with the principle of the 'presumption of innocence' a Crown court jury will not be told if the defendant has any previous conviction(s). But a defendant's criminal record may be revealed in a preliminary hearing – for example, to help magistrates decide on bail. If a media report of that hearing were able to reveal that record, it could be remembered by a juror, and so prejudice the jury against the defendant.

ch. 4, p. 39 explains this principle

Other material with potential to create prejudice could include the suggestion by the prosecution in a preliminary hearing that a defendant is guilty of more offences than the crime he/she is charged with. For example, in a rape case police may be checking other unsolved rapes if they suspect the defendant is a serial rapist. Magistrates may be told of these inquiries by a prosecutor opposing bail. Those inquiries may come to nothing. Yet if the media could report from the preliminary hearing these unfounded suspicions a juror may remember this in the trial, and prejudicially tell other jurors that the defendant may be a serial offender.

The scope of the section 8 restrictions

The section 8 restrictions function by listing categories of information which *can* be published from such preliminary hearings. The list is expressed here in simplified format (with explanation in italics):

- the name of the court (*for example, Doncaster magistrates court*) and the magistrates' names;
- the names, addresses and occupations of the parties, *including the defendant(s)*, and of witnesses, and the ages of the defendant(s) and witnesses;
- the charge(s) in full or summarised;
- the names of legal representatives engaged in the proceedings, *for example, solicitors or barristers acting for the defence or prosecution*;
- if proceedings are adjourned, the date and place to which they are adjourned;
- 'arrangements as to *bail*', *that is whether bail was granted or refused, and, if it was granted, any bail conditions and* ***surety*** *arrangement. For cases in which bail is refused, the usual interpretation of the restrictions is that in most instances the media should not report why the prosecution opposed bail or any reason the magistrates gave for refusing it – because such matter could be prejudicial. But it would be safe to report that someone was remanded in custody for his/her own protection*;

- whether **legal aid** was granted;
- the fact that reporting restrictions are in force.

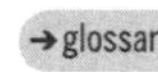

As explained below, **committal hearings** are a type of preliminary hearing which take place for some either-way cases in the magistrates courts and – as chapter 9 explains – in the youth court. Section 8 says that a report of a committal hearing can include, in addition to the eight categories of information specified above:

- any decision of the magistrates to commit any defendant to Crown court for trial; if a defendant is committed for trial, the charge(s) on which he/she is committed, and the name of the Crown court;
- when there is more than one defendant, and one is committed for trial, any decision on the 'disposal' of the case of any defendant not committed for trial, *for example, that there was a discharge because of insufficient evidence*.

The scope given to report the names, ages and address of witnesses is now largely redundant. Witnesses no longer give evidence in person at committal hearings. But if such detail of any witness is aired in a preliminary hearing, section 8 permits it to be reported. It will usually not be prejudicial to add the witness's occupation. It is possible, though, that restrictions in other law, explained in chapters 9, 10 and 11, may grant a witness anonymity.

The scope given in section 8 to report whether a charge has been committed for trial permits, on any logical interpretation, reporting that a case has been 'sent for trial' or 'transferred' – procedure which replaced committal for some categories of charge.

transfer is explained on p. 3

If, in a hearing in which there is more than one defendant, one unsuccessfully asks for the section 8 reporting restrictions to be lifted, section 8 permits the reporting of the bare fact that the court declined to lift them.

see pp. 68–69 on lifting procedure

Reporting denials of guilt and choice of jury trial

The media, when reporting preliminary hearings covered by section 8, routinely publish:

www.mcnaes.com ch. 7 provides more advice on the section 8 reporting restrictions

- *basic protestations of innocence*, made by the defendant from the dock or through a solicitor. In an indictable-only case no formal plea is taken at the magistrates court, but it may be made clear there that the charge is denied. In either-way cases defendants are asked to indicate how they will plead;
- *that a defendant, in an either-way case, has chosen trial by jury.*

Although publication of protestations of innocence and choice of jury trial is beyond what strict application of section 8 would permit, the media are safe in reporting these facts, because:

- it seems only fair to the defendant to quote denial of guilt – if made in relation to the only charge faced, or to all charges – and that jury trial was chosen, which too indicates denial of the charge(s);
- publishing such matter cannot be prejudicial – a jury, obviously, will know if a charge is denied.

But the media should be wary, when the restrictions apply, of reporting anything which suggests that a defendant will later enter a mixture of pleas – for example, quotes suggesting he/she will admit one charge while denying another. This could be prejudicial if at trial jurors are not told of the admission but remember it from pre-trial coverage.

Describing the courtroom scene

The media routinely report, even when section 8 restrictions apply, scene-setting information; that the hearing lasted ten minutes, what the defendant wore, that he/she 'spoke only to confirm their name and address', that guards stood on either side of him/her. Such bland material will not cause prejudice to the case.

Background material

Media organisations publishing reports of preliminary hearings usually add some background material about the defendant and/or the alleged crime. Background material, from sources other than the court hearing, is not itself a report of those proceedings and so does not contravene section 8 of the 1980 Act. The Contempt of Court Act 1981 would cover such material, so nothing should be published which creates a substantial risk of serious prejudice, as chapter 18 explains. Mingling background material into a court report without sufficient care could create such a risk – for example, potential jurors who see/hear the report could draw wrong inferences about what the case evidence is.

An option for the media, when they want to report on an alleged crime which has occurred, say, in the previous 24 hours *and* that the alleged perpetrator has already appeared in a preliminary hearing, is to publish items segregated by page design or separate narrative. Each item could have its own headline/introduction. One item would be a story on the alleged incident, conforming to contempt law, not citing information from the court hearing, and the other item would be a separate report solely of the preliminary hearing, conforming to the section 8 restrictions.

Liability for breach of the section 8 restrictions

'Any proprietor, editor or publisher' of a newspaper or periodical can be prosecuted if it breaches the restrictions. In the case of a TV or radio programme, 'the body corporate which provides the service' and any person whose 'functions in relation to the programme correspond to those of an editor of a newspaper' can be prosecuted. The maximum fine is £5,000.

If a breach occurs after a trial has begun, and is serious enough – because of what is published – to cause it to be aborted, a media organisation may also become liable for huge costs under section 93 of the Courts Act 2003.

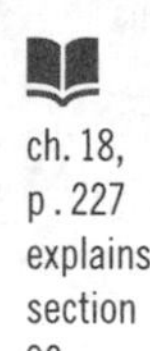

ch. 18, p. 227 explains section 93

Case study

In 1996 Graham Glen, the former editor of *The Citizen*, Gloucester, and the paper's owners were each fined £4,500 by Gloucester magistrates for breach of section 8 in a report of the first appearance in Dursley magistrates court of Fred West, accused of several murders. This report breached section 8 by including a statement made in the hearing that West had confessed to police to killing one of his daughters – that is, a reference to evidence (*Media Lawyer* Issue No. 3, May 1996).

When do the section 8 restrictions cease to apply?

These restrictions cease to apply in four circumstances.

(1) ***The restrictions are lifted if a defendant requests this*** Under the 1980 Act magistrates are required to make an order lifting restrictions if the sole defendant wants

this. If a case has more than one defendant, each must be allowed to make representations before a decision on lifting is taken. If any defendant objects, the restrictions may only be lifted if the magistrates decide this is in the interests of justice.

A defendant may want restrictions lifted so his/her solicitor can publicise, by means of a full media report of the hearing, a request for witnesses to come forward, to help corroborate any **alibi** – for example: 'My client was at the funfair, not the crime scene. Did anyone see him at the fair?' →glossary

! Remember

Even if the restrictions are lifted at a defendant's request, the media should not, for as long as the case has potential of jury trial, publish the previous convictions of any defendant in it, even if these were revealed in the preliminary proceedings.

Pre-trial publication of previous convictions is so foreseeably prejudicial that, arguably, the section 4 defence in the Contempt of Court Act 1981, which normally protects fair and accurate reports of court hearings, may not apply.

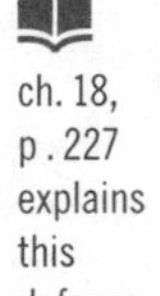

ch. 18, p. 227 explains this defence

The 1980 Act says that if there is disagreement between defendants on whether section 8 restrictions should be lifted, their representations to magistrates on this issue, even if a lifting order is then made, should not be reported– that is, while the case retains potential for jury trial. However, the fact that such a lifting order was made can be included immediately within the report.

Once lifted, the restrictions cannot be re-imposed (*R v Blackpool Justices, ex p Beaverbrook Newspapers Ltd* [1972] 1 All ER 388; [1972] 1 WLR 95). If magistrates decide, after a request from one defendant, to lift the restrictions this means they are lifted in respect of all defendants in the hearing – even if any objected (*R v Leeds Justices, ex p Sykes* [1983] 1 WLR 132).

(2) ***The section 8 restrictions automatically cease to apply if and when, for an either-way charge, it becomes clear that the defendant is to be dealt with summarily*** This means that the restrictions no longer apply to an either-way charge if a defendant pleads guilty to it at a magistrates court. But other reporting restrictions apply to pre-trial hearings if he/she denies the charge and chooses **summary** trial, see below. →glossary

(3) ***The section 8 restrictions automatically cease to apply if magistrates decide there is insufficient evidence to commit a sole defendant or all the defendants in an either-way case for Crown court trial*** Committal hearings are explained below. Section 8 has not been updated to cover the 'sending for trial' procedure, which replaced committal for indictable-only offences. Magistrates can refuse to send a charge for trial if they decide there has been abuse of legal process in the prosecution (though such a decision will be rare). If there is only one defendant in the case, and this decision means that he/she will not face a jury trial on any charge in it, then the section 8 restrictions can be regarded as ceasing to apply. If a hearing involves other charges on which the defendant is sent for jury trial, or involves any other defendant being sent for trial, or awaiting a committal hearing, the safest approach is to regard the restrictions as applying to it.

(4) ***The restrictions automatically expire when the proceedings against all defendants in the case have been concluded – that is, no jury trial remains pending for any defendant in the case*** After such conclusion, evidence aired or submissions made at any preliminary hearing at a magistrates court – including any committal hearing – weeks or months earlier can be fully reported, if still thought newsworthy. The media may wish to highlight evidence which, for legal reasons, the jury did not hear. This may provide a fuller picture of the defendant or throw light on how the crime was investigated.

See www.mcnaes.com ch. 7 for an example of a newspaper reporting evidence aired at a preliminary hearing months after it occurred.

Libel considerations

A report of preliminary proceedings published as soon as practicable after the section 8 restrictions are lifted or expire will be regarded as a contemporaneous report and so can enjoy the protection of absolute privilege in libel law, explained in chapter 21.

Section 8 also applies to either-way cases

There are preliminary hearings in magistrates courts for either-way cases. These included theft, burglary and sexual assault charges. A defendant in an either-way case has a right of jury trial, but may choose not to exercise it. These hearings include procedures which determine if the defendant intends to deny the charge, and whether it is tried by magistrates or by a jury. For as long as an either-way case retains potential for jury trial, the section 8 restrictions apply to its preliminary hearings. To know if this potential exists, journalists must understand court procedure (see also Figure 2, which shows how an either-way case is processed).

Procedure in either-way cases

In an either-way case, the defendant is asked, usually in its first hearing in the magistrates court (that is, a preliminary hearing), to indicate how he/she intends to plead. ***If the defendant indicates an intention to plead guilty,*** this is automatically treated as a formal plea of guilty, convicting him/her of that offence.

The section 8 restrictions automatically lapse in respect of that charge, because there will be no trial. The defendant will at that hearing or later be sentenced by magistrates, unless, after hearing more detail of the offence, and of any previous conviction(s) the defendant has, they decide their punishment powers are insufficient, and that he/she should be **committed for sentence** to the Crown court. →glossary

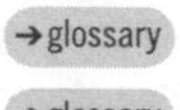

If the defendant indicates he/she will plead 'not guilty', a **mode of trial** hearing follows, usually immediately. In this the magistrates are told some detail of evidence which gave rise to the charge, so they can decide if the case can be dealt

Figure 2 Processing of either-way cases in magistrates courts.

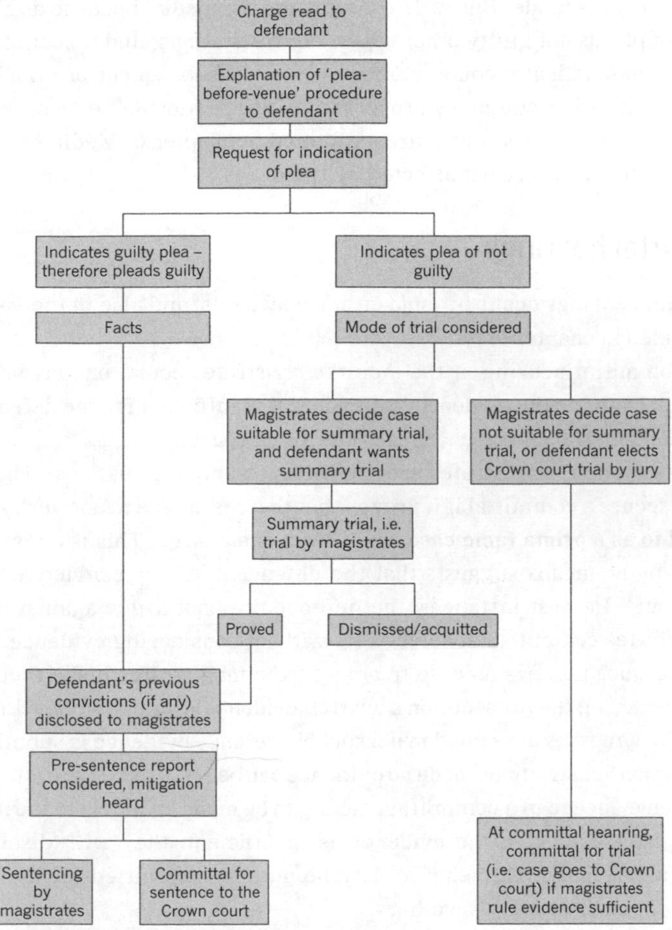

Copyright: Design of figure used by permission of Judicial College.

with in a summary trial – that is, by magistrates. They may decide the alleged crime is too serious for summary trial, because, in the event of a conviction, magistrates' punishment powers would be insufficient. If that is the decision, the case will be adjourned for a committal hearing for another set of magistrates to decide if there is sufficient evidence for the case to go to the Crown court. While the committal hearing is pending, there remains potential for jury trial, so the section 8 restrictions continue to apply, limiting what can be reported from the mode of trial procedure.

magistrates' sentencing powers are explained in ch. 6

If magistrates agree to offer a summary trial – which is known as the magistrates 'accepting jurisdiction' – the defendant is asked if he/she wants that or jury trial. If the choice is jury trial, magistrates will adjourn the case for a committal hearing, and the section 8 restrictions continue to apply.

If summary trial is chosen, the defendant is asked to enter a formal plea of not guilty, and that trial will take place in the magistrates court, most likely after adjournment to permit preparations.

The section 8 restrictions cease to apply to a charge as soon as the choice of summary trial is made. But little changes for the media, because as soon as the defendant pleads not guilty other reporting restrictions, under section 8C of the 1980 Act, automatically come into force to cover subsequent pre-trial proceedings, now classed as summary proceedings. The section 8C restrictions, similar in format to those of section 8, are explained in chapter 6. Media reports of the summary trial itself are not affected by them.

Committal hearings

Committal hearings occur in some either-way cases, and also in the youth court, as explained in chapter 9.

In a committal hearing at the (adult) magistrates court, one or more magistrates will examine the evidence to decide if it is sufficient for the defendant to be committed for trial on any charge to the Crown court.

In this function, magistrates are known as 'examining justices'. The prosecution will secure a committal if it proves that there is 'a case to answer', sometimes referred to as a **prima facie** case, on at least one charge. This is a low burden of proof. It by no means suggests that the defendant will be convicted of it at the Crown court. In most instances, the defence does not argue against committal, so magistrates commit such defendants without considering evidence. But if the defence argues there is no case to answer, the magistrates make their decision after considering the prosecution's written evidence – for example, witness statements. No witnesses are called in person. No defence evidence is submitted.

→glossary

The section 8 restrictions mean no evidence can be reported. There is no provision for written evidence in a committal hearing to be made available to the media.

If magistrates decide the evidence is insufficient, they will 'discharge' the defendant as regards that charge. He/she may be committed for trial on some charges but be discharged on others.

! Remember

A discharge should not be described as an acquittal – because there has been no trial. A discharged defendant will not normally be prosecuted again for that charge, but in rare cases he/she might be, if further evidence comes to light. It is also possible – though again, rare – for the prosecution, after a discharge, to seek to resurrect the charge on the existing evidence by seeking 'a voluntary bill of indictment' as explained in mcnaes.com ch. 7.

The section 8 reporting restrictions will automatically be in force at the start of the committal hearing, and only lapse if all defendants are discharged on all charges.

Section 5B of the 1980 Act says that, if magistrates decide to discharge a defendant, as much of the written statements as has been accepted as evidence shall be read aloud unless the court otherwise directs; and that when such a direction is given (against reading the evidence aloud), an 'account' must still be given orally in court of such evidence.

Committal hearings are to be abolished. When this becomes law an either-way case which, in the mode of trail procedure, magistrates refuse to try or one in which the defendant wants a jury trial will be 'sent for trial' to the Crown court. See this book's Late News section.

Transfer of cases to Crown court

Committal hearings were abolished some years ago for two types of either-way charges: those alleging serious and complex fraud, and those alleging sexual and/or violent crimes in which a child (for example, the alleged victim) is due to be a witness. The Criminal Justice Act 1987, as regards fraud cases, and the Criminal Justice Act 1991, as regards relevant cases involving children, introduced procedure whereby such charges are swiftly 'transferred' by magistrates, without consideration of the strength of evidence, to the Crown court. Parliament passed this law to minimise delay in the pre-trial processing of such cases because:

- complex fraud cases will already have undergone many months, perhaps several years, of investigation, and need to be tried while witnesses' memories of events remain as fresh as possible;
- children's welfare, and their ability to give accurate evidence, can suffer if they have to wait many months to testify and the delay is stressful.

Transfer procedure is due to be replaced by the 'sending for trial' process used for indictable-only offences. Reporting restrictions under section 8 of the 1980 Act apply to preliminary hearings in magistrates courts which concern cases subject to transfer.

Recap of major points

- An indictable-only case will be 'sent for trial' to the Crown court.
- A denied either-way case can be tried by magistrates or by a jury. The defendant can choose trial by jury.
- Reporting restrictions under section 8 of the Magistrates' Courts Act 1980 automatically apply to media reports of all preliminary hearings in the magistrates court if the case retains potential for jury trial.

Useful Websites

www.cps.gov.uk/legal/s_to_u/sending_indictable_only_cases_to_the_crown_court/
Crown Prosecution Service guidance on 'sending for trial' and committals

8

Criminal cases in the Crown courts and appeal courts

Chapter summary

Crown courts deal with the most serious criminal cases, including murder. Their trials lead to the tense moment when the jury announces the verdict, with the press bench full for major cases. This chapter details the work of Crown courts, and explains the jury's role. It explains how reporting restrictions ban the media from publishing full reports of pre-trial hearings. It outlines the work of the High Court, Court of Appeal and Supreme Court in criminal cases.

Roles at Crown courts

There are Crown courts at 77 locations in England and Wales, in administrative regions referred to as 'circuits'. The most famous is the Central Criminal Court in London – known as the Old Bailey.

In Crown court trials:

- juries decide if each charge is proved;
- judges rule on law, and sentence convicted defendants.

In very rare circumstances – for example, if there is a real risk that criminals could intimidate jurors to acquit a defendant – a Crown court trial can proceed with no jury, leaving the judge to decide the verdict(s).

Who are jurors?

A Crown court jury consists of 12 people, aged between 18 and 70, selected randomly from electoral rolls for the local districts. They are sent a summons to turn up for jury service. Some categories of people are barred from being jurors – for example, anyone jailed in the previous ten years.

Types of Crown court judge

Three types of judge sit in Crown courts:

- High Court judges: those who can sit in the High Court and Crown courts. They are referred to as, for instance, Mr Justice Smith or Mrs Justice Smith. They wear red robes for criminal cases. Only they can try the most serious offences, such as murder, as they are the most experienced judges.
- Circuit judges, referred to as Judge John Smith or Judge Mary Smith. They are barristers of at least ten years' standing or solicitors who have been Recorders.
- Recorders, who are part-time judges. They are barristers or solicitors who have held 'right of audience' (that is, the right to represent clients) at Crown court. Recorders are usually referred to as the Recorder, Mr John Smith or Mrs Mary Smith.

! Remember

Some cities have bestowed the title of 'Honorary Recorder of –' on the senior circuit judge, who carries out ceremonial duties.

Lawyers at Crown court

Prosecutions at Crown court are conducted by barristers. Barristers also usually appear for the defence. Solicitors have 'right of audience' in some circumstances. A court clerk sits in each Crown court in front of the judge, to assist in procedures.

see also ch. 1, pp. 6–7 on solicitors and barristers

Routes to Crown court

A case yet to be tried reaches a Crown court because it has been:

- *sent for trial,* from a magistrates court because it is an indictable-only charge; or
- *committed for trial,* from a magistrates court if it is an either-way charge; or
- committed for trial, from a youth court; or
- transferred by a magistrates court, if it is an either-way fraud case deemed serious or complex, or an either-way case involving an alleged sexual or violent offence and a child witness.

These procedures are explained in chapter 7, or in chapter 9. In rare circumstances a High Court judge, by means of a voluntary bill of indictment, can send a case to the Crown court for trial, as mcnaes.com ch. 7 explains.

A case can also be heard by the Crown court if the defendant has been **committed for sentence** or been subject to 'section 70' committal which are procedures explained in chapter 6, or is an appeal, see below.

→glossary

Arraignment

A defendant whose case is sent or committed for trial or transferred to a Crown
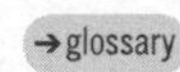
court is asked to plead guilty or not guilty to each charge on the **indictment** for formal pleas to be recorded. This process is known as arraignment. At Crown court charges are referred to as 'counts'. See also 'Reporting the arraignment' below.

Hearings prior to jury involvement: automatic reporting restrictions

In cases in which a defendant denies guilt, there will be at least one hearing at Crown
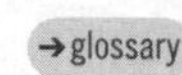
court before the jury is involved. Statutes have applied **automatic** reporting restrictions to media coverage of certain types of these hearings. The hearings are for the judge to make rulings, some of which may determine what the jury, if the case
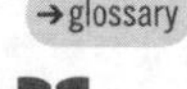
proceeds to trial, will be told, and may include **bail** decisions.

bail decisions are explained in ch. 6, pp. 54–55

The reporting restrictions are to prevent information being published which could prejudice a trial, the principle being that members of the public should not learn contemporaneously through the media about that information, as discussed in these hearings held prior to trial, because it could relate to a case which some may try if they are subsequently selected as jurors. Material which could prejudice a jury's verdict, and which could be discussed in these hearings, includes a defendant's previous conviction(s), or evidence ruled to be inadmissible. Types of prejudicial matter are outlined in chapter 7, pp. 65–66 in relation to similar restrictions in section 8 of the Magistrates' Courts Act 1980, which apply – for the same reason – to media coverage of preliminary hearings in magistrates courts.

The scope of the automatic reporting restrictions

The automatic restrictions which limit media reports of some types of pre-trial hearings at Crown courts are in various statutes, but of the same format. They restrict these reports to seven categories of information:

- the name of the Crown court and the judge's name;
- the names, ages, home addresses and occupations of the defendant(s) and witnesses;
- the charge(s), or a summary of it/them;
- the names of solicitors or barristers in the case;
- if proceedings are adjourned, the date and place to which they are adjourned;
- arrangements as to bail – that is, whether bail was granted or refused, and, if it was granted, any bail conditions and **surety** arrangement;
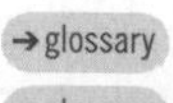
- whether **legal aid** was granted.

Witnesses are unlikely to take part in a hearing prior to trial. But if they do, or are mentioned in court, under these restrictions they can be named in reports, unless other law gives them anonymity.

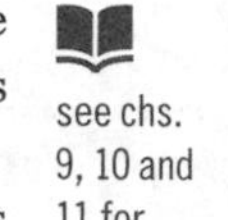
see chs. 9, 10 and 11 for anonymity law

In cases in which bail is refused, the usual interpretation of the restrictions is that the media should not report why the prosecution opposed bail or reasons the judge gave for refusing it, as such information could be prejudicial.

Home addresses can include past addresses in events which gave rise to the charges – see chapter 6, p. 57 on care needed in references to former addresses.

Which types of hearings?

The types of hearings for which the above format of restrictions apply are:

Unsuccessful applications for a case to be dismissed prior to arraignment A defendant whose case is 'sent for trial' or 'transferred' to Crown court may apply to a judge, before arraignment, for it to be dismissed because of insufficient evidence. The reporting restrictions on such hearings in cases sent for trial are detailed in Schedule 3 of the Crime and Disorder Act 1998. The restrictions for hearings in 'transferred' cases are detailed in Schedule 6 of the Criminal Justice Act 1991 and section 11 of the Criminal Justice Act 1987.

'Preparatory hearings' A Crown court may hold a 'preparatory hearing' in a case which involves a serious offence or which will involve a complex or lengthy trial. A preparatory hearing must be held in a terrorism case. The hearings are so that the judge can rule on case matters. If such a hearing is held, it marks the start of the trial, and takes place shortly before the jury is sworn. If the arraignment has not yet been held, it must take place at the start of the preparatory hearing. The reporting restrictions – again, in the format set out above – are in section 11 of the Criminal Justice Act 1987 for preparatory hearings in serious and complex fraud cases, and in section 37 of the Criminal Procedure and Investigations Act 1996 in respect of preparatory hearings in other types of case.

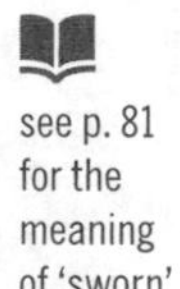
see p. 81 for the meaning of 'sworn'

The same restrictions apply, generally under section 37 of the 1996 Act and – for fraud cases – under section 11 of the 1987 Act to media reports of any application to a Crown court judge for leave to appeal against rulings made at a 'preparatory hearing', and to any such appeal in a higher court.

'Relevant business information'

Section 11 of the Criminal Justice Act 1987 allows journalists covering an application at the Crown court to dismiss transferred fraud charges to include 'relevant business information' in reports of the hearing, even when the automatic restrictions are in place. This means the media can report:

- any address used by the defendant for carrying on business on his/her own account;
- the name of the business at 'any relevant time', that is, when events which gave rise to the charge(s) occurred;

- the name and address of any firm in which he/she was a partner, or by which he/she was engaged, at any such time;
- the name of any company of which he/she was a director, or by which he/she was otherwise engaged, at any such time, and the address of its registered or principal office;
- any working address of the defendant in his/her capacity as a person engaged by any such company ('engaged' means under a contract of service or a contract for services).

What else can be reported?

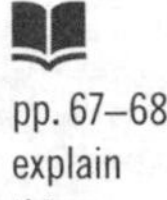

pp. 67–68 explain this

In addition to the information which the format of restrictions lists as safe to publish, it is safe to include in reports of pre-trial Crown court hearings neutral descriptions of the court scene, and non-prejudicial background facts of the type outlined in chapter 7 in relation to preliminary hearings before magistrates.

'Pre-trial' hearings – automatic reporting restrictions

The Criminal Procedure and Investigations Act 1996 defines a pre-trial hearing as any hearing at a Crown court before a guilty plea is accepted (that is, before it becomes clear there will be no trial) or, in cases which remain contested, all hearings which occur before a jury is sworn or before the beginning of a 'preparatory' hearing in the case. Reporting restrictions in section 41 of the Act automatically ban publication, before the conclusion of all proceedings in the case, of what is said in a 'pre-trial hearing' in:

- applications for rulings on the admissibility of evidence or any other question of law, including any rulings made by the judge;
- applications for such a ruling to be varied or discharged, including any order made.

The safest course to obey the restrictions

As can be gleaned from the passages above, the law enshrining these various sets of restrictions developed piecemeal. The definitions of hearings held at the Crown court before a trial overlap, and the extent to which the restrictions apply to all types of these hearings is unclear. To avoid any illegal publication a journalist's safest course is to include only the categories of information listed under the heading 'The scope of the automatic reporting restrictions' (plus, in fraud cases 'relevant business information') and non-prejudicial background information in a contemporaneous report of any Crown court hearing held before a jury becomes involved – that is, a contested case. However, see also 'Reporting the arraignment' below.

When do the automatic reporting restrictions cease to apply?

A Crown court judge can lift the restrictions, or lift them in part, to allow the media to publish contemporaneously fuller reports of such hearings.

If any defendant objects to this, the judge may lift them only if satisfied that doing so is in the interests of justice. Argument in court about whether the restrictions should be lifted cannot be reported until the 'conclusion' of all relevant trials, even if restrictions are lifted in other respects.

If the judge leaves the restrictions in place, they automatically cease to apply at the 'conclusion' of relevant proceedings. In the statutes, this is stated to be, or can safely be construed to be, the acquittal or conviction of a sole defendant or, for multiple defendants, all defendants in respect of all charges in all trials in the case, or when it becomes clear that, for some other reason, no relevant trial remains pending. This might be when the prosecutor decides not to proceed with the case, or when all charges are dismissed for lack of evidence. But reporting restrictions under other law may still apply – see chapters 9, 10 and 11.

Case study

In 2010 the media successfully argued that reporting restrictions covering a pre-trial appeal should be lifted. The case concerned three MPs and a peer charged with fiddling parliamentary expenses. A pre-trial issue was whether 'parliamentary privilege' protected them from prosecution. The Crown court judge ruled it did not, and allowed this pre-trial ruling to be published contemporaneously. The defendants appealed against the ruling to the Court of Appeal, which agreed – at the media's request – to lift the reporting restrictions in section 37 of the Criminal Procedure and Investigations Act 1996 to allow contemporaneous publication of submissions made in the appeal and the court's decision upholding the Crown court ruling. Explaining the decision to lift the restrictions, the Lord Chief Justice, Lord Judge, said the appeal had nothing to do with whether the defendants were dishonest but was 'confined to a narrow but important issue of constitutional law'. So, he said, there was no realistic prospect that a future trial of the defendants might be prejudiced by the lifting of the reporting restrictions (*R v Chaytor and others* [2010] EWCA Crim 1910).

Liability for breach of the automatic reporting restrictions

Liability and penalty for breach of the reporting restrictions under the Acts cited above are the same as for breach of restrictions under the Magistrates' Courts Act 1980 – (see chapter 7, p. 68). If a breach occurs after a trial has begun, and is serious enough – because of what is published – to cause it to be aborted, a media organisation may also become liable for huge costs under section 93 of the Courts Act 2003 (see chapter 18, p. 227).

Appeals against rulings by judge: reporting restrictions

The Criminal Justice Act 2003 gives the prosecution the right to appeal against a ruling made by a Crown court judge which would terminate all or part of the case – for example, that there is no case to answer – no matter what stage the case has reached when the ruling is made. Section 71 of the Act, intended to prevent prejudice to the trial, or to any linked trial, automatically bans reporting of any Crown court discussion (which, if the trial has begun, would be in the jury's absence) about such an appeal. It also restricts reports of the Court of Appeal hearing, and any further appeal made to the Supreme Court, to the same seven categories of information allowed under the automatic reporting restrictions. These restrictions apply, unless lifted earlier, until the conclusion of all trials in the case.

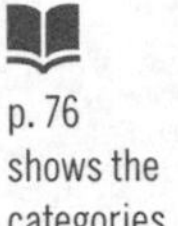

p. 76 shows the categories

Reporting the arraignment

If defendants in a case plead guilty to each charge at the arraignment, they are convicted of all charges in the case and so the restrictions detailed on pp. 76 and 78 cease to apply, as there will be no trial.

If a sole defendant or all defendants deny the charge or charges at the arraignment, the media can safely report those pleas contemporaneously if there is be just one trial in the case.

But if a defendant or co-defendants enter a mixture of guilty and not guilty pleas, or if denied charges are to be dealt with in more than one trial, a judge may – to avoid what he/she considers a substantial risk of prejudice – make an order under section 4(2) of the Contempt of Court Act 1981 postponing publication of that information. A judge could do this, for example, to ban media reports of an arraignment from mentioning, until the trial ends, any charge which has been admitted (if the jury is not to be told about it) or – if the case will involve more than one trial – any charge not due to be dealt with in the first trial. Or the judge could use section 4(2) to ban any reporting of the arraignment, and of the first trial, until any further trial in the case is concluded.

See ch. 18, pp. 228–230 for detail on section 4(2) orders, and for considerations to be borne in mind even if a judge does not make such an order.

Procedure in Crown court trials

The media may publish contemporaneous, full reports of what the jury is told at a Crown court trial once it has started, as long as any discretionary reporting restriction or any automatic anonymity for a complainant of a sexual offence is complied with (see chapters 9, 10 and 11).

! Remember

Until the jury has returned all verdicts in the trial, no report should include – unless the judge says otherwise – any ruling, discussion or argument which occurs while the jury is not in the courtroom. This is explained in chapter 18. To avoid libel dangers, reporting must be fair and accurate, as explained in chapter 21.

Selection of the jury and the giving of evidence

A Crown court trial can be regarded as under way when the jury is 'empanelled' – a group of potential jurors is brought into the courtroom, and the court clerk selects 12 at random. These will be 'sworn' – that is, required to swear a legal oath to try the case according to the evidence.

Soon after this the prosecution counsel 'opens the case' by outlining it. Prosecution witnesses then testify. A Crown court trial usually follows the sequence used in magistrates' trials, as regards the giving of evidence, including cross-examination, and speeches by lawyers.

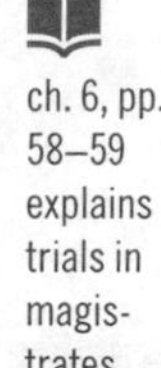

ch. 6, pp. 58–59 explains trials in magis-trates courts

At the Crown court, defence counsel may choose to make a speech 'opening' the defence case prior to calling the defence witnesses. After all these have been heard, prosecuting counsel in most cases makes a closing speech to the jury, which is followed by the defence's closing speech.

The judge then sums up the case to remind jurors of evidence and direct them on law. The judge will, if he/she decides that evidence is not sufficient to support a charge, direct the jury to bring in a verdict of not guilty on that charge.

Otherwise, and to consider any other charge, the jury 'retires' to a jury room to decide its verdict(s). A jury bailiff escorts jurors to and from the room and is the only official allowed contact with them in it. The jury will have been directed to elect a foreman or forewoman to be its spokesperson.

Majority verdicts

A judge initially asks a jury to reach a unanimous verdict on each charge – that is, a unanimous vote to acquit or convict.

- However, if a jury has retired to discuss the case for at least two hours and ten minutes and has failed to reach a verdict, the judge can recall it to the courtroom to tell it that a majority verdict is acceptable (for each charge).
- For a full jury of 12, majority verdicts of the ratios 11–1 or 10–2 are acceptable.
- If a jury is reduced in number for any reason, for example because one or two jurors have fallen ill during the trial, a majority of 10–1 or 9–1 is allowed.
- If a defendant is convicted by a majority, rather than by a unanimous vote, the media should ideally – to be fair – report the fact that it was by a majority

decision, as this indicates that one or two people in the jury disagreed with the 'guilty' verdict.

ch. 11 explains the ban on interviewing jurors

If the verdict is an acquittal, the court asks no questions of the jury about the ratio of the vote, so no indication is usually given of how many jurors concurred in the verdict. If the foreman/woman volunteers the fact that acquittal was by a majority it is by convention regarded as unfair to publish this fact, because stating that one or two jurors voted against acquittal could leave a stain on the defendant's character even though he/she was cleared of the charge.

A jury which cannot reach a verdict by a sufficient majority is known as a 'hung jury'. The prosecution then has to decide if it wants to seek a re-trial.

 For media access to preosecution material, see ch. 14, pp. 160–161.

Sentencing at Crown court

If a defendant pleads guilty at a Crown court to all charges, the judge will pass sentence, often after an adjournment. First, the judge will hear the prosecution's summary of the case facts, and be told if the defendant has previous convictions, and of any offences to be **taken into consideration**. The judge will also consider any statement about the impact of a crime from the victim(s) or – in a homicide case – a statement by bereaved relatives on how that killing affected them. The judge will also hear **mitigation**.

→glossary

→glossary 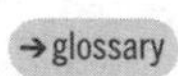

Sentencing after a Crown court trial follows a similar pattern, though the judge, having presided in it, will not normally need to hear detail of the offence(s) again.

The same sentencing procedure is used for a defendant who, after conviction in the magistrates court, has been **committed for sentence** to the Crown court.

→glossary

Crown courts frequently impose jail terms, but have the same range of other sentencing options as magistrates – see chapter 6.

If no other factors apply – for example, the defendant is not sentenced to life or deemed 'dangerous' – he/she can expect, if he/she behaves well in prison, to be released 'on licence' half-way through the term imposed by the court. On release, he/she will be monitored by a probation officer. A released prisoner who breaks any condition of the licence, for instance by committing a further crime, can be returned to prison to serve the remainder of the jail term.

see Useful Website below on probation

Life sentences, 'dangerous' offenders and indeterminate sentences

Life sentences may be imposed for murder and other very serious offences. The judge will state, when sentencing, a minimum term of the life sentence which the defendant should serve, and may recommend that it should actually be for life.

A defendant convicted of a sexual or violent offence, as specified in statute, that was committed on or after April 4, 2005, can be categorised as a 'dangerous offender'.

This law is complex, but in summary: an offender can be categorised as 'dangerous' if a Crown court judge considers there is significant risk of him/her committing further offences which might cause serious harm to members of the public.

This means he/she must be given a life sentence if the circumstances of the offence of which he/she is convicted are deemed particularly serious and the law allows that penalty. Some 'dangerous offenders' have been given an 'indeterminate sentence for public protection', meaning he/she will not be released from prison until a stated minimum term is served and until and unless the Parole Board deems the level of risk he/she poses to the public is manageable in the community. If it continues to be the case that the risk is deemed too high, the prisoner will remain in jail indefinitely, even though the sentence imposed was not a life sentence. However, in October 2011 the Government announced plans for the system of indeterminate sentences to be replaced by a new regime of 'tough, determinate sentences'.

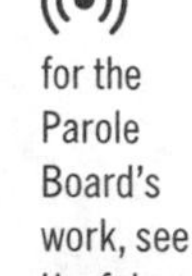

for the Parole Board's work, see Useful Websites below

The Court of Appeal

A defendant who wishes to appeal against a conviction or the severity of the sentence imposed by a Crown court can seek permission to appeal to the Court of Appeal, Criminal Division, based in London. Permission to appeal can be granted by the Crown court trial judge or by the Court of Appeal itself.

figure 1 in ch. 1, p. 4 shows the hierarchy of the court system

The Court of Appeal may, if it allows the appeal, quash a conviction. It may decide there must be a re-trial of the case, by another Crown court jury.

Appeals are usually heard by three judges. A reporter covering a Court of Appeal hearing in which its judgment is delivered may, in cases decided by a majority rather than a unanimous decision, have to wait until each of the three judges has announced his/her own decision for that majority, and therefore the appeal result, to be revealed.

Appeals beyond the Court of Appeal go to the Supreme Court.

Journalists can visit prisoners

The right of a convicted prisoner to be visited in jail by a journalist investigating whether there has been a miscarriage of justice was upheld in *R v Secretary of State for the Home Department, ex p Simms* [1999] 3 All ER 400.

The Supreme Court

The Supreme Court, formerly known as the House of Lords, is the highest court in criminal and civil law. Its judges – colloquially referred to as the law lords – now have the formal title of Justices of the Supreme Court. The court only hears appeals of high significance, usually no more than 40 to 50 each year. Appeals are heard by several Justices, with a majority decision being binding. The Supreme Court sits in the former Middlesex Guildhall.

see Useful Websites below

Retrials after 'tainted acquittal' or after compelling new evidence emerges: reporting restrictions

Under what is known as the 'double jeopardy rule', the law – as a protection of civil liberties – usually prevents someone who has been acquitted of an offence being tried for it again. But there are two major exceptions:

- If a Crown court trial convicts a person of interference with or intimidation of a juror, witness or potential witness in an earlier trial in which the same or another defendant has been acquitted, the prosecution can apply to the High Court for an order quashing that acquittal, to allow a retrial.
- Under the Criminal Justice Act 2003 (the 2003 Act), if 'new and compelling evidence' emerges after a defendant has been acquitted at Crown court of a serious charge as defined by the Act, the prosecution can apply to the Court of Appeal for the acquittal to be quashed and a new trial to be held.

In the 2003 Act procedure, the Court of Appeal can make an order under the Act's section 82 imposing reporting restrictions, making it an offence to publish anything which would create a substantial risk of prejudice to a retrial. The order can ban the media from reporting the application to quash the acquittal, or anything relating to it– for example, the media can be banned from reporting evidence from the original case or the fact that there are ongoing police investigations about the new evidence. The reporting restrictions are in force until the end of any retrial, or until the matter is otherwise dropped.

The Crown court as an appeal court

Defendants can appeal to a Crown court judge against a refusal by magistrates to grant bail.

Defendants can appeal to the Crown court against conviction by magistrates, including in youth courts. In the appeal there is no jury: a judge will sit normally with two lay magistrates. The Crown court also hears appeals against the severity of sentences imposed by magistrates, and may confirm a sentence, substitute a lesser penalty or increase it, but not to more than the highest sentence magistrates could have imposed.

The High Court

The High Court's Queen's Bench Division, which deals with criminal and other matters, has about 60 judges, headed by the Lord Chief Justice. It hears cases in London and Cardiff and major regional cities.

A defendant convicted by magistrates, or who has appealed unsuccessfully from them to the Crown court, may appeal on a point of law to the Queen's Bench Division on the ground that a decision was wrong in law. This procedure is known as appeal by way of 'case stated', because no evidence is given verbally to the High Court, which considers a written record of the case. The prosecution can also use this procedure to challenge an acquittal by magistrates. The High Court has wide powers to reverse, affirm or amend magistrates' decisions, including those taken in youth courts. It can order the case to be retried summarily.

ch. 15 covers media challenges to court decisions

Judicial reviews

Part of the High Court's work involves judicial reviews, hearings which can consider other types of challenges to decisions made by magistrates. The media can also use the judicial review procedure to challenge discretionary reporting restrictions imposed by magistrates.

Courts martial

People in the armed forces are subject to UK law in the courts martial system, even if the alleged offence was committed in another country. This military court is presided over by a civilian judge advocate who sits with three to seven service personnel. Courts martial are usually open to the public and the media.

((•)) For more information on courts martial, see Useful Websites below.

Recap of major points

- Crown courts deal with the most serious criminal cases.
- At the Crown court judges rule on law and decide on punishment, and in trials juries decide whether each charge is proved.
- Automatic reporting restrictions limit what the media can report from most Crown court hearings held prior to trial.
- A defendant convicted in a Crown court can seek to appeal to the Court of Appeal, and thereafter to the Supreme Court.
- Crown courts hear appeals from magistrates courts against conviction or sentence.
- The High Court is also an appeal court for certain matters.

((•)) Useful Websites

www.direct.gov.uk/en/CrimeJusticeAndTheLaw/Juryservice/index.htm
Government guidance on jury service

www.justice.gov.uk/guidance/prison-probation-and-rehabilitation/before-after-release/probation.htm
Ministry of Justice information on probation

www.justice.gov.uk/about/parole-board/index.htm
Parole Board

www.supremecourt.gov.uk/
Supreme Court website

www.judiciary.gov.uk/about-the-judiciary/the-judiciary-in-detail/jurisdictions/military-juisdiction
Judiciary website on courts martial

9

Juveniles in criminal and ASBO cases

Chapter summary

Juveniles – the term covers those aged under 18 – charged with crimes are dealt with in youth courts by magistrates. The public cannot attend these courts, but journalists can. Reporting restrictions automatically ban media reports of youth court cases from identifying the juveniles involved. The anonymity is to protect their welfare. Some juveniles are tried in the (adult) magistrates courts or Crown courts, depending on the seriousness of the offence. Adult courts can also ban media reports from identifying a juvenile involved in a case. An anti-social behaviour order can be imposed on a juvenile, and a media report of this may be able to name him/her.

Juveniles and the age of criminal responsibility

In law relevant to this chapter a 'child' is defined as being younger than 14. A 'young person' is 14 or over, but under 18. Children under the age of 10 have not reached 'the age of criminality', and so cannot be prosecuted for a crime as they are considered too young to distinguish between right and wrong. But they may be placed under the supervision of social workers, by family courts.

ch. 13 explains family law cases

The legal distinction between a 'child' over 10 and a 'young person' is not relevant in court reporting. Lawyers use the term 'juvenile' to describe defendants aged from 10 up to, but not including, the age of 18, and witnesses under 18.

Juveniles in youth courts

Most juveniles who are prosecuted are dealt with by youth courts, presided over by magistrates. Youth courts – though usually in the same building as magistrates courts (where adult defendants appear) – have smaller courtrooms, to make juveniles feel less nervous than they might be in an adult court. Magistrates who sit in youth courts receive special training. Procedures there, including trials, are similar to those in adult magistrates courts, described in chapters 6 and 7.

→glossary A juvenile denied **bail** may be sent to non-secure accommodation run by the local authority, or – if the alleged offending is persistent or serious – to custody, as explained below.

Youth courts' powers

A youth court, because its sentencing powers are limited, cannot try extremely serious cases such as homicide, and in these cases must commit juvenile defendants to a Crown court. But a youth court has discretion, if it considers its punishment powers sufficient in a particular case, to try other offences – such as robbery – which, had the defendant been an adult, could only be tried by a Crown court.

Sentencing

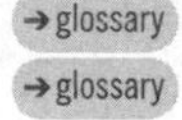

A youth court can impose **community punishment**, **absolute** and **conditional discharges**, order offenders to pay compensation to victims, and can fine. A parent must pay the fine if the offender is aged under 16. A youth court can also make a 'youth rehabilitation order', which can involve community punishment and other requirements, such as a curfew.

Many young offenders who admit a first offence are merely made subject to 'a referral order', which means they must cooperate with a referral to a youth offender panel, comprising of trained youth workers, and agree with it a 'contract' which seeks to prevent reoffending. This includes agreeing to do unpaid work in the community. An offender who fails to cooperate can be given a more severe punishment.

Youth courts can make 'a detention and training order' in a serious case. This can be imposed for between four months to two years. Normally this means that the juvenile spends half the period in custody with training, and the other half supervised in the community.

The court can make 'a parenting order' requiring a parent to attend counselling and guidance sessions, and to cooperate with other steps to help the juvenile avoid reoffending. A parent failing to comply will face court punishment.

Juveniles in custody

A juvenile refused bail by a youth court or sentenced there to detention and training can be held on remand or for that sentence in a secure children's home, a secure training centre or a young offenders' institution.

Committal for trial for homicide, 'grave' and other cases

A juvenile charged with a homicide offence, such as murder or manslaughter, or one of a range of firearms offences, cannot be tried or sentenced by a youth court because of the seriousness of the charge. In these cases defendants make initial appearances there for decisions on bail and procedure but are then **committed for trial** to a Crown court. →glossary

Grave offences

Some crimes, such as causing death by dangerous driving and certain sexual offences, are classed as 'grave'. In these cases, the youth court considers in **mode of trial** proceedings whether its maximum power of punishment – that is, a two-year detention and training order – would be sufficient if it convicts the defendant. If it considers this power insufficient, the case is committed to Crown court for trial. These mode of trial/committal hearings differ from those in magistrates courts because in the youth court a juvenile has no right to choose jury trial, and the court does not consider if there is sufficient evidence, but considers the facts of the alleged offence and can take account of a juvenile's previous offending. →glossary

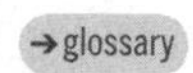

ch. 7 explains these procedures in the magistrates court

The youth court will also send a case for Crown court trial if it considers that the defendant would, if convicted, meet the 'dangerous' offender criteria, explained in chapter 8.

Section 8 reporting restrictions

A youth court case which must or may be committed for trial to the Crown court, or which is sent for trial there, has the potential of being tried by jury, so the **automatic** reporting restrictions of section 8 of the Magistrates' Courts Act 1980 (the 1980 Act) apply to all preliminary hearings of such a case in the youth court for as long as that potential exists. For a case committed or sent for trial, these restrictions normally continue in force until the Crown court finishes dealing with it. →glossary

See ch. 7, pp. 65–73 for detail of the section 8 restrictions and how on rare occasions they may be lifted. They are explained there in relation to cases in the (adult) magistrates courts – but apply identically in respect of such preliminary hearings at the youth court.

Section 8C restrictions

Pre-trial hearings of a case to be tried by the youth court are covered by the automatic reporting restrictions in the 1980 Act's section 8C.

ch. 6 explains section 8C

! Remember

Other reporting restrictions apply automatically to almost all types of criminal cases at youth courts, as explained below, preventing the media from identifying juveniles involved. So, for some hearings, section 8 or 8C and anonymity will apply.

Committal for sentence

A youth court which convicts a juvenile of a serious crime can at this stage too consider whether he/she should be regarded as a 'dangerous offender'. If the

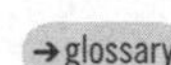

answer is yes, the youth court can **commit** him/her to Crown court **for sentence**. The 1980 Act restrictions do not apply in respect of a trial at a youth court or a hearing which decides whether to commit for sentence – because sections 8 and 8C only apply to preliminary/pre-trial hearings.

Admission to youth courts

Parliament has decided that the public should not be allowed inside any youth court, to avoid juveniles being stigmatised in their communities by allegations of or conviction for immature law-breaking. Exceptions can be made – a victim may be allowed to see an offender being sentenced.

Journalists can cover youth court cases because section 47 of the Children and Young Persons Act 1933 (the 1933 Act) says that 'bona fide representatives of newspapers or news agencies' can attend.

Section 49 automatic restrictions on identifying juveniles

Parliament decided – again, to stop juveniles being stigmatised – that defendants in youth courts should not usually be identified in media reports of their cases. This anonymity also applies to juvenile witnesses in them, helping make giving evidence less of an ordeal. The anonymity also protects the reputation of juvenile witnesses if their character is scrutinised in cross-examination.

Juveniles involved in youth courts are given this automatic anonymity by section 49 of the 1933 Act.

Section 49 says that a report of youth court proceedings must not reveal:

- the name;
- address;
- school; or
- any particulars likely to lead to the identification of any person aged under 18 'concerned in the proceedings' – which means as a defendant, witness or a victim/alleged victim and must not include:

- any picture (including in any television programme) of, or including, any such juvenile.

In the Act, the definition 'concerned in the proceedings' also covers a juvenile 'in respect of whom the proceedings are taken', which means that section 49 anonymity also applies to a juvenile who is the victim/alleged victim in the case, as stated in the charge, even if not a witness – for example, because he/she is too young to give evidence.

But a juvenile victim/alleged victim who is dead can be identified by the media, as explained on p. 183.

No identifying detail should be published

The section 49 restrictions mean that normally media reports of youth court cases should not include any detail that could identify a juvenile concerned in the proceedings. Describing a defendant as 'a 14-year-old Bristol boy' would not identify him because Bristol is large. But naming a small village as a defendant's home could well identify him to people who know he lives there. Including a juvenile's nickname or an unusual physical characteristic in a report may also identify him/her to some people. Another example: saying in a report that a juvenile is the 12-year-old twin son of a policeman may identify him to anyone who knows of such twins. The test must always be whether any member of the public could realise, as a result of the report, who the juvenile is. Adults who figure in youth court cases as witnesses or because mentioned in evidence can be named in reports, as long as doing so does not identify a juvenile protected by section 49 (or breach any restriction under other statute in respect of the adult). But a journalist may need to exclude from a report a name and detail identifying an adult, to avoid identifying a juvenile – for example, a father who gives evidence about his son, the defendant, cannot be named.

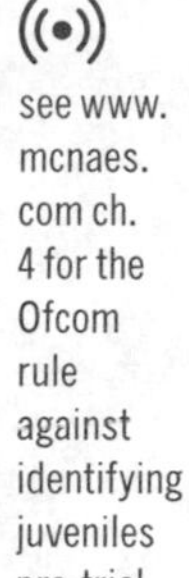

see www.mcnaes.com ch. 4 for the Ofcom rule against identifying juveniles pre-trial

see www.mcnaes.com ch. 9 for 'Example of section 49 anonymity'

Section 49 is a blanket ban on identifying the juvenile's school, however large, unless the youth court permits this. It may do, for example, to let the media highlight a problem of drug-dealing at a particular school.

Appeal proceedings – anonymity retained

ch. 8, pp. 84–85 explains these appeal routes

Section 49 anonymity also applies to reports of Crown court hearings of appeals from the youth court against conviction or severity of sentence, and to reports of High Court hearings of appeals from the youth court (or from the Crown court appeal hearings) on a point of law. The section 49 restrictions do not apply to reports of the Crown court proceedings involving a juvenile committed there for trial or for sentence. But the Crown court may make a discretionary order giving him/her anonymity under section 39 of the 1933 Act, see below.

Breaches of section 49

It is illegal to publish material which breaches section 49 – that is, material which identifies a juvenile who should have anonymity. The Criminal Justice and Public Order Act 1994 says the proprietor, editor or publisher of a newspaper, magazine or website can be prosecuted. For a TV or radio programme the case will be against 'the body corporate which provides the service' and any person whose 'functions in relation to the programme correspond to those of an editor of a newspaper'. The maximum fine is currently £5,000. The Attorney General has to consent to such prosecutions.

Case study

In 2003 a district judge fined the Plymouth *Evening Herald* £1,500 for publishing a photograph of a 15-year-old boy convicted at youth court of stabbing a fellow pupil. The district judge said evidence by friends and relatives that they had recognised the boy, even though his face was pixellated, meant that the paper had breached section 49 (*Media Lawyer*, March 4, 2004).

Section 49 anonymity only applies to a report referring to a youth court case.

Case study

In 2010 Ian Carter, formerly Group Editor of East Surrey and Sussex Newspapers, was acquitted of breaching section 49. The *Croydon Advertiser* had published an interview in which a juvenile victim of a stabbing told of his experience. It included a photo of the teenager, and was published eight days after another juvenile had appeared in a youth court charged with the stabbing. But District Judge Suzanne Bayne, at South Western magistrates court, Battersea, acquitted Mr Carter after accepting the defence argument that the interview had not mentioned the courts or that a juvenile was being prosecuted. Ms Bayne said there was nothing in the article which identified the stabbing victim 'as a witness in current proceedings' (*Media Lawyer*, July 16, 2010).

When section 49 anonymity ceases to apply

Section 49 gives a youth court the power to lift a juvenile's anonymity to allow the media to identify him or her, 'to any specified extent', in three types of circumstance.

(1) *To avoid injustice* This power is rarely exercised. A youth court could use it to allow a media report of a preliminary hearing to identify a juvenile defendant whose lawyer says he/she wants publicity to help trace witnesses

to prove an **alibi** – 'My client John Doe was at the funfair that night, not the crime scene. Did anyone see him at the funfair?' 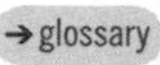

(2) *Unlawfully at large* A youth court, if asked to do so by or on behalf of the Director of Public Prosecutions, can lift the section 49 anonymity to help to trace a juvenile who is 'unlawfully at large' after being charged with or convicted of a violent or sexual offence, or any offence for which a person aged 21 or over could be jailed for 14 years or more. This would allow the media to name and publish a photograph of a juvenile who has failed to answer bail or escaped from secure accommodation, and who is a potential threat to public safety.

(3) *In the public interest* A youth court can lift the anonymity of a juvenile it convicts of any offence if satisfied that doing so is 'in the public interest'. Before taking this decision it must give the prosecution and defence the opportunity to argue for or against lifting the anonymity.

This power to lift the anonymity in the public interest is in section 49(4A) of the 1933 Act, inserted there by section 45 of the Crime (Sentences) Act 1997. It can be used when a youth court feels that the media should be able to identify a juvenile who has persistently offended or committed a notorious crime. The court may decide that allowing the media to identify the defendant will alert the community to the risk that he/she will commit further crime – for example, if they are able to recognise him as a prolific burglar. The court may also believe that allowing the media to 'name and shame' such a juvenile will deter other youngsters from committing crime and reassure the community that justice has been done.

See also ch. 15, pp. 185–186, for grounds the media can cite, from official guidance for courts and prosecutors, to argue in court for the removal of such a juvenile's anonymity.

! Remember

A court can only lift section 49 anonymity 'in the public interest' if the juvenile has been convicted.

Case study

The ability of youth courts to lift section 49 'to any specified extent' is illustrated by a decision of Newbury youth court in 2006. It decided it was in the public interest to allow media reports to name a 14-year-old girl convicted of drink-driving. But it refused to permit publication of recent photographs of her or to allow her school to be named. Shortly after the court decided this, the girl, who was first convicted of drink-driving when she was 12, threw a punch at the prosecutor and hurled a two-litre jug of water at the magistrates (*Media Lawyer*, March 28, 2006).

Anonymity expires when the juvenile turns 18

Section 49 anonymity automatically expires when the juvenile concerned reaches the age of 18, whether he/she is a defendant, witness or victim/alleged victim. This was made clear in 2003 when the High Court upheld the decision of South Shields youth court that a defendant who was 17 when proceedings against him began no longer had anonymity when the case resumed after his 18th birthday (*Todd v Director of Public Prosecutions* [2003] All ER (D) 92 (Oct)).

Juveniles in adult courts

A juvenile may appear in the (adult) magistrates court if jointly charged with an adult, or if the charges the juvenile and adult face arose from the same incident. The juvenile may be tried there as a co-accused, or the magistrates can remit the juvenile's case to the youth court for trial or sentencing. If the adult is committed for trial to the Crown court, the juvenile may be sent there too if the magistrates think a joint trial is in the interests of justice – for example, to avoid witnesses having to testify in two trials. Also, a juvenile defendant can be committed or sent by a youth court to a Crown court, as this chapter has explained.

Section 39 reporting restrictions in adult courts

There is no automatic ban on identifying a juvenile who appears as a defendant, witness or victim/alleged victim in a criminal court other than a youth court.

However, the adult courts have discretion to impose anonymity under section 39 of the Children and Young Persons Act 1933.

If a section 39 order is made, its scope normally is that no report of the case shall reveal the:

- name;
- address;
- school; or
- any particulars 'calculated' (that is, likely) to lead to the identification of any person aged under 18 'concerned in the proceedings', either as a defendant or witness or a victim/alleged victim; and should not contain:
- any picture of, or including, any such juvenile.

('Calculated' survives from the Act's original wording.)

As with the section 49 restriction, a journalist must take care not to breach a section 39 order by including too much detail about a juvenile protected by it.

There is a blanket ban on identifying the juvenile's school unless the court decides otherwise.

Ch. 15, pp. 180–185 gives guidance on how the media can challenge section 39 orders which are invalid or unnecessary.

- A court, to pay proper heed to the principle of open justice, should not make a section 39 order merely because of the juvenile's age, or as an order arbitrarily covering all juveniles in the case. It should consider for each whether there is good reason for anonymity.
- Section 39 or 49 of the 1933 Act can only provide anonymity for a living juvenile, not one who is dead – for example, a murder victim.
- A court cannot use section 39 to specify that an adult, rather than a juvenile, have anonymity.

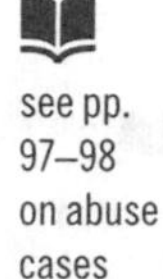
see pp. 97–98 on abuse cases

But anonymity for a juvenile under section 39 may mean that an adult defendant or adult witness in a case cannot be identified either.

For example, if a father is charged with assaulting his child, and if the child's identity is protected by a section 39 order, the family relationship cannot be included in any report which names the father as the defendant, because giving the relationship would identify the child. Even mentioning the child's age could in some cases reveal a familial relationship.

Section 39 orders can also be made in civil courts and by coroners as explained in chapters 12 and 16.

! Remember

A section 39 order can apply to a juvenile 'in respect of whom the proceedings are taken'. It can be used to prevent a media report of a truancy case from identifying a child whose parent is prosecuted in the (adult) magistrates court for failing to ensure the child attends school. The effect would be that the report could not identify the parent either, or, unless the court made an exception, the school.

Recent breaches of section 39 orders

A person or organisation breaching a section 39 order can be fined up to £5,000.

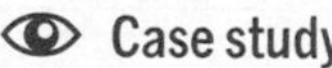

The Sun, *Daily Mirror* and the *Wigan Evening Post* apologised to a judge at Chester Crown court in 2008 after each breached, to some extent, a section 39 order made in a murder case. *The Sun* published details of a disability condition of one of the convicted juvenile defendants, and the *Evening Post* published an address for him, although the order covered both matters. The judge had also said in the order that only one particular photograph could be published of two juvenile witnesses (the murder victim's teenage daughters). But the *Mirror* published a different photograph. The judge said that, in view of the apologies, he would not refer the breaches to the Attorney General for possible prosecution. The judge also said: 'The common theme of these things is that it almost always seems to be a sub editor or features editor who is not aware of something which the news department are' (*Media Lawyer*, February 12, 2008).

When does section 39 cease to apply to a juvenile?

see p. 94 on *Todd*
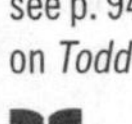
ch. 1, p. 5 explains Article 10
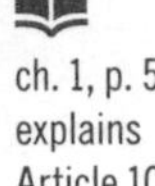

It seems that section 39 anonymity automatically expires when the juvenile reaches the age of 18. The 1933 Act does not specify this, but it can be inferred from the decision on the scope of section 49 in *Todd v Director of Public Prosecutions*. Also, it is a recognised legal principle that Article 10 of the European Convention on Human Rights requires any statutory restriction on reporting to be construed as narrowly as possible.

Jigsaw identification

The term 'jigsaw identification' describes the effect when someone to whom the law has given anonymity is nevertheless identified by the media to the public by mistake, because of a combination or accumulation of detail published. It can occur when two or more media organisations are covering the same case. Each may publish a report which in itself preserves the anonymity. But jigsaw identification will occur if a member of the public who reads, views or hears the reports of more than one organisation can, by combining the different detail in each, recognise the person who should be anonymous.

Jigsaw identification can also occur if a media organisation publishes a series of sequential reports in which it allows too much detail gradually to accumulate. The term is also used to describe such an accumulation in a single report.

The examples given below relate to anonymity for juveniles. But jigsaw identification can also destroy anonymity granted under other law – for example, the anonymity automatically granted to alleged victims of sexual offences.

Sexual offence law is explained in ch. 10. Chs. 11, 13 and 17 explain other law giving anonymity.

Example 1 A juvenile in a youth court, who has anonymity under section 49 of the Children and Young Persons Act 1933, admits causing criminal damage to a sports car owned by local millionaire John Doe. One local paper reports: 'A 15-year-old boy vandalised a sports car owned by London tycoon John Doe, costing him £5,000 in repairs'. Another local paper reports: 'A 15-year-old boy vandalised his rich neighbour's sports car, causing £5,000 damage'. Neither paper names the boy. The second paper does not name Doe. But anyone reading both will know the boy is Doe's neighbour, which identifies the boy locally.

Example 2 A juvenile, who should have anonymity after a section 39 order was made under the 1933 Act, is giving evidence at Crown court in a murder trial. A local radio station describes her as 'a 16-year-old who works as a shop assistant in London'. Another radio station does not mention her job but describes her routine as 'commuting each morning to work in Charing Cross'. A newspaper gives the detail that she lives in Islington. This accumulation of detail could lead to those who know her, and who listen to both stations and read that newspaper, to realise that she is the witness.

Cases of abuse within a family

There is a particular danger of jigsaw identification in media coverage of court cases concerning violence or sexual abuse allegedly inflicted on a child by a relative or family 'friend' – for example, when a father, stepfather or a mother's live-in partner is the adult defendant. In such cases, when the alleged abuse is physical but not sexual, it is standard practice for magistrates or the Crown court judge to make a section 39 order to forbid media reports from identifying the child. In cases of alleged sexual abuse, the child has automatic anonymity under other law explained in chapter 10. When covering such abuse cases in courts, a media organisation has two options:

(a) *the report can name the adult defendant* – but, if the defendant is a relative, or 'friend', the report must not, in order to protect the child's anonymity, include any detail of the defendant's relationship to the child. This can severely restrict what evidence is published – for example, about how the defendant had opportunity to abuse the child, or even the child's age. Lord Justice Maurice Kay made this comment in the Court of Appeal in 2005, alluding to a case in which a father was convicted of conspiracy to rape a child and of distributing indecent photographs of her: 'Offences of the kind established in this case are frequently committed by fathers and step-fathers. . . . If the offender is named and the victim is described as "an 11-year old schoolgirl", in circumstances in which the offender has an 11-year old daughter, it is at least arguable that the composite picture presented embraces 'particulars calculated to lead to the identification' of the victim' (*R v Teesside Crown Court, ex p Gazette Media Company Ltd and others* [2005] All ER (D) 367 (Jul)).

(b) the report does not identify the adult defendant in any way, and therefore can refer to the familial or household relationship between the defendant and child, can definitely refer to the child's age and can include greater detail of evidence, while preserving the child's anonymity.

An editor's instinct is usually that it is in the public's best interests for people charged with crime – and particularly those convicted of it – to be named, as a deterrent and so that a community can be wary of that individual. This is achieved by the approach in (a), if it is possible to construct a meaningful report without revealing the family relationship. But another editor may feel that the public interest is best served by the approach in (b) which can make clear that the alleged abuse was – for example – by a relative. Approach (b) allows more evidence to be published and more questions to be raised about why the community, social services or the police remained unaware of the abuse within that household.

Jigsaw identification would occur if two media organisations covering the case adopted different approaches. If one followed policy (a), naming the adult defendant but obscuring his relationship to the child victim, and the other followed approach (b), not identifying the defendant but reporting, for example, that he was the child's father, anyone reading both reports would be able to identify the child, even though neither report named the child. To avoid jigsaw identification of the child, all the newsrooms involved need to adopt the same approach.

Ch. 10, pp. 109–111 explains the ethical ban on identifying children in sex cases.

Anti-social behaviour orders on juveniles

A court can make an anti-social behaviour order – ASBO – against a person to stop behaviour, criminal or not, which causes harassment, alarm or distress to one or more people not in the person's household. ASBOs, introduced by the Crime and Disorder Act 1998, can be imposed on an adult or a juvenile aged 10 or over.

The order may seek to stop the person engaging in activity which may lead to crime. A persistent shoplifter can, by means of an ASBO, be banned from going into any shop. ASBOs have banned juveniles from entering streets where they have habitually been creating a nuisance, or from getting into any car, if they tend to 'joy-ride'.

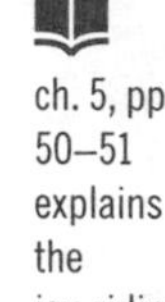
ch. 5, pp. 50–51 explains the joy-riding offence

An ASBO is an order made in civil law, but breaching it is a criminal offence. So, for example, if a person banned from any shop ignores the ban, this is an offence in itself, even if he/she cannot be proved to have shoplifted there. The minimum duration of an ASBO is two years.

There are two main types of court hearing which can impose an ASBO on a juvenile.

ASBO applications in civil proceedings in magistrates courts

the role of the county courts is explained in ch. 12

An (adult) magistrates court, sitting in civil proceedings, can impose an ASBO on an adult or juvenile, if persuaded to do so by an application by a local authority, a registered social landlord (for example, a housing association), the

Environment Agency or the police. County courts have similar powers to make ASBOs.

There is no automatic ban on the media identifying a juvenile in a report of an ASBO application in a magistrates or county court, whether or not it results in an ASBO. But these courts have discretion to use section 39 of the Children and Young Persons Act 1933 to stop the media reports identifying a juvenile 'concerned in such proceedings', whether this is a juvenile being considered for an ASBO, or a witness.

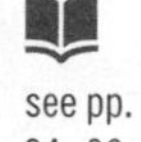
see pp. 94–96 on section 39

 See www.mcnaes.com, ch. 9 for 'interim' ASBO orders.

'Bolt-on' ASBO hearings

A criminal court, including a youth court, can decide to make an ASBO against a defendant it has convicted of an offence, whether or not any agency has applied for one. Such a hearing – on whether an ASBO is needed – is a consequence of that conviction (for example, for theft or taking vehicles), and may proceed immediately after that criminal case concludes. This type of ASBO, because of this linkage to the conviction, is sometimes known as a 'bolt-on' ASBO (it remains an order made in civil law).

- In youth courts, the automatic anonymity given by section 49 of the 1933 Act prevents the media identifying the juvenile defendant, and any juvenile witness, in any report of the actual criminal case which precedes the 'bolt-on' ASBO hearing, unless the court specifically removes a juvenile's anonymity in that criminal case – for example, 'in the public interest' as regards the convicted juvenile defendant.
- But if a 'bolt-on' hearing follows then if (and only if) the youth court imposes an ASBO on the defendant, the section 49 anonymity ceases to apply to that juvenile in relation to reports of the 'bolt-on' hearing, so he/she can be identified as the subject of an ASBO, unless the youth court in that 'bolt-on' hearing decides to preserve the juvenile's anonymity by using its discretion to make a section 39 order.
- The section 49 anonymity automatically continues to apply to any other juvenile concerned in the 'bolt-on' proceedings, for example as a witness, whether or not an ASBO is made.

see pp. 92–93 on when section 49 anonymity ceases

 Ch. 15, pp. 186–187 explains how reporters can challenge anonymity being given in ASBO cases.

The default position in law

This complex law on ASBOs can be understood as follows: Parliament has, by amending the Crime and Disorder Act 1998 by section 86 of the Anti-Social Behaviour Act 2003, made the 'default' position in law to be that, unless a section 39 order is made, the media can identify a juvenile on whom a 'bolt-on' ASBO is imposed. However, that juvenile may well still have anonymity under section 49 as regards any report of the earlier hearing in a youth court in which he/she was convicted (for example, of theft).

The media can argue that the section 49 anonymity should be lifted in respect of that earlier conviction hearing, 'in the public interest'.

Another option for a reporter who knows an application for an ASBO is to be made is to approach beforehand the person making the application to ask them to repeat in the ASBO hearing information given to the court during the criminal hearing, and to detail the conviction – meaning it can then be reported as part of the ASBO application, and the juvenile can be identified if the ASBO is imposed.

see Useful Websites, below, for the Society's guidance

It may also assist the media that the Justices' Clerks Society has issued guidance to its members that when a court draws up an ASBO it should include details of the anti-social behaviour which led to the order being made.

Alleged breach of an ASBO by a juvenile

A juvenile alleged to have breached an ASBO will face a criminal charge, because a breach is a criminal offence. The charge will normally be dealt with at a youth court. The usual anonymity under section 49 of the 1933 Act for juveniles appearing in a youth court does *not* apply to a juvenile accused of breaching an ASBO. So the media *can* identify such a juvenile when reporting such a case in a youth court, unless the youth court decides to give the juvenile defendant anonymity by using its discretion to make a section 39 order under the 1933 Act. If the youth court does make such a section 39 order, it must give its reasons. These requirements are stated in section 141 of the Serious Organised Crime and Police Act 2005.

Again, the media can choose to challenge the section 39 anonymity – see pp. 186–187.

! Remember

In 2011 the Government announced plans to replace ASBOs with new types of measures – Criminal Behaviour Orders and Crime Prevention Injunctions. See www.mcnaes.com for updates.

see www.mcnaes.com ch. 9 and Useful Websites for more details

Drinking banning orders

The Violent Crime Reduction Act 2006 created 'drinking banning orders' (DBOs). These can be used to ban a person from entering premises which sell alcohol or from other conduct which could lead to drink-related misbehaviour or crime. The law on whether media reports can identify juveniles in DBO proceedings is in essence the same as for ASBO proceedings.

➡ Recap of major points

- Most juveniles charged with a crime are dealt with by youth courts. The public cannot attend these courts, but reporters can.
- Section 49 of the Children and Young Persons Act 1933 bans media reports from identifying anyone aged under 18 involved in youth court cases, whether as defendant, witness or crime victim.
- This section 49 anonymity can be lifted, in the case of a convicted juvenile, to allow the media to identify him/her in the public interest – for example after persistent offending.
- There is no automatic anonymity for juveniles involved in adult court proceedings. But an adult court can make an order under section 39 of the 1933 Act to ban the media from identifying a juvenile.
- If the law or ethics require that an individual has anonymity in reports, media organisations should be alert to the danger of jigsaw identification.
- Anti-social behaviour orders (ASBOs) can be imposed by magistrates sitting in civil proceedings (an adult court) or by a youth court. The default position in law is that a juvenile made subject to an ASBO, or accused of breaching one, can be identified, unless a section 39 order is made.

((•)) Useful Websites

www.direct.gov.uk/en/YoungPeople/CrimeAndJustice/index.htm
Government guidance on the youth justice system

www.jc-society.com/File/ASBO_updated_GPG_May_2006.pdf/
Justices' Clerks' Society Good Practice Guide on ASBOs

www.cps.gov.uk/legal/d_to_g/drinking_banning_orders/
Crown Prosecution Service guidance on DBOs

10

Sexual offences

Chapter summary

The law gives victims of sexual offences, including rape, lifetime anonymity in media reports of these crimes and of any prosecutions which follow. In recent years several media organisations have been fined for inadvertently publishing detail which breached this anonymity, causing considerable distress to those identified. As this chapter explains, the anonymity is removed in some circumstances, allowing the media to identify the individual. Even when the law lets the media identify the person, a journalist should consider if this would be ethical.

The scope of automatic anonymity for complainants of sexual offences

Section 1 of the Sexual Offences (Amendment) Act 1992 (the 1992 Act) says that after an allegation of a sex offence is made, it is illegal to include in any publication:

- any matter which is likely to lead members of the public to identify, during his/her lifetime, the person who is the victim/alleged victim of that offence.

It says the ban includes in particular:

- his/her name;
- his/her address;
- the identity of any school or other educational establishment attended by him/her;
- the identity of his/her place of work;
- any still or moving picture of him/her.

The anonymity is automatic, and the effect of section 1 is that it applies from the time an allegation is made, by the alleged victim or anyone else. It remains in place regardless of whether the allegation is later withdrawn, or whether the police are told, whether an alleged offender is prosecuted, and whether anyone is convicted.

Section 6 of the 1992 Act defines publication as any speech, writing, relevant programme, or other communication in whatever form addressed to the public at large or to any section of the public, and a 'picture' as 'a likeness however produced'.

So, for example, the anonymity applies in respect of a news website report that a rape may have or has occurred – for example, 'Police in Southampton are investigating a rape' – and to any report of the trial of the alleged rapist (who can be named).

The anonymity also applies to anyone who is the target of an attempt or conspiracy to commit a sex offence.

The anonymity applies in the cases of babies, or adults with a mental incapacity – anyone unable to complain for themselves – as soon as anyone makes the allegation on their behalf; for example, when a parent alerts police, or tells a journalist.

Anonymity applies in all contexts

Parliament decided in 1976 that the violation of rape and the potential for victims to suffer embarrassment, and further trauma when testifying in court, justified giving them anonymity. The anonymity has since been extended to victims and alleged victims of other sexual offences. It applies to crime stories and reports of criminal trials, courts martial and civil cases, so that if a woman who alleges she was raped sues the alleged rapist in a civil court, she must remain anonymous, irrespective of whether she wins damages.

ch. 17 explains employment tribunals

Similarly, anyone who claims at an employment tribunal he/she was the victim of a sexual offence should have anonymity in reports of the case.

The anonymity applies in contexts other than reporting of crimes or court cases. If a journalist is interviewing someone for a biographical feature, and that person says that as a child he/she was sexually molested, it applies – unless the individual gives valid, written consent to be identified.

see pp. 108–109 on consent

Care needed with detail

Section 1 prohibits publication of matter 'likely to lead' to identification. A report of a sexual offence which refers to the alleged victim's school or workplace and gives their age could prompt speculation likely to lead to identification. Naming a large university and saying the victim is a student there is unlikely to identify him/her. But including further detail could do so, for example by saying the victim is a 25-year-old music student. In 1983 the then Solicitor General said that a report of a rape case could be illegal if the detail included was sufficient to identify the victim in the minds of some people even though not in the minds of the community generally.

Jigsaw identification

for a definition of jigsaw identification, see ch. 9, p. 96

Jigsaw identification could occur if in reports of a rape trial a town's newspaper describes the alleged victim only as 'a mother of three' who lives and works locally, a TV station describes her only as 'a nurse', and a radio station describes her only as 'a woman in her thirties' who works at night. A member of the public could then know she is a local nurse in her thirties, who has three children and works locally at night, detail which could identify her to colleagues and acquaintances.

see also ch. 9, pp. 97–98, on abuse cases

If a case involves sexual abuse of a child by an adult in the same family (or household), media organisations covering it should agree whether their reports (a) name the adult defendant, but omit any detail of any relationship to the child, or (b) do not identify the adult defendant, and report that the alleged abuse was familial. Journalists should also pay heed to the Editors' Code of Practice or the Ofcom Broadcasting Code which, as explained below, forbid the identification of children in sex cases, even on the very rare occasions when law permits this.

Invalid orders purporting to give an adult defendant anonymity

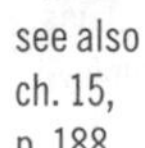

see also ch. 15, p. 188

The media may decide, when covering a court case involving alleged sexual abuse within a family, that the only way to preserve anonymity for the alleged victim(s) is not to publish anything identifying the adult defendant. But occasionally magistrates courts and Crown court judges have sought to make that choice for the media by passing an order, purportedly under the Sexual Offences (Amendment) Act 1992, stating that the adult defendant should not be identified. The reason usually given is the order is needed to protect the anonymity of the alleged victim(s), but the Act gives no power to courts to impose such an order.

Sexual offences for which alleged victims have anonymity

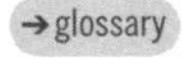

→glossary

The 1992 Act and the Sexual Offences Act 2003 apply the anonymity for victims and alleged victims to almost all offences with a sexual element. The most serious are **indictable-only**, with a maximum sentence of life imprisonment. These include:

- *rape* – penetration of vagina, anus or mouth without consent, by penis. If the victim is aged under 13, any such conduct is defined as rape, even if the victim says there was no compulsion, because the victim is so young. Males and females can be rape victims but only males can be rapists; females can be guilty of inciting or aiding rape;

- *assault by penetration* – of vagina or anus, without consent and otherwise than by penis – for example, by finger or object;
- *causing or inciting a child under 13 or a person who has 'a mental disorder impeding choice' to engage in sexual activity* in which the activity caused or incited involves penetration by penis or otherwise;
- *an attempt, conspiracy or incitement* to commit any of the above offences;
- *aiding, abetting, counselling or procuring* the commission of any of them.

Some sexual crimes are **either-way** charges. For some, an offender can be sentenced to a jail term of up to 14 years. Either-way charges include: →glossary

- *sexual assault* – intentional sexual touching, without consent;
- *administering a substance* – for example, spiking someone's drink with a drug – to enable the perpetrator to engage him/her in sexual activity;
- *trespass with intent to commit a sexual offence*;
- *sexual intercourse with a girl* who has reached the age of 13 but *who is under 16* – this offending is not classed as rape if there is no compulsion, but could be very serious and exploitative if the perpetrator is much older;
- *abuse of a position of trust through sexual activity* with someone aged under 18 – so, for example, if a male teacher has consensual sex with a 17-year-old girl, this may not be a crime because she is over 16 (the age of sexual consent), unless she was a pupil at the school where he works, in which case the sexual relationship is criminal abuse of his position of trust as a teacher;
- *sexual activity by a care worker*, for example in a hospital, if it involved such activity with a person in his/her care who has a mental disorder, and not involving penetration (which would be indictable-only);
- *engaging in sexual activity in the presence of a child*, or causing a child to watch a sexual act, for the perpetrator's sexual gratification;
- *arranging or facilitating commission of a sex offence against a child*, anywhere in the world;
- *meeting or intending to meet a child following sexual grooming*;
- *sexual activity by an adult with a child family member* (NB: it is incorrect to describe such an offence as incest, because incest is a consensual relationship);
- *abducting a woman* with the intention that she shall marry or have unlawful sexual intercourse;
- *indecent conduct towards a child*;
- *taking an indecent photograph of a child*;

- *causing or inciting child prostitution*;
- *procuring a woman by threats or false pretences*;
- *trafficking a person into or within the UK for sexual exploitation*, for example, prostitution; causing or inciting an adult to be a prostitute, or controlling such a prostitute, for gain. Some journalists may not realise that the 2003 Act extended anonymity to cover adults who are or have allegedly been, for example, 'controlled' prostitutes or have been trafficked to be prostitutes;
- *exposure* (colloquially called 'flashing') of genitals with the intent to cause alarm or distress;
- *voyeurism* – observing for sexual gratification someone else or people doing something private (for example, taking a shower, or having sex), knowing they did not consent to being observed.

Buggery is no longer illegal between consenting adults, but is an offence if perpetrated on someone aged under 16 – a victim who should therefore have anonymity.

A sexual offence which allegedly occurred before May 1, 2004 will be charged according to older definitions, with the anonymity applying. One such older offence is 'indecent assault'.

The anonymity does not apply to two adult relatives charged with consensual, illegal sexual activity with each other – which would have been charged as 'incest' under the old law – or to adults accused of sexual activity in a public lavatory. But if only one of them is charged, the other retains anonymity.

Liability for breach of the anonymity provision

Section 5 of the 1992 Act says those who can be prosecuted if a publication/broadcast breaches the anonymity are the newspaper or periodical's proprietor, editor and publisher, or any 'body corporate' (for example, a company) providing the programme service and any person whose functions in relation to the programme correspond to those of an editor of a newspaper, or as regards any other form of publication, any person publishing it.

It is a defence for the person accused to show that he/she was not aware, and neither suspected nor had reason to suspect that the material published would be likely to identify the victim/alleged victim of a sexual offence. The maximum fine is £5,000.

Case study

In 2006 the *Daily Telegraph* was fined £2,000, and ordered to pay £5,000 compensation and the *Daily Express* was fined £2,700 and ordered to pay £10,000 compensation after both newspapers published photographs of a servicewoman. She was a complainant at a court martial at which a serviceman was cleared of a serious sexual assault. The photos pictured her from behind, so her face was not shown. After being prosecuted, the newspapers admitted the photos identified her, but said at the time they were published it had been genuinely believed her anonymity was preserved. The *Daily Mail*, which also used a similar photo of the woman but changed the colour of her hair, was not prosecuted (*Media Lawyer*, February 23, 2006).

See www.mcnaes.com ch. 10 for more case studies of anonymity being breached.

When does the anonymity cease to apply?

Anonymity ceases to apply in the following circumstances.

After death

The anonymity does not apply to dead people, so will not apply to someone raped and murdered.

By court order, at the request of a defendant

A court due to try someone for a sexual offence can, on the application of a defendant or a co-defendant, remove an alleged victim's anonymity if it is satisfied that:

- it should be lifted to induce people likely to be needed as witnesses to come forward; and that
- otherwise the conduct of the applicant's defence at the trial is likely to be substantially prejudiced.

A defendant may argue that he needs witnesses to come forward to support an **alibi**. →glossary

Allowing the media to identify the alleged victim when reporting the alibi defence could jog the memories of members of the public about where and when he/she was seen, and who, if anyone, was with him/her at the time of the alleged offence.

Courts are rarely asked to lift anonymity on this ground, specified in section 3 of the 1992 Act. If the alleged offence is indictable-only – for example, rape – a Crown court has power to waive the anonymity. A magistrates court does not because it cannot try the case.

By court order, to lift 'a substantial and unreasonable' restriction on reporting

The court trying a sexual offence can lift an alleged victim's anonymity if it is satisfied that:

- the anonymity would impose a substantial and unreasonable restriction on media reporting of the trial; and that
- it is in the public interest to remove or relax it.

Again, if the alleged offence is indictable-only, only a Crown court has power to waive the anonymity. Courts are rarely asked to lift anonymity on the above ground, which is also specified in section 3.

Case study

Police were hunting a known criminal, Arthur Hutchinson, after three members of the same family were murdered in Sheffield after a wedding party at their home. To help trace Hutchinson, police publicly named him as the suspect, and he was captured. The media had also named the murder victims. Some time after being charged with the murders, Hutchinson was also charged with raping a teenage girl from the same family, in the same terrible attack. The media had not previously been told of the rape allegation. At Hutchinson's trial on the murder and rape charges, lawyers acting for newspapers argued that it would be impossible for them to report it at all if they could not identify the family involved and name the girl as the alleged rape victim. It was pointed out that publishing Hutchinson's name or that he was charged with three murders would in itself be enough for the Sheffield public to remember who the victim's family was, and that evidence of the rape and murders was inextricably linked. The judge agreed that the media could identify the girl, and thus the family, because anonymity would otherwise impose a substantial and unreasonable restriction on reporting of the trial, and it was in the public interest for the trial to be fully reported (*R v Arthur Hutchinson* (1985) 129 SJ 700; (1985) 82 Cr App R 51). Hutchinson was convicted.

If the victim/alleged victim gives written consent

The media can identify someone as being the victim/alleged victim of a sexual offence if he/she agrees to this. But section 5 of the 1992 Act specifies that to be valid:

- the consent must be in writing;
- the person waiving his/her anonymity must be aged 16 or over; and
- the consent will not be valid if it is proved that anyone 'interfered unreasonably with the peace and comfort' of the individual, with the intention of obtaining it.

So, the law guards a victim against being pressured into giving consent, and makes clear that any child under 16 is regarded as too immature to consent.

A court's permission is not needed for this consent to be given. Instances occur fairly regularly of written consent being given, particularly after a perpetrator is jailed. For example, a woman who has suffered rape may feel that by allowing the media to identify her she is sending a powerful signal to other rape victims that they can find the courage to seek justice, and that there is no stigma in being a victim.

If someone is prosecuted for making a false allegation

Anonymity for anyone alleged to be the victim of a sexual offence normally continues to apply even if no one is prosecuted or convicted of an offence, or if the allegation is withdrawn. But people alleged to have falsely claimed to have been victims of sexual offences have been charged with wasting police time, or perjury, or perverting the course of justice.

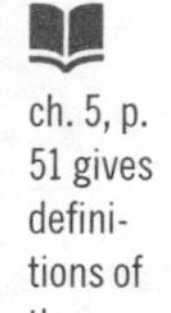

ch. 5, p. 51 gives definitions of these offences

A person appearing in court on such a charge in relation to a false allegation of a sexual offence can be identified in reports of those proceedings as someone who was previously alleged to be the victim of a sexual offence. Section 1(4) of the 1992 Act says an alleged victim of a sexual offence can be identified in articles which consist 'only of a report of criminal proceedings other than' proceedings for the sexual offence.

Sexual offences prevention orders

The Sexual Offences Act 2003 gives courts the power to make, in civil law, a sexual offences prevention order (SOPO), which restricts the behaviour of a sexual offender to protect the public from the risk of 'serious sexual harm'. An order can ban an offender from loitering near schools or inviting children back to his/her house, or making unsolicited approaches to women. The court can make a SOPO when sentencing for a sexual offence. Police may also apply to magistrates for an order at a later stage if an offender's behaviour causes concern – for example, after he has been released from jail. Breaching a SOPO is a crime.

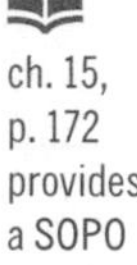

ch. 15, p. 172 provides a SOPO case study

Ethical considerations

The Editors' Code of Practice, policed by the Press Complaints Commission (PCC) makes clear that, even if the law says a victim/alleged victim of a sex offence may be identified, an ethical decision should be made on whether this should be done.

- Clause 11 (Victims of sexual assault) says: 'The press must not identify victims of sexual assault or publish material likely to contribute to such identification unless there is adequate justification and they are legally free to do so'.

The term 'sexual assault' here includes all sexual attacks including rape.

- Clause 7 (Children in sex cases) says: 'The press must not, even if legally free to do so, identify children under 16 who are victims or witnesses in cases involving sex offences'.

It adds that in any press report of a case involving a sexual offence against a child:

- the child must not be identified;
- the adult may be identified;
- the word 'incest' must not be used where a child victim might be identified;
- care must be taken that nothing in the report implies the relationship between the accused and the child.

Clause 7 is subject to the code's public interest exceptions, but clause 11 is not, though the term 'adequate justification' arguably embraces the idea of the public interest. The code says there would have to be 'exceptional public interest' to override the normally paramount interests of a child under 16.

Ch. 2 explains the code and the PCC's role. Appendix 2, pp. 429–433 shows the code in full.

Case study

In 2011 the PCC upheld a complaint against the *Staffordshire Newsletter* because a report about a man being jailed for sexual activity with a child contained detail with potential to enable members of the public to identify the victim. The victim's grandfather complained that the report breached clauses 7 and 11 of the Editors' Code of Practice. The report named the offender, and included the child's gender, the child's age when the abuse started and the period of time for which it continued. The grandfather said the victim's identity was now common knowledge in the local community and at the child's school. The PCC said that the newspaper was fully entitled to identify the convicted man. But it added that while each of the details reported might have seemed relatively insignificant, they had the potential to imply the connection between the accused and his victim. It took into account that the report had been supplied by an outside agency, and so the paper did not know all the case details. But, overall, the PCC 'did not agree that the newspaper had taken sufficient care to avoid this implication'. The result has been 'a serious, albeit inadvertent, error' (*A Man v Staffordshire Newsletter*, adjudication published May 3, 2011).

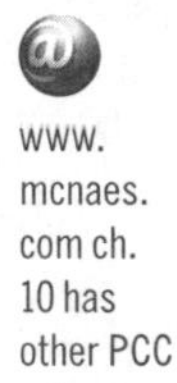
www. mcnaes. com ch. 10 has other PCC rulings

In the first seven months of 2011 there were five PCC adjudications against publications which unintentionally breached the anonymity of sexual offence victims.

The PCC guidance – see Useful Websites, below – says that 'editors should err on the side of caution' on what detail is published.

Rule 1.8 of the Ofcom Broadcasting Code says broadcasters should 'be particularly careful not to provide clues' which may lead to the identification of children when by law they should have anonymity 'as a victim, witness, defendant or other perpetrator in the case of sexual offences featured in criminal, civil or family court proceedings'. This rule also warns against jigsaw identification and that inadvertent use of the term 'incest' may identify such a child.

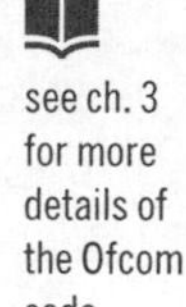

see ch. 3 for more details of the Ofcom code

Relatives of alleged and convicted sex offenders

In guidance on reporting cases involving paedophiles, the PCC has drawn attention to the rights of relatives and friends of people who have been accused of sex crimes: 'Not only do they also have a right to respect for their private lives under clause 3, but the code also makes clear [under clause 9] that the "press must avoid identifying [them] without their consent" – or unless there is a public interest in doing so.'

Recap of major points

- It is illegal for the media to identify the victims or alleged victims of sexual offences.
- The offences involved include rape, assault by penetration, sexual assault, indecent assault, sexual activity with children.
- The law also gives anonymity to the victims and alleged victims of voyeurs and 'flashing', and to people allegedly or actually trafficked to be prostitutes.
- The anonymity can be removed by a court if a defendant requests this, and the court is satisfied that the identity of an alleged victim should be published to induce witnesses to come forward, and that otherwise the defence is likely to be substantially prejudiced.
- There is a danger of 'jigsaw identification', particularly when several media organisations are covering a case of alleged sex abuse within a family.
- At a trial of a sexual offence, the court can lift the anonymity of the alleged victim to remove a substantial and unreasonable restriction on the reporting of the trial, if it is satisfied it is in the public interest to do this.
- A victim/alleged victim can waive the anonymity, by giving a media organisation written consent to identify him/her, if aged 16 or over.

((•)) Useful Websites

www.cps.gov.uk/legal/s_to_u/sexual_offences_rape/index.html/
Crown Prosecution Service guidance on prosecution of rape offences – see its Legal Guidance for information on other offences

www.pcc.org.uk/news/index.html?article=NzM0Nw==/
PCC guidance on reporting court cases involving sexual offences

www.pcc.org.uk/advice/editorials-detail.html?article=OTQ=/
PCC guidance to editors on the reporting of paedophile cases

www.editorscode.org.uk/
Editors' Codebook – gives advice on Editors' Code

http://stakeholders.ofcom.org.uk/broadcasting/broadcast-codes/broadcast-code/
The Ofcom Broadcasting Code

11

Court reporting – other restrictions

Chapter summary

Earlier chapters show that reporting on crime and court cases is not a job for an untrained amateur. Reporting restrictions can dictate what is published. Breaching them is an offence. This chapter details more restrictions, which include permanent bans on using cameras and audio-recording devices in any court. Revealing how individual jurors voted in verdicts is also illegal. Reporting what a court has heard in private can be punished as contempt of court. The chapter also outlines how courts can ban the media from identifying some adult witnesses, and blackmail victims. Courts can also order the media to postpone reporting a case. Chapter 15 shows how to challenge a reporting restriction as invalid or unnecessary. Chapter 21 deals with defamation dangers in court reporting.

Ban on photography, filming and sketching in courts and precincts

More than eighty years ago, Parliament banned the photographing of court proceedings. Case law means the ban includes filming in courts.

A primary reason for the ban is that photography and filming, and any publication of images gained, would put added strain on witnesses and defendants.

Section 41 of the Criminal Justice Act 1925 makes it illegal to:

- take or try to take any photograph or film; or
- make or try to make – with a view to publishing it – any portrait or sketch of:
  - any person in any court, its building, or within its precincts,
  - any person 'entering or leaving' a court building or its precincts;
- publish such a photo, or film, portrait or sketch.

Section 41 applies to criminal and civil courts, and inquests. 'Any person' includes judges, magistrates, coroners, jurors, witnesses, defendants and any other party.

The Act does not define 'precincts', which has caused practical difficulties.

The term includes rooms, foyers or corridors within the courthouse property. It is unclear to what extent it includes areas immediately outside, not part of the property. If unsure, check with the particular court.

Journalists standing on the public pavement frequently photograph and film judges, lawyers, defendants and witnesses entering or leaving court buildings, for example the Royal Courts of Justice in London. Where this practice has become customary, it is rare for a court to object, though it would seem to breach the section 41 ban on showing people 'entering or leaving'. Jurors should not normally be photographed, as this might be regarded as a contempt in common law, as explained below.

Breaches of section 41 can be punished with fines up to £1,000.

Artists' sketches of court cases

The media publish artists' sketches of scenes in court, including the face of the defendant, to illustrate newsworthy cases. To comply with section 41, these artists visit the court's public gallery or press bench, memorise the scene and characters, but do the actual sketching elsewhere. A Government consultation paper made no objection to sketching in a courthouse press room.

Jury visits to the scene of crime or death

If a judge or coroner decides that a jury should visit an outside location such as a crime or accident scene to help jurors understand evidence, the visit should not be filmed, photographed or sketched without the court's permission. The court may allow this, as long as no juror can be identified through what is published.

Photography and filming could be contempt of court

see also ch. 18, p. 214 on common law contempt

Despite the existence of the 1925 Act, a court may deem photography or filming in court or in its precincts, or even elsewhere, for example on the pavement outside, to be a contempt of court in common law.

A photographer's conduct could be regarded as contempt if it amounted to 'molestation' – interference with the administration of justice. Case law suggests that running after a defendant for a short while in order to photograph him/her would not usually be seen as molestation. But stalking a defendant or witness further, or jostling them, could be contempt as it might deter them or other witnesses from giving evidence.

Case study

In 2009 Mr Justice Keith warned photographers to stop taking pictures of two young brothers as they arrived at Sheffield Crown court in cars under blankets, saying he would take action if he thought a contempt of court had taken place. The brothers had admitted inflicting, when aged 10 and 11, horrific violence on two boys in a village near Doncaster (*Press Gazette*, September 7, 2009).

The fine or prison sentence to punish such a contempt is at the judge's discretion. Members of the public have been swiftly punished, particularly for attempts to intimidate a witness.

Case study

In 2004 a man was jailed for nine months for using a mobile phone to take pictures in Birmingham Crown court. The judge believed there was a 'sinister motive' (*Media Lawyer*, October 8, 2004).

In 2005 Parliament amended section 41 to ensure that the Supreme Court – which has replaced the House of Lords – can permit broadcasting of its proceedings which, being concerned with points of law, are argued from documentary evidence, and are rarely likely to involve witnesses in person. In September 2011 Justice Secretary Ken Clarke announced that the law would be changed to allow broadcasters to screen footage of judges giving judgment in the Court of Appeal, and the Government would begin consultations on how such a scheme could also cover judges' 'summary remarks' in Crown court trials. But he stressed that victims, witnesses, offenders and jurors will not be filmed.

see mcnaes.com for updates

Ban on audio recording in court

It is illegal to use any audio-recording device in a court, including a tape-recorder, or a mobile phone's recording facility, without the court's permission. One aim of this ban is to prevent witness testimony being broadcast, which for some witnesses would increase the strain of giving evidence. It is also to stop secret recordings being made in the public gallery by, for example, a defendant's criminal associates, who could use it to intimidate or humiliate a prosecution witness or to help dishonest witnesses collude in false corroboration.

For example, one witness could listen to a recording of the other's evidence, and repeat the same information in his/her own evidence but claim to have recalled it independently.

The ban is contained in section 9 of the Contempt of Court Act 1981, which makes it a contempt to:

- use a tape-recorder or any other audio-recording device in court, or to take one into a court for use, unless the court gives permission;
- broadcast any audio recording of court proceedings, or play any of it in the hearing of any section of the public;
- make any unauthorised use of a recording, if recording has been allowed.

A court can allow audio-recordings for note-taking purposes, including by a journalist. Part I.2 of the Consolidated Criminal Practice Direction says that when considering a request for permission to record, a criminal court should consider 'the existence of any reasonable need on the part of the applicant . . . whether a litigant or a person connected with the press or broadcasting' and whether use of a recorder 'would disturb the proceedings or distract or worry witnesses or other participants'.

ch. 14, p. 156 explains what the Direction is

The Lord Chief Justice, Lord Judge, has suggested that the same factors can be considered if a request is made to audio record in civil cases – see his interim guidance on text-based communications, referred to below.

The Criminal Procedure Rules, issued in a new version in 2011 (SI 2011/1709), which cover magistrates and Crown courts and the Criminal Division of the Court of Appeal, say in Rule 16.9 that a court can permit use of a device for recording sound and can give permission 'to publish a sound recording made during a hearing' – the first time such rules have expressly stated this. However, a person wanting such permission must 'apply as soon as reasonably practical', explaining why permission should be given, and notify each party in the case, and anyone else the court specifies, of the application. The rule specifically allows courts to grant permission to journalists to use such devices, but the courts can impose limitations on their use – for example, it could ban their use during witness testimony.

see Useful Websites below for the Rules

The penalty for a contempt arising from breach of section 9 of the Contempt of Court Act 1981 is a jail term of up to two years and/or an unlimited fine.

Tweeting, emailing and texting 'live' reports from court

Reporters should not make or receive calls on mobile phones during court hearings – these acts could be punished as a contempt because they are disrespectful and potentially disruptive and damaging to the administration of justice. A judge could punish a reporter whose mobile phone ringtone interrupts a witness's testimony, by fining or jailing the journalist, particularly if the witness is already finding it difficult to testify. The normal rule is that mobile phones must be turned off in court. The rule derives from the **inherent jurisdiction** courts have to govern their own proceedings.

→glossary

However, in December 2011 the Lord Chief Justice issued guidance that journalists in courts could use 'text-based communications' to provide 'live' running coverage of a case, including by use of the Twitter micro-blogging system. His guidance, in summary, is:

- Journalists can give live coverage of a case by tweeting or filing text from a court during a hearing, and mobile phones, laptops or similar equipment can be used for this purpose. Use of such devices must be silent and not disruptive.

The guidance applies to reporting of proceedings, not any other type of message. His December guidance followed a consultation about live, text-based communications from courts, so as to draw up a permanent rule on the issue. In October 2011 the new version of the Criminal Procedure Rules said in Rule 16.9 that a court could permit use of a device for 'communicating by electronic means'. Guidance issued with this new rule made clear it had been drawn up to cover journalists' use of laptops and mobile phones to transmit text (including tweets) when reporting from courtrooms. But the rule requires application to be made in each case for use of such devices. However, as this book's Late News section explains, the Lord Chief Justice's December guidance said journalists do not need to apply for permission.

The Supreme Court has a general rule allowing the use of live, text-based communications, though not in some types of case.

See Useful Websites below for the Lord Chief Justice's guidance and the Rules.

Case studies

In 2011 a district judge allowed journalists to tweet from an extradition hearing at the City of Westminster magistrates court. Also, the Court of Appeal agreed tweeting was generally to be approved for its cases, but refused to allow Twitter to be used in a case in which a claimant sought an injunction on privacy grounds, because of the risk that private information might be published. Later that year West Midlands police press officers tweeted summaries of every case heard during a morning in Birmingham magistrates court, with its permission, and a judge at Bristol Crown court allowed reporters to tweet from a bail hearing in a murder case. However, a judge at Newcastle Crown court refused to allow journalists to tweet from a murder trial (*Media Lawyer*, January 18, 20 and 26, February 3 and April 19, 2011).

Confidentiality of jury deliberations

It is a contempt of court to breach the confidentiality of a jury's deliberations, whether the jury is in a Crown court, an inquest or a civil case. Juries arrive at their verdicts in secret discussions, in rooms guarded against intrusion. The secrecy helps jurors to be frank in discussions, without fear of a public backlash for an unpopular decision or retribution from a vengeful defendant they convict.

For the role of juries in criminal trials, civil cases and inquests see ch. 8, ch. 12 and ch. 16.

Section 8 of the Contempt of Court Act 1981 says it is a contempt of the court to obtain, solicit or disclose any detail of:

- statements made;
- opinions expressed;
- arguments advanced; or
- votes cast

by members of a jury during its deliberations.

The prohibition applies even if what is published does not identify any individual juror or even a particular trial. The penalty for a contempt arising from breach of section 8 is a jail term of up to two years and/or an unlimited fine.

After a trial the media is safe to publish a juror's general impressions of the experience of jury service, provided the individual is willing to volunteer these, and is not asked about statements made, opinions expressed, arguments advanced or votes cast in the course of the deliberations, and does not refer to such matters in what is published. A juror could be interviewed, for example, on whether he/she felt in general that evidence was clearly presented. Journalistic investigations of alleged miscarriages of justice such as a controversial murder conviction sometimes prompt jurors from the trial to speak up months or years later. Some have contacted journalists to say that, in the light of new evidence which has emerged, they are no longer certain of the accused's guilt. The safest course is to seek legal advice before conducting or publishing such an interview.

Case study

In 2009 the High Court fined *The Times* £15,000 and ordered it to pay £27,426 costs for breaching section 8. The newspaper had published an article about the 10–2 majority verdict by a Crown court jury which convicted a childminder of a child's manslaughter. It quoted but did not name the jury foreman, who had approached the newspaper, as expressing doubt about the case's medical evidence. He also said that, early in its deliberations, the jury voted 10–2 in an initial indication of its consensus. He said the majority of jurors – because of what he called 'common sense' rather than 'logical thinking' – held to their initial view that the defendant was guilty. *The Times* denied contempt. But the High Court ruled that *The Times* had, by using these quotes, breached section 8 by disclosure of 'votes cast', 'opinions expressed' and 'statements made' during the jury's deliberations, even though jurors' identities were not disclosed, and the foreman's descriptions of the jury's deliberations were brief and possibly inaccurate (*Attorney General v Michael Alexander Seckerson and Times Newspapers Ltd [2009] EWHC 1023* (Admin)). Mike Seckerson, the jury foreman, was fined £5,000 for his part in the breach (*Media Lawyer*, December 20, 2009).

Contempt risk in identifying or approaching jurors

There is a risk of a media organisation being accused of common law contempt if it identifies a juror against his/her wishes, even after a trial. The disclosure could be held to interfere with the judicial process by putting the juror at risk of harm from anyone unhappy with a verdict. A reporter deemed to have harassed a juror for an interview might be held to be in contempt, because harassment could discourage people from serving as jurors.

See ch. 18 about common law contempt. See also ch. 37, p. 425 on the statutory ban on identifying jurors who have served in trials in Northern Ireland.

A juror discharged during a case for late attendance or being drunk may well be named in court, and could be punished by the judge. In the absence of any court order to the contrary, the media can safely identify the juror, if named, and say how the court dealt with him/her.

Section 11 orders – blackmail, secrets, personal safety

A court can ban the media from reporting a person's name, or other information, in coverage of a case.

Section 11 of the Contempt of Court Act 1981 says:

- A court can ban the publication or a name or other information in connection with the proceedings as long as it has first allowed that information to be withheld from the public.

Section 11 orders are not used routinely, but a typical use would be:

- To protect the identity of victims/alleged victims of blackmail. Someone who is the target of blackmail involving a threat to reveal an embarrassing secret will be less likely to report the threat to police, and then to be a witness, if it is likely that his/her identity will be given in open court, and reported by the media when the secret emerges in evidence. In blackmail trials, the alleged victim is usually referred to in open court simply by a letter of the alphabet, for example, Ms X. This also protects the administration of justice as a continuing process, because identifying any alleged victim of

ch. 5, p. 50, gives the definition of blackmail

blackmail publicly in court reporting makes it less likely that other victims of blackmail will report it to the police.

- To protect commercially sensitive information or secret processes – for example, a company sues another for damages over breach of confidence about valuable research data. The court may hear evidence about the data in private, to preserve its confidentiality – if it does not stay confidential, the case would be pointless. A section 11 order could be made to ban reports of the case publishing details of the data.

ch. 33 explains official secrets law

- To protect national security or state secrets – for example, in a prosecution under the Official Secrets Act 1911 someone is accused of betraying UK military secrets to a foreign power. The court may well go into private session to hear evidence about those secrets. A section 11 order could be used to ban publication of such material, should it leak out. It could also ban the media from identifying UK intelligence officers who are witnesses, as identification would end their usefulness as undercover agents and might put them at risk.

ch. 15 explains how to challenge such orders

- To protect a person from the risk of attack. A court might be persuaded that the name and address of a witness, or the address of a defendant – for example, a sex offender – should not be published, to prevent an attack on that person by criminals or vigilantes. But the media can oppose such orders on the ground that they are unnecessary.

Two-stage process

A section 11 order is the second step in a two-stage process. The court first has to rule that a name or other information should not be given in proceedings held in public. Only then can it impose a section 11 order. If the name or information then slips out by mistake in a public session – for example in what a witness or lawyer says – or if the media have discovered it by other means, it is illegal to publish it in any context which connects it to the case. A section 11 order remains in force indefinitely, unless a court revokes it.

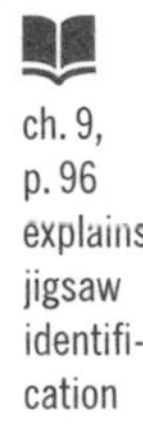

ch. 9, p. 96 explains jigsaw identification

When a section 11 order is in force, journalists need to guard against 'jigsaw identification'.

Breaching a section 11 is an offence of contempt of court punishable by a jail term of up to two years and/or an unlimited fine.

But section 11 only bans the reporting of the name or matter 'in connection with the proceedings'.

Ban on reporting a court's private hearing

Courts sit in private, with the public and media excluded, for some cases including when considering whether mentally ill people should be confined in hospitals, and hearings involving state secrets. The media is automatically banned from publishing what is said in some categories of case heard by a court **in private** – that is, **in chambers** or **in camera**. →glossary

Section 12 of the Administration of Justice Act 1960 makes it an offence of contempt of court to publish, without the court's permission, a report of proceedings it has heard in private if they:

- relate to the exercise of the inherent jurisdiction of the High Court with respect to children;
- fall under the Children Act 1989 or the Adoption and Children Act 2002 or which otherwise relate wholly or mainly to the maintenance or upbringing of a child;
- fall under the Mental Capacity Act 2005, or under any provision of the Mental Health Act 1983 authorising an application or reference to be made to the First-tier Tribunal, the Mental Health Review Tribunal for Wales or to a county court;
- involve national security;
- involve a secret process, discovery or invention;
- are those, of any kind, where the court expressly bans the publication of all or specified information relating to the private hearing.

Ch. 13 explains children cases in family courts, and ch. 17 explains mental health tribunals.

A reporter may be told what has happened in a private hearing by one of the parties. But in these particular types of case section 12 automatically prohibits the publication of anything heard by a court in private, to protect the welfare, including the privacy, of children and the mentally ill or incapacitated; and state or commercial secrets.

A breach of section 12, if proved as contempt, is punishable by a jail term of up to two years, and/or an unlimited fine.

Any document 'prepared for use' in a court's private hearing is deemed part of those proceedings. If a case falls into the section 12 categories, the court will regard publication by the media of information or quotations from such a document, such as a psychiatric report or a report on a couple's fitness as parents, as a contempt.

Some detail can be published about a private hearing

Some material about a private hearing in these types of case can be published. Section 12 makes clear that publishing the text, or a summary, of any order made in such a hearing is not contempt unless the court has specifically prohibited its publication.

In *Re B (A Child)* [2004] EWHC 411 (Fam), Mr Justice Munby stated that section 12 did not itself ban publishing a reference to 'the nature of the dispute' being heard in the private hearing. He added that what could be published without breaching section 12 included:

- the names, addresses or photographs of parties and witnesses involved in the private proceedings;
- the date, time or place of hearings in the case; and
- 'anything which has been seen or heard by a person conducting himself lawfully in the public corridor or other public precincts outside the court'.

But he added that a court could ban publication of even these details, or that automatic restrictions under other law could apply.

ch. 13 explains anonymity in family cases

If the court hearing in private does not fall into the section 12 categories, a media organisation may safely be able to publish an account of it, for example if guided by a person who was in it. But a media report of a case heard in private is not protected by any statutory privilege in relation to libel law, and is not protected by section 4 of the Contempt of Court Act 1981 if it creates a substantial risk of serious prejudice to an 'active' case.

Ch. 18 explains contempt law and ch. 21 explains privilege.

Ban on publishing material from court documents

Even if a case is heard in public, a journalist should exercise care before quoting from a document used in it if the material has not been read out in court.

Civil cases are conducted mainly by reference to documents as chapter 12 explains.

In a civil case, it is safe to quote from any document the journalist obtains with the court's permission, or from any case document he/she is able to inspect by right. If the civil case is heard in public, it will be safe to quote from any skeleton argument provided to a journalist by lawyers involved, unless the court forbids this. Any reporting restriction, for example protecting the identity of a child or alleged victim of a sexual offence, must be observed in what is reported from such documents.

ch. 14 explains inspection rights

In criminal cases, the media has no automatic right to inspect case documents.

Journalists should beware of the risk of contempt incurred by publishing material from a document which they have obtained from one side or the other in criminal or civil proceedings, without the court's permission, and which one party was compelled or had a duty to produce as part of the 'disclosure' process and which has not been read out in open court. 'Disclosure' is the pre-trial exchange of evidence and information. Contempt law applies because of the danger that parties who feared that material they provided to the other side might be published, even though it was not used in court, would refuse to cooperate fully with the disclosure process.

Again, publishing material not aired in open court is not protected by statutory privilege in relation to libel law, or by the Contempt of Court Act 1981 if the strict liability rule is breached.

Lifetime anonymity for adult witnesses

A criminal court can ban the media from revealing the identity of an adult witness, if there is concern that he/she is scared or distressed about testifying. This discretionary power is in section 46 of the Youth Justice and Criminal Evidence Act 1999 (the 1999 Act). Section 46 says that a court can order that an adult witness has lifetime anonymity in reports of the case if the court is satisfied that:

- the quality of the witness's evidence, or his/her level of cooperation in preparations for the case, is likely to be diminished by fear or distress in connection with being identified by members of the public as a witness in that case; and that
- granting anonymity is likely to improve the quality of the witness's evidence or the level of his/her cooperation.

A main purpose of this law is to provide better protection for witnesses who fear that the fact that they have given evidence, or are due to testify, will provoke hostility from criminal elements in their communities.

Section 46 says a party in the proceedings in a criminal court – including the defence, though it is usually the prosecution – can ask the court to make the anonymity order, called a 'reporting direction', to cover a witness aged 18 or over. The court may hear this request in camera.

The scope of a section 46 order

A section 46 order makes it illegal to include in any publication during the witness's lifetime any matter likely to lead members of the public to identify him/her as a witness in the proceedings.

It says information likely to identify such a witness, includes in particular:

- the witness's name and address;
- the identity of any educational establishment he/she attends;
- the identity of any place where he/she works; and
- any still or moving picture of him/her.

However, a section 46 order cannot be used to give a defendant anonymity.

Any detail which risks revealing the witness's identity should be left out. The witness may be the alleged victim of the offence(s) being tried. If so, the effect on reports will be major and similar to that of the lifetime anonymity automatically given to victims/alleged victims of sexual offences who, therefore, do not need section 46 anonymity. When a section 46 order is made, journalists should ensure they avoid jigsaw identification.

For more on jigsaw identification see ch. 9, p. 96. Ch. 10 explains anonymity for victims of sexual offences.

Factors a court must consider

When deciding whether to grant section 46 anonymity, the court must take into account the witness's view about anonymity; the nature and circumstances of the alleged offence(s) being tried; the witness's age, social and cultural background and ethnic origins; his/her domestic and employment circumstances, religious beliefs or political opinions; and any behaviour towards the witness on the part of the defendant, or the defendant's family or associates, or anyone else likely to be a defendant or witness in the proceedings.

The court must also consider:

- whether it would be in the interests of justice to make the anonymity order; and
- whether it would be in the public interest in avoiding imposing a substantial and unreasonable restriction on reporting the proceedings.

Breaches of section 46 orders

Publication of material which breaches the section 46 anonymity brings the same liability as breaching a sex offence victim's anonymity, with the same maximum fine.

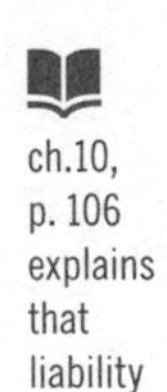
ch.10, p. 106 explains that liability

Anyone prosecuted for breach of section 46 has a defence if he/she can prove that:

- he/she was not aware, and neither suspected nor had reason to suspect, that the publication included the matter or report in question; or that
- the witness concerned gave written consent for the matter to be published.

This 'written consent' defence will fail if it is proved that a person 'interfered with the peace or comfort' of such a witness to get that consent.

see ch. 15, pp. 187–188 on challenging section 46 orders

The court which bestowed the section 46 anonymity, or a higher court, can make 'an excepting direction' to remove the anonymity entirely or relax it to some extent, if satisfied that this is necessary in the interests of justice, or that the restriction imposes a substantial and unreasonable restriction on the reporting of the proceedings, and that it is in the public interest to remove or relax the restriction.

Other anonymity orders

The High Court has power to ban publication of the identities of people concerned in its proceedings, and uses it to give anonymity to children involved in family law cases. The court also usually gives anonymity to mentally incapacitated adults when protecting their interests in civil cases. A media organisation which publishes information identifying such people, in breach of such an order, could be punished for contempt of court. The High Court's powers derive from its inherent jurisdiction and from Article 8 of the European Convention on Human Rights concerning privacy.

For further detail of use of such orders in family law, see ch. 13, p. 148. For their use in privacy cases, see ch. 26. For information about the Court of Protection, see ch. 13, p. 145.

The Civil Procedure Rules govern the conduct of civil cases in county courts and the High Court. Rule 39.2(4) states: 'The court may order that the identity of any party or witness must not be disclosed if it considers non-disclosure necessary in order to protect the interests of that party or witness'. But, as chapter 15 explains, case law is that anonymity orders should not be made merely to spare them embarassment.

Ch. 35, p. 415 covers anonymity for suspected terrorists subject to 'control orders'.

Indefinite anonymity for convicted defendants

In exceptional instances, the High Court has banned the media from publishing the new identities and whereabouts of people who became notorious after committing, or being associated with, horrific crimes. The aim was to help rehabilitate them after their release from prison, and protect them from public hostility and possible vengeance attacks.

Mary Bell The first such case concerned Mary Bell. In 1968, when she was 11, she was convicted of the manslaughter of two young boys, and was sentenced to detention for life. When released on licence in 1980, the Home Office gave her a new identity to help her rehabilitation.

Venables and Thompson In 2001 Dame Elizabeth Butler-Sloss granted indefinite anonymity to Jon Venables and Robert Thompson. In 1993, when they were 11, they were convicted of murdering two-year-old James Bulger in Merseyside.

Maxine Carr Similar anonymity was given to Maxine Carr, former girlfriend of school caretaker Ian Huntley, who in 2003 was convicted of murdering two schoolgirls in Soham. Carr was convicted of conspiring to pervert the course of justice, having given Huntley a false **alibi**. She was acquitted of knowing, when she gave it, that he had murdered the girls.

Kenneth Callaghan In 2009 Mr Justice Stephen in the High Court in Belfast banned all the media from publishing any photograph which would identify Kenneth Henry Callaghan, then 39, and any information identifying his address, place of work, or any location where he stays or which he frequents. He had become eligible for parole after serving 21 years for raping and murdering a woman. The judge also ordered that no photo should be published which identified any serving prisoner being assessed for release at a unit run by the Northern Ireland Office without giving the NIO 48 hours' notice of the intention to publish.

see www.mcnaes.com ch. 11 for more detail of these cases

Ban on publishing 'indecent' matter

Section 1 of the Judicial Proceedings (Regulation of Reports) Act 1926 prohibits publication in any court report of any 'indecent matter or indecent medical, surgical or physiological details . . . the publication of which is calculated to injure public morals'. It is unlikely that mainstream media organisations would be prosecuted today under this law.

Section 4(2) of the Contempt of Court Act 1981

A court has power, under section 4(2) of the Contempt of Court Act 1981, to order the postponement of publication of reports of a court case, or any part of a case, where this appears necessary to avoid a substantial risk of prejudice to the administration of justice in that case, or any other case which is pending or imminent.

This restriction is best understood in the context of contempt law, so is explained in ch. 18, see pp. 228–229. See also ch. 15, pp. 176–180 for grounds on which a section 4(2) order may be challenged.

Postponed reporting of 'special measures' and section 36 orders

Courts can make special arrangements to help a 'vulnerable' or 'intimidated' witness give evidence, and can also ban a defendant from personally cross-examining a witness. Thc law temporarily bans the media from reporting that a court made such an arrangement, and why, because in some cases a jury might be influenced in its verdict if it knew why such a measure was taken – for example, knowing a witness was allegedly intimidated by people suspected of being the defendant's associates might prejudice jurors against the defendant.

Special measures

Section 19 of the Youth Justice and Criminal Evidence Act 1999 allows courts to make a 'special measures direction' in a case involving a 'vulnerable' or 'intimidated' witness. Such measures can include:

- letting a witness give evidence behind a screen so he/she cannot see or be seen by the defendant;
- allowing a witness to give evidence by live video link in a video recording;
- excluding the public and all but one reporter while a witness testifies;
- having lawyers and the judge remove wigs and gowns to make the court less strange to a child witness.

ch. 14, p. 155 explains this exclusion power

The definition of 'vulnerable' can include (other than the defendant) any witness aged under 18, or one with a mental disorder or physical disability. The definition of an 'intimidated' witness can include an alleged victim of a sex offence, a witness in which the alleged crime is said to involve a gun or knife, and a witness the quality of whose evidence is, in the court's view, likely to be diminished because of fear or distress connected with testifying.

A special measures direction is not automatic, so a witness aged under 18 or the alleged victim of a sexual offence will not necessarily be thought to need a special measure.

Section 36 orders banning cross-examination by defendants

A defendant has the right to conduct his/her own defence in court – and cross-examine witnesses – rather than employ a lawyer. But after some notorious incidents in which defendants used this right to intimidate victims who testified against them, section 36 of the Youth Justice and Criminal Evidence Act 1999 introduced provisions which automatically bar defendants from personally cross-examining some categories of witnesses, including the alleged victim in a sexual offence case. Courts can arrange for a lawyer to conduct the cross-examination if the defendant fails to appoint one.

Section 36 also gives courts discretion, in some circumstances, to make an order in any type of criminal case stopping a defendant from cross-examining witnesses.

Restrictions on reporting special measures and section 36 orders

Section 47 of the 1999 Act contains automatic reporting restrictions which temporarily ban the media from publishing the fact that a section 19 (special measures) order or section 36 order has been made, varied or discharged; or anything from discussion or argument in court about such orders. The restrictions apply to proceedings in magistrates courts as well as to jury trials. Their purpose is to stop jurors (who would not be in court when an order was made or discussed) being prejudiced against the defendant or a witness by learning, before they reach all verdicts in the case, why the court considered making or made the order.

It will be safe to report, during a trial, anything the jury can see anyway – for example, that a witness is giving evidence by video, and anything the judge says to the jury to explain the effect of a section 19 or section 36 order – for example, why a lawyer steps in to act for a defendant who is otherwise representing himself.

But it would, for example, be illegal to publish the fact, beyond any explanation the judge gives to the jury, that most reporters had been ordered to leave the courtroom. These reporting restrictions cease to have effect when the relevant case, against all defendants involved, is determined by acquittal, conviction or otherwise, or is abandoned, or if the court lifts the restrictions during the trial itself.

Liability for breaching the section 47 reporting restrictions is the same as for breaching an order under section 46.

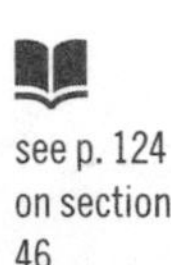
see p. 124 on section 46

It is a defence for a person charged with breaching section 47 to prove he/she was not aware and neither suspected nor had reason to suspect that such matter was included in what was published. An adult witness subject to a special measures direction under section 19 of the Act may also have been granted lifetime anonymity, in respect of media reports of the trial, under section 46.

! Remember

Decisions on special measures and cross-examination issues are likely to be taken in pre-trial hearings, or when a jury is kept out of the courtroom, so other statute or contempt law will probably restrict contemporaneous reporting anyway, see chapters 6, 7, 8 and 18. So the 1999 Act restrictions can be seen as legislative 'overkill'.

Postponing reports of 'derogatory' mitigation

A court can postpone a media report of a derogatory allegation made in a 'speech in mitigation', if it feels that someone's reputation may have been unfairly besmirched.

This restriction, in section 58 of the Criminal Procedure and Investigations Act 1996, is rarely used.

Ch. 6, p. 59 explains when a speech of mitigation is made. More details of this postponement power can be read in www.mcnaes.com ch 11.

Extradition hearings

Media coverage of hearings in the UK on whether a person should be extradited to another country are not affected by any automatic reporting restriction. These hearings usually take place in Westminster Magistrates' Court.

➡ Recap of major points

- It is illegal to take photographs of, film or sketch people in a court or its precincts.
- It is also illegal to make an audio recording of a court case without permission.
- Journalists can tweet, email or text from the courtroom to report cases, unless the court forbids this.
- It is illegal to seek to discover, or to publish, what a jury discussed in deliberating on a verdict, or how an individual juror voted in the verdict.
- It may also be ruled to be a contempt offence if a media organisation publishes material identifying a juror.
- It is contempt of court to publish material heard by a court in private, in certain categories of case.
- An order made under section 11 of the Contempt of Court Act 1981 prohibits publication of a name or information withheld from the public proceedings of the court – for example, the name of a blackmail victim.
- Section 46 of the Youth Justice and Criminal Evidence Act 1999 allows a court to give an adult witness in a criminal case lifelong anonymity in media reports of it.
- In exceptional cases, the High Court has given convicted offenders indefinite anonymity, so the media cannot reveal their whereabouts after they are released.

((•)) Useful Websites

www.judiciary.gov.uk/publications-and-reports/guidance/2011crown-court-reporting-restrictions-guidance-2009/

Guidance on reporting restrictions, published by the Judicial College (formerly the Judicial Studies Board), the Newspaper Society, the Society of Editors and Times Newspaper Ltd

www.justice.gov.uk/guidance/courts-and-tribunals/courts/procedure-rules/criminal/rulesmenu.htm

Criminal Procedure Rules 2011

www.judiciary.gov.uk/Resources/JCO/Documents/Consultations/cp-live-text-based-forms-of-comms.pdf/

Consultation on use of live-text communications in court reporting

www.judiciary.gov.uk/Resources/JCO/Documents/Guidance/ltbc-guidance-dec-2011.pdf

Lord Chief Justice's guidance on use of live-text communications

www.supremecourt.gov.uk/docs/pr_1102.pdf/

Supreme Court guidance on use of live-text communications

12

Civil courts

Chapter summary

Civil law cases are a rich source of news. Civil courts resolve private disputes and redress private wrongs. Some cases involve companies or individuals suing for damages; some are brought against the state and public bodies, for example when a hospital trust is sued for medical negligence by a patient. Most civil litigation is dealt with in county courts. The High Court deals with complex or high-value claims. Juries are not used in most civil cases. Bankruptcies and company liquidations are civil law matters. Magistrates have some civil law functions.

Types of civil litigation

Most civil litigation is concerned with:

- breaches of contract, including recovery of debt;
- torts – that is, civil wrongs for which monetary damages can be awarded. Torts include negligence, trespass and defamation;
- breach of statutory duty;
- proceedings by financial institutions against mortgagors;
- possession proceedings by landlords against tenants, usually for failure to pay rent;
- 'Chancery' matters;
- insolvency, including bankruptcy and the winding up of companies;
- family law cases, including divorce; disputes between estranged parents over residence arrangements for and contact with their children;

- applications by local authorities to take into care children considered at significant risk of violence or neglect.

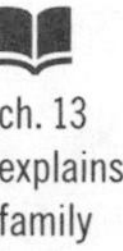
ch. 13 explains family law

County courts

County courts deal with most civil cases. They cover areas no longer based on counties. There are more than 200 throughout England and Wales.

The High Court

The High Court deals with the most complex or serious civil cases, and those of highest value. The administrative centre of the High Court is at the Royal Courts of Justice in London. Outside London it is divided administratively into 132 'district registries'. These have offices and courtrooms, mostly in cities, and share buildings with the larger county court centres.

The High Court is made up of three divisions:

- The *Queen's Bench Division* (QBD), within which there are also specialist courts: the Admiralty Court, the Commercial Court and the Technology and Construction Court.
- The *Chancery Division*, which deals primarily with company work, trusts, estates, insolvency and intellectual property. County courts also have limited jurisdiction in this area.
- The *Family Division*

High Court judges normally sit singly to try cases. The High Court is also an appeal court in civil law.

In appeals and for some other functions two or three judges hear the case, and it is then known as the Divisional Court. A QBD court carrying out certain functions is referred to as the Administrative Court. It handles judicial review of the administrative actions of government departments and of other public authorities, and of the decisions of some tribunals.

ch. 17 explains tribunals

Ch. 8, p. 85 explains the High Court's role as a criminal court.

Court of Appeal

The Court of Appeal, Civil Division, is for most cases the court of final appeal in civil law. It hears appeals from the county courts and the High Court. Some are heard by three judges, but usually by two. When there are three, each may give a judgment but the decision is that of the majority. In a limited number of cases, appeals can be made to the Supreme Court. The Court of Appeal's procedures in civil cases are similar to those in its criminal cases.

The hierarchy of the civil and criminal courts is shown in Figure 1 in chapter 1, p. 4.

Types of judge in civil courts

Three types of judge preside in the county courts and High Court:

- *District judges* – appointed from among practising solicitors and barristers. Their casework includes many of the fast-track and small claims cases, family disputes and insolvency. They may be referred to in media reports as, for example, District Judge John Smith, but are increasingly being referred to as, in this instance, Judge John Smith. Deputy district judges are part-time appointments.
- *Circuit judges* – in the busier county courts there may be two or more senior judges known as circuit judges; in some regions they travel round to hear cases in several towns or cities – hence the origin of the term 'circuit'. Circuit judges may also sit in Crown courts in criminal cases. Recorders are barristers and solicitors who sit part time in the jurisdiction of a circuit judge. Retired circuit judges who sit part time are known as deputies. Circuit judges hear some fast-track and most multi-track trials. They may also hear appeals against the decisions of district judges. Appeals from a circuit judge lie direct to the Court of Appeal.
- *High Court judges* – they are more experienced, and so more senior, than circuit judges.

Legal terms for parties in civil cases

divorce law is explained in ch. 13

In many types of civil actions, the party, whether a person or organisation, who initiates the action – for example, claims damages for a tort – is known as the 'claimant'. He/she was formerly called the 'plaintiff'. The party against whom the action is taken is the 'defendant'. In some actions, for example in bankruptcy and divorce cases, the person initiating it is the 'petitioner' and the other party the 'respondent'.

Media coverage of civil cases

The media have privilege against libel actions for reports of what is said in open court. In civil cases, there is also privilege for media reports based on case documents made available by the court, see below.

ch. 21 explains privilege

Settlements

A case in which one party sues another may well be settled before a full trial, usually by one side paying the other a sum of money. The settlement means there will be no court judgment on the facts. A media report of a settlement should not suggest that the side paying the money has admitted liability – that is, fault – for the wrong allegedly suffered by the other, unless liability is admitted. Wrongly suggesting that a settlement indicates an admission of liability could be defamatory. For example, a private health clinic may sue for libel if a report wrongly suggests it has admitted liability for medical complications after cosmetic surgery, even though it has paid out to settle the case.

Reporting restrictions and contempt law

Judges in civil cases have, if they decide to impose a reporting restriction, some of the same powers used by criminal courts, outlined in earlier chapters. A judge in a civil court can, under section 39 of the Children and Young Persons Act 1933, ban the media from identifying a juvenile concerned in the case as a claimant or witness, or victim. Judges in civil cases – particularly in family law cases – can also use their **inherent jurisdiction** to order that certain people, especially children, are protected by anonymity in reports.

→glossary

The Contempt of Court Act 1981 applies to media reports of civil cases, in that once a case is 'active' nothing must be published which creates a substantial risk of serious prejudice to it. But as juries are rarely used in civil cases, the Act is generally much less restrictive over pre-trial coverage than it is for criminal cases.

ch. 18 explains contempt law

The bans on taking photographs, sketching, filming or audio recording in court apply to civil courts, as do other statutory and common law protections of the confidentiality of jury deliberations, and of jurors and witnesses generally.

see ch. 11

'Payments into court'

The defendant being sued in certain types of civil action, for example a contract dispute or in a defamation case, may make a 'payment into court' before the start of the trial. This is a formal offer of payment made in the hope that the claimant, who will be told of the sum offered – will accept it as a settlement. If the media discovers that such an offer has been made, it should not be reported unless and until it is referred to in open court at the end of the trial, if the case goes to trial. Disclosing that an offer has been made at any earlier stage may be regarded as contempt of court as it could potentially prejudice the court's decision at trial. The judge in the case, or the jury, if there is one, is not told of the offer before reaching a judgment or verdict. If at the end of the trial the court finds for the claimant, but awards less than the amount in the defendant's pre-trial offer, the claimant will have to pay that part of his/her own costs which was incurred after the date the payment into court was made.

Starting civil proceedings

Most civil actions in the High Court and county courts are begun by the court issuing a claim form – it used to be called a writ. The claim form, which is prepared by the claimant, sets out the nature of the claim against the defendant, and the remedy, or remedies, sought. The remedy wanted may be an **injunction** – a court order compelling the other party to do something, or stop doing something – or an order for the defendant to pay a debt or damages. The claim form is served on the defendant.

→glossary

The vast majority of money claims – for example, over debts – do not proceed to trial as the defendant usually does not file any defence. The claimant simply writes to the court asking for judgment to be entered 'in default'. If damages are claimed there may have to be a hearing to decide the sum. Once a judgment is entered in the court's records the claimant can enforce it, seeking the money from the defendant. The court's enforcement procedures could include bailiffs taking the defendant's goods to sell to pay the money owed.

Trials in civil cases

A defendant who wants to dispute a civil claim must file a defence within 28 days of service of the claim form. A civil trial is confined to issues that the parties set out in their statements of case (previously known as pleadings), these being the particulars of claim, the defence made to it, any counterclaims or reply to the defence, and 'further information documents'. As a general rule, the public, including journalists, have the right to see these documents.

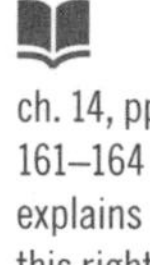

ch. 14, pp. 161–164 explains this right

Each case is allocated to an appropriate 'track' based upon various factors including the value of the claim and its complexity.

There are three tracks:

- the small claims track;
- the fast track;
- the multi-track.

While the monetary value of the claim is not necessarily the most important factor, the general approach is that a claim which exceeds £5,000 (or £1,000 for personal injuries) but is not more than £25,000 will be allocated to the fast track. Claims below these levels are allocated to the small claims track, although it cannot deal with possession claims. The Government has announced an intention to increase the limit for small claims track cases.

((•)) See Useful Websites, below, for the Government's consultation paper.

Cases allocated to the fast track are intended to be heard within 30 weeks and to be concluded in a hearing lasting no more than one day.

The multi-track covers a wide range of claims. Many are only a little more complicated than those on the fast track. Others will require more preparations, and the judge will normally arrange a case-management conference (which sometimes he/she conducts by telephone) at which the issues are clarified and efforts made to encourage a negotiated (or mediated) settlement.

Most civil cases are resolved without reaching trial.

Small claims hearings

Cases on the small claims track are decided at a county court by the district judge and are intended to be heard within three months. The procedure is designed to allow litigants to present their own case, without the need for a lawyer. Proceedings are informal. The judge must give reasons for the final decision. These cases are now heard in public, though this will often be in the district judge's 'chambers' (that is, a private room) with access allowed.

Full trials

In fast-track and multi-track claims there is, if necessary, a formal trial. This is by a judge with no jury, unless the case is in the few categories where there may be a jury.

Most parties involved in trials at county courts and the High Court instruct solicitors to prepare their cases. The solicitors either brief counsel (that is, instruct a barrister to provide further advice and to argue the case in court) or may represent the client themselves in a county court trial. Solicitor-advocates have 'rights of audience' in the higher courts – that is, they can appear for their client without needing to brief a barrister.

ch. 1 explains the legal profession

Full trial procedure

A claimant or defendant may represent himself/herself in court and may be assisted by some other lay person (often called a 'McKenzie friend'). Unless there is a jury, civil trials are now largely based on documents, read beforehand by the judge, with each party disclosing its documents to the other side before the trial. The documents are those listed above, plus witness statements, and each party also supplies a 'skeleton argument' setting out their cases. In the trial, the witnesses may do no more than confirm that their written statement is true, although usually the judge allows some supplementary questions. The claimant's witnesses testify first, and are cross-examined by the defendant or his/her advocate. If the defendant calls witnesses there will be the same process of (a short) examination and cross-examination. Expert evidence may be admitted only with the court's permission. An expert owes a duty of impartiality to the court and unless expert evidence is likely to be strongly contested, the court appoints a single expert who is jointly instructed by the parties.

After all the evidence, the advocates make their submissions on the evidence and law. Finally, the judge gives his/her judgment and explains his/her reasons for it.

In civil law, the standard of proof – the test used by a judge (or jury) to decide which of any competing pieces of evidence will be accepted as the truth – is 'the balance of probabilities'.

see ch. 4, p. 39 on that standard

This is a lower standard of proof than that needed for criminal convictions. In more difficult cases a judge may 'reserve' – that is, delay – giving judgment, to have more time to weigh evidence and check the law. He/she may read the judgment out in court at a later date or have it typed and 'hand it down' at a subsequent hearing. Court reporters are usually provided with copies of written judgments. After the judgment (or, in jury trials, the verdict) there is usually argument about costs, an issue on which the judge must make an appropriate order, as it is not simply a question of the loser paying the winner's costs, though the loser can expect to pay a major part of these.

See ch. 14, p. 163 for information on access to judgments in civil cases.

Trials with juries

In civil law, there is a right to apply for trial by a jury if the claim:

ch. 19 explains defamation trials

- involves an allegation of fraud; or
- is for defamation; or
- false imprisonment; or
- malicious prosecution.

The reasons why juries can be used in these categories of case have been described in a House of Lords judgment as 'historical rather than logical'. But those historical reasons include the notion that defamation cases, and those involving fraud claims particularly, concern allegations against someone's integrity and honour; that in a defamation case, a jury may understand nuances in current meanings of words which a judge – who may be remote from everyday 'street language' – may not; that false imprisonment or malicious prosecution cases usually involve allegations against an arm of the state such as the police, and a jury is needed to give the public confidence that the case has been independently decided as a judge alone might be seen as another arm of the state.

A judge has discretion to allow jury trial in other types of civil case, but such instances are exceptional.

If there is a jury, the judge will sum up the case after each side has made final submissions in the trial. In some cases the judge may ask the jury for a general verdict, but in more complicated cases the judge will set out a series of questions for jurors to answer in the verdict. Juries decide the level of damages if the verdict is for the claimant. Juries in civil cases are selected at random from the electoral role, as are juries in criminal trials. A county court jury consists of eight people and a High Court jury of 12.

Civil functions of magistrates

Magistrates have various civil powers. The role of magistrates courts in family law cases, for example divorce and care proceedings, is outlined in chapter 13. Magistrates also hear appeals from decisions of local authority committees on licensing public houses, hotels, off-licences and betting shops.

Bankruptcy

The civil courts deal with bankruptcy cases. Some yield news stories of wild extravagance at the expense of creditors or the accumulation of large bills for unpaid tax. Reporters should note that in law the term bankruptcy only applies to people. Companies go into liquidation. The Government's Insolvency Service is a useful source of information on bankruptcy and insolvency.

see Useful Websites, below, for the Service's site

Bankruptcy petitions

A petition can be filed at the county court for a bankruptcy order to be made by a district judge against an individual who owes at least £750 in unsecured debts. A creditor will file a petition if this seems the best way to get the debt, or some of it, repaid, by realising – taking and selling – any of the debtor's assets. A debtor may file for his/her own bankruptcy to stop the hassle of bailiffs and creditors calling at his/her home, because after bankruptcy he/she can refer them to a trustee or Official Receiver. Also, filing for bankruptcy offers the prospect of starting anew, with debt wiped out, when the bankruptcy is discharged – that is, the duration of the bankruptcy ends.

A bankruptcy order will be granted by the district judge unless, if the petition is from a creditor, the debtor's offer to repay the debt has been unreasonably refused. Instead of a bankruptcy order, an 'individual voluntary arrangement' may be made, in the hope that the debtor can avoid bankruptcy by gradual repayment of debt, if the creditors agree.

Otherwise, after a bankruptcy order the district's Official Receiver (a civil servant in the Insolvency Service, who is also an officer of the court) takes over legal control of all the debtor's property, apart from basic domestic necessities, tools and other items necessary for the bankrupt to work.

Libel danger in wrongly stating someone is bankrupt

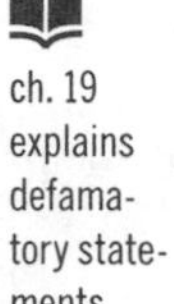

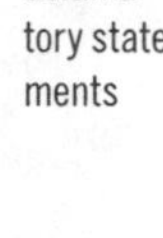

ch. 19 explains defamatory statements

Suggestions that someone is insolvent may well be regarded as defamatory. Therefore it may not be safe, as regards danger of a libel action, for a media organisation to report – until and unless a bankruptcy order is made – the filing of a bankruptcy petition by a creditor, because the county court may find that the alleged debtor is solvent.

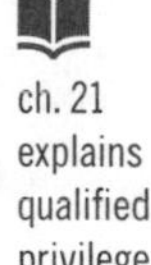

ch. 21 explains qualified privilege

However, a debtor who files his/her own petition is admitting insolvency, so it is safe to report this. When a bankruptcy order has been made, it is open to public inspection at the court, announced in the *London Gazette* (a government newsletter) and the Official Receiver issues a notice for the public. Also, a public register, which is online, shows who is currently bankrupt. There is no libel risk in reporting the bankruptcy from any of these official sources, as the report is protected by qualified privilege under the 1996 Defamation Act, if that defence's requirements are met. The register's address is under Useful Websites, below.

A judge can make a bankruptcy order following the conviction of a criminal, for example a fraudster.

Effects of bankruptcy

A bankrupt cannot obtain credit of £500 or more without disclosing his/her bankruptcy, nor trade under any name other than the name in which he/she went into bankruptcy without disclosing that name and the bankruptcy. A bankrupt may not open new bank accounts, act as a company director or take part in the management of any company without the leave of the court. He/she cannot sit in Parliament or on a local authority, nor take any public office.

Discharge from bankruptcy

Whereas in the past a bankruptcy would not be discharged for at least three years, the period is now usually 12 months.

An Official Receiver who considers that a bankrupt has been dishonest or otherwise blameworthy over debt incurred can ask the court to make a Bankruptcy Restrictions Order, which can increase the duration of the restrictions on the bankrupt by between two and 15 years.

See www.mcnaes.com ch. 12 for further details on bankruptcy cases, including the right anyone has to inspect bankruptcy documents.

Company liquidation

Care should be taken, when reporting that a limited company has gone into liquidation, to make the circumstances clear. Misuse of terms could create a libel problem.

(1) *A members' voluntary liquidation* takes place where the company is solvent, but the directors and shareholders decide to close it down, possibly in the case of a small firm because of impending retirement, or because of a merger. To imply that such a company is in financial difficulties in these circumstances is defamatory.

(2) *A creditors' voluntary liquidation* takes place for a voluntary winding up to proceed under the supervision of a liquidator.

(3) *A compulsory liquidation* follows a hearing in public in the High Court or county court of a petition to wind up the company. This is usually because a creditor claims it is insolvent, but can also happen when a company fails to file its statutory report or hold its statutory meeting on being set up; where it does not start, or suspends, business; or where members of the company are reduced to below the number required in law. Once a winding-up order is made, a liquidator is appointed to collect the assets and pay off the creditors.

Recap of major points

- County courts handle most civil litigation. The High Court deals with the more serious or high-value claims.
- Civil case hearings are mainly conducted by reference to documents. A journalist has rights to see the key documents of cases heard in public.
- Civil courts can impose reporting restrictions. Contempt law applies to media coverage reports of their cases, but is less restrictive if no jury is involved.
- Magistrates handle some types of civil case.
- The county courts deal with bankruptcy cases.
- Journalists need to take care before suggesting a person is bankrupt or a company is insolvent, because this could be defamatory if untrue.

((•)) Useful Websites

www.direct.gov.uk/en.MoneyTaxAndBenefits/ManagingDebt/Makingacourtclaimformoney/index.htm

Government guidance: 'Making a court claim for money'

www.direct.gov.uk/

Directgov site – explains aspects of civil law for users

www.judiciary.gov.uk/

The Judiciary website – judges' roles explained, including 'A Day in the Life'

www.justice.gov.uk/consultation-cp6-2011.htm

The Government's 2011 consultation paper 'Solving disputes in the county courts', on changes to the civil court system

www.bis.gov.uk/insolvency

The Insolvency Service website – explains bankrupty and compulsory liquidation

www.bis.gov.uk/insolvency/personal-insolvency/individual-insolvency-register

Individual Insolvency Register – shows who is currently bankrupt

13

Family courts

Chapter summary

Family law, a branch of civil law, includes many cases involving disputes between estranged parents after marital breakdown – for example, about contact with a child – or those brought by local authorities seeking to protect children. A court can remove a child from his/her parents because of suspected abuse or neglect. Reporting restrictions and contempt of court law severely limit what the media can publish about most family cases, to protect those involved, particularly children, who in most instances cannot be identified in media reports. This chapter examines the main restrictions. However, because of the complexity of court rules and the restrictions, a fuller version of this chapter is provided in www.mcnaes.com.

Introduction

The term 'family cases' covers a range of matters dealt with by magistrates courts, county courts or the High Court Family Division. Cases can be transferred between these courts.

Types of case in family courts

Two major categories in family court proceedings are 'private' and 'public' law cases.

Private law cases include:

- Matrimonial cases – proceedings for divorce, judicial separation or nullity, or to end a civil partnership. Cases concerning dissolution of marriages or civil partnerships may also involve ancillary proceedings about financial and property disputes between estranged couples.

- Enforcement of financial arrangements between estranged couples, including unmarried couples.
- Other disputes between estranged parents about their children, such as where they live, and the absent parent's rights to contact, leading to the courts making residence and contact orders under the Children Act 1989.
- Applications for court orders to enforce the return of a child abducted, for example, by one parent in defiance of the other's rights.
- Paternity disputes.
- Applications in domestic violence cases for 'non-molestation' orders.
- Applications to protect a person from a 'forced marriage'.

Public law

Public law cases include:

- Applications, mainly by local authorities, for court orders allowing social workers to intervene to protect a child they suspect is being neglected or abused in his/her home. The orders are made under the Children Act 1989, in magistrates courts or county courts. The courts can also make emergency protection orders for police or social workers to remove a child if there is immediate concern for his/her safety.
- Applications for orders for children to be taken into local authority care if they are beyond parental control.

Adoption cases – a court can sanction adoptions of children who have been removed from their birth parents by a local authority in public law cases. Other adoptions may formalise existing relationships, such as a stepfather becoming the adoptive father, and therefore are private law cases.

! Remember

The Editors' Code of Practice and the Ofcom Broadcasting Code say that normally journalists should not interview children aged under 16 on matters concerning their welfare (Editors' Code) or privacy (Ofcom Code) without the consent of a parent or responsible adult. The Editors' Code also says that 'minors' must not be paid for material involving children's welfare, nor parents or guardians for material about their children or wards, unless it is clearly in the child's interest. See chapter 27, pp. 328–329 and www.mcnaes.com ch. 13.

Reporting family law cases

Reporting family law cases is fraught with difficulties because of the effects of anonymity provisions under the Children Act 1989, the contempt of court provisions in section 12 of the Administration of Justice Act 1960 (the 1960 Act), and other extremely tight restrictions on reporting court hearings.

The result is that much of what reporting there is involves anonymised articles involving, for example, claims by parents that they have suffered a miscarriage of justice at the hands of social workers, medical experts or the courts.

Disputes between parents over where a child will live – which, in cases which attract media attention, usually involve celebrities – are almost invariably shrouded in anonymity almost as soon as they arise, because of the 1989 Act's restrictions. Also, the High Court has the power to issue injunctions intended to protect the privacy of any children involved in such cases.

Anonymity under the Children Act 1989

Section 97 of the Children Act 1989 restricts media coverage of family law cases by making it an offence to publish:

- a name or other material intended or likely to identify a child – a person under the age of 18 – who is involved in any current case in a magistrates court, a county court or the High Court in which any power under the Act has or may be exercised with respect to that or any other child;
- an address, as being that of a child involved in such an ongoing case; or
- detail identifying the child's school.

Section 97 anonymity automatically applies to children in unresolved residence and contact disputes between parents, and those who are the subject of intervention by social workers. It applies to any report of what is said in court or a written judgment, as well as to any wider feature about a child who is involved in an ongoing case. Clearly, it also means the child's family cannot be identified to avoid jigsaw identification.

ch. 9, p. 96 explains jigsaw identification

Breaching section 97 by publishing material identifying a child covered is punishable by a fine of up to £2,500. It is a defence for an accused person to prove that he/she did not know, and had no reason to suspect, that the published material was intended or likely to identify the child.

Adoptions

Section 97 also bans reports of adoption proceedings from identifying the child concerned while he/she is under the age of 18.

! Remember

It is an offence under section 123 of the Adoption and Children Act 2002 for anyone other than an officially recognised adoption agency, or someone acting on its behalf, to publish information, or an advertisement, that a child is available for adoption.

When does anonymity under the Children Act 1989 cease?

Court waiver

Section 97(4) of the Children Act 1989 says that, if a child's welfare requires it, a court may waive to any specified extent the anonymity otherwise automatically bestowed on a child. The Lord Chancellor may also do so, with the Lord Chief Justice's agreement.

Judges have waived the anonymity to allow the media to identify and picture children who have been abducted by a parent, or been removed to avoid them being taken into care, in the hope – usually successful – that the public will help find them.

Anonymity ends when the case concludes

The Court of Appeal has held that section 97 anonymity only applies while Children Act proceedings are going on, and ends with the case (*Clayton v Clayton* [2006] EWCA Civ 878). The then President of the Family Division said that if a court felt that anonymity should continue beyond a case's conclusion to protect a child's

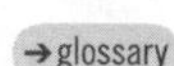

welfare or privacy it should issue an **injunction** to continue it. The High Court or a county court can order that the anonymity continue until the child is 18.

! Remember

A consequence of *Clayton v Clayton* is that a journalist who wants to identify a child as having been involved in a case under the 1989 Act – for example in a 'true life' story about a mother's battle with social workers, or a celebrity's account of the break-up of their marriage – should be sure that the proceedings have ended and that no order has been made to continue a child's anonymity.

Wards of court

Children who have been made wards of court by the High Court, or who are the subject of proceedings to make them wards, or who are involved in similar cases are automatically protected by section 97 anonymity while the case is ongoing (*Kelly v British Broadcasting Corporation* [2001] Fam 59).

Case study

In 2001 Bobby Kelly, aged 16, ran away from home and joined the 'Jesus Christians' cult. His family made him a ward of court. A BBC reporter traced and interviewed him. Mr Justice Munby ruled in the High Court that the media did not require the court's permission to interview a ward of court or to publish the interview. But he warned that the media should take care to avoid any breach of reporting restrictions (*Kelly v British Broadcasting Corporation*). For example, anonymity might apply, and a published interview should not breach contempt law in respect of matter heard by a court in private. The BBC was allowed to identify Bobby, who said he was homesick but that 'it says in the Bible that you have to give everything up to work for God'.

((•)) see Useful Websites, below, for the Bobby Kelly story

Anonymised judgments

In county courts and the High Court the texts of family case judgments, if made public, are usually anonymised to prevent a child or adult being identified. A media organisation would commit an offence if it reported an anonymised judgment in a way which identified any protected person.

The Court of Protection

for more detail, see www.mcnaes.com ch. 13

The Court of Protection is a specialist court established by the Mental Capacity Act 2005 to make decisions for people who lack the mental capability to decide for themselves – for example, on financial or welfare matters or medical treatment. It usually sits in private, in London and at other venues, and has its own procedural rules. Its judgments are usually anonymised.

Contempt danger in reporting on private hearings

Section 12 of the Administration of Justice Act 1960 makes it a contempt of court to publish, without a court's permission, a report of a private hearing if the case falls into certain categories, including those which:

- relate to the exercise of the inherent jurisdiction of the High Court with respect to children;
- are under the Children Act 1989 or the Adoption and Children Act 2002 or which otherwise relate wholly or mainly to the maintenance or upbringing of a child;
- are under the Mental Capacity Act 2005, or any provision of the Mental Health Act 1983 authorising an application or reference to be made to the First-tier Tribunal, the Mental Health Review Tribunal for Wales or to a county court;
- are of any kind where the court expressly bans publication of all or specified information relating to the private hearing.

ch. 17 explains mental health tribunals

The section 12 prohibition applies broadly across family cases heard in private. The definition of 'private' includes some cases which journalists may attend. It could also be a contempt to publish information from a document prepared for use in a private hearing (*Re F (A Minor) (Publication of Information)* [1977] Fam 58;

[1977] 1 All ER 114). This would include a witness statement in a dispute between parents over contact arrangements regarding children, or a social worker's report for a court about a child taken into local authority care, irrespective of whether the information published was anonymised.

It might also be a contempt to publish any of the judgment, unless the judge has agreed to publication.

Section 12 does allow publication of any order a court makes in private proceedings, unless the court specifically bans publication of the order.

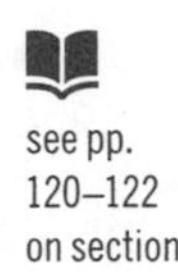

see pp. 120–122 on section 12

Also, section 12 does not stop the media making basic reference to a case being heard in private, although Children Act anonymity may well apply.

The definition of 'private'

Section 12 reporting restrictions apply if a family case is heard in private.

The current position is that if a county court or High Court excludes the public from a family case, it is classed as private, even if journalists attend. The section 12 restrictions apply unless the judge lifts them. If they are not lifted, a journalist can only report limited detail about the hearing.

If magistrates exclude the public from a family case, journalists have an automatic right to attend it under section 69 of the Magistrates' Courts Act 1980 (the 1980 Act), under which a hearing is not classed as private unless journalists are also excluded by specific order of the court. But Part 27.11 of the Family Procedure Rules 2010 (SI 2010/2955) classes such hearings at magistrates courts as private, even if journalists attend.

This clash of definition between the 1980 Act and the 2010 Rules arises because Part 2 of the Children, Schools and Families Act 2010 has not been put into effect. The safest course for a journalist wanting to report such a case at a magistrates court would be to ask it to lift the 1960 Act's restrictions, which would establish if the court considered that they applied at all.

See also p. 147 on media coverage of magistrates courts.

! Remember

There is a particular risk of defamation when publishing a report of court proceedings held in private, because no privilege applies. Chapter 21 explains privilege.

Disclosure restrictions

Part 12.73 of the Family Procedure Rules 2010, reflecting section 12 of the 1960 Act, says no information 'relating to' court proceedings concerning children and held in private, whether or not the information is in documents filed with the court, may be communicated to the public, or to anyone other than lawyers, officials or other specified categories of people, without the court's permission. Part 14.4

contains a similar ban for adoption cases. These Parts therefore implicitly forbid, for example, a parent of a child taken into local authority care, or a lawyer, giving a journalist information about the proceedings (other than the few details permitted by section 12 of the 1960 Act), unless the court authorises it. The ban applies whether or not journalists attend the private hearing.

See also www.mcnaes.com ch. 13 for courts' powers to authorise journalists to see case documents: 'Can journalists see documents?'

The ban does not stop a parent telling in general terms how they feel about the court case or of the wider experience of, for example, a child being removed from them – though any anonymity applying under the Children Act 1989 must be preserved in any report.

! Remember

A full explanation of reporting restrictions under the 1989 Act and 1960 Act, with case studies, and of journalists' rights under statute and court rules to attend family cases is provided in www.mcneas.com, chapter 13. Also, the High Court Family Division has published a detailed guide to reporting family proceedings – see Useful Websites below.

Other reporting restrictions in family cases

Although journalists now have a presumptive right to attend family proceedings in magistrates courts, county courts and the High Court, even though they are generally held in private, with the public barred, the media are still bound by strict reporting restrictions. Those applying to current cases involving the Children Act 1989, and to private hearings, contained in the Administration of Justice Act 1960, are referred to above. But other restrictions can apply, depending on the type of case.

Section 71 of the Magistrates' Courts Act 1980 restricts what may be published from evidence given in 'family proceedings' in a magistrates court – and the 1989 Act anonymity restrictions could also apply to the same hearings if the case concerns that Act.

Automatic reporting restrictions under section 2 of the Domestic and Appellate Proceedings (Restriction of Publicity) Act 1968 cover some types of family case – for example, about neglect to pay maintenance, or for declarations about parentage, legitimacy or marital status – in any court which hears such a case or an appeal, including the magistrates courts, county courts and High Court.

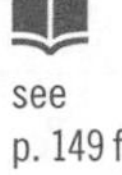
see p. 149 for reporting restrictions in divorce cases

See www.mcnaes.com ch. 13 for full details of the 1980 Act and 1968 Act restrictions.

Anti-publicity injunctions in family cases

The High Court has inherent jurisdiction to order that a person must be anonymous in published reports of its proceedings and judgments. It is a contempt to breach such an injunction. Injunctions can be issued to protect children and mentally or physically incapacitated adults in cases in which the court is ruling on their care, medical treatment or whether they should be kept alive. County courts should refer applications for these injunctions to the High Court. Injunctions can also be issued to protect children who become involved in high-profile news stories, for example when their father is charged with murdering their mother, or their mother is charged with murdering one of the youngsters.

See www.mcnaes.com ch. 13 for the procedure to alert the media to family law injunctions, and for instances of them restricting media coverage of a criminal trial and an inquest.

News-gathering activity can be banned

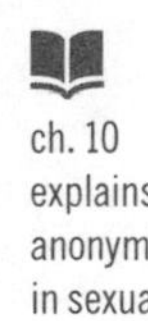

ch. 10 explains anonymity in sexual offence cases

An injunction can forbid news-gathering or other activity which is deemed likely to jeopardise a person's welfare or privacy, or could lead to the subjects feeling harassed. Mr Justice McKinnon made such an order in 2008 banning the media from approaching two women whose father, after repeatedly raping them, as children and adults, fathering children, was jailed for life at Sheffield Crown court. Nobody involved was named in reports of the father's trial, but lawyers for the daughters said news-gathering activities could lead to them and their children being identified in local communities.

See the case study on www.mcnaes.com ch. 13 for more details.

Coverage of divorce, nullity, judicial separation and civil partnership cases

Divorce, judicial separation or nullity cases, or proceedings to end a civil partnership, are usually dealt with by county courts, although some are transferred to the High Court.

Most divorce proceedings are uncontested. Lists of petitioners granted a decree nisi – the first stage of a divorce – are read out in open court. The decree ends the marriage when made absolute, usually after six weeks. In a contested case, the husband, wife and possibly other witnesses may give evidence in court.

Reporting restrictions apply to divorce, judicial separation and nullity cases, and proceedings to end a civil partnership – whether the report is of a hearing in a contested case or of case documents.

The reporting restrictions are explained in www.mcnaes.com ch. 13.

In matrimonial cases there may be hearings on financial orders (previously known as 'ancillary relief') – that is, the division of property and other financial arrangements between estranged couples.

Copy of decree

Part 7.36 of the Family Procedure Rules 2010 permits any person, on payment of a fee, to obtain from the court a copy of the decree absolute.

Recap of major points

- Family courts are difficult to report, because reporting restrictions apply in virtually all cases.
- A child involved in ongoing proceedings under the Children Act 1989 must not be identified in media reports of such cases, unless the court authorises it. The same anonymity applies to any wider feature referring to the child's involvement in such a case.
- The High Court has wide-ranging powers to protect the welfare of children and others, including anonymity orders.

Useful Websites

www.judiciary.gov.uk/publications-and-reports/guidance/2011/family-courts-media-access-reporting

'The Family Courts: Media Access and Reporting', an official guide for journalists, judges and practitioners explaining the law on reporting family courts, endorsed by the President of the Family Division Sir Nicholas Wall, the Society of Editors and the Judicial College

http://news.bbc.co.uk/1/hi/uk/852109.stm/ and **http://news.bbc.co.uk/1/hi/uk/853876.stm/**

BBC reports on Bobby Kelly, when he was a ward of court

14

Open justice and access to court information

Chapter summary

Open justice is vital to a democracy. If justice is done in secret the public can have no confidence in it, because the secrecy may hide injustice. Journalists are the wider public's eyes and ears in courtrooms, so need to know their rights of admission to courts. This chapter explains these rights, and that the law allows courts to sit in private on occasion. This chapter also explains the rights that citizens, and therefore journalists, have to see court documents needed to understand civil cases, and outlines the help criminal courts must give to reporters covering cases. Other chapters refer to the admission rights for particular types of court – youth courts in chapter 9, family courts in chapter 13, coroners courts in chapter 16, and employment tribunals in chapter 17.

A fundamental rule in common law

In 1913, the House of Lords in *Scott v Scott* [1913] AC 417 **affirmed the common law rule that normally courts must administer justice in public. One law lord in that case, Lord Atkinson said:**

> "The hearing of a case in public may be, and often is, no doubt, painful, humiliating, or deterrent both to parties and witnesses, and in many cases, especially those of a criminal nature, the details may be so indecent as to tend to injure public morals, but all this is tolerated and endured, because it is felt that in public trial is to found, on the whole, the best security for the pure, impartial, and efficient administration of justice, the best means for winning for it public confidence and respect."

See www.mcnaes.com ch. 14 for more detail on *Scott v Scott*.

A major benefit of open justice is that a witness who testifies in public proceedings is less likely to lie. A public lie is more likely to be exposed than one told behind closed doors. Other benefits of open justice were categorised by Lord Woolf in the Court of Appeal judgment in *R v Legal Aid Board, ex p Kaim Todner* [1998] 3 All ER 541:

> It is necessary because the public nature of proceedings deters inappropriate behaviour on the part of the court. It also maintains the public's confidence in the administration of justice. It enables the public to know that justice is being administered impartially. It can result in evidence becoming available which would not become available if the proceedings were conducted behind closed doors or with one or more of the parties' or witnesses' identity concealed. It makes uninformed and inaccurate comment about the proceedings less likely.

As Lord Woolf noted, any reporting restriction is a departure from the open justice principle, and so must have an overriding justification. Chapter 15 explains the specific grounds on which reporting restrictions can be challenged by journalists, and explains how a journalist can challenge a court's decision to exclude him/her from a hearing. But the foundation of such challenges is that general benefits always flow to society from open justice.

In private, in chambers and in camera

- The term **in chambers** refers to occasions when a judge holds a hearing, usually a preliminary one in a case, in a courthouse room, not a formal courtroom. →glossary
- The term **in camera** tends to be used when the public and media are excluded from all or part of the main hearing in a case – for example a criminal trial – being held in a courtroom. The hearing is effectively being held in secret. →glossary
- The term **in private** is used to cover both the above terms. But a hearing may be held in chambers for administrative convenience, rather than because of a decision or rule that it should be private – see p. 158. →glossary

The media's role

The court reporter's vital role as trustee for the wider public has been recognised in many judgments. In *R v Felixstowe Justices, ex p Leigh* [1987] QB 582; [1987] 1 All ER 551, Lord Justice Watkins said:

> The role of the journalist and his importance for the public interest in the administration of justice has been commented upon on many occasions. No-one nowadays surely can doubt that his presence in court for the purpose of reporting

proceedings conducted therein is indispensable. Without him, how is the public to be informed of how justice is being administered in our courts?"

The limited scope of common law exceptions to open justice

It is generally acknowledged that excluding the press and public from a court case is only justified in common law in three types of circumstance:

- When their presence would frustrate the process of justice – for example, when a woman or child cannot be persuaded to give evidence of intimate sexual matters in the presence of many strangers.
- When unchecked publicity would defeat the whole object of the proceedings, for example:
  - when a case concerns ownership of a trade secret, and publicity would reveal the secret to commercial rivals; or
  - when a case concerns a matter relating to national security which could be damaged by publicity.
- When the court is exercising a parental role to protect the interests of vulnerable people, mainly:
  - children, for example, in family law cases, or
  - people with mental incapacity or mental illness;

  and unchecked publicity could harm the welfare of those involved.

ch. 13 explains family law

Statutes and procedural rules allow courts to exclude the public and, in some instances, journalists too, in specified circumstances, as this chapter explains. These statutory powers cover, to an extent, the same kinds of occasion for which common law justifies exclusion. Common law can be used if no statutory power covers the occasion, but does not give courts a general licence to sit in private.

Lord Diplock, emphasising that common law rarely justified departing from the open justice rule, said in a 1979 House of Lords judgment that the rule should only be set aside when:

> "the nature or circumstances of the particular proceeding are such that the application of the general rule in its entirety would frustrate or render impracticable the administration of justice or would damage some other public interest for whose protection Parliament has made some statutory derogation from the rule (*Attorney General v Leveller Magazine Ltd* [1979] AC 440 at 449, 450)."

See www.mcnacs.com ch. 14 for more detail of this case.

Case study

Magistrates in Surrey were persuaded to exclude press and public when the court heard a speech in mitigation. This included reference to the defendant having assisted police inquiries. Some who help the police do not want this publicised. But the magistrates were strongly criticised in the High Court when their exclusion of the media was challenged by a newspaper group. Lord Justice Ackner said hearing a matter in private was a course of last resort to be adopted only if the proceedings in open court would frustrate the process of justice (*R v Reigate Justices, ex p Argus Newspapers* (1983) 5 Cr App R (S) 181).

Other cases which can be cited

Scott v Scott, Attorney General v Leveller Magazine Ltd and other cases referred to in this chapter can be cited by a journalist when challenging exclusion from a court hearing. A journalist can also direct the court to guidance issued by the Judicial College (formerly the Judicial Studies Board): 'Reporting Restrictions in the Criminal Courts', see Useful Websites below. This guidance states: 'The test is one of necessity. The fact, for example, that hearing evidence in open court will cause embarrassment to witnesses does not meet the test for necessity.' It also reminds courts that imposing a reporting restriction to stop some detail being published might avoid the need for exclusion.

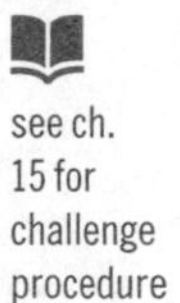
see ch. 15 for challenge procedure

A defendant's embarrassment is insufficient reason to exclude the media

A High Court judge criticised Malvern magistrates' decision to sit in camera to hear mitigation for a woman who admitted driving with excess alcohol. Her solicitor had asked the court to sit in private because she would refer to embarrassing details of her pending divorce which – the court was told – had made her suicidal and drink to excess. The solicitor said her emotional state meant she could not speak about this in open court. The High Court agreed that magistrates did have power to sit in camera but Lord Justice Watkins said that in this case their reason for doing was 'wholly unsustainable and out of accord with [the open justice] principle' (*R v Malvern Justices, ex p Evans* [1988] QB 540; [1988] 1 All ER 371, QBD).

The public and press should not be excluded for longer than necessary

The Court of Appeal said in 1989 that a judge should be alive to the importance of adjourning into open court as soon as exclusion of the public was not plainly necessary (*Re Crook (Tim)* (1991) 93 Cr App R 17).

Journalists can sometimes stay when the public is excluded

If the public are lawfully excluded, it does not follow that journalists must necessarily go too.

Rowdy supporters of a defendant may be banned or ejected from a court's public gallery. But journalists are not going to be rowdy, so should be let into the court. In 1989 in the Court of Appeal Lord Lane said it would not be right generally to distinguish between excluding the press and excluding the public. There might be cases, however, during which the press should not be excluded with the other members of the public, such as a prosecution for importing an indecent film, where the film was shown to the jury and some members of the public might gasp or giggle and make the jury's task more difficult (*Re Crook (Tim)* [1991] 93 Cr App R 17).

Criminal courts cannot sit in private to protect a defendant's business interests

The risk that publicity may severely damage a defendant's business does not justify a criminal court sitting in private (*R v Dover Justices, ex p Dover District Council and Wells* (1991) 156 JP 433).

Articles 6 and 10

Article 6 of the European Convention on Human Rights says everyone is entitled to a fair and public hearing. But the rights which Article 6 primarily protects are not those of the media or wider public, but those of parties in civil litigation and defendants in criminal cases.

A journalist challenging exclusion from a court should cite Article 10, which protects the right to freedom of expression and to impart information.

Ch. 1 explains the Convention's effect, and Articles 6 and 10 are set out in Appendix 1, pp. 427–428.

Statute on open and private hearings

Magistrates' cases

Section 121 of the Magistrates' Courts Act 1980 says magistrates must sit in open court when trying a case or considering jailing someone, or hearing a civil law complaint, unless another statute permits them to sit in private. Section 4 of the Act requires magistrates sitting as examining justices at a committal hearing, and in hearings leading up to it, to sit in open court, except when another statute permits them to sit in private or 'the ends of justice' would not be served by an open hearing.

ch. 7, p. 72 explains committal hearings

Indecent evidence

Section 37 of the Children and Young Persons Act 1933 gives any court the power to exclude the public – but not journalists – when a witness aged under 18 is giving evidence in a case involving indecency.

Sexual history

Section 43 of the Youth Justice and Criminal Evidence Act 1999 requires a court hearing an application to introduce evidence or questions about a complainant's sexual history, for example in a rape case, to sit in private. This reflects the sensitivity of someone who may have suffered rape being questioned about such matters. The court must give its decision on whether such evidence will be allowed, and its reasons, in open court.

One journalist can stay

Section 25 of the 1999 Act allows a court to make a 'special measures direction' to exclude the public and some journalists when a witness is due to testify in a sex offence case or when the court decides there are reasonable grounds for believing that a person other than the defendant wants to intimidate the witness. But it says one journalist must be allowed to stay in court.

ch. 11, pp. 126–128 explains special measures directions

The 1999 Act says that even if, under this section, some journalists and the public are excluded from a courtroom, the proceedings are still legally deemed to be held in public 'for the purposes of any privilege or exemption from liability available in respect of fair, accurate and contemporaneous reports'. This is a reference to contempt and libel law explained in chapters 18 and 21.

Sentence review for informants

Section 75 of the Serious Organised Crime and Police Act 2005 says a Crown court may exclude the public and press when reviewing a sentence previously imposed on a defendant who pleaded guilty, and who has given or offered assistance - for example, information - about a crime to a prosecuting or investigating agency such as the police. But the public and press can only be excluded if the judge considers this in the interests of justice and necessary to protect someone's safety. This might be, for example, because the informant would be at risk of retaliation from criminals if the fact that he/she gave such assistance was publicised. In the review, the original sentence could be reduced as a reward for the assistance offered. If the original sentence was lenient because the defendant had already offered such assistance, the review can increase it if he/she knowingly failed to provide it. If a defendant has failed to honour a pledge of assistance, a journalist has strong grounds for arguing that a lenient sentence should be reviewed in open court. The public would want to be confident that the defendant received an appropriate sentence. The Act allows the court to ban publication of anything about the proceedings 'as it thinks appropriate'.

Official secrets trials

Journalists and the public can be excluded from such trials.

see ch.33, p. 391

Procedural rules and open justice

Courts have rules of procedure which add detail to statute. The wording of some rules gives courts wide discretion to sit in private. A journalist facing exclusion because of a procedural rule should argue that the court's interpretation of it must fully recognise the common law protection of open justice, and Article 10, and cite *Scott v Scott*, in which Lord Shaw stressed that judges must be vigilant to ensure that the open justice principle is not usurped. Lord Shaw said: 'There is no greater danger of usurpation than that which proceeds little by little, under cover of rules of procedure, and at the instance of judges themselves.'

Criminal cases: rules on open and private hearings

Procedure for criminal cases in magistrates courts, Crown courts and the Court of Appeal (Criminal Division) is governed by the Criminal Procedure Rules 2011 and the Consolidated Criminal Practice Direction.

((•)) See Useful Websites, below, for these rules and the Direction.

Rule 16.2 says that a court must have regard to the importance of dealing with criminal cases in public and of allowing them to be reported. Rule 37.2 states specifically that the general rule is that a trial or sentencing in a magistrates court must be in public.

Rule 16.6, for magistrates and Crown courts, says that if the prosecution or defence want to argue that a trial or part of it should be heard in private (that is, in the limited circumstances when a court has power to waive the open justice rule) they must apply in writing to the court not less than five business days before the trial is due to begin, and that the court officer must at once display a notice of the application prominently in the courtroom's vicinity, and give the media notice of it. The application itself shall be heard in private, unless the court orders otherwise, and, if in a Crown court, shall be heard after the **arraignment** but before the jury is sworn. The rule adds that if a court orders that a trial will be heard wholly or partly in private it must not begin until the day after the application was granted, which gives the media some time to challenge the order.

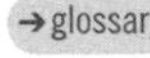

Ch. 8 explains Crown court procedure and ch. 15 explains how a journalist can in any court oppose or challenge an access restriction.

Civil cases: rules on open and private hearings

The Civil Procedure Rules (CPR) cover civil proceedings in the Queen's Bench and Chancery Divisions of the High Court and the county courts.

See Useful Websites, below, for these rules. For general information on civil courts, see ch. 12. Other rules apply to the family court – see ch. 13.

Part 39(2) of the CPR says that the general rule is that a hearing is to be in public but that a hearing, or part of it, may be in private if:

- publicity would defeat the object of the hearing;
- it involves matters relating to national security;
- it involves confidential information (including information relating to personal financial matters) and publicity would damage that confidentiality;
- it is necessary to protect the interest of any child or protected party;
- it is an application **without notice** and it would be unjust to any respondent for there to be a public hearing – that is, one party is not yet aware of the proceedings; →glossary
- it involves uncontentious matters arising in the administration of trusts or of a deceased's estate;
- the court considers a private hearing necessary in the interests of justice.

The Practice Direction which supplements this rule lists types of case which shall, 'in the first instance', be listed as private. These include a claim by a mortgagee for possession of land; landlords' applications for possession of residential property because rent is allegedly owed; and proceedings brought under the Consumer Credit Act 1974 and the Protection from Harassment Act 1997 (the latter would include some domestic violence cases).

! Remember

A journalist can try to persuade the judge that cases in these categories should be heard in public. The Practice Direction states that the judge should have regard to 'any representations' made.

The CPR also provide for other types of hearing to be held in private. A journalist excluded from a civil court should ask which rule applies.

Contempt and libel issues in reports of private hearings

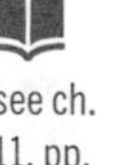

see ch. 11, pp. 120–122

If a case falls into certain categories it could be a contempt for a journalist who discovers what has been said in a private court hearing to publish such information and material from documents prepared for use in the case.

Publishing information from a private hearing in any court case:

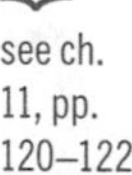

chs. 18 and 21

- is not protected by section 4 of the Contempt of Court Act 1981 if the publication creates a substantial risk of serious prejudice to an 'active' case;
- is not protected by privilege if someone defamed by it sues for libel.

Hearings in chambers are not always private

ch. 11 pp. 120–122 explains the 1960 Act. See also p. 163 on judgments

A hearing may be in chambers, rather than in public in a courtroom, merely because of routine, administrative convenience. Lord Woolf (later Lord Chief Justice) said in the Court of Appeal in 1998 that the public had no right to attend hearings in chambers. But members of the public and journalists who asked should be given permission to attend if this was practical and the case was not in a category listed in section 12 of the Administration of Justice Act 1960. He said that a judgment or order made in a case in chambers was normally a public document, but there was no right to inspect it without the court's permission (*Hodgson v Imperial Tobacco* [1998] 2 All ER 673; [1998] 1 WLR 1056).

Bail applications at Crown court

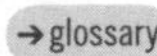

Bail hearings in the Crown court, including those in which a defendant wants to overturn a refusal by magistrates to grant bail, should normally be held in public. The Criminal Procedure Rules (Rule 16.11) state that Crown court bail applications may be held in chambers. But Mr Justice Gray, in a High Court ruling in 2006, said this did not mean there was a presumption that they should be held in private (*Malik v Central Criminal Court* [2006] EWHC 1539 (Admin)).

Case study

Warrington Guardian reporter Jo Lean wrote to a judge to protest after court staff refused to let her into a Crown court bail hearing in a robbery case. A few hours later the judge agreed she could have information on what was decided in the hearing (*Media Lawyer*, July 3, 2008).

What information and help must criminal courts provide?

see Useful Websites below for the Direction

The Consolidated Criminal Practice Direction, which applies to criminal courts, makes little reference to media facilities, but does say in Part III.30.16–18, in relation to treatment of 'vulnerable defendants', including juveniles: 'Facilities for reporting the proceedings... must be provided'. It says the court may restrict the number of reporters attending to such number as is judged 'practicable and desirable'. If it is decided to limit access to the court by journalists and the public 'arrangements should be made for the proceedings to be relayed, audibly and if possible visually, to another room in the same court complex to which the media and the public have access if it appears that there will be a need for such additional facilities.'

Magistrates' names

The names of magistrates dealing with a case must be given by the court to the media and public. The High Court made this clear in 1987 in *R v Felixstowe Justices, ex p Leigh,* cited above. In that judgment, Lord Justice Watkins said any attempt to give magistrates anonymity was inimical to the proper administration of justice, adding: 'There is, in my view, no such person known to the law as the anonymous JP'.

Defendants' names, charges and other details

The Ministry of Justice commends the practice of magistrates courts making available to journalists the daily lists of defendants due in court. A Home Office circular (no. 80/1989) said these should contain each defendant's name, age, address, the charge he/she faces and, where known, his/her occupation. The Judicial College's guidance makes clear that court staff will not breach data protection law by giving the media this information. The guidance allows the information to be provided by phone or by a clerk in court.

see Useful Websites below for guidance and protocol

A protocol issued by the Courts Service in 2009 says: 'Crown Court staff are encouraged to cooperate with local newspapers when they make enquiries'.

It is unclear if qualified privilege protects a fair and accurate media report of court list information, should anyone sue for libel if an error in it is published. A journalist at a court hearing should quote the defendant's details and charge(s) as given at the hearing, and not rely on the list. A report of the hearing will be protected by privilege, if the defence's requirements are met.

see ch. 21 on privilege

Crown court lists can be accessed from an internet service, www.courtserve.net/ as well as being seen at the courts, but give less information than those of magistrates courts.

The Ministry also approves of magistrates courts supplying local media with copies of court 'registers', which briefly record each day's details of convicted defendants and punishments. It is unclear whether privilege protects a media report based on a register, should the register be inaccurate. But it is common for newspapers to publish reports based on the information supplied. In 2008 the Government announced that magistrates courts would give the media lists and registers free of charge.

A defendant's details should be given in court

The Home Office, in circular no. 78/1967 and in a similar circular in 1969, recommended that defendants' names and addresses should be stated orally in magistrates courts. The 1967 circular said: 'A person's address is as much part of his description as his name. There is, therefore, a strong public interest in facilitating press reports that correctly describe persons involved.' The High Court ruled in 1988 that a defendant's address should normally be stated in court (*R v Evesham Justices, ex p McDonagh* [1988] QB 553; [1988] 1 All ER 371).

The Judicial College guidance says: 'Announcement in open court of names and addresses enables the precise identification vital to distinguish a defendant from someone in the locality who bears the same name and avoids inadvertent defamation.'

Facts of an admitted case should be stated

If a defendant pleads guilty to a charge the prosecution should state in open court the facts of the offence, before any sentence is imposed, so that the public and media can know the circumstances. This requirement is imposed by Part III.26 of the Consolidated Criminal Practice Direction.

Details of witnesses in criminal cases

A Home Office statement on standards of witness care, issued in 1998, said that unless it was necessary for evidential purposes, defence and prosecution witnesses should not be required to disclose their addresses in open court.

Fines

A public register shows if fines imposed by criminal courts are unpaid, see below.

Journalists' access to documents used in court cases

Journalists can safely report information from documents as read out in a court's public proceedings or officially provided by the court, provided any reporting restriction in place is obeyed. But there are contempt risks in publishing other information gleaned from case documents, as explained in chapter 11.

see ch. 21 on privilege

A media organisation may face a libel action if it publishes defamatory matter from a document not read out in open court, unless the document was officially made available.

Access to material in criminal cases

Journalists covering court cases and preparing background features for when they end often have help from the police and prosecutors because it is in the public interest for cases to be fully aired in media reports. The Crown Prosecution Service (CPS) in 2005 issued a protocol which says that material which the prosecution had relied on in a trial, and which *should* normally be released to the media included:

see Useful Websites, below, for the protocol

- maps and photographs, including custody photos of defendants, and diagrams produced in court;
- videos showing crime scenes;
- videos of property seized, for example weapons, drugs, stolen goods;
- sections of transcripts of interviews which were read to the court;
- videos or photographs showing reconstructions of the crime;
- CCTV footage of the defendant, subject to copyright issues.

The protocol also says that material which *might* be released following consideration by the CPS, in consultation with the police, victims, witnesses and others directly affected by the case, such as family members, included:

- CCTV footage showing the defendant and victim, or the victim alone, which the jury and public had seen in court, subject to copyright;
- video and audio tapes of police interviews with defendants, victims and witnesses;
- victim and witness statements.

The protocol also enables the media to ask the CPS head of strategic communications to become involved in the event of a dispute over disclosure.

But in 2010 the High Court confirmed that the media had no automatic right of access to documents in criminal cases. It refused to allow *The Guardian* access to documents used in an extradition hearing, even though such hearings rely heavily on documents (*R (on the application of Guardian News and Media Ltd) v City of Westminster Magistrates Court* [2010] EWHC 3376 (Admin)).

Access to documents in civil cases

The Civil Procedure Rules (CPR) cover county courts, the High Court and the Court of Appeal, Civil Division. These allow non-parties, such as journalists, access to documents filed with the court in civil claims lodged after October 2, 2006, when rule changes took effect.

see Useful Websites, below, for these rules

This access is important, as civil cases are now largely conducted by reference to documents rather than by the systematic taking of oral evidence. As chapter 12 explains, a civil trial may be impossible to report meaningfully if a reporter has not read key documents.

Pending and ongoing civil trials

Part 5.4C of the CPR says any person who pays the prescribed fee may see a civil court's register of claims – that is, its list of cases – and, as a general rule, can obtain a copy of any 'statement of case' if the relevant claim has been listed for a hearing and all defendants have filed acknowledgements of service or defences.

'Statement of case', which is defined in Part 2.3, means the claim form, particulars of claim (if not in the claim form), defence, and also any counterclaim or reply to the defence. For further detail, see Part 16 of the CPR.

'Further information documents' supplied in response to a request under Part 18 of the rules are also included in a statement of case.

Case study

The Journal newspaper was able to publish the story of a footballer's dispute with his former landlords because reporter Emma King asked Newcastle county court if she could see the claim form.

Former Sunderland player El Hadji Diouf had been taken to court by the landlords. They said he owed them £12,000 but agreed a settlement with him before the case was due to start, which included a confidentiality clause. Emma asked the court if she could see the claim form as it was a public document. She argued it was in the public interest to publish the allegations in it. Diouf's barrister initially opposed her request, citing the confidentiality agreement. But he was told by Judge Christopher Walton that a report of the case would be in the public interest because the footballer was a well-known figure (*Holdthefrontpage* website, May 13, 2011).

The Court of Appeal has ruled that if a party to a civil court case objects to a document being made available for publication, a court will require 'specific reasons' why the party will be damaged by its publication, and that 'simple assertions of confidentiality', even if supported by both parties in the case, should not prevail (*Lilly Icos Ltd v Pfizer Ltd* [2002] EWCA Civ 02).

A non-party may obtain a copy of any other document filed with the court if it gives permission. But a party or any person identified in a statement of case may apply to the court for restrictions on access to such documents.

Witness statements

A statement of case does not include witness statements. But Part 32.13 says: 'A witness statement which stands as evidence-in-chief is open to inspection during the course of the trial unless the court otherwise directs'. This enables public access during the course of the trial to written evidence relied on in court but not read out. But the court may rule that a witness statement should not be made available because of the interests of justice, the public interest or the nature of medical evidence or confidential information, or because of the need to protect the interests of any child or protected party.

See also p. 164 on access to documents after a civil case is concluded.

Interlocutory hearings and judicial reviews

The CPR rules on access to documents apply to interlocutory hearings (*Cleveland Bridge UK Ltd v Multiplex Constructions (UK) Ltd [2005] EWHC 2101 (TCC)*). They also apply to judicial reviews (*R (on the application of Corner House Research and Campaign Against Arms Trade) v Director of the Serious Fraud Office and BAe Systems plc* (Interested Party) [2008] EWHC 246 (Admin)); *Media Lawyer*, February 19, 2008).

! Remember

Qualified privilege will protect media reports of documents made available to the media as copies, or for public inspection, by a court, if the defence's requirements are met. (See chapter 21 on privilege.) Family courts have their own procedural rules, which say that no document shall be disclosed other than to a limited range of people – see chapter 13.

Skeleton arguments

Each side in a civil case draws up a skeleton argument, a document summarising their arguments in law. Lord Justice Judge, as he then was, said in the Court of Appeal in 2003 that barristers should give journalists copies of the skeleton arguments if asked to do so. He said the principle of open justice led inexorably to the conclusion that skeleton arguments, or those parts adopted by counsel and treated by the court as forming part of an oral submission, should be disclosed (*R v Howell* [2003] EWCA Crim 486).

Judgments and orders

The Practice Direction which supplements Part 39 of the Civil Procedure Rules states that when a hearing takes place in open court members of the public can obtain a transcript of any judgment given or a copy of any order made, subject to payment of the appropriate fee. When a judgment is given or an order is made in a private hearing, a non-party wanting a copy will need permission from the judge involved.

Case study

Mr Justice Jacob said in the Chancery Division in January 1998 that, with very rare exceptions, and even when a hearing had been in private, no judgment could be regarded as a secret document (*Forbes v Smith* [1998] 1 All ER 973).

See www.mcnaes.com ch. 12 for information about bankruptcy records and www.mcnaes.com ch. 13 for divorce records.

Access to statements of case and witness statements after a civil case concludes

The High Court ruled in 2004 that anyone, including a journalist, can obtain access to witness statements relating to a case which has concluded – including a case settled without a judgment (*Chan U Seek v Alvis Vehicles Ltd and Guardian Newspapers* [2004] EWHC 3092 (Ch)).

see www.mcnaes.com ch. 14 for an outline of this case

However, a party to a case can object to such access. If a judge holds a hearing to decide the access issue, costs could be awarded against a journalist or media organisation whose application fails.

Public register of monetary judgments, orders and fines

see Useful Websites, below

A public register shows the names and addresses of people and businesses with county court and High Court monetary judgments against them, if these sums were not paid within a required timescale. The register also shows if these are recorded as being paid later or as still unpaid. This information stays on the register for six years. It is run by the Registry Trust and can be searched online. Not all High Court judgments are shown.

The register has been extended to include records of:

- fines which were not paid quickly, or which remain unpaid, after being imposed in criminal cases by magistrates courts or Crown courts;
- Child Support Agency liability orders;
- tribunals' 'enforced' awards – sums owed after a tribunal has ordered them to be paid, for example after a successful claim at an employment tribunal.

see ch. 17 on tribunals

A fair and accurate report of matter on the register is protected from a libel action by qualified privilege if the requirements of the defence are met. Take care to understand what the register shows.

see ch. 21, p. 268

Recap of major points

- A journalist arguing against being excluded from a court represents the wider public's interest in open justice.
- Common law, statute and courts' procedural rules enshrine the open justice principle, but do allow courts to sit in private in some circumstances.
- Courts should normally give reporters magistrates' names, and defendants' details in open court.
- Court staff should help the media check defendants' details.

- A protocol enables the media access to some types of prosecution material, for example photos and video footage, to help them report a trial.
- The Civil Procedure Rules enable journalists to get copies of and inspect documents in civil cases.

((•)) Useful Websites

www.judiciary.gov.uk/publications-and-reports/guidance/2011/crown-court-reporting-restrictions-guidance-2009/

Guidance on reporting restrictions, published by the Judicial College (formerly the Judicial Studies Board), the Newspaper Society, the Society of Editors and Times Newspapers Ltd

www.justice.gov.uk/guidance/courts-and-tribunals/courts/procedure-rules/criminal/rules-menu.htm

Criminal Procedure Rules 2011

www.justice.gov.uk/guidance/courts-and-tribunals/courts/procedure-rules/criminal/practice-direction/pd_consolidated.htm

Consolidated Criminal Practice Direction

www.justice.gov.uk/guidance/courts-and-tribunals/courts/procedure-rules/civil/menus/rules.htm

Civil Procedure Rules and Practice Directions

www.newspapersoc.org.uk/sites/default/files/PDF/Protocol-pub-crim-just-oct05.pdf

'Publicity and the Criminal Justice System' – protocol for release of prosecution material to the media

www.societyofeditors.co.uk/page-view.php?pagename=Count-registers

'Protocol for sharing court registers and court lists with local newspapers'

www.trustonline.org.uk/about-us/

Registry Trust public register which shows unpaid fines

15

Challenging the courts

Chapter summary

Courts often restrict media coverage of cases, and journalists must be prepared to challenge invalid or overly broad restrictions – they may be the only people in court arguing for the open justice principle discussed in the previous chapter. This chapter explains the case law journalists can cite when opposing reporting restrictions, and how to make challenges.

Why a challenge may be needed

A criminal or civil court may try to restrict reporting of a case when it has no power to do so, or to impose a restriction which is valid but wider than necessary.

The benefits of open justice are best protected by unrestricted reporting. A journalist challenging a proposed or existing reporting restriction should remind the court of those benefits as well as raising specific points about the particular case. Journalists challenging possible exclusion from a court should also refer to the explanation of those benefits in chapter 14.

It is an established principle that any court should only impose the minimum reporting restriction needed to achieve its objective. The Master of the Rolls, Lord Neuberger, said in the Court of Appeal in 2011: 'As has been stated on many occasions, court hearings should take place in public and should be freely reported unless justice cannot be done on that basis in the particular case, and in that event, *the court should ensure that the restrictions on access and reporting are the minimum necessary to enable justice to be done in that case*' (emphasis added) (*Elena Ambrosiadou v Martin Coward* [2011] EWCA (Civ) 409).

A reporting restriction must be obeyed

Reporting restrictions, even if they are invalid or too broad, must be obeyed unless the court amends or lifts them (*Lakah Group and Ramy Lakah v Al Jazeera Satellite Channel* [2002] EWHC 2500; [2002] All ER (D) 383 (Nov) (QB)).

The media's right to be heard

A court considering imposing reporting restrictions should hear representations from a media organisation or a journalist opposing or querying a reporting restriction or a decision to sit in private.

Lord Bingham, then Lord Chief Justice, said in the High Court in 2000 that there was nothing to stop magistrates from hearing a representative of the press and that a reporter could 'save the court from falling into error' (*McKerry v Teesdale and Wear Valley Justices* (2000) 164 JP 355; [2000] Crim LR 594).

The principle that a court should give the media the opportunity to make representations about restrictions is recognised in Part 1.3.2 of the Consolidated Criminal Practice Direction and Part 16 of the Criminal Procedure Rules 2011 (SI 2011/1709), which cover magistrates and Crown courts.

see Useful Websites below for Direction and Rules

Notice of applications for restrictions and of opposition to them

Part 16 requires that parties applying for the imposition of a reporting restriction, or for a court hearing to be held partly or entirely in private, should give the media advance notice if the court directs this. This version of the rules came into force in October 2011. It may be some time before giving the media notice – and therefore allowing it time to prepare argument against such applications – becomes established, general practice in all courts. The rules also impose obligations on media organisations to apply 'as soon as reasonably practicable' if they wish to oppose the imposition of a reporting or access restriction, or its continuation, and to give notice to the parties (for example, the defence and prosecution in a criminal case) that such representations are to be made. The rules give the courts discretion to hear applications for restrictions, or media representations against them, made without notice and made verbally rather than in writing.

see www.mcnaes.com ch. 15 for the details of these Rules

! Remember

A journalist opposing the application for a reporting or access restriction, or its continuation, should tell the court if he/she was disadvantaged because no notice was given of it. The court may allow more time for him/her to prepare argument.

The media should be told of a restriction made

The Court of Appeal has said that when an oral order is made restricting reporting, a written copy should be drawn up as soon as possible and made available for inspection at the relevant court's office. Each court's daily list should make clear that an order applies to a case (*R v Central Criminal Court, ex p Crook and Godwin* [1995] 1 All ER 537).

Part 16 of the Criminal Procedure Rules 2011 says that if a reporting or access restriction is made, a notice of this should be displayed somewhere prominent in the courtroom's vicinity and communicated to reporters 'by such other arrangement as the Lord Chancellor directs'.

Judicial College guidance for criminal courts

((•)) see Useful Websites below for this guidance

Guidance entitled 'Reporting Restrictions in the Criminal Courts', published by the Judicial College, has been drawn up by media organisations and the judiciary, and endorsed by the Lord Chief Justice, Lord Judge. It is extremely useful in supporting challenges to actual or proposed reporting restrictions or threatened exclusions.

It says (its page numbers given):

- courts should invite media representations when first considering making orders to restrict reporting or exclude the media (pp. 4, 5 and 14);
- courts should hear media representations as soon as possible, because of the importance of contemporaneous court reporting and the perishable nature of news (pp. 6 and 14);
- courts should recognise that the media have expertise in reporting restrictions and are well placed to represent the wider public interest in open justice (p. 14);
- courts should check, before making an order, that no automatic reporting restriction already applies – if one does, an order is unnecessary (p. 14);
- the need for an order must be 'convincingly established' (pp. 6 and 15);
- any order should put in writing as soon as possible, giving its precise terms, legal basis, scope and duration (pp. 5 and 14);
- courts should have procedures to notify the media that an order has been made, and give them copies of the written notice (p. 5);
- any media argument for changing or lifting an order already made should be heard as soon as practicable (p. 14).

D Common law

A court has no common law power to restrict reporting – see *Independent Publishing Company Limited v Attorney General of Trinidad and Tobago and*

Another ((PC) [2005] 1 AC 190; *The Times*, June 24, 2004). A court has no common law power to order that something said in open court cannot be reported, or to make orders limiting what the media may report other than by way of court reporting. The Privy Council said at paragraph 67 of the judgment: 'Their Lordships likewise conclude that if the court is to have the power to make orders against the public at large it must be conferred by legislation; it cannot be found in the common law.' As explained in chapter 14, courts do have limited common law power to exclude the public (and journalists).

Methods of challenge

Journalists intending to challenge proposed or actual reporting restrictions or exclusion of the media from a court should raise the issue as soon as possible.

An approach to the court by a reporter or editor

In court, the reporter should approach the clerk as the first step. This can be done, if a hearing is under way, by asking an usher to pass the clerk a note.

Journalists can and should refer to the Judicial College guidance.

If an order has already been made the clerk can be asked to:

- supply it in written form, if it has not already been provided or displayed;
- specify in writing why it was made, if the order does not make this clear;
- state in writing the statute and section under which it was made, if the order does not state this – although a court may have used, or purported to have used, common law power to make the order.

Such a request might prompt the court to reconsider the order, especially if a reporter – or an editor, by fax, letter or email – quotes case law against it.

Article 10 of the European Convention on Human Rights guarantees the right to freedom of expression and to receive and impart information. Journalists opposing a restriction or exclusion should remind the court of these rights.

ch. 1 explains Article 10

Raising a query or challenge in person, or by an editor writing to the court, has the advantage that doing so may resolve the matter quickly, and is the cheapest method as there is no need to involve a lawyer.

A reporter whose argument is being opposed by both the defence and prosecution should remind the court of the warning by Court of Appeal judge Sir Christopher Staughton that '...when both sides agreed that information should be kept from the public, that was when the court had to be most vigilant' (*Ex p P* [1998] CA Transcript 431, (1998) *The Times*, 31 March, quoted with approval in the Supreme Court in the second paragraph of *Guardian News and Media Ltd's Application* [2010] UKSC 1).

Costs

Courts do not normally make costs orders against journalists or a media employer when these informal challenges are made, even if they fail. But it is important to make the challenge as early as possible.

Challenges taken to a higher court

If a challenge by a reporter or an editor fails, the court's decision can be challenged in a higher court.

Judicial review of restrictions imposed by magistrates

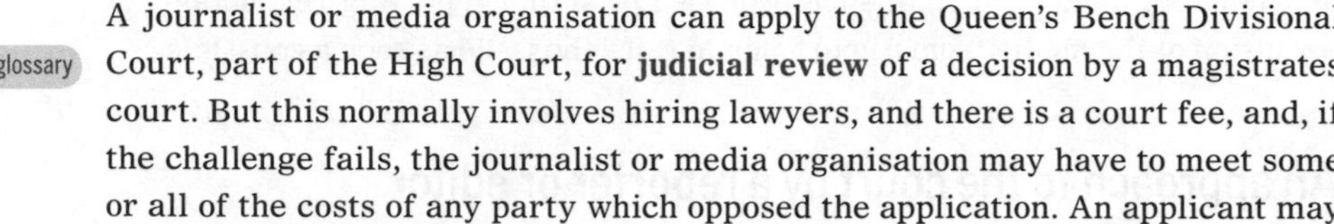

→glossary

A journalist or media organisation can apply to the Queen's Bench Divisional Court, part of the High Court, for **judicial review** of a decision by a magistrates court. But this normally involves hiring lawyers, and there is a court fee, and, if the challenge fails, the journalist or media organisation may have to meet some or all of the costs of any party which opposed the application. An applicant may have to bear its own costs even when successful.

Crown court restrictions can be challenged at the Court of Appeal

Decisions by Crown court judges to impose reporting restrictions or exclude the media can be challenged under section 159 of the Criminal Justice Act 1988, which gives the media a route of appeal to the Court of Appeal.

The disadvantages are that the appeal may not be considered quickly, so a story may have lost any news value, and will normally involve hiring lawyers, paying a court fee, and, even if it succeeds, costs.

An appeal against a decision to hear a case in private can only be made in writing – appellants or their lawyers have no right to appear in person before the Court of Appeal to argue the case (Criminal Procedure Rules 2011, Rules 65 and 69 (SI 2011/1709).

ch. 8, p. 85 explains courts martial

A provision similar to section 159 was included in the Armed Forces Act 2006 to allow media appeals against an order restricting reporting of, or banning journalists from, courts martial.

Convention rights of anonymity

see also p. 125

As explained in chapter 11, the High Court has banned the media from reporting new identities given to a few notorious defendants after release from prison.

It is exceptionally rare for courts to use this power, and rare for a court to ban the media from identifying a defendant facing trial.

The Supreme Court has said that in an extreme case, a court has power to ban the media from identifying a witness or 'a party', such as a defendant, if doing so is necessary to protect that person or his/her family from peril to their lives and safety (*Application by Guardian News and Media Ltd and others in Ahmed and others v HM Treasury* [2010] UKSC 1). The risk could arise because of what the person had said about, for example, 'some powerful criminal organisation'. It said the sources of a court's power to make an anonymity order to protect such a person from 'a threat of violence arising out of its proceedings' were the person's rights under Article 2 (the right to life) and Article 3 (the right which protects against torture) of the European Convention on Human Rights. But it removed anonymity that lower courts had given four men who were appealing against orders made under anti-terrorism law to freeze their assets, ruling that, in the case's circumstances, the men's right to respect for privacy and family life under Article 8 of the Convention did not override the media's rights under Article 10, because there was a 'powerful, public interest' in identifying them in any report of the 'important' proceedings about their frozen assets.

Case study

A man was charged in 2009 with withholding information after a policeman's murder in Northern Ireland. He wanted anonymity in reports of his court appearances. Police had told him he was at risk of violence from the Continuity IRA. A district judge at Lisburn magistrates court said evidence showed the man's identity was already known to those who might wish to harm him, so there was no justification for giving him anonymity. The High Court rejected the man's appeal. But it also ruled that a magistrates court *did* have power to make an anonymity order if one was needed under Article 2 to protect a defendant from 'a real and immediate risk' of violence. (*Re RA's Application for Judicial Review* [2010] NIQB 27).

p. 175 explains such risk

! Remember

The High Court has used the Convention in the context of family law to ban media reports from identifying a defendant.

see www.mcnaes.com ch. 13

Discretionary reporting restrictions

Courts have discretionary powers to restrict reports of proceedings. The main ones are those under sections 11 and 4(2) of the Contempt of Court Act 1981, and section 39 of the Children and Young Persons Act 1933. Orders under section 11 of the Contempt of Court Act 1981 allow a court to prohibit publication of information – such as a defendant's name or address – which has already been withheld from the public, while section 4(2) allows a court to order the postponement of reports of all or parts of proceedings because of the risk of prejudicing those or other pending proceedings.

Other discretionary restrictions are contained in other legislation.

Section 11

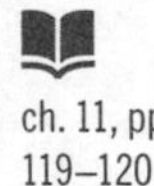

ch. 11, pp. 119–120 explains section 11 orders

Courts have common law powers to order that a name or other information should be withheld from the public during proceedings. A court which uses this power can make an order under section 11 of the Contempt of Court Act 1981 indefinitely banning publication of the name or information such as a defendant's address in connection with reports of the proceedings.

'In connection with the proceedings'

A section 11 order only bans publication of a name or matter 'in connection with the proceedings'. It does not – for example – stop the media referring to someone by name, or to their address, in other contexts.

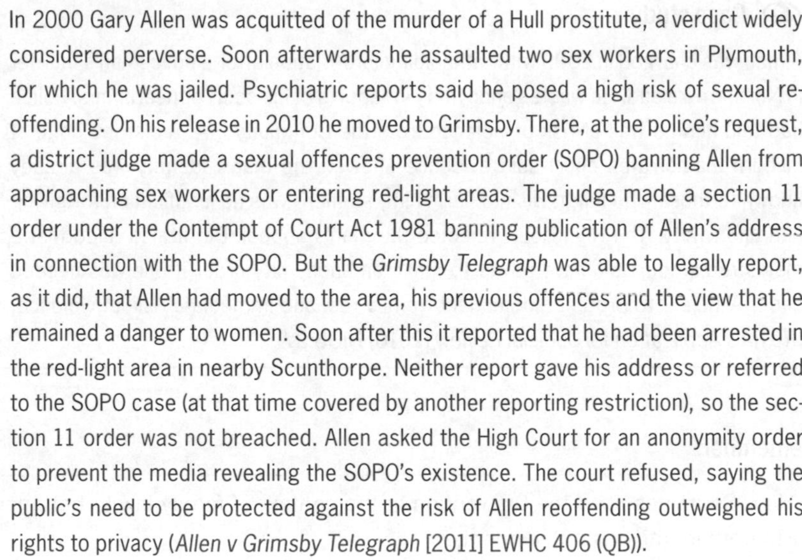

see also ch. 10, p. 109 on SOPOs, and p. 176

Case study

In 2000 Gary Allen was acquitted of the murder of a Hull prostitute, a verdict widely considered perverse. Soon afterwards he assaulted two sex workers in Plymouth, for which he was jailed. Psychiatric reports said he posed a high risk of sexual re-offending. On his release in 2010 he moved to Grimsby. There, at the police's request, a district judge made a sexual offences prevention order (SOPO) banning Allen from approaching sex workers or entering red-light areas. The judge made a section 11 order under the Contempt of Court Act 1981 banning publication of Allen's address in connection with the SOPO. But the *Grimsby Telegraph* was able to legally report, as it did, that Allen had moved to the area, his previous offences and the view that he remained a danger to women. Soon after this it reported that he had been arrested in the red-light area in nearby Scunthorpe. Neither report gave his address or referred to the SOPO case (at that time covered by another reporting restriction), so the section 11 order was not breached. Allen asked the High Court for an anonymity order to prevent the media revealing the SOPO's existence. The court refused, saying the public's need to be protected against the risk of Allen reoffending outweighed his rights to privacy (*Allen v Grimsby Telegraph* [2011] EWHC 406 (QB)).

Has the name or matter been withheld from the public?

A section 11 order cannot be made if the name or matter has already been mentioned in public proceedings in the case. In *R v Arundel Justices, ex p Westminster Press* ([1985] 2 All ER 390; [1985] 1 WLR 708) the magistrates made a section 11 order banning publication of the name and address of a man charged with burglary offences. The High Court held in a judicial review that the magistrates had no power to make the order as the defendant's details had already been given in public – when the clerk routinely checked the information with the defendant in the first hearing.

A court which *has* made a deliberate decision to withhold a name or matter from its public proceedings can use a section 11 order to forbid its publication after it is mentioned by mistake (*Re Times Newspapers Ltd* [2007] EWCA Crim 1925, *Re Trinity Mirror plc and others* [2008] QB 770; [2008] EWCA Crim 50).

Is anonymity necessary for justice to be done?

Section 11 orders may only be made when they are necessary in the interests of the administration of justice. In *Attorney General v Leveller Magazine Ltd* ([1979] AC 440 at 449–450), Lord Diplock said that departure from the open justice rule was only justified:

www. mcnaes. com ch. 14 explains this case

> “where the nature or circumstances of the particular proceeding are such that the application of the general rule in its entirety would frustrate or render impracticable the administration of justice or would damage some other public interest for whose protection Parliament has made some statutory derogation from the rule.”

The High Court in Northern Ireland said in 1997: 'The use of the words "some other public interest" indicates that Lord Diplock had in mind the protection of the public interest in the administration of justice rather than the private welfare of those caught up in that administration' (*R v Newtownabbey Magistrates court, ex p Belfast Telegraph Newspapers Ltd, The Times,* August 27 [1997] NI 309).

Someone else may be wrongly perceived as the defendant

The Judicial College guidance says banning publication of a defendant's address creates the risk that the public might think, wrongly, that someone entirely unconnected with the case, but with the same or a similar name, is the defendant. Judge David Clarke, Honorary Recorder of Liverpool, said in *R v Thomas Carroll* (*Media Lawyer,* January 2001): 'This is a real danger, particularly where the defendants bear common names such as my own'.

Section 11 is not to protect the 'comfort and feelings' of defendants

A section 11 order should not be made for the 'comfort and feelings' of a defendant – *R v Evesham Justices, ex p McDonagh* [1988] QB 553; [1988] 1 All ER 371. Evesham magistrates agreed that a defendant's address should not be given in court because he feared harassment from his ex-wife, and made a section 11 order banning its publication. But in a judicial review, Lord Justice Watkins said that while no statutory provision said a defendant's address had publicly to be given in court, 'it is well established practice that, save for a justifiable reason, it must be'. He said:

> “There are undoubtedly many people who find themselves defending criminal charges who for all manner of reasons would like to keep unrevealed their identity, their home address in particular. Indeed, I go so far as to say that in the vast majority of cases, in magistrates' courts anyway, defendants would like their identity to be unrevealed and would be capable of advancing seemingly plausible reasons why that should be so. But section 11 was not enacted for the comfort and feelings of defendants.”

It was, he added, only in rare circumstances, conforming to those set out in *Attorney General v Leveller* (see above), that a court would protect a defendant from publicity.

Section 11 is not to protect a defendant's business interests

A section 11 order cannot not be used to protect a defendant's business interests, the High Court held in *R v Dover Justices, ex p Dover District Council and Wells* (1991) 156 JP 433.

Section 11 anonymity is not to protect a defendant's children

A section 11 order cannot be used to protect the children of a defendant in a criminal case. The Court of Appeal ruled in 2008 that Croydon Crown court was wrong to use an order to stop the media naming a man who had admitted 20 charges of downloading child pornography from the internet. He had been named in open court throughout the case. The judge who made the order justified it by saying the defendant's daughters, aged 6 and 8, who were neither victims nor witnesses in the case, would suffer significant harm if their father was identified. The Court of Appeal said the judge was wrong to conclude that the children's privacy rights under Article 8 of the European Convention outweighed those of the media and the public under Article 10. At the Court of Appeal Sir Igor Judge, who was then President of the Queen's Bench Division said: 'there is nothing in this case to distinguish the plight of the defendant's children from that of a massive group of children of persons convicted of offences relating to child pornography', adding that allowing the defendant anonymity would be 'to the overwhelming disadvantage of public confidence in the criminal justice system' (*In Re Trinity Mirror and others,* cited above).

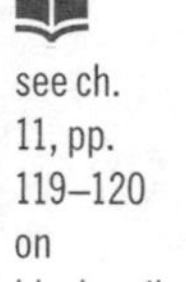

see ch. 11, pp. 119–120 on blackmail cases

Anonymity for witnesses in criminal cases

Courts routinely use section 11 to provide anonymity for alleged blackmail victims. Lord Woolf, then Master of the Rolls, said in 1998 that, apart from in blackmail and rape cases, there had to be 'some objective foundation' to a claim for entitlement to section 11 anonymity (*R v Legal Aid Board, ex p Kaim Todner* [1999] QB 966; [1998] 3 All ER 541, CA).

Case study

A section 11 order made by a Crown court judge giving anonymity to a witness on the grounds that the stress of publicity might cause her to relapse into heroin addiction was criticised in the High Court in 1984. Lord Justice Brown said: 'There must be many occasions when witnesses in criminal cases are faced with embarrassment as a result of facts which are elicited in the course of proceedings and of allegations made which are often without any real substance. It is, however, part of the essential nature of British criminal justice that cases shall be tried in public and reported and this consideration must outweigh the individual interests of particular persons' (*R v Central Criminal Court, ex p Crook* (1984) *The Times*, November 8).

Anonymity and risk of attack?

Lawyers sometimes urge courts to give a defendant or witnesses anonymity, or ban publication of their address, on the ground that the individual is at risk of violence from criminals or vigilantes.

Case law says:

- A court asked to give a defendant or witness anonymity, or ban publication of their address, on safety grounds must be satisfied that the risk to their safety is 'real and immediate'.
- This risk must have an objective, verifiable basis, be backed by evidence to the court, and not be assessed merely on the person's subjective fears.

If allegations against a defendant are already public knowledge, there is no justification for restricting media reports.

The test of whether a claimed risk is real and immediate is 'not readily satisfied'. See *Re Officer L*, discussed below. The test is the same, whether the person said to be at risk is a defendant or witness, and whether the anonymity sought is by use of section 11 or an order based directly on Convention rights.

Police and prison officer defendants – risk of attack

Lawyers defending police or prison officers often argue that they should have anonymity or that the media should not publish their home addresses, claiming that the crime of which they are accused or the general nature of their job or duties, put them at risk of attack or harassment from vengeful criminals.

Case study

Two senior police officers were charged in 2010 with misconduct in a public office after alleged improper interference in prosecutions for speeding. Aldershot magistrates, after hearing an objection from a reporter, refused the officers' request for a section 11 order banning publication of their home addresses. The officers sought judicial review, arguing that publication would put them at risk because of their past involvement in investigating serious crime, including undercover operations. The High Court, refusing to make an order, noted that the Press Association, which with a regional media group had argued against a ban, had shown that anyone could use internet records of electoral registers, at a cost of £4.95, to discover the officers' addresses within five minutes. Any risk to the officers' safety, if it existed, would be from someone who targeted them, who would be not be deterred merely because the media had not published the addresses, it said, adding that the type of charges the officers faced were unlikely to provoke a vigilante attack (*R (on the application of Harper and Johncox) v Aldershot Magistrates' Court and others* [2010] EWHC 1319 (Admin)).

Police officers as witnesses: risk of attack

In 2007 the House of Lords approved the approach taken by a tribunal of inquiry established to investigate the murder of a Catholic in Northern Ireland which decided not to allow anonymity for some police witnesses who said they feared for their lives. One allegation was that police could have prevented the murder. Lord Carswell referred to the established criterion that there should be 'a real and immediate risk' to life to justify anonymity. A real risk was one which was objectively verified and an immediate risk was one which was present and continuing, he said, adding: 'It is in my opinion clear that the criterion is and should be one that is not readily satisfied: in other words, the threshold is high' (*Re Officer L* [2007] UKHL 36; [2007] 4 All ER 965; [2007] All ER (D) 484 (Jul)).

Police firearms officers involved in fatal shootings while on duty have been given anonymity at inquests – *R (on the application of Officer A and another) v HM Coroner for Inner South London* [2004] All ER (D) 288 (Jun).

Section 11 and sexual offences prevention orders

see also ch. 10, p. 109 on SOPOs, and p. 172, below, on the *Allen* case

Police can apply in civil law for a 'sexual offences prevention order' (SOPO) to be made against a convicted sexual offender whose behaviour suggests he may reoffend. Home Office guidance issued in 2010 says it is normal practice for some police forces to ask magistrates, at the outset of the application hearing, to make a section 11 order to stop the offender being identified in reports, and suggests that any disorder arising from public knowledge of his involvement in the SOPO hearing would make him more likely to abscond. But it adds: 'It is, of course, for the court to decide whether such a prohibition is necessary'. The media can argue that a SOPO case needs unrestricted reporting because the public should be able to recognise such offenders.

Section 11 anonymity in civil cases

In *R v Legal Aid Board, ex p Kaim Todner*, cited above, Lord Woolf said that in general, parties and witnesses in civil cases had to accept the embarrassment, damage to their reputation and possible consequential loss which could be inherent in being involved in litigation, and that their protection was that normally a public judgment would refute unfounded allegations.

In a few civil cases courts have ruled that the potential psychological harm to a claimant of his/her medical condition being made public justified an anonymity order. See *H v Ministry of Defence* [1991] 2 QB 103; [1991] 2 All ER.

Section 4(2) orders

Courts have power to postpone publication of media reports of all or part of a case under section 4(2) of the Contempt of Court Act 1981, to 'avoid a substantial risk of prejudice' to later stages of the same case or to other cases pending or imminent.

ch. 18, pp. 228–229 explains section 4(2)

Postponement orders frequently mean that when the restriction no longer applies the case receives substantially less coverage than it would otherwise have done, especially if the order means that coverage of a sequence of trials has, because of the practicalities of media production, to be compressed into one day's publication on the day the last trial ends. Many details will never be published and the benefits of open justice will have been eroded.

see ch. 14 on the benefits of open justice

In 2006 the head of the Metropolitan Police's counter-terrorism branch, Peter Clarke, said section 4(2) orders were causing long delays in publication of reports of terrorism trials, which had led to myths about the terrorism threat being exaggerated.

Some legal observers say recognition of such concerns has made senior members of the judiciary willing to give greater weight to arguments that juries can be trusted, even in a series of related trials, to consider each charge on its own merits, whatever has been published previously.

see also the ruling in *R v B*, the *Dhiran Barot* case, explained on p. 179

Journalists challenging a section 4(2) order should refer the court to pp. 20 and 21 of the Judicial College guidance.

A court should hear media representations on section 4(2) orders

The High Court has said that any court, including a magistrates court, has discretionary power to hear media representations when it is considering making or continuing a section 4(2) order, and said the media were the best qualified to represent the public interest in publicity (*R v Clerkenwell Metropolitan Stipendiary Magistrates, ex p Telegraph plc* [1993] QB 462; [1993] 2 All ER 183).

In *R v Beck, ex p Daily Telegraph* ([1993] 2 All ER 177, 181) Lord Justice Farquharson said the best course was for a judge to make a limited order under section 4(2) for, say, two days, to give the press time to make representations.

The terms of section 4(2) orders must be precise

see Useful Websites below for the Direction

The Consolidated Criminal Practice Direction says a section 4(2) order must be put in writing either by the judge personally or by the clerk of the court under the judge's directions, and must include:

- its precise scope;
- the time at which it ceases to have effect; and
- the specific purpose of the order.

The risk of prejudice must be substantial

A section 4(2) order should only be made if the risk of prejudice to current or pending proceedings is substantial.

In 1993 in the Court of Appeal the Lord Chief Justice, Lord Taylor, said that in determining whether publication of information would cause a substantial risk of prejudice to a future trial, a court should credit that trial's jury with the will and ability to abide by the judge's direction to decide the case only on the evidence before it. The court should also bear in mind that the staying power and detail of publicity, even in cases of notoriety, were limited and that the nature of a trial was to focus the jury's minds on the evidence put before them rather than on matters outside the courtroom (*R v Beck, ex p Telegraph plc* [1993] 2 All ER 971). See also Sir Igor Judge's comments in *R v B* on juries' ability to be focused and fair, cited below.

Principles for decisions on section 4(2) orders

In *R v Sherwood, ex p Telegraph Group* [2001] EWCA Crim 1075; [2001] 1 WLR 1983, the Court of Appeal set out three principles on section 4(2) orders:

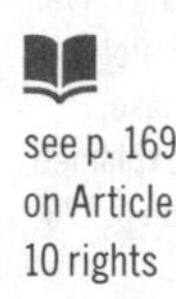

see p. 169 on Article 10 rights

(1) Unless the perceived risk of prejudice was demonstrated, no order should be made.

(2) The court had to ask whether an order was necessary under the European Convention on Human Rights. Sometimes wider considerations of public policy would come into play to justify refusing to make a section 4(2) order even though there was no other way of eliminating the prejudice anticipated.

(3) Applications for postponement orders should be approached as follows:
   (i) would reporting give rise to a substantial risk of prejudice? If not, that would be the end of the matter;
   (ii) if such a risk was perceived to exist, would an order eliminate it? If not, obviously there could be no necessity to impose such a postponement. But even if the judge was satisfied that an order would achieve the objective, he/she would have to consider whether the risk could satisfactorily be overcome by less restrictive means;
   (iii) the judge might still have to ask whether the degree of risk of prejudice contemplated should be regarded as tolerable in the sense of being the lesser of two evils, when compared to the harm which a section 4(2) order could cause to the benefits of open justice.

Risk of prejudice in sequential cases

Lord Justice Farquharson said in *R v Beck, ex p Daily Telegraph* (cited above) that the fact that an accused expected to face a second indictment after a trial of the first did not in itself justify making a section 4(2) order. It depended on all the circumstances, including the nature of the charges, the timing of the second trial and where the second trial would be heard. If substantial prejudice to the accused could be avoided by extending the period between trials, or transferring the case to another court, then that course should be followed.

Case study

In 2011 the Court of Appeal lifted a section 4(2) order which had imposed a blanket postponement on reporting a series of three murder trials, involving a total of 20 defendants, until after the end of the final trial. The trials concerned the alleged murder of a 15-year-old boy who was repeatedly stabbed by a gang who chased him into Victoria underground station, London, during the rush hour. An Old Bailey judge made the order after prosecution lawyers argued that contemporaneous media reports would increase stress for young witnesses due to testify in more than one trial, who also faced hostility for giving prosecution evidence. They also argued that the testimony of witnesses in the later trials could be influenced by media reports of the earlier ones. The Court of Appeal said that a postponement order would not prevent the witnesses' identities being known to the defendants, or to the community, and said other measures could be taken to help them give evidance. Witnesses could also be cross-examined about changes in their evidence. The principle of open justice meant that media reporting of the trials should not be postponed unless it was necessary for justice (*Re MGN and others* [2011] EWCA Crim 100, and *Media Lawyer*, January 28, 2011).

Risk of prejudice if one defendant is sentenced before others tried

In 2006 the Court of Appeal overturned a section 4(2) order postponing reporting of the sentencing of terrorist Dhiran Barot. The judge made the order on the ground that reports would prejudice the forthcoming trial of other defendants. Lawyers for the media argued that five months would elapse before that jury trial and so the 'fade factor' would mean that contemporaneous reporting of Barot's sentencing would not create a risk of serious prejudice.

ch. 18, pp. 224–225 explains the term 'fade factor'

Sir Igor Judge said in the Court of Appeal that although there was a primacy in the right to a fair trial it did not follow that a section 4(2) order should have been made. The right to a fair trial had to be balanced with the hallowed principle that the media had the freedom to act as the eyes and ears of the public. Juries had a 'passionate and profound belief in, and a commitment to, the right of a Defendant to be given a fair trial', he said, adding: 'They know that it is integral to their responsibility. It is, when all is said and done, their birthright; it is shared by each one of them with the Defendant. They guard it faithfully. The integrity of the jury is an essential feature of our trial process. Juries follow the directions which the judge will give them to focus exclusively on the evidence and to ignore anything they may have heard or read out of court' (*R v B* [2006] EWCA Crim 2692).

The possibility of retrial does not mean a hearing is 'pending or imminent'

In 2006 in Scotland Lord Macfadyen, giving the opinion of the Extra Division of the Inner House of the Court of Session, rejected convicted murderer William Beggs's argument that section 4(2) orders should postpone media reports of a court hearing in which he sought to be moved to a different jail. He claimed publicity about that case could cause a substantial risk of prejudice to any

ch. 18, p. 217 explains when appeals become 'active'

retrial in the murder case, over which he had appealed. Lord Macfadyen said a retrial, should there be one, 'cannot at this stage be said to be "pending or imminent"'.

Risk of reports of a civil case prejudicing a criminal case

In 1994 Mr Justice Lindsay refused to make a section 4(2) order postponing reporting of civil cases involving pension funds, although criminal proceedings were pending. He said: 'By framing [section 4(2)] as it did, the legislature contemplated that a risk of prejudice which could not be described as substantial had to be tolerated as the price of an open press and that if the risk was properly to be described as substantial, a postponement order did not automatically follow' (*MGN Pension Trustees Ltd v Bank of America* [1995] 2 All ER 355, Ch D).

Section 4(2) cannot be used for other types of ban

Magistrates' and Crown court judges have occasionally made section 4(2) orders for a purpose other than avoiding a substantial risk of prejudice to a current or future hearing. Such orders are invalid. For example, a section 4(2) order cannot be used to ban publication of a name or material to encourage a witness to give evidence, or to protect anybody's general welfare or safety. The Court of Appeal made this clear in *Re Trinity Mirror plc and others* and in *Re Times Newspapers Ltd*, which are cited above.

Section 4(2) orders cannot restrict reports of events outside the courtroom

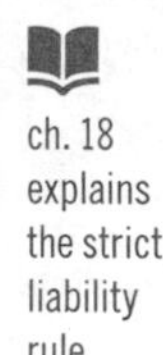

ch. 18 explains the strict liability rule

Section 4(2) refers only to postponing reports of a court's proceedings – but some courts have tried to use it temporarily to ban reporting of an external event, or a statement not made in the proceedings. Such orders are beyond the section's scope, and unnecessary because a media organisation can face proceedings under the Contempt of Court Act's strict liability rule for publishing anything which creates a substantial risk of serious prejudice to an active case. The Court of Appeal accepted in *R v B*, cited above, that editors should be trusted to make their own decisions about what was safe under that rule, saying that an important safeguard was that no responsible editor would wish to commit contempt.

The Children and Young Persons Act 1933

The Children and Young Persons Act 1933 contains two provisions dealing with anonymity for juveniles – people under the age of 18 – appearing in courts. Section 39 allows an *adult* court to make an anonymity order for a juvenile 'concerned in the proceedings', while section 49 imposes *automatic* anonymity for any juvenile appearing in a youth court. The anonymity given under either provision may be challenged.

Challenging section 39 orders

see ch. 9, pp. 94–95 for more details on section 39 orders

Section 39 gives a court discretion to order that reports of a case should not identify any specified juvenile 'concerned in the proceedings' in court. In a criminal case this covers a juvenile who is a defendant, witness or the victim/alleged victim. In a civil case it covers a juvenile who is a claimant, respondent or witness.

Courts often make section 39 orders without properly considering whether they are necessary, and make invalid orders.

Lord Justice Glidewell said a judge has discretion to hear representations from parties – including the press – with a legitimate interest in a section 39 order (*R v Central Criminal Court, ex p Crook and Godwin* [1995] 1 All ER 537).

Crown court judges tend to protect a juvenile defendant's identity with a section 39 order made pre-trial. They may consider lifting it if the juvenile is convicted. A court is less likely to lift the order after an acquittal.

Crown Prosecution Service guidance on lifting section 39 anonymity

Guidance issued by the Crown Prosecution Service to prosecutors says that the following circumstances are examples of when there is a strong public interest in favour of lifting the section 39 restrictions in the case of a convicted juvenile:

see Useful Websites below for this CPS guidance

- significant public disorder where the public will rightly need to be satisfied that offenders have been brought to justice and there is a need to deter others;
- serious offences which have undermined the public's confidence in the safety of their communities;
- hate crimes which can have a corrosive impact on the confidence of communities.

See www.mcnaes.com chapter on 'Incitement of Hate' for an outline of hate crimes.

Is the juvenile 'concerned in the proceedings'?

Some courts have made section 39 orders purporting to ban the identification of children not 'concerned in the proceedings'.

Case study

A judge at Leeds Crown court agreed to lift a section 39 order which, in effect, stopped the media identifying a woman accused of attempting to murder her 54-year-old mother. Social workers wanted the order to continue, to give anonymity to the woman's children who – the court heard – had been taunted in their community because of the case. Media organisations argued that the children were not 'concerned in the proceedings'. The woman was later acquitted (*Media Lawyer*, June 3, 2009).

Which proceedings are covered by a section 39 order?

In *R v Lee*, cited above, Lord Justice Lloyd said that the word 'proceedings' in section 39 must mean proceedings in the court making the order and not any proceedings anywhere. So, a section 39 order made in a magistrates court does not apply to reports of the case when it reaches Crown court – but the Crown court can make a new order.

An order must be clear about whom it protects

The child or children covered by a section 39 order should be clearly identified (*R v Central Criminal Court, ex p Godwin and Crook*, cited above).

There must be a good reason for a section 39 order

A court should not make a section 39 order merely because of a juvenile's age, or unthinkingly as a 'blanket' order covering all juveniles in the case.

In *R v Lee* ([1993] 2 All ER 170; [1993] 1 WLR 103, CA) Lord Justice Lloyd said in the Court of Appeal: 'There must be a good reason for making an order under section 39'. Orders should not be made automatically, he warned, adding: 'If the discretion under section 39 is too narrowly confined, we will be in danger of blurring the distinction between proceedings in the juvenile [now youth] court and proceedings in the Crown court, a distinction which Parliament clearly intended to preserve.'

In *R v Central Criminal Court, ex p W, B and C* [2001] 1 Cr App R 7, the High Court stressed the value of the deterrent effect on a juvenile robber's contemporaries of his being publicly identified as having been punished by a court.

Principles to guide a court about section 39 orders

Lord Justice Simon Brown in *R v Crown Court at Winchester, ex p B* ([2000] 1 Cr App R 11) identified seven principles a court deciding whether to make a section 39 order should consider:

(1) In deciding whether to impose or lift reporting restrictions, the court will consider whether there are good reasons for naming the defendant.

(2) It will give considerable weight to the offender's age and the potential damage to the child or young person of public identification as a criminal before he/she has the benefit or burden of adulthood.

(3) It must have regard to the welfare of the child or young person.

(4) The prospect of being named in court with the accompanying disgrace is a powerful deterrent and naming a defendant in the context of his punishment serves as a deterrent to others. These deterrents are proper objectives for the court.

(5) There is a strong public interest in open justice and in the public knowing as much as possible about what has happened in court, including the identity of those who have committed crimes.

(6) The weight to be attributed to different factors may shift at different stages of the proceedings, and, in particular, after the defendant has been found, or pleads, guilty and is sentenced. It may then be appropriate to place greater weight on the interests of the public in knowing the identity of those who have committed crimes, particularly serious and detestable crimes.

(7) The fact that an appeal has been made may be a material consideration.

Decided cases have established a number of other principles relating to the use of section 39 orders, as follows:

A section 39 order cannot validly be made in respect of a dead juvenile

Courts sometimes make section 39 orders attempting to ban the identification of dead children. Several High Court judges have said the courts do not have this power. The Judicial College guidance says that for section 39 to apply the juvenile 'must be alive' and cites in support *Re S (a child) (Identification: Restrictions on Publication)* [2005] 1 AC 593.

But a court can advise a reporter that publishing a dead child's name could infringe a section 39 order made to protect living siblings, such as where parents are accused of charges of cruelty.

((•)) See Useful Websites, below, for the Judicial College guidance.

Section 39 orders cannot specifically give adults anonymity

The Court of Appeal held in 1991 that section 39 orders could not be used to ban the publication of the identity of an adult defendant (*R v Southwark Crown Court, ex p Godwin* [1992] QB 190; [1991] 3 All ER 818).

Lord Justice Glidewell said:

> In our view, section 39 as a matter of law does not empower a court to order in terms that the names of [adult] defendants should not be published. It may be that on occasions judges will think it helpful to have some discussion about the identification of particular details and give advice.... If the inevitable effect of making an order is that it is apparent that some details, including names of [adult] defendants, may not be published because publication would breach the order, that is the practical application of the order; it is not a part of the terms of the order itself.

See ch. 9, pp. 97–98 on the reporting of familial abuse cases.

In 2005 the Court of Appeal ruled there was no power under section 39 to prohibit identification of adults charged with sexual offences against children. But it warned of the danger of publishing material which might identify the children if the adult's name was published (*R v Teesside Crown Court, ex p Gazette Media Co* [2005] EWCA Crim 1983).

Victim is too young to need section 39 anonymity

The Judicial College guidelines say: 'Age alone is not sufficient to justify imposing an order as very young children cannot be harmed by publicity of which they will be unaware ...'.

Courts have accepted that a baby or a toddler who is the victim/alleged victim of a crime does not need section 39 anonymity, because by the time they are old enough to be harmed by the case's publicity it is likely to have been forgotten.

The identity of the juvenile is already in the public domain

In *R v Cardiff Crown Court, ex p M (a minor)* (1998) 162 JP 527, DC, the High Court ruled that if a section 39 order was not made when the case was first listed, publicity identifying the juvenile might make it inappropriate to make an order at a later stage.

Section 39 cannot be used to spare a defendant's children from embarrassment

In 2008 the High Court lifted section 39 orders imposed by Highbury Corner magistrates and Inner London Crown court giving anonymity to the children of a barrister who was summarily convicted of harassing his former wife, then lost an appeal to the Crown court against the conviction. The section 39 orders prevented the media from identifying the barrister in reports of those cases, although his children were not 'concerned in the proceedings'. Lord Justice Thomas said in the High Court: 'There was no evidence of any particular harm to his children other than the obvious embarrassment of their father having been convicted of a criminal offence' (*Crawford v Director of Public Prosecutions* (2008) *The Times*, February 20). Lord Justice Thomas made clear that in making this judgment the High Court had followed the ruling in *Re Trinity Mirror plc and others* in respect of a section 11 order.

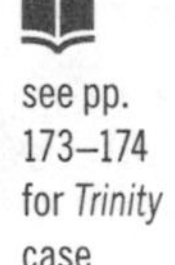
see pp. 173–174 for *Trinity* case

A section 39 order cannot be in force if the juvenile has turned 18

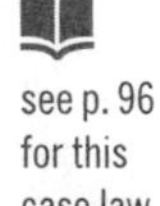
see p. 96 for this case law

A section 39 order can only be made to give anonymity to a person aged under 18. Case law on section 49 of the Act, and the wording of section 39 itself, make clear that section 39 anonymity expires when a juvenile turns 18. An order cannot be made simply because a defendant was under the age of 18 when the offence was committed.

Effect on a juvenile defendant's family

In 2000 Mr Justice Elias said in the High Court that normally there was no justification for making a section 39 anonymity order for a juvenile offender simply to spare his/her relatives from being identified in publicity about a case.

He said: 'Sadly, in any case where someone is caught up in the criminal process other members of the family who are wholly innocent of wrongdoing will be innocent casualties in the drama. They may suffer in all sorts of ways from the publicity given to another family member. But I do not consider that in the normal case that is a relevant factor or a good reason for granting a direction under section 39' (*Chief Constable of Surrey v JHG and DHG* [2002] EWHC 1129 (Admin); [2002] All ER (D) 308 (May)).

Challenges to youth court anonymity

Section 49 of the Children and Young Persons Act 1933 gives all juveniles involved in youth court proceedings, and appeals from youth courts, automatic anonymity in media reports.

A youth court which convicts a juvenile can, by using section 49(4A) of the 1933 Act, inserted by section 45 of the Crime (Sentences) Act 1997, make an order that the anonymity should be lifted if it is satisfied that it is 'in the public interest' to do so.

See ch. 9, pp. 90–94 for more detail of this power to lift section 49 anonymity.

In 1998 the Home Office and Lord Chancellor's Department issued a joint circular 'Opening up youth court proceedings' which said that lifting the anonymity would be particularly appropriate in respect of a juvenile defendant:

- whose offending was persistent or serious; or
- whose offending had had an impact on a number of people; or
- in circumstances when alerting people to his/her behaviour would help prevent further offending.

It said occasions when it would *not* be in the best interests of justice to lift section 49 anonymity included:

- when publicity might put the offender or his/her family at risk of harassment or harm;
- when the offender was particularly young or vulnerable;
- when the offender was contrite and ready to accept responsibility for his/her actions;
- when public identification of the offender would reveal the identity of a vulnerable victim and lead to unwelcome publicity for that victim.

Case study

In 2001 in *McKerry v Teesdale and Wear Valley Justices*, the High Court made clear that youth courts have discretion to consider applications from journalists about lifting section 49 anonymity. The High Court upheld the youth court's decision to lift the

p. 167 cites *McKerry*

section 49 anonymity in the case of a 15-year-old offender following a request by the *Northern Echo*. The teenager had admitted taking a car without the owner's consent, had previous, similar convictions for 'joy-riding', and the media had been told he had been arrested 130 times. The youth court had said he was a serious danger to the public and had shown a complete disregard for the law.

The guidance issued by the Crown Prosecution Service on circumstances when there is a strong public interest in favour of lifting section 39 anonymity also applies to the lifting of section 49 anonymity for a convicted juvenile – for example, if the offence is of significant public disorder, has undermined public confidence in safety, or is a hate crime.

see p. 181 for the guidance

ASBOs: arguments for identifying juveniles

Courts have power to make anti-social behaviour orders (ASBOs) – which are civil orders – banning repetition of criminal and other objectionable conduct. In 2011 the Government announced plans to replace ASBOs with Criminal Behaviour Orders and Crime Prevention Injunctions.

 Ch. 8, pp. 98–100 explains when anonymity applies for juveniles in ASBO cases.

A journalist who wants a court to permit a report to identify a juvenile in an ASBO case can cite Home Office guidance, 'Publicising anti-social behaviour orders', issued to local authorities in 2005. This says:

see Useful Websites, below, for this guidance

> ASBOs protect local communities: Obtaining the [ASBO] order is only part of the process; its effectiveness will normally depend on people knowing about the order. Publicity should be expected in most cases. It is necessary to balance the human rights of individuals subject to an ASBO against those of the community as a whole when considering publicising ASBOs.

The guidance said the benefits of publicity included:

- public reassurance that action was being taken to protect the community's human rights;
- enforcement – local people have the information to identify individuals who breached ASBOs;
- deterrence – if a person subject to an ASBO knew people might identify him/her for breaching it, a breach would be less likely, while others who saw publicity about ASBOs might be deterred from anti-social behaviour.

Mr Justice Elias said in 2002 that, when a court was considering imposing or lifting a section 39 order, the public interest in allowing the media to identify the juvenile was reinforced, in some cases strongly, by the fact that he/she was subject to an ASBO (*Chief Constable of Surrey v JHG and DHG*, cited above).

Mr Justice Wilson said in the High Court in 2001 that in most cases magistrates should not ban identification by the media of a child subject to an ASBO, because the effectiveness of such orders would often depend on the local community knowing that the ASBO applied to that child (*Medway Council v BBC* [2002] 1 FLR 104).

Section 46 anonymity for adult witnesses

Section 46 of the Youth Justice and Criminal Evidence Act 1999 gives courts the power to stop the media identifying an adult witness during his/her lifetime. The court must be satisfied that the quality of the witness's evidence, or level of cooperation in connection with preparations for the case, is likely to be diminished by reason of his/her fear or distress in connection with being identified as a witness by members of the public. It must also be satisfied that anonymity is likely to improve the quality of his/her evidence or the level of his/her cooperation.

for more details about such orders, see ch. 11, pp. 123–124

Rule 16.5 of the Criminal Procedure Rules 2011 says an application for a section 46 order to be lifted or varied can be made by any person 'directly affected' by it – which would include a journalist covering the case. The application must explain why the restriction should be varied or removed.

see Useful Websites, below, for these rules

Would the quality of evidence be improved?

Home Office explanatory notes to the 1999 Act state: 'Neither "fear" nor "distress" is seen as covering a disinclination to give evidence on account of simple embarrassment'. They also say that a witness eligible under the Act for 'special measures' protection (for example, testifying from behind a screen or by video link) is not necessarily also eligible for section 46 anonymity.

ch. 11, pp. 126–128 explains special measures

Case study

At Blackpool magistrates court in 2009 a journalist successfully opposed a prosecution application that a section 46 order should be made to provide anonymity for a barrister. He was a prosecution witness in an assault case in which – the prosecution said – the defendant was expected to make derogatory allegations. David Graham, head of Watsons freelance agency, argued that no other complainant in the court's cases that day would have such anonymity, and that the court should not be seen as having a special rule for lawyers (*Media Lawyer*, April 7, 2009).

Does the section 46 order serve much purpose?

If a prosecution witness's identity is known to the defendant – almost always the case – the defendant will tell associates who he/she is. In such cases, the only purpose of section 46 anonymity would be to shield the witness's identity from the rest of the population. A journalist can ask the court why a witness's identity has to be shielded if the defendant already knows it and can tell others.

Case study

In 2007 a judge at Kingston Crown court made a section 46 order banning identification of witnesses due to testify as the victims of an attempted robbery. But she lifted it after the Newsquest newspaper group and local reporters pointed out that the defendants knew the witnesses, whose identities were already in the public domain as they had previously been named in open court, and that if the order remained in force the media would no longer be able to identify the victims or say where the offence occurred (*Holdthefrontpage* website and *Media Lawyer*, September 19 and 20, 2007).

Sexual offence law does *not* give anonymity to defendants

As chapter 10 explains, the Sexual Offences (Amendment) Act 1992 automatically bans media reports from identifying the victims or alleged victims of sexual offences – but gives courts no power to ban media reports from identifying a defendant. Occasionally magistrates and judges assert that it does, insisting that anonymity for a defendant is necessary as an extra precaution to prevent media reports including detail likely to identify a victim/alleged victim.

Case study

Mr Justice Aikens stressed at Maidstone Crown court in 2004 that defendants accused of sexual offences have no right to anonymity under the 1992 Act. He overturned an order made by West Kent magistrates and confirmed by Judge Anthony Balston at Crown court, purporting to give anonymity to the chief executive of a charity facing one charge of rape and eight of indecent assault. Mr Justice Aikens said he was satisfied the alleged victims' anonymity could be protected without giving the defendant anonymity (*R v Praill* (2004) *Media Lawyer*, November 19, 2004).

Postponement of reports of derogatory mitigation

Section 58 of the Criminal Procedure and Investigations Act 1996 allows courts to ban, for 12 months, publication of an assertion which is derogatory of a person's character and is made during a speech in mitigation. The order cannot be made if the assertion was made during the trial or at any other stage during the proceedings.

See www.mcnaes.com ch. 11 for more details of this restriction and for grounds of challenge if it is made invalidly.

Recap of major points

- Challenges to reporting restrictions can be made by a reporter addressing the court, or by an editor writing to it. If this fails, the challenge can be taken to a higher court.
- An order under section 11 of the Contempt of Court Act 1981 should only be made if the relevant name or matter has already been deliberately withheld by the court from its public proceedings.
- A court order bestowing anonymity on safety grounds is only justified if the risk which publicity would create for that person is 'real and immediate', verified by evidence.
- An order under section 4(2) of the Contempt of Court Act to postpone media reporting of a case should only be made to avoid a substantial risk of prejudice to a pending or imminent hearing.
- A section 39 order cannot be made in respect of an adult or a dead juvenile. It can be argued that a baby or toddler is too young to need it.
- Journalists can request a youth court to remove, after a juvenile is convicted, the anonymity provided by section 49 of the Children and Young Persons Act 1933, and can cite Home Office and CPS guidance on this.
- Journalists arguing that a juvenile subject to an ASBO should be identified in their reports can point to Home Office guidance on when such identification is justified.
- An anonymity order under section 46 of the Youth Justice and Criminal Evidence Act 1999 should only be made if the witness is eligible and if the order is needed to achieve one of the section's purposes.

((•)) Useful Websites

www.justice.gov.uk/guidance/courts-and-tribunals/courts/procedure-rules/criminal/rulesmenu.htm/

Criminal Procedure Rules 2011

www.justice.gov.uk/guidance/courts-and-tribunals/courts/procedure-rules/criminal/practice-direction/pd-consolidated.htm

Consolidated Criminal Practice Direction

www.judiciary.gov.uk/publications-and-reports/guidance/2011/crown-court-reporting-restrictions-guidance-2009/

Guidance on reporting restrictions, published by the Judicial College (formerly the Judicial Studies Board), the Newspaper Society, the Society of Editors and Times Newspapers Ltd

www.cps.gov.uk/legal/p_to_r/reporting_restrictions_-_cases_involving_convicted_youths/

Crown Prosecution Service guidance to prosecutors on section 49 anonymity

http://tna.europarchive.org/20080530130433/http://www.respect.gov.uk/members/article.aspx?id=11490/

Home Office guidance: 'Publicising anti-social behaviour orders'

16

Coroners courts

Chapter summary

Coroners investigate certain types of death to establish the cause. The inquests they hold are court hearings, often newsworthy. This chapter outlines coroners' duties and explains why some inquests have juries. The Contempt of Court Act affects what can be reported, and coroners may also impose reporting restrictions to provide anonymity for a witness. Media coverage of inquests into deaths must be sensitive to the grief of the bereaved. In another role, coroners courts decide whether a found object should be classed as historical 'treasure'.

Changes to the coroner system

A coroner – the office dates from the twelfth century – is appointed to serve a district, and must be a barrister, solicitor or doctor of at least five years' standing. Coroners investigate the causes and circumstances of certain types of death, holding hearings in their courts to do this in some cases. The other role of the coroner system is to decide whether found objects from bygone centuries should be classed as 'treasure'. Both types of hearing are called an inquest. From April 2012 the Coroners and Justice Act 2009 (the 2009 Act) is due to make changes to the system. Coroners' districts will become known as 'areas', some being merged to form larger ones. The former offices of coroner, deputy coroner and assistant deputy coroner will become, respectively, senior coroner, area coroner and assistant coroner.

Investigations into deaths

Under the 2009 Act a coroner must investigate certain categories of death: those for which he/she has reason to suspect that the cause is unknown, if the death is 'violent or unnatural' or if the person died while in custody or was otherwise held in state detention. The definition of 'violent or unnatural' includes deaths caused by crime, accidents, suicide, neglect or lack of care, excessive alcohol, drug abuse or any other form of poisoning. People in 'state detention' includes those held in police stations, prisons, immigration detention centres and mental hospitals. Anyone concerned about the circumstances of a death can report it to the local coroner. Usually deaths in the above categories are reported by police or doctors, who have a duty to do so. A coroner has the right at common law to take possession of a body to make his/her inquiries.

Deaths leading to inquests

Not all investigations require an inquest. In many circumstances there would be no need if, for example, a post mortem examination showed that a death was from natural causes. But holding an inquest means a coroner can require witnesses to testify – usually in public – about the death. Inquests help keep communities and institutions vigilant about fatal dangers, and reassure the public that suspicious deaths are investigated. Inquest determinations on how people died are included in national statistics – for example, on road accidents.

! Remember

An inquest is a fact-finding hearing to establish the reason for a death. It does not rule on who, if anyone, may be criminally responsible, which is the role of the criminal courts, for example, in murder cases. It remains the role of the civil courts to decide if any party must pay damages to a deceased person's family.

A coroner's jurisdiction to hold an inquest arises from the fact that the body is in his/her district. A coroner must hold an inquest if a body has been brought into his/her district from abroad and he/she has reason to suspect the death was violent or unnatural. This is why, for example, the deaths of British service personnel overseas give rise to inquests in the UK.

Purpose of inquests into deaths

The purpose of a coroner's investigation into a death, and therefore an inquest, if one is held, is to determine:

- who the deceased was; and
- how, when and where he/she came by his/her death; and
- to make findings on the particulars about the death which have to be registered according to statute.

Establishing a deceased's identity is usually straightforward, but may require lengthy investigation if, for example, a decomposed body is found. The particulars, which have to be communicated to the Registrar of Births, Marriages and Deaths, include the deceased's name, the date and place of death and his/her gender, age, address and occupation.

In most inquests the decisions are made by a coroner alone. But juries figure in some inquests to decide on facts, with a coroner presiding to rule on law and procedure.

Inquests which have juries

The legal tradition of having juries in some types of inquests is to help safeguard civil liberties and public health – for example, to provide scrutiny, other than by officialdom – of police, prisons and workplace safety regimes.

Under the 2009 Act, an inquest must be held with a jury if the senior coroner has reason to suspect that the death falls into one of the following categories:

- the deceased was in custody or otherwise in state detention, and the death was either violent or unnatural, or the cause is unknown;
- the death resulted from an act or omission of a police officer or member of a police force of the armed services in the execution of his/her duty;
- the death was caused by those types of accident, poisoning or disease which by law must be notified to a government department or inspector, such as workplace fatalities.

Also, an inquest into any other type of death can be held with a jury if the senior coroner thinks there is 'sufficient reason'. An inquest jury is of at least seven and not more than 11 people. Jurors are selected randomly from electoral rolls.

Information about inquests

A Home Office circular in May 1980 urged coroners to make arrangements to ensure that the media were properly informed of all inquests. A reminder was sent out in 1987. This role often falls to the coroner's officer – a police officer with special duties to assist a coroner in investigations.

Case study

Lincolnshire county coroner Stuart Fisher showed in 2006 how helpful some coroners can be. After he was rung by a Press Association reporter about an inquest he had held the previous day into the death of a baby, Mr Fisher fetched the file on the hearing from the boot of his car, and proceeded to read his 'narrative verdict' as well as evidence from witnesses (*Media Lawyer*, April 13, 2006).

Procedure at inquests

check www.mcnaes.com for updates about these new rules

The 2009 Act enables reform of inquest procedure, but the full scope of these changes will not be clear until new Coroners Rules, due to be made under the Act's section 45, are finalised. The Ministry of Justice published a consultation paper covering these in 2010. They will replace the Coroners Rules 1984.

Rule 17 of the Coroners Rules 1984 states that every inquest should be held in public, with the only exception being that the coroner can exclude the public (and journalists) from an inquest on grounds of national security. For example, an inquest into the death of military personnel may need to consider facts about weaponry or military bases which are official secrets.

Section 45 of the 2009 Act says that the new rules can also provide for the exclusion of 'specified persons' – a definition which would cover journalists and members of the public – 'in the interests of national security'. It also says the new rules can empower coroners to exclude specified persons during the giving of evidence by a witness aged under 18, if the coroner is of the opinion that this would be likely to improve the quality of the witness's evidence.

Openings

The usual practice has been for an inquest to have an initial, brief hearing – the opening – for the coroner formally to ascertain the identity of the deceased. The inquest can then be adjourned to permit burial or cremation – there having already been a post mortem examination – and is usually resumed after a period of weeks or months to hear evidence gathered about the circumstances of the death. The 2010 consultation paper aired the idea that, under the new system, 'openings' to identify the deceased might not be necessary, if a coroner's investigation had already done this.

Evidence

see ch. 6, p. 59 on leading questions in criminal trials

Unlike the criminal courts, where the process is accusatorial, adversarial and subject to strict rules on how evidence is given, an inquest is inquisitorial. The coroner can 'lead' witnesses through their evidence. Rule 37 of the Coroners Rules 1984 has allowed a coroner to take documentary rather than oral evidence from any witness where such evidence is unlikely to be disputed – so, for example, a busy hospital doctor may not need to attend an inquest to give evidence in person. Rule 37 has required a coroner to:

- announce publicly at the inquest the name of anyone whose evidence is accepted in documentary form; and
- read aloud at the inquest this documentary evidence, unless the coroner otherwise 'directs' – that is, makes a formal decision – that it will not be read out.

The 2010 consultation paper proposes that these procedures should be retained. But it will remain the case that coroners do not usually read out suicide notes, to spare the bereaved further anguish.

Determinations and 'verdicts'

An inquest produces a decision on what caused a death, determined by the coroner, or the jury if one is involved. These decisions, announced at the inquest, have traditionally been referred to as verdicts. It has become the journalistic convention to report that a coroner's jury *returns* a verdict and that a coroner sitting without a jury *records* a verdict. The 2009 Act abolishes the term 'verdict' and instead uses the term 'determination' to denote a decision as to the identity of the deceased, and how, when and where he/she died. But it seems likely that the term 'verdict' will continue to be used colloquially.

Under the former legislation, most verdicts have been expressed in 'short form', comprising of a single word or short phrase such as 'natural causes', 'accidental death', 'misadventure', 'dependence on drugs', 'non-dependent drug abuse', 'industrial disease', 'unlawful killing', or 'suicide'. An 'open verdict' has been used when an inquest decides there is insufficient evidence for any other verdict. The new rules being drawn up are likely to replace or amend some of this terminology, in the categorisation of 'short-form determinations'.

Recent years have seen increasing use of 'narrative verdicts' – statements summing up the coroner's or jury's conclusions on how the deceased came to die, providing some detail in factual conclusions, in contrast to short-form verdicts. It seems likely that under the new rules a coroner or a jury will be able to deliver a 'narrative determination' rather than a 'short-form determination'. A narrative determination will also fulfill a requirement from case law that a coroner should allow a jury to express a brief conclusion about disputed facts at the centre of the case, so that inquest procedure complies with Article 2 of the European Convention on Human Rights, protecting the right to life. The principle is that a jury must be able to express conclusions in a way which can help avoid similar loss of life. Also, a coroner usually makes concluding remarks to focus public attention on lessons to be learnt from a death.

The Convention is explained in ch. 1, pp. 4–6. Article 2 is set out in Appendix 1, p. 427.

When a person is suspected of crime in connection with a death, an inquest is usually opened, then adjourned until after any criminal proceedings have ended. The inquest may then be resumed if there is sufficient cause. For example, if someone accused of a murder is acquitted, an inquest may subsequently return a determination of unlawful killing (or whatever similar determination is permitted under the new rules) while not attributing blame. If a public inquiry is instigated under the Inquiries Act 2005 to consider why a person or people died – for example, in a train crash – the Lord Chancellor can direct that any inquest should be adjourned. It will not be reopened unless there is an exceptional reason.

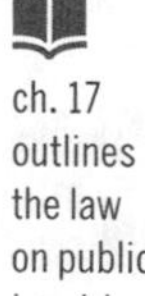
ch. 17 outlines the law on public inquiries

Review of inquest decisions

There is no direct route of appeal against an inquest decision, but an aggrieved person with sufficient legal interest in the case – for example, a deceased's next

→glossary

of kin – can apply to the High Court for **judicial review**. This could result in that court making an order to quash an inquest determination and to order that a fresh inquest be held in the interests of justice.

The 2009 Act created a national post of Chief Coroner to hear appeals against inquest decisions. But the Government decided in 2010 that this post should be scrapped to save costs.

Media coverage of inquests

privilege is explained in ch. 21

An inquest is a type of court proceeding, so fair, accurate and contemporaneous reports of an inquest held in public are protected from libel actions by absolute privilege. Non-contemporaneous reports are protected by qualified privilege if the requirements of that defence are met.

An inquest is covered by the Contempt of Court Act 1981 (the 1981 Act). As explained in chapter 18, it is illegal to publish material which creates 'a substantial risk of serious prejudice' to an active case. The Court of Appeal has ruled that an inquest becomes 'active' when it is opened (*Peacock v London Weekend Television* (1986) 150 JP 71). It seems unlikely that a coroner, being an experienced professional, could be prejudiced in his/her considerations by media coverage. But the media should take care, in an inquest case in which a jury is or could be involved, not to publish material which creates a substantial risk of serious prejudice to its deliberations. The media should also avoid publishing material which could breach the Act by affecting a witness's testimony.

An inquest may precede a hearing in a criminal court into the same events – for example, an inquest may be opened and then adjourned because someone is charged with murder. The media can safely report that inquest hearing contemporaneously, if it is held in public, because the report – provided it is fair, accurate and published in good faith – will be protected by section 4 of the 1981 Act unless the coroner has made an order to postpone reporting of the hearing.

Reporting restrictions

section 39 is explained in ch. 9

Coroners can make orders restricting media reports of inquests, for example by using section 39 of the Children and Young Persons Act 1933 to give a juvenile witness anonymity.

→glossary

Coroners also have **inherent jurisdiction** in common law to order that a witness should have anonymity in reports of inquest proceedings – for example, to prevent a real and immediate risk to their safety (*R (on the application of Officer A) v HM Coroner for Inner South London and others* [2004] EWHC Admin 1592).

see also ch. 15, pp. 175–176 on anonymity for police officers

---

Case study

At the 2008 inquest into the death of Jean Charles de Menezes, the innocent Brazilian shot dead by police in London after he was mistaken for a terrorist, the coroner Sir

Michael Wright granted anonymity to the police firearms officers involved, warning that any attempt to photograph witnesses granted anonymity would be punished as a contempt of court (*Media Lawyer*, October 28, 2008).

section 11 is explained in ch. 11

A coroner who allows the name of a witness – for example, a police or MI5 officer – to be withheld from the public in the inquest can make an order under section 11 of the Contempt of Court Act 1981 banning publication of it.

Under section 45 of the Coroners and Criminal Justice Act, the new rules for coroners will be able to give them powers to direct that a name or information from an investigation must not be disclosed except to specified people. The 2010 consultation paper said the main aim of this provision was to enable coroners to protect the names or other details of UK Special Forces personnel, and that, having given such a direction, the coroner will be able to make an order under section 11 of the 1981 Act.

Publication of material heard in any part of an inquest held in private could be deemed a contempt of court and will not be protected by privilege in libel law.

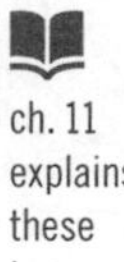

ch. 11 explains these laws

Common law and statutory protections of witnesses and jurors, including section 8 of the 1981 Act, apply to inquest proceedings, as does the ban on photography, filming and audio recording in courts.

Media challenges to reporting restrictions or lack of access

Any media challenge to a reporting restriction imposed by a coroner, or to a decision to exclude the media from an inquest, must – if the coroner will not reconsider – be made to the High Court as an application for judicial review.

Ethical considerations when covering deaths

chs. 2 and 3 introduce the codes

The Editors' Code of Practice and the Ofcom code set out ethical standards, explained in chapter 27, to minimise media intrusion into bereaved people's grief and shock. These are particularly pertinent to coverage of inquests. The Editors' Code and the Ofcom code also say that excessive detail about suicide methods should not be published.

see Useful Websites, below

In 2008 the Ministry of Justice published a discussion paper, 'Sensitive Reporting in Coroners' Courts', which gives examples of bereaved people being upset by media coverage. The Samaritans have also published media guidance on reporting suicides.

Treasure inquests

Historically, coroners courts have decided whether historical objects found on or buried in the ground should be classed as 'treasure'. The Crown or a franchisee has legal rights to take possession of valuable objects ruled to have been treasure deliberately hidden by a past generation – for example, buried for safety during warfare. The Treasure Act 1996 amended this ancient law to encourage those who use metal-detectors to declare discoveries so that museums can decide if they want the objects found. The Act has various definitions of treasure, including:

- a found object which is not a single coin and which contains at least 10 per cent of gold or silver, and which is at least 300 years old, and any other object found with it;
- a find of ten or more coins found together whatever their metallic content, which are at least 300 years old.

District coroners have been responsible for holding inquests to decide if an object is treasure. The Coroners and Justice Act 2009 was due to remove this duty from them, because it contains law to create a national post of Coroner for Treasure, the idea being that an individual with particular expertise could preside at all treasure inquests. However, in September 2011 the Government said it was continuing to consider the feasibility of having such a national post. Anyone with reasonable grounds for believing an object they have found might be classed as treasure is required to notify a coroner within 14 days of the discovery or this realisation. Failure to do so is punishable by a fine, or a jail term of up to three months.

The coroner, once notified, or if he/she has reason to suspect any other found object is treasure, must hold an investigation, which could involve an inquest, with a jury if there is 'sufficient reason'.

If the find is ruled to be treasure the British Museum or National Museum of Wales is given the opportunity to acquire the find. There is a system for the finder to be paid a reward, based on the treasure's market value, from public money. It is also possible for some of it to be awarded to the owner of the land where the treasure was found.

The reward may be reduced, or not even offered, if the finder was trespassing or illegally disturbing an archaeological site. If the object is not classed as treasure or no museum wants it, the finder can keep or sell it, subject to any rights of the land's owner or occupier.

➡ Recap of major points

- The purpose of an inquest is to find out who a deceased person was and how he/she died.
- A treasure inquest decides if a found, historical object should be classed as 'treasure', in which case a museum is given the opportunity to acquire it.
- A coroner can exclude the public and journalists from an inquest on grounds of national security.
- Coroners can impose reporting restrictions.

- Inquests are court hearings, and so are covered by the law of contempt of court, which can affect media coverage.

((•)) Useful Websites

www.direct.gov.uk/en/Governmentcitizensandrights/Death/WhatToDoAfterADeath/DG_066713/
Government guidance on inquests into deaths

www.coronersociety.org.uk/
The Coroners Society of England and Wales

www.justice.gov.uk/consultations/docs/coroner-reform.pdf/
Ministry of Justice 2010 consultation on reform of coroners' system

www.inquest.org.uk/
Inquest – a charity providing free advice to the bereaved on contentious deaths

www.justice.gov.uk/publications/sensitive-reporting-coroners.htm
Ministry of Justice discussion paper: 'Sensitive Reporting in Coroners' Courts'

www.samaritans.org/media_centre/media_guidelines.aspx
The Samaritans' media guidelines on reporting suicides

www.culture.gov.uk/what_we_do/cultural_property/3291.aspx/
Government guidance on treasure

17

Tribunals and public inquiries

Chapter summary

The term 'tribunal' denotes a legal body which adjudicates on disputes in specialised areas of law. In the UK there is a wide range of tribunals, with a huge annual caseload, some of which can yield news and 'human interest' stories. For example, tribunals adjudicate – usually in public hearings – on asylum and immigration cases; on what rent can be charged to tenants; on whether a patient in a secure mental health hospital is safe to return to the outside world; on entitlement to state benefits; on employment disputes. Some tribunals are termed a 'commission' or 'panel'. Some regulate professions, for example, when deciding if a doctor or lawyer should, because of misconduct, be banned from practising. The term 'public inquiry' denotes other kinds of legal, investigatory processes.

Tribunals in the administrative justice system

Most tribunals are official bodies, other than the courts, which make decisions determining someone's legal rights. There are more than 70 types of tribunal. The majority rule on disputes between an individual, or a private organisation, and a state agency, for example, about tax obligations; entitlement to benefits; immigration status. The annual workload of tribunals in this 'administrative justice' system can exceed 800,000 cases.

The tribunals listed here are some that may be of particular interest to journalists:

The Immigration and Asylum Chamber hears appeals against decisions made by the Home Secretary and his/her officials in asylum, immigration and nationality matters.

The Special Immigration Appeals Commission hears appeals against decisions made by the Home Office to deport, or exclude, someone from the UK on national security grounds or for other public interest reasons, and appeals against decisions to deprive someone of UK citizenship.

The Social Entitlement Chamber of the First-tier Tribunal hears appeals from disputes about social security and child support payments, criminal injuries compensation, and asylum support.

The Health, Education and Social Care Chamber of the First-tier Tribunal hears, for example, appeals from doctors and dentists who have not been included on lists which allow them to provide work in NHS primary care, and appeals from people who have been banned from working for organisations concerned with children and vulnerable adults.

This chamber includes the First-tier Tribunal (mental health) for England (formerly the mental health review tribunals) which hears appeals from patients, detained under the Mental Health Act 1983, to be released from secure, mental hospitals. There is a separate mental health review tribunal for Wales.

Rent assessment panels hear, for example, appeals against rent levels fixed by a rent officer for regulated tenancies.

Reforms in the Tribunals, Courts and Enforcement Act 2007 created the First-tier Tribunal as a generic tribunal to merge the administration of most tribunals dealing with appeals against decisions made by state officials. A decision of the First-tier Tribunal may, in some instances, be appealed to, or be reviewed by, the Upper Tribunal, also created by the 2007 Act.

www.mcnaes.com ch. 17 gives an outline of the procedural rules of these tribunals, who can attend them, powers they have to prohibit the disclosure or publication of specified documents or information relating to their proceedings.

Examples of disciplinary tribunals

The disciplinary tribunals listed below, being those of regulated professions, are not part of the 'administrative justice' system.

The General Medical Council hears complaints against doctors in its Fitness to Practice Panels. These have usually sat in public, except when they are considering confidential information concerning a doctor's health or are considering making an interim order. But in 2011 the GMC consulted on its proposals for a greater proportion of hearings to be in private.

The Solicitors' Disciplinary Tribunal must, in general, sit in public to hear allegations of professional misconduct made against solicitors. But the tribunal can in some circumstances exclude the public from all or any part of the hearing – for example if it decides this is necessary to avoid 'exceptional prejudice' to a party, witness or other affected person.

The Bar Standards Board's Disciplinary Tribunal considers allegations of misconduct made against barristers practising in England and Wales. Its hearings take place in public unless there has been a specific order that a hearing be held in private.

Defamation and contempt issues in reporting tribunals

Tribunals, including the disciplinary tribunals of professions regulated by statute, derive their powers from an Act of Parliament. Consequently, as specified by paragraph 11 of Part 2 of Schedule 1 to the Defamation Act 1996 (the 1996 Act), fair and accurate published reports of the public proceedings of these tribunals are protected by qualified privilege if the requirements of that libel defence are met. The requirements are that the report is:

- fair and accurate; and
- published without malice; and
- about a matter of public concern, and its publication is for the public benefit.

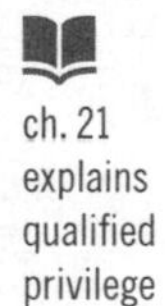
ch. 21 explains qualified privilege

Also, a requirement is that, at the request of anyone defamed by the published report, a reasonable letter or statement of explanation or contradiction must be published.

The proceedings of many tribunals are not as formal as those in an ordinary court of law. An appellant might not be represented by a lawyer. Journalists should remember that qualified privilege does not extend to any published matter which is not 'of public concern' and the publication of which is not 'for the public benefit' – so a flare-up at a hearing of irrelevant, personal abuse may well be such matter.

! Remember

Qualified privilege protects fair and accurate reports of the findings (but not of the proceedings) of the disciplinary committees of certain private associations – for example, in the field of sport, business, and learning. Chapter 21, p. 271 explains how this privilege arises from paragraph 14 of Schedule 1, Part 2 to the 1996 Act.

Absolute privilege for coverage of tribunals which are courts

Some tribunals are classed as courts. This means that media reports of their hearings held in public, if fair, accurate and contemporaneous, are protected by absolute privilege – the libel defence explained in chapter 21.

In 2009 the High Court judge Mr Justice Eady said that a media account of the proceedings of the Solicitors' Disciplinary Tribunal enjoyed absolute privilege (*Imran Karim v Newsquest*, case number HQ09X00357 and *Media Lawyer*, October 29 and December 21, 2009).

A tribunal is classed as a court if it wields 'the judicial power of the state', but there is no comprehensive case law on which tribunals can be regarded as wielding this power.

Contempt issues in coverage of tribunals which are courts

If a tribunal is classed as a court the Contempt of Court Act 1981 applies to media coverage of its cases, which means that once a case is 'active' the media should not publish material which could create 'a substantial risk of serious prejudice' to the tribunal's hearings. The 1981 Act is explained in the next chapter.

Case study

In 2011 a district tribunal judge in Exeter ruled that the First-tier Tribunal, which includes a wide range of tribunals in the administrative justice system, is an 'inferior court' and therefore that the 1981 Act applied to its cases. The judge said that, as a consequence of this ruling, the BBC needed permission to film a hearing in the First-tier Tribunal's Social Security Entitlement Chamber in which a woman was appealing against a decision that she was no longer entitled to employment support allowance. She supported the BBC's request to film the hearing but the judge refused it, adding that section 9 of the 1981 Act banned the broadcasting of any recording of a court's proceedings. The BBC had argued that the First-tier Tribunal was not a court (*Re: The Appeal of L*, August 8, 2011).

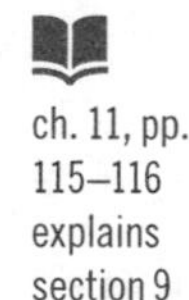

ch. 11, pp. 115–116 explains section 9

Earlier case law has established that mental health review tribunals are courts – these are now in the First-tier Tribunal (Mental Health). Also, the Upper Tribunal, the Special Immigration Appeals Commission and the Employment Appeal Tribunal were each created by statute to be a 'superior court of record'.

In many instances, it would be unlikely that media stories about an 'active' tribunal case – for example, published before its full hearing – could create a substantial risk of serious prejudice, in that judges and/or professionals such as doctors or lawyers preside in tribunals, and are unlikely to be influenced by media reports. But there is a possibility that media reports could affect witnesses in their testimony.

Also, media contact with a witness prior to such a hearing could be punished as contempt in common law if it was ruled to amount to interference with him/her, as chapter 18 explains.

A further consideration is that if a tribunal classed as a court holds a hearing in private, it may be ruled to be a contempt if a media organisation reports what was said in that hearing, if the case concerns mental health, national security, the welfare or upbringing of children, or secret processes, and in any other case where the tribunal has expressly prohibited publication of information.

See www.mcnaes.com ch. 17: 'Tribunals which are courts' for further detail of relevant contempt law.

Employment tribunals

Employment tribunals adjudicate on complaints against employers – for example, unfair dismissal, including 'constructive dismissal' in which a person claims that he/she had to quit the job because of improper conduct by another/others in the workplace. These tribunals also adjudicate on complaints of discrimination by employers on grounds of gender, race or age.

Each employment tribunal has normally had three members: a lawyer who is chair, and who is now officially known as an 'employment judge'; and two lay members – someone with experience as an employer and someone with background as an employee, a trade unionist. Employment tribunals, for example formerly known as industrial tribunals, are based in regional centres.

The Government announced in November 2011 that from April 2012 tribunal hearings would have less oral evidence, with witness statements 'taken as read'. It was unclear how the media could see these. New procedural rules are planned. A judge alone will preside in unfair dismissal claims.

check www.mcnaes.com for updates

Employment tribunal staff are instructed to provide journalists with the details of the parties in a case, and the nature of the claim, once it is listed for a hearing. Hearings tend to be informal.

In judgments, employment tribunals first decide on *liability* – whether the complaint against the employer is justified. The decision may be announced in summary on the same day that the hearing ends, but may not be revealed until sent out later in a written judgment. If the employer is held liable, subsequently – often after an adjournment of some weeks – the tribunal decides the '*remedy*', for example requiring the employer to pay compensation to someone sacked unfairly.

see Useful Websites, below

Under regulation 17 of the Employment Tribunals (Constitution and Rules of Procedure) Regulations 2004 (SI 2004/1861) a public register of judgments must be maintained. This is based in Bury St Edmunds.

Appeals on points of law from employment tribunal decisions can be made to the Employment Appeal Tribunal (EAT) based in London. EAT judgments can be read online at its website.

Admission to employment tribunal cases

Sections 10 and 10A of the Employment Tribunals Act 1996 say that an employment tribunal can decide to sit in private:

- in the interests of national security; or
- when a witness's evidence is likely to contain:
  - information which he/she cannot disclose without breaking statutory law or without breaking an obligation of confidence; or
  - information which would cause substantial injury to his/her or the employer's interests, other than interests in collective negotiations over pay and conditions.

A Minister of the Crown, under section 10, can direct an employment tribunal to hear a case in private in the interests of national security – if the tribunal has not already decided to do so.

Case study

The High Court has ruled that an employment tribunal is not empowered to sit in private merely because there is to be evidence of a sensitive or salacious nature when sexual misconduct is alleged (*R v Southampton Industrial Tribunal, ex p INS News Group Ltd and Express Newspapers plc* [1995] IRLR 247).

Sexual misconduct cases: restricted reporting orders

Section 11 of the Act gives employment tribunals discretionary power to make temporary anonymity orders, known as 'restricted reporting orders', in cases involving allegations of sexual misconduct – for example, that a woman was forced to leave her job because her boss sexually harassed her. Sexual misconduct is defined as a sexual offence or sexual harassment or other adverse conduct (of whatever nature) related to sex, or to the sexual orientation of the person at whom the conduct is directed.

In a restricted reporting order, an employment tribunal can prohibit the inclusion in reports of any matter likely to lead members of the public to identify:

- the person making the allegation of sexual misconduct; and/or
- anyone 'affected' by it, for example the person(s) accused of such misconduct or any witness due to give evidence in such proceedings.

The tribunal can decide in each such case who should have such anonymity, if anyone. It may, for example, decide not to grant anonymity for the accuser but order it in respect of the person accused, to safeguard his/her reputation until judgment on whether the accusation is proved. Such an order cannot specifically bestow such anonymity on an employer that is a company or institution, so its corporate name can be published if this does not identify a person named in the order (*Leicester University v A* [1999] IRLR 352). But in a case where the employing organisation is small, for example a small firm, it may be that to preserve anonymity for the person the firm itself cannot be identified in media reports while the order remains in force, because reference to the person's gender or age or job description would in itself be enough to identify him/her to people who know he/she works there.

see also ch. 9, p. 96 on the dangers of jigsaw identification

In 1997 the Court of Appeal said it was important that tribunals should recognise that their power to make these orders in cases of sexual misconduct was not to be exercised automatically, and that the public interest in the media's ability to communicate information should be considered (*Kearney v Smith New Court Securities* [1997] EWCA Civ 1211).

Under Schedule 1 (rule 50) of the Employment Tribunals (Constitution and Rules of Procedure) Regulations 2004 a tribunal chair can make the restricted reporting order as an interim measure prior to any hearing, and at the first hearing the tribunal can decide whether the order should continue in force as a 'full' order. The order must specify who must not be identified, and should be displayed on the noticeboard which lists the hearing and on the door of the hearing room.

Media rights to challenge a restricted reporting order or its scope

Under rule 50 of the 2004 Regulations, any person – including a journalist – can apply to make representations about an interim restricted reporting order. Also, the Extra Division of the Inner House of the Court of Session has ruled in a Scottish case that an employment tribunal has discretion to hear representations from a journalist or media organisation about revocation of a full order without them having to become a 'party' to the case (*Fiona Davidson v Dallas McMillan* [2009] CSIH 70). This is an important ruling for journalists, because a party might be held liable for costs of a hearing, though it is unusual for employment tribunals to order one party to pay another's costs.

Case study

An employment tribunal can take account of previous publicity when refusing to make a restricted reporting order. In 2000 a tribunal refused to make such an order which would have granted temporary anonymity to a businessman accused of sexual harassment. Both parties wanted the order made. But the *Daily Record* successfully argued that both parties had previously willingly given information about the case to the media (*Scottish Daily Record and Sunday Mail Ltd v Margaret McAvoy and others*, EAT/1271/01).

Lifting or cessation of a restricted reporting order

Section 11 of the Act says that once the employment tribunal has made a restricted reporting order:

- it can revoke (that is, cancel) the order at any stage – for example, while the case is ongoing, or when it makes a verbal announcement of its decision on liability – to permit media reports to immediately identify the person formerly covered by the order;
- but, anyway, as soon as the tribunal's written judgment in the case is 'promulgated', that is, sent to the parties, the order is automatically no longer in force, and so anyone covered by it can then be identified in media reports, unless they are the alleged victim of a sexual offence.

see p. 208 on sexual offences

The 2004 Regulations (rule 50) say that in sexual misconduct cases in which an employment tribunal decides there is 'liability' (that is, the complaint against the employer is justified) a restricted reporting order, if not revoked then or earlier, remains in force until the subsequent judgment on the 'remedy' (for example, on the amount of compensation which the employer must pay) is sent to the parties, at which point the order automatically lapses. This may be some weeks or months after the case's final hearing.

Case study

Where a restricted reporting order is imposed, but a settlement is reached without the case proceeding to judgment, the restriction remains in place indefinitely (*Fiona Davidson v Dallas McMillan* [2009] CSIH 70). However, in 2008 six media organisations persuaded a tribunal and the Employment Appeal Tribunal that a restricted reporting order should be lifted to allow reports to identify two sisters who had alleged sexual misconduct in a claim against a firm of City brokers. The case had ended in a settlement, and the sisters wanted the media to be able to identify them. At the EAT, Mr Justice Underhill said the tribunal was justified in lifting the restriction because there had been a change in circumstances – the media's application and the change in the sisters' position (*Tradition Securities & Futures SA and another v Times Newspapers Limited and others*, UKEATPA/1415/08/JOJ; UKEATPA/1417/08/JOJ).

Liability for breach of anonymity

Publishing matter which breaches a restricted reporting order is a summary offence punishable by a fine of up to £5,000. Any proprietor, editor or publisher held responsible will be liable to pay it. It is a defence for the person or company prosecuted to show that he/she/it was not aware, and neither suspected nor had reason to suspect that the published matter breached the order.

Automatic anonymity for alleged victims of sexual offences

An automatic reporting restriction, under the Sexual Offences (Amendment) Act 1992, means that anyone in employment tribunal proceedings who states that they are, or who is alleged to be, a victim of a sexual offence – for example, rape or sexual assault – must not be identified in media reports of the case in his/her lifetime, unless the person gives valid, written consent to be identified.

ch. 10 on sexual offences explains this anonymity

This is the position irrespective of whether a restricted reporting order has been imposed under the Employment Tribunals Act 1996 or whether such an order has expired.

Disability cases: restricted reporting orders

Section 12 of the 1996 Act and rule 50 of the 2004 Regulations allow employment tribunals to make restricted reporting orders when considering claims that an employer unlawfully discriminated on disability grounds, if evidence 'of a personal nature' is likely to be heard and is likely to cause significant embarrassment if published.

National security restrictions

Section 10 of the 1996 Act says that a Minister of the Crown can order an employment tribunal to conceal the identity of a witness in a case concerning national security issues, and order it to keep secret all or part of the reasons for its decision in such a case, or the tribunal on its own initiative can take either of these courses of action. When the tribunal has taken such steps, it is an offence to publish anything likely to lead to the identification of the witness or to publish any part of a decision the tribunal intended to keep secret. The maximum fine is £5,000.

Contempt and defamation law affecting coverage of employment tribunals

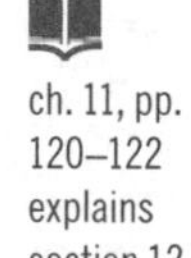

ch. 11, pp. 120–122 explains section 12

As this chapter has explained, both employment tribunals and the EAT are classed as courts. Therefore:

- unauthorised publication of matter aired in their private hearings could be deemed to be contempt of court under section 12 of the Administration of Justice Act 1960 if the particular case falls into any of the relevant categories, which include national security;
- the Contempt of Court Act 1981 applies to their proceedings;
- the ban in section 9 of the 1981 Act on unauthorised use of audio-recording devices (and, it can be construed, cameras) applies to an employment tribunal hearing (*Neckles v Yorkshire Rider Ltd* [2002] All ER (D) 111 (Jan)).

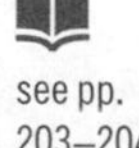

see pp. 203–204

It can be construed that contemporaneous reports of their proceedings in public are protected by absolute privilege from libel actions, and that non-contemporaneous reports will be protected by qualified privilege under Part 1 of Schedule 1 to the Defamation Act 1996, if the respective requirements of these defences are met.

ch. 21 explains privilege

Public inquiries

Public inquiries can be broadly categorised either as local inquiries, set up routinely in certain circumstances, or those which are set up ad hoc to consider a matter of national concern.

Local public inquiries

Some Acts of Parliament provide that an inquiry hearing must be held before certain decisions are made affecting the rights of individuals or of public authorities. An inquiry might be held, for example, before land is compulsorily acquired for redevelopment, and also before planning schemes are approved. In some cases, an 'inspector' appointed by a Minister to chair the inquiry decides the matter at issue. In others, he/she must report to the Minister, who subsequently announces a decision and the reasons for it. Some statutes under which inquiries are held stipulate that they must be held in public. In others, this is discretionary. Local authorities and health trusts also have general statutory powers under which they can fund an ad hoc inquiry into a matter of local (or national) concern, though it will be at their discretion whether it is held in public.

Public inquiries into matters of national concern

Public inquiries initiated ad hoc by government Ministers have in recent years included:

- The inquiry which began in 2010 to investigate the role of official bodies in the monitoring of Mid Staffordshire Foundation NHS Trust, after poor standards of hospital care led to between 400 and 1,200 more patients dying than would have been expected in a three-year period from 2005 to 2008. The inquiry was established under the Inquiries Act 2005 (the 2005 Act). See www.midstaffspublicinquiry.com/.
- The Hutton inquiry set up in 2003 into the death of Dr David Kelly, who committed suicide after investigation by his employer, the Ministry of Defence, into his contact with BBC journalists about the Government's stated justification for the Iraq war. This inquiry was held on a non-statutory basis by a chair appointed by the Secretary of State for Constitutional Affairs. See www.the-hutton-inquiry.org.uk/.

If an inquiry is held on a non-statutory basis, it has no legal powers to compel witnesses to give evidence, but is seen as a flexible option when full cooperation is anticipated.

If the inquiry is established under the 2005 Act, under section 19 a Minister or an inquiry's chair can decide on various grounds – for example, national security or to protect the 'efficiency' of the inquiry – that it should hear evidence in private. The various powers granted in the Act to Ministers, including those to impose or continue restrictions on media reports of an inquiry's proceedings, have led to criticism that the Act fails to embody sufficiently the idea that the proceedings of a public inquiry should be independent of the Government.

www.mcnaes.com ch. 17 sets out the reporting restrictions which can be imposed under the Act, including by the chair of such an inquiry. It also outlines the powers of the chair to compel production of evidence – including from a journalist – and explains how section 18 of the Act gives journalists some rights to obtain or view a record of evidence and documents when covering an inquiry hearing, but says that audio recording and televising of the proceedings need the chair's permission.

Coverage of public inquiries: defamation law

Reports of public inquiries held under the Inquiries Act 2005 have, under its section 37, the same privilege 'as would be the case if those proceedings were proceedings before a court', which means that, as regards proceedings held in public, absolute privilege applies to contemporaneous reports and qualified privilege, under Part 1 of Schedule 1 to the Defamation Act 1996, to non-contemporaneous reports, if the respective requirements of these defences are met.

Media reports of public inquiries held under any other statute enjoy qualified privilege under paragraph 11 of Part 2 of Schedule 1 to the Defamation Act 1996. This means that if requested by a person defamed by such a report, its publisher must publish a reasonable statement or letter by way of explanation or contradiction.

www.mcnaes.com ch. 17 has further detail on this privilege

Privilege will not apply to media reports of any matter aired in a private session of an inquiry. As is the case with administrative tribunals, proceedings of public inquiries are not as formal as those in an ordinary court of law, so some extra care must be exercised in what is reported.

The findings of a public inquiry are usually published by a government department, by Parliament or by the relevant local authority. Under the Defamation Act 1996:

- a fair and accurate media report of such findings, when they have been officially published by a government or legislature anywhere in the world is protected by qualified privilege which, in that it arises from Part 1 of Schedule 1 to the Act (paragraph 7), has no requirement for anyone's explanation or contradiction to be published;
- a fair and accurate media report of findings officially published by a UK local authority is protected by qualified privilege under Part 2 of the Schedule (paragraph 9), and is therefore subject to a reasonable letter or statement by way or explanation of contradiction being published, if this is requested.

➡ Recap of major points

- Most types of tribunals adjudicate in disputes in specialist areas of law. Some are regulatory tribunals for professions, for example doctors, lawyers.
- Employment tribunals can make temporary anonymity orders in cases involving sexual misconduct. They can sit in private in certain circumstances, for example to protect national security.
- Media reports of the public proceedings of tribunals are protected by qualified privilege and, as regards those classed as courts, by absolute privilege when reports are contemporaneous.
- For any tribunal classed as a court, contempt law applies.
- Media reports of the public proceedings of public inquiries are, as regards libel actions, protected by either qualified privilege or absolute privilege.
- The Inquiries Act 2005 empowers either a Minister or the chair of the relevant public inquiry to impose reporting restrictions. Journalists have some rights to view documents and other evidence.

((•)) Useful Websites

www.justice.gov.uk/guidance/courts-and-tribunals/tribunals/rules.htm
Procedural rules for the First-tier Tribunal and the Upper Tribunal

www.employmenttribunals.gov.uk/
Employment Tribunals

www.justice.gov.uk/guidance/courts-and-tribunals/tribunals/employment/rules-and-legislation.htm
Procedural rules for employment tribunals

www.justice.gov.uk/guidance/courts-and-tribunals/tribunals/employment-appeals/index.htm
Employment Appeals Tribunal

www.direct.gov.uk/en/Employment/index.htm
Government guidance on employment rights

www.employmenttribunalsni.co.uk/
Northern Ireland industrial tribunals

www.legislation.gov.uk/ukpga/2005/12/notes/contents/
The Government's explanatory notes to the Inquiries Act 2005

18

Contempt of court

Chapter summary

The law of contempt protects the integrity of the administration of justice, and the fundamental principle that a defendant is presumed innocent until proven guilty. Contempt law most affects journalists when they publish material which might affect a trial, by making a juror more likely to find a defendant guilty – or innocent – or influence a witness's evidence. It also considers the effect of publications held to 'impede' the course of justice by creating a risk that witnesses will refuse to come forward to help the prosecution or defence. Media organisations which have committed contempt by publishing prejudicial material have been fined heavily. The law of contempt applies as much to material which appears on the internet as it does to print and broadcast coverage.

What does contempt of court law protect?

The law of contempt of court protects the judicial process. Anyone who is disruptive or threatening in a courtroom can be punished immediately for contempt, by being sent by the magistrates or judge to the court's cells, and in some cases subsequently to jail, as contempt is a criminal offence.

The greatest risk of the media committing contempt is by publishing material which could prejudice a fair trial, by:

- giving the impression that a defendant or suspect is the sort of person who is likely to have committed the crime, or vilifying a suspect to the extent that witnesses might refuse to come forward to help his/her defence or the prosecution case.

The media can also commit contempt by:

- seeking to discover or publishing information from the jury's confidential discussions about a verdict – see chapter 11, pp. 117–119;

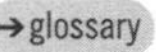

- publishing material which breaches the **common law** of contempt, for example by 'vilifying' a person for being a witness at a trial – see below;
- contaminating a witness's evidence by interviewing him or her in detail – see below;
- publishing material in breach of a court order made in common law or under the Contempt of Court Act 1981 (the 1981 Act), for example by naming a blackmail victim in reports of a trial – see chapter 11, pp. 119–120.

! Remember

The Court of Appeal has ruled that the punishment for publishing material in breach of an order made under a statute other than the 1981 Act – for example, under the Children and Young Persons Act 1933, explained in chapter 9 – should be that specified by that statute, rather than as a contempt (*R v Tyne Tees Television* [1997] EWCA Crim 2395, *The Times*, October 20).

Types of contempt

There are two types of contempt – common law contempt and strict liability contempt. Common law contempt can consist of publishing material which creates a substantial risk of serious prejudice to proceedings which are imminent or pending *with the intention* of creating that risk, or of behaviour or conduct which interferes with the administration of justice.

Strict liability contempt, which is governed by the 1981 Act, consists simply of publishing material which creates a substantial risk of serious prejudice to 'active' proceedings – the court decides whether the publication has created the risk, and the motives of the writer and publisher are irrelevant.

pp. 219–222 explain material that could create that risk

The media's approach to contempt has caused concern. In March 2011, the Attorney General, Dominic Grieve QC, expressed alarm about the media's approach to crime reporting, saying there was 'frenzied interest' in high-profile arrests which stopped abruptly only when a suspect was charged or released, and warning that the law might have to be changed to give arrested people anonymity until they were charged.

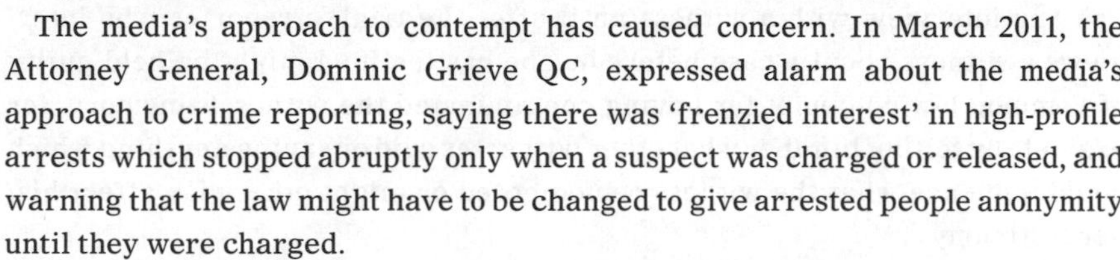

Contempt in common law

Common law contempt makes it an offence to publish material which creates a substantial risk of serious prejudice to legal proceedings which are 'imminent or pending', if it can be proved that there was intent to create such a risk.

- The term 'intent' could mean either deliberate intent to create such a risk, or recklessness in publishing material which the person responsible for the publication should have foreseen would create such a risk.

The Contempt of Court Act 1981 largely superseded the common law by creating the strict liability rule in respect of a case which is active under the Act. Common law contempt still applies to material published before proceedings become active (and arguably may apply to material published at later stages in the proceedings). Prosecutions of the media for common law contempt are extremely rare as the prosecution has to prove that the journalist or editor *intended* to create a serious risk of prejudice.

Case study

In 2010 the Police Service of Northern Ireland sought a High Court injunction to stop the BBC broadcasting a documentary about the 1972 bombings in the village of Claudy in which nine people died and 30 were injured. Police argued that even though no proceedings were active, the programme – which the BBC refused to allow an officer to see before it was broadcast – was a contempt, would interfere with the administration of justice or could breach confidentiality. Mr Justice Seamus Treacy rejected the 'unprecedented' application, saying it was based on pure speculation, was not supported by any legal authority, and, if allowed, would significantly extend the boundaries of the law (*Media Lawyer*, November 3, 2010).

Witness interviews and 'molestation'

see ch. 11, pp. 114–115 on molestation

Publishing detailed accounts of a witness's evidence while a case is active could breach the strict liability rule. But even if the intention was not to publish any interview with a witness until after the trial, a reporter who interviews a witness about a case before he/she has testified might be held guilty of common law contempt for having contaminated the witness's memory, for example by telling him/her what other witnesses said or saying anything which could influence what the witness remembered or might otherwise affect his/her testimony.

A media organisation's offer to 'buy up' a witness who has yet to give evidence to tell his/her story after the trial could amount to common law contempt if held to have influenced how he/she testified. It could also be a contempt by 'molestation' to pester a witness so much for a pre-trial interview, or in photographing him/her, against his/her wishes, that the witness is deterred from testifying.

Ch. 2 gives detail of clause 15 of the Editors' Code of Practice, governing payments to witnesses. There is similar provision in the Ofcom Broadcasting Code, see ch. 3.

Vilifying a witness

Media organisations which publish, after the end of a trial, criticism of a witness which was so abusive that a judge could rule that it was likely to deter others from being witnesses in future could be punished for common law contempt for 'vilifying' the witness.

Scandalising the court

'Scandalising the court' punishes the publication of scurrilous or very abusive comment about a judge. There has been no successful prosecution for this offence for nearly a century. A judge whose good faith or conduct in court was questioned by a media organisation would these days be more likely to sue for defamation than seek a prosecution for contempt. Judges accept that their decisions may be criticised.

Ch. 11 explains that publishing information from some types of court document, photography or filming in a courtroom, or harassment of a defendant by photographers or film crews could be ruled to be a contempt in common law.

Contempt of Court Act 1981 – strict liability

A primary purpose of the 1981 Act was to replace some aspects of the common law of contempt, and give greater certainty about what constitutes a contempt. Section 1 of the Act made contempt by publication a strict liability offence in the case of 'active' criminal or civil proceedings. The strict liability rule says it is a contempt to publish material which creates a substantial risk of serious prejudice or impediment to 'active' legal proceedings.

Strict liability means that the prosecution, when seeking to prove that a contempt has occurred, does not have to prove that the editor or media organisation responsible *intended* to create the risk. The court simply judges the actual or potential prejudicial effect of what was published. Prosecutions for contempt are usually of an editor and/or the relevant publishing company.

The Act defines publication as any writing, speech, broadcast or other communication addressed to any section of the public – which includes material on websites.

Breaching the strict liability rule is punishable by an unlimited fine and/or a maximum of two years in jail.

ch. 1, p. 7 explains the Attorney General's role

Who can prosecute for contempt of court?

Proceedings for contempt under the strict liability rule can be initiated only by a Crown court or higher court, by the Attorney General or by some other person with the Attorney General's consent.

Magistrates cannot punish contempt of court by publication. Such a contempt in respect of proceedings in a magistrates court (although none appears to have been recorded) would have to be dealt with by the High Court.

→glossary

A judge trying a Crown court case has **inherent jurisdiction** to deal with contempt by publication arising during such proceedings. But in 1997 the Court of Appeal ruled that only in exceptional circumstances should trial judges deal with such an alleged contempt themselves (*R v Tyne Tees Television* (1997) *The Times*, October 20). Crown court judges usually refer such matters to the Attorney General, who decides if the case should be referred to the High Court.

When are criminal proceedings active?

The strict liability rule applies only if proceedings are 'active'.

ch. 4 explains these early stages of a criminal case

The Act says a criminal case becomes active when:

- a person is arrested; or
- an arrest warrant is issued; or
- a summons is issued; or
- a person is charged orally.

These steps all mean that there is a definite prospect of an individual facing trial. A criminal case, if not already active because one of the above four events has occurred, also becomes active when the accused is served with a document specifying the charge(s). A potential problem for the media is that the police may not make clear, after a crime is committed, if a person is under arrest or simply 'helping police with their inquiries'. Journalists must press for clarification.

When do criminal proceedings cease to be active?

Criminal proceedings cease to be active when any of the following events occur:

- the arrested person is released without being charged (except when released on police bail);
- no arrest is made within 12 months of the issue of an arrest warrant;
- the case is discontinued;
- the defendant is acquitted or sentenced; or
- the defendant is found to be unfit to be tried, or unfit to plead, or the court orders the charge to lie on file.

Ch. 4, p. 41 and pp. 42–43 explain police bail and arrest warrants.

A defendant can be ruled to be unfit to be tried or unfit to plead if he/she suffers acute physical ill-health or mental illness. An order that a charge should 'lie on file' means the defendant has not been acquitted or convicted, but that the court agrees that the charge is no longer worth proceeding with. If after a lengthy trial a defendant is convicted of four charges but the jury cannot agree on the fifth, the judge may order that charge to 'lie on file' if the expense of a retrial for that charge would be excessive, or a conviction would not lead to a longer prison sentence.

Period between verdict and sentence at Crown court

A Crown court case remains active, even though all the verdicts have been reached, until the defendant is sentenced. It is technically possible for a media organisation to breach the strict liability rule during this period, although the jury's involvement has ended. But Crown court judges are regarded as too experienced to be influenced by media coverage, so it is thought unlikely that there will be any substantial risk of serious prejudice, whatever is published after all verdicts but before an adjourned sentencing. Media organisations are generally safe in publishing background features about such a case, including material which did not feature in the trial, as soon as the last verdict is given, although judges have been known to order the postponement of publication of such material until after sentencing.

Proceedings become active again when an appeal is lodged

The 1981 Act states that:

- when an appeal is lodged, the case becomes active again, so strict liability contempt resumes;
- the case ceases to be active when the hearing of any appeal is completed – unless in that appeal a new trial is ordered or the case is remitted to a lower court.

Lawyers often announce at the end of a criminal or civil case that their clients will appeal, but it usually takes some weeks for an appeal to be prepared and lodged.

Thus there is a time when the case is not active between, in a criminal case, the sentence and the lodging of an appeal.

Even if an appeal is lodged against a Crown court conviction, the media still have considerable freedom with regard to what can be published about such a case, even though it has become active again, as the appeal will be heard by the judges of the Court of Appeal.

ch. 8, p. 83 explains appeals from Crown courts

It can safely be assumed that nothing the media publishes will create a substantial risk of serious prejudice to the way these judges approach the case. But if they order a retrial – that is, another jury trial – the media must be wary of publishing anything which creates a risk of serious prejudice to the retrial, as witnesses and potential jurors will be considered susceptible to publicity about the case before and during the retrial.

Where to check if an appeal has been lodged

Appeals to the Court of Appeal from Crown courts may be lodged at the Crown court office. Appeals on a point of law to the Queen's Bench Divisional Court (the High Court) from a Crown court appeal hearing must be lodged at the Royal Courts of Justice in London. Appeals from magistrates court summary trials may be lodged at a local Crown court office.

see also ch. 15, p. 179 for Lord Macfadyen's ruling in similar circumstances

Case study

The High Court in Belfast in 2002 refused to issue an injunction to stop Ulster Television broadcasting a programme featuring new material which had not been put before the jury in a trial in which two men were convicted of murder. The men's lawyers said they intended to appeal and the material could prejudice the jury at any retrial. But Mr Justice Kerr said the possibility of a retrial was a matter of speculation.

Police appeals for media assistance

Sometimes when police have obtained a warrant for someone's arrest, they seek media help in tracing him/her. The warrant makes the case active under the 1981 Act. Police may supply the suspect's photograph and/or description for publication, even though visual identification may be an issue in the case. If the person is armed or likely to be violent, police may say so, to warn the public.

Technically, a media organisation publishing such a photograph, description, or warning about the person's character could be accused of creating a substantial risk of serious prejudice to such an active case.

But in the House of Commons during the debate on the Contempt of Court Bill in 1981, the then Attorney General said:

> "The press has nothing whatever to fear from publishing in reasoned terms anything which may assist in the apprehension of a wanted man and I hope that it will continue to perform this public service."

There is no known case of a media organisation being held in contempt for publishing such a police appeal. But there is no defence in the 1981 Act for assisting the police in this way.

The Attorney General's comments would not apply to information supplied by police which was published or repeated after the person's arrest.

Section 3 defence of not knowing proceedings were active

Section 3 of the Act provides a defence for an alleged breach of the strict liability rule which applies if:

- the person responsible for the publication, having taken all reasonable care, did not know and had no reason to suspect when the material was published that relevant proceedings were active.

The person accused of contempt must prove that all reasonable care was taken. So, to be sure that the section 3 defence can be used, a journalist reporting a crime story must check regularly with police, especially before a deadline, about whether someone has been arrested or charged, as either event would make the case active, and the story would need to be re-edited to remove any detail likely to breach the Act's strict liability rule. For some news stories it might be necessary for journalists to check with magistrates courts whether arrest warrants or summonses have been issued. If the police or court spokesperson says the case is not active, the journalist should keep a note of what was said, by whom and when, to prove that he/she took reasonable care to establish if the case was active.

See www.mcnaes.com ch. 17 for detail of when cases before certain types of tribunal are active. See p. 232, for detail of when a civil case is active.

What type of material can cause a substantial risk of serious prejudice?

The 1981 Act does not define what creates a substantial risk of serious prejudice to an active case. But cases in which editors and media organisations have been convicted of contempt show that material which could be held to be in contempt of court in active cases includes:

- references to a suspect or defendant's previous convictions;
- information suggesting he/she is dishonest or of bad character in other ways;
- any evidence seeming to link him/her directly to the crime of which he/she is suspected or accused;
- any other suggestion that he/she is guilty.

ch. 6 explains when 'bad character' evidence is admissible

If the person is tried, the magistrates or jury will probably not be told of his/her previous convictions, while character evidence may be admissible only in certain circumstances.

It could also be strict liability contempt in an active case to publish:

- a witness's detailed account of a relevant event – the risk this presents is explained below;
- a photograph, or footage or physical description of a suspect when visual identification of the alleged perpetrator is or is likely to be an evidential issue because:
  - a police identity parade is to be held; and/or
  - a witness is expected to testify at the trial on such identification.

! Remember

Contempt law is enforced more strictly in Scotland. This means particular care must be taken in cross-border publication, including on the internet. See the www.mcnaes.com chapter on Scotland.

Information suggesting a suspect or defendant is dishonest or of bad character

The *Daily Mirror* and *The Sun* were fined £50,000 and £18,000 respectively in 2011 over coverage in December 2010 and January 2011 of the arrest of former teacher Chris Jefferies, the landlord of murdered landscape architect Joanna Yeates. The court heard that one *Daily Mirror* front page carried the headline 'Jo Suspect is Peeping Tom' beneath a photograph of Mr Jefferies, and another front-page headline read 'Was Killer Waiting In Jo's Flat?', with sub-headings below reading 'Police seize bedding for tests' and 'Landlord held until Tuesday'. *The Sun's* front-page headline read 'Obsessed By Death' next to a photograph of Mr Jefferies and below the words 'Jo Suspect "Scared Kids"'. Attorney General Dominic Grieve QC said material in the articles gave an 'overall impression' that Mr Jefferies had a 'propensity' to commit the kind of offences for which he had been arrested. The Lord Chief Justice, Lord Judge, said section 2(2) of the Contempt of Court Act 1981 provided that the strict liability contempt rule applied only to a publication which created a substantial risk that the course of justice in the proceedings in question 'will be seriously impeded or prejudiced' and went on: 'Dealing with it briefly, impeding the course of justice and prejudicing the course of justice are not synonymous concepts. If they were, they would not have been identified as distinct features of the strict liability rule.' The issue of impeding the course of justice outside the trial process was 'less well trodden'. Vilification of a suspect under arrest was a potential impediment to the course of justice, he said, adding:

> At the simplest level publication of such material may deter or discourage witnesses from coming forward and providing information helpful to the suspect, which may, (depending on the circumstances) help immediately to clear him of suspicion or enable his defence to be fully developed at trial. This may arise, for example, because witnesses may be reluctant to be associated with or perceived to be a supporter of the suspect, or, again, because they may begin to doubt whether information apparently favourable to the suspect could possibly be correct.

Mr Jefferies won damages from newspapers for libel, see ch. 4

It was not an answer to argue that on the evidence actually available, the combination of the directions of the judge and the integrity of the jury would ensure a fair trial – the evidence at trial may be incomplete 'because its existence may never be known, or indeed may only come to light after conviction' (*Attorney-General v MGN Ltd and another* [2011] All ER (D) 06 (Aug)). Both newspapers said they intended to appeal to the Supreme Court. Mr Jefferies was released without charge after his arrest. Another man was charged with murdering Joanna, and convicted.

Case study

In 2011 the *Daily Mail* and *The Sun* were found guilty of strict liability contempt, after both mistakenly published on their websites a photograph which showed a man who was on trial for murder posing with an automatic pistol. The photograph had been taken from a social networking web page. It was the first time website operators in the UK had been found guilty of contempt. Lord Justice Moses, sitting with Mr Justice Owen in the High Court said: 'The criminal courts have been troubled by the dangers to the integrity and fairness of a criminal trial, where juries can obtain such easy access to the internet and to other forms of instant communication. This case demonstrates the need to recognise that instant news requires instant and effective protection for the integrity of a criminal trial.' The newspapers were found to have created a 'a substantial risk' of prejudicing the trial of Ryan Ward, who was eventually convicted of murdering father-of-two Craig Wass by hitting him on the head with a brick when he intervened in a row to protect Ryan's girlfriend. The offending photograph of Ward appeared on the two newspapers' websites alongside their reports of the first day of the trial. They were removed immediately the newspapers were alerted to the risk – the *Daily Mail* had used the picture uncut, but *The Sun* had cropped it, although part of the barrel of the gun could still be seen. No juror saw the pictures. The Divisional Court said that although the jury was warned against researching material on the internet, a juror would not have understood the trial judge's instructions to have prohibited reading online news reports of the case. The trust put in juries 'to put aside extraneous material' during a trial 'cannot always be relied upon by those whose publications put the prospects of a fair trial at substantial risk', and a publisher who created such a risk 'cannot always rely upon the steps taken to allay the very risk it has created'. The court was satisfied that there was 'a substantial risk that a juror would see the photograph and that there was a substantial risk of serious prejudice, namely that the jury would have had to be discharged, had that occurred' (*Attorney General v Associated Newspapers Ltd and another* [2011] All ER (D) 45 (Mar)). The court fined each paper £15,000 and ordered them to pay the Attorney General's costs of £28,117 (*Media Lawyer*, July 19, 2011).

Publishing a witness's detailed account

Publishing a witness's detailed account of a relevant event, after a case becomes active, may be deemed a contempt because of the risk that:

- **the witness may, because such a detailed account has been published, feel obliged to stick to it and therefore be less able honestly to retract or vary some detail after further reflection; or**
- **the witness's evidence may not figure in the trial at all, because it is ruled inadmissible or has been retracted – but if it has already been published other witnesses or jurors in the case may have read or heard it and been influenced by it.**

Visual identification

Publishing a photo footage or description could influence or confuse a witness who gives identification evidence so that the court may not be sure if the witness's evidence is based on what was seen during the crime or on recollection of a subsequently published photograph, footage or description.

Police investigating crimes often ask the media to publish a sketch or computer generated image of an alleged offender's face, as described by a witness, or issue a physical description, in an attempt to get the public to give information about the individual's identity.

The strict liability rule means that the image and description must usually not be published again after the case becomes active.

In 2004, the Queen's Bench Divisional Court ruled that a newspaper article which named two well-known Premier League footballers who were being questioned by police over allegations of gang rape at a London hotel created a substantial risk of serious prejudice, because visual identification of the alleged attackers was at issue at the time. The *Daily Star* was fined £60,000, and ordered to pay costs. Lord Justice Rose said the aggravating feature was that the media had been repeatedly told not to name or use pictures of the players under investigation. The Crown Prosecution Service eventually said there was insufficient evidence to prosecute the footballers.

! Remember

The examples of prejudicial material in this chapter relate mainly to the contempt risk of saying or suggesting that a suspect or defendant is guilty – but the strict liability rule can be breached by publishing material suggesting or asserting a suspect's innocence.

Injunctions

p. 214 explains the contempt risk from interviewing

The Attorney General can ask the High Court to grant an injunction forbidding publication of material which it has been told is about to be published and which could in its view create a substantial risk of serious prejudice to a criminal case. Such an injunction could also be issued to restrain other media activity seen as capable of creating serious prejudice, for example reporters' attempts to interview witnesses before a trial. It has been ruled that a Crown court has some power to grant such injunctions (*Ex p HTV Cymru (Wales) Ltd*, Crown Court at Cardiff (Aikens J) [2002] EMLR 184).

What can be published after a criminal case becomes active?

Contempt law does not mean that the media cannot publish anything about a crime after a case becomes active.

Non-prejudicial, basic information about the crime can be published. For example, the media can report that there was an alleged robbery, where it took place, and that later someone was arrested. Do not report that 'the robber was later arrested' as this says the arrested person is guilty of the offence. Note the Attorney General's concern about 'frenzied interest' in high-profile cases.

In most cases, it will not be contempt to name the arrested person, because he/she will be named at the trial. But it may be unsafe in libel law to name an arrested person before he/she is charged, and new law gives pre-charge anonymity to teachers accused by pupils, as chapter 4 explains.

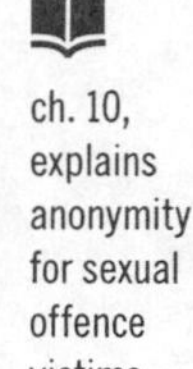

ch. 10, explains anonymity for sexual offence victims

In contempt law it is safe to identify the alleged victim of crime before any prosecution begins. But after court proceedings begin, anonymity law explained in chapters 9 and 11 may apply.

Common ground

It is not prejudicial to publish material which will be common ground between the defence and prosecution at the trial, such as non-prejudicial background material about a defendant and any alleged victim. Also, in a murder case, there will rarely be dispute about where the body was found. In contested cases, the nature and extent of a victim's injuries will probably be common ground because much of the forensic or medical evidence will be beyond dispute – the trial issue will be how the injuries were caused or who caused them.

How the courts interpret the strict liability rule

In *A-G v MGN Ltd* ([1997] 1 All ER 456) Lord Justice Schiemann set out the principles a court should follow when deciding whether published material created a substantial risk of serious prejudice in cases with a potential for jury trial. The court, he said, should consider what risk occurred at the time the material was published. The mere fact that by reason of earlier publications there was already some risk of prejudice did not in itself prevent a court finding that the later publication had created a further risk. The court should consider:

- the likelihood of the publication coming to a potential juror's attention;
- its likely impact on an ordinary reader; and
- crucially, the residual impact on a notional juror at the time of the trial.

Juries are told to put pre-trial publicity out of their minds

At the start of Crown court trials judges tell juries to decide their verdicts only on the evidence presented to them, and to put pre-trial publicity about the case, or media coverage of the trial, out of their minds. They are also warned not to research the internet for material.

Judges have made clear that juries must be trusted. In 1996 the then Lord Chief Justice, Lord Taylor, dismissed an appeal by Rosemary West, who was convicted of a series of murders, which was based in part on claims that she had not had a fair trial because of adverse publicity. He said:

> But, however lurid the reporting, there can scarcely ever have been a case more calculated to shock the public who were entitled to know the facts. The question raised on behalf of the defence is whether a fair trial could be held after such intensive publicity adverse to the accused. In our view it could. To hold otherwise would mean that if allegations of murder are sufficiently horrendous so as inevitably to shock the nation, the accused cannot be tried. That would be absurd.

More recently, senior judges have firmly re-stated the view that jurors given directions by a judge are capable of looking at the evidence fairly. In *Re B* ([2007] EMLR 5; *The Times*, November 6, 2006), Sir Igor Judge, as he then was, presiding at the Court of Appeal, stressed the robustness and independence of juries in a case in which the court lifted an order postponing reporting of a hearing at which Dhiren Barot, self-confessed terrorist, was to be sentenced.

He said, at paragraphs 31 and 32 of the judgment, that 'juries up and down the country have a passionate and profound belief in, and a commitment to' the defendant's right to a fair trial and went on:

> They know that it is integral to their responsibility. It is, when all is said and done, their birthright; it is shared by each one of them with the defendant. They guard it faithfully. The integrity of the jury is an essential feature of our trial process. Juries follow the directions which the judge will give them to focus exclusively on the evidence and to ignore anything they may have heard or read out of court.

The judge at the trial would give the jury appropriate directions, he said, adding: 'We cannot too strongly emphasise that the jury will follow them, not only because they will loyally abide by the directions of law which they will be given by the judge, but also because the directions themselves will appeal directly to their own instinctive and fundamental belief in the need for the trial process to be fair.'

There were, he added, at least two safeguards against the risk of prejudice – the media's responsibility to avoid inappropriate comment which might interfere with the administration of justice, and the trial process, including the integrity of the jury.

Ch. 15, pp. 178–179, refers to similar rulings on integrity of juries.

The 'fade factor' and limited publication

The 'fade factor' recognises that the public will probably have forgotten detail in reports published in the early stages of a criminal case, for example soon after the crime, or about the time that someone is arrested or charged, by the time a jury is selected. Other factors a court takes into account include the area

where the material was published, and the likely extent to which it was read – or, if broadcast, seen or heard – in that area.

A leading textbook, *Arlidge, Eady and Smith on Contempt* (2005) observes:

> “... a long gap between publication and the anticipated trial date may significantly reduce any risk of contamination. Also the fact that publication takes place in the local media, outside the anticipated area of trial, would be a major consideration in reducing the risk of prejudice.
>
> On the other hand, some facts are so striking, even when published some time in advance of the hearing, as to render it impossible to be confident that the conscientiousness of jurors, or the directions of a trial judge, would prevent a substantial risk that the course of justice in the trial would be seriously impeded or prejudiced ... This is especially so in the case of the revelation of a criminal record.”

see p. 219 on previous convictions

Case study

The lapse of time was a factor in assessing the substantial risk of serious prejudice in a contempt case in 1997. The *Daily Mail* and *Manchester Evening News*, which carried stories describing how a home help was caught on video film stealing from an 82-year-old widow, were found not guilty of contempt of court in the Queen's Bench Divisional Court. Mr Justice Owen said his initial view was that the stories were a plain contempt of court as they carried the clearest statements that she was guilty at a time when proceedings against her were active. The key issue was whether the stories created a substantial risk that the criminal proceedings against her would be seriously prejudiced. But the stories were several months old by the time of the trial, and he had concluded that the contempt allegation was not made good. But Lord Justice Simon Brown warned the media against thinking that when someone was apparently caught red-handed there was no possibility of a not guilty plea at trial (*A-G v Unger* [1998] 1 Cr App R 308).

! Remember

The 'fade factor' alone might not be enough to avoid liability for contempt if the court holds that published material has created an impediment to the course of justice – see the *Jefferies* case, above.

Publishing material shortly before or during a trial

The 'fade factor' offers no protection if the material concerned is published shortly before a trial begins or after it has started. In 2008 ITV Central was fined £25,000 for contempt for broadcasting an item on the morning on which the trial

of five men was due to start which reported that one defendant was in jail serving a sentence for murder.

Case study

In 2002 the *Sunday Mirror* was fined £75,000 for publishing an article which led to the collapse of the first trial of two Leeds United footballers on assault charges. The two-page spread was published while the jury was deliberating and had been sent home for the weekend. It contained an interview in which the victim's father said his son was the victim of a racial attack – the jury had been told that there was no evidence of a racial motive – and a story commenting on a major witness's credibility. In the contempt proceedings, counsel for the Attorney General estimated the cost of the aborted trial at £1,113,000 and the cost of the subsequent retrial £1,125,000 (*Attorney General v Mirror Group Newspapers Ltd* [2002] EWHC 907 (Admin)).

Archive material on news websites

The protection of 'the fade factor' does not apply to material which, since it was originally published, remains accessible to the public in a media organisation's online archive. Although judges instruct juries not to do research on defendants, jurors (and witnesses) might nevertheless search the internet for such material. Jurors might find stories in news archives referring to a defendant's previous convictions, or accounts of the crime they are trying which were published before the case became active. They might also find accounts published by foreign media which ignore UK contempt law.

UK media organisations say it would be impossible to keep checking whether anything in their online archives refers to people who have since become involved in any of the thousands of cases which are active at any time.

- But if a media organisation's attention is drawn to archived material which, in the view of the defence or prosecution creates a substantial risk of serious prejudice to a particular active case, the safest course to avoid a contempt problem is to remove it or block public access to it until the case is no longer active.

Lord Falconer, the former Lord Chancellor, suggested in 2008 that the Attorney General should be able to identify 20 or so high-profile cases where there was a distinct contempt risk and write to warn the media to remove prejudicial material from their websites.

In 2012 a juror was jailed for six months for contempt because she used the internet to research the defendant, despite the judge forbidding this. The trial at Luton Crown court had to be halted, and the defendant re-tried.

Media could face huge costs if 'serious misconduct' affects a case

Under the Courts Act 2003 the Lord Chancellor made regulations in 2004 allowing a magistrates court, a Crown court or the Court of Appeal to order a third party (which could be a media organisation) to pay costs which were incurred in a court case as a consequence of that party's 'serious misconduct' (Costs in Criminal Cases (General) (Amendment) Regulations 2004 (SI 2004/2408)). The 'serious misconduct' could be held to have occurred through publication of material, or through a reporter's action, even if there was no strict liability contempt. The measure was largely inspired by the costly abandonment of the trial in the Leeds footballers case following a *Sunday Mirror* article. If 'serious misconduct' not amounting to a contempt was held to have occurred in future, the media organisation involved could become liable for huge costs.

see case study on p. 226

Regulation 3F(4) says the court must allow the third party against whom such a costs order is sought to make representations, and it may hear evidence. An appeal against such an order made by magistrates may be made to the Crown court, an appeal against a Crown court order may be heard in the Court of Appeal. There is no appeal against such an order made in the Court of Appeal.

Court reporting – the section 4 defence

In some circumstances, a media report of a court hearing might create a substantial risk of prejudice to a later stage of the same case or to another case due to be tried.

Before the Contempt of Court Act 1981, even a fair and accurate report of proceedings in open court could be held to create such risk of prejudice, and so be contempt. But section 4 of the 1981 Act gives the media a defence, saying a person cannot be found guilty of breaching the strict liability rule in respect of a report of a court hearing held in public which is:

see ch. 21, pp. 265–266 for the definition of 'contemporaneous'

- a fair and accurate report of that hearing;
- published contemporaneously; and
- in good faith.

The Act does not define 'good faith', but the overall effect of section 4 is that courts are expected to make a specific order restricting the media if they do not want all, or part, of any hearing in public to be reported contemporaneously.

The section 4 defence does not protect reports of a court hearing held in private.

Inaccurate reporting of a current jury trial

The section 4 defence does not protect an unfair or inaccurate court report. The Queen's Bench Divisional Court fined the BBC £5,000 in 1992 for an inaccurate report of a continuing trial before a jury, saying it contained errors which created a substantial risk of serious prejudice since it was foreseeable that publication would delay and obstruct the course of justice (*A-G v BBC* [1992] COD 264).

Section 4(2) orders

In some circumstances, it might be argued that fair, accurate and contemporaneous reporting of a trial could prejudice a later stage of that case, or another case.

If several defendants are to be dealt with in a series of trials, publishing reports of the first in the series could arguably influence people who read or see them and who are then selected as jurors for the next or subsequent trials, which could concern different allegations against the same defendant(s).

ch. 4, p. 1 explains this principle

The jury in the second trial, because of the principle of the presumption of innocence for defendants, may well be told nothing about the earlier trial. But a juror in the second trial who remembers media reports of the first might be more likely to find a defendant guilty, especially if he/she was convicted in the first trial.

To avoid this danger, section 4(2) of the 1981 Act gives a court power to postpone publication of reports of a hearing or trial. In the example above, a judge could order that no report of the first trial should be published until the second has finished.

Section 4(2) says a court may order the postponement of the reporting of a case, or part of a case:

- where this appears to be necessary for avoiding a substantial risk of prejudice to the administration of justice in those proceedings; or
- in any other proceedings, pending or imminent; and that
- the period of postponement may be as long as the court thinks necessary for this purpose.

Note that a court may make a section 4(2) order if there is a substantial risk of *any* prejudice, not necessarily 'serious' prejudice. Publishing material which breaches a section 4(2) order is punishable as contempt, with an unlimited fine and/or a maximum of two years in jail.

Normally all charges against a defendant can be reported prior to any trial, even under the automatic reporting restrictions of other statutes as described in chapters 6, 7 and 8. But in cases involving a defendant who faces more than one trial, a Crown court judge may at a stage prior to trial – for example, at the →glossary **arraignment** – make a section 4(2) order postponing publication of the charge(s) the defendant is due to face in any subsequent trial until after the end of the first trial, to stop potential jurors in the first trial knowing that the same defendant is to face another trial.

Ch. 15, pp. 176–180, explains the grounds on which the media may challenge the imposition of a section 4(2) order.

What if a section 4(2) order is not made?

Pleas made in a hearing before the trial

Sometimes, a defendant facing a number of charges will, when arraigned, plead guilty to some but deny the others, so the jury will try him/her on the charge(s) he/she has denied. If a media organisation carries a report before the end of that trial which mentions that the defendant has admitted, or faces, other charge(s), and if the jury has not been told of other charges and/or any such guilty plea (that is, a previous conviction), the judge might feel obliged, to ensure fairness to the defendant, to stop the trial and order a retrial before a fresh jury elsewhere. Had the judge made a section 4(2) order before the trial began, postponing reporting of the other charge(s) or guilty plea(s), the media's position would have been clear, and they would have obeyed the order. But if the judge did not make such an order, the legal position would be less clear on whether reporting the other charge(s)/guilty plea(s) during the trial was a contempt.

In the view of some legal experts, the section 4 defence should protect the media in such circumstances. Their view is that the defence should apply, unless the court makes clear, by making a section 4(2) postponement order, that information aired in open court should not be contemporaneously reported. But the section 4 defence is subject to 'good faith' in publishing, so it would fail if it could be proved that the person responsible for publication deliberately intended to create prejudice to the subsequent trial. Proof of such intent could lead to the offence being regarded not as a breach of the 1981 Act but as a graver contempt at common law.

Proceedings in court in the absence of the jury

During trials judges often have to rule on the admissibility of evidence or other matters after hearing argument from defence and prosecution lawyers, while the jury is kept out of the courtroom. The process of making such a ruling is still classed as a public proceeding. But the judge may tell the lawyers not to mention the matters discussed to the jury if the matters are prejudicial. Publishing reports of those discussions and rulings before the verdicts are given could lead to the trial being aborted. But the judge might not make a section 4(2) postponement order covering things discussed or ruled in court in the jury's absence, because he/she expects the media to realise that such prejudicial matters should not be published prematurely.

The law is not clear

The application of the law of contempt in both the circumstances outlined above – that is, publication before a trial of any guilty plea(s)/other charge(s), or contem-

poraneous reporting of discussions in a jury's absence during a trial – is unclear if no section 4(2) order has been made.

***Arlidge, Eady and Smith on Contempt* (2005), says:**

> “ Suppose that through oversight or other reason no such [section 4(2)] order is made. Suppose also that information comes to light in the absence of the jury – guilty pleas, or an inadmissible confession for example – which journalists readily appreciate would be likely to prejudice the jury if its members were to find out about it. It may well be in such circumstances that publication of that information would give rise to a substantial risk of serious prejudice, and thus to a *prima facie* contempt under the strict liability rule. It would seem that in principle, provided the publication took place in good faith, the [section 4 defence] protection would prevail. Even if the journalists were conscious of the risk of serious prejudice at the time of publication, it would be difficult to infer any intention on their part to interfere with the administration of justice sufficient to found a common law contempt, since they would presumably (in accordance with the majority view in *R v Horsham Justices, ex p Farquharson* [1982] QB 762) be entitled to assume that the court, having the power to order a section 4(2) postponement, knew its own business and had decided on good and sufficient grounds to make no such order. ”

 See pp. 213–214 for more detail of the common law of contempt.

Journalists should not, even if no section 4(2) order is made, contemporaneously report things discussed or rulings made when the jury is not in the courtroom during a Crown court trial. Even if the publication cannot be held to be contempt, there is a risk that a media organisation might be accused of 'serious misconduct' under section 93 of the Courts Act 2003 and be held liable for the costs of an aborted or delayed trial. The material can be published after all verdicts are reached, unless the judge orders otherwise. But judges have been known to make clear on occasion that they have no objection to contemporaneous reporting of what happened in the jury's absence because they did not think it would be prejudicial. Arguably, a cautious approach should be taken to publication of any other charge(s) faced, or guilty plea(s) entered, by a defendant who is shortly to be tried on other matters, unless it is clear that the jury will be told about them.

Section 5 defence of discussion of public affairs

Section 5 of the Contempt of Court Act 1981 says:

> “ a publication made as, or as part of, a discussion in good faith of public affairs will not be treated as contempt of court under the strict liability rule if the risk

of impediment or prejudice to particular legal proceedings is merely incidental to the discussion. ”

The defence was introduced because of complaints that freedom of expression in the UK was unnecessarily restricted by a ruling in a case in 1973.

Case study

The *Sunday Times* wanted to publish an article raising important issues of public interest about the way the drug Thalidomide was tested and marketed – at a time when civil actions were pending against the manufacturers, Distillers Company (Biochemicals) Ltd, on behalf of children born with deformities because their mothers took the drug during pregnancy. The House of Lords ruled that the proposed article would be contempt in respect of those pending cases (*Attorney General v Times Newspapers Ltd* [1974] AC 273; [1973] 3 All ER 54). The Government-appointed Phillimore Committee said of the decision: ‘At any given moment many thousands of legal proceedings are in progress, a number of which may well raise or reflect such issues (matters of general public interest). If, for example, a general public debate about fire precautions in hotels is in progress, the debate clearly ought not to be brought to a halt simply because a particular hotel is prosecuted for breach of the fire regulations.’

The European Court of Human Rights held in 1979 that the Lords’ ruling violated the right to freedom of expression under Article 10 of the European Convention on Human Rights.

The Government responded by introducing the section 5 defence. The time of liability for contempt in civil proceedings was also changed, and is now explained below.

Two newspapers were prosecuted in 1981 for contempt arising from comments published during the trial of Dr Leonard Arthur, a paediatrician accused of murdering a new-born baby with Down’s syndrome. It was alleged at the trial that the doctor, complying with the parents’ wishes, let the infant starve. Dr Arthur was acquitted of murder. The *Sunday Express* admitted that a contempt was committed in a comment article by the editor, John Junor, which said the baby had been drugged instead of being fed and had died ‘unloved and unwanted’. The editor was fined £1,000 and Express Newspapers £10,000.

But the *Daily Mail* denied contempt, arguing that its article, which discussed ‘mercy killing’ generally, was protected by section 5. The House of Lords held on appeal that while the article did create a substantial risk of serious prejudice to Dr Arthur’s trial, it was written in good faith and, because it was written in support of a ‘pro-life’ candidate at a by-election, was a discussion of public affairs. Lord Diplock said the article made no express mention of Dr Arthur’s case and the risk of prejudice would be properly described as merely incidental (*The Times*, December 16 and 19, 1981; *Attorney General v English* [1983] 1 AC 116).

Safest course

To be sure of section 5 protection a media organisation should not, when publishing a general feature or discussion about a social issue, refer in it to any active case in which the issue figures, and in particular should not suggest that the defendant in such a case is or is not guilty.

Contempt of civil proceedings under the 1981 Act

Under the strict liability rule:

- civil proceedings are deemed to be active from the time a date for the trial or a hearing is fixed; and
- a civil case ceases to be active when it is disposed of, abandoned, discontinued or withdrawn.

There is generally less possibility of media coverage creating a substantial risk of serious prejudice to active civil cases than to active criminal cases, as most civil cases are tried by a judge alone, and judges are regarded as highly unlikely to be affected by media coverage.

 Ch. 12 explains civil courts, and which cases could involve juries.

But there remains the possibility that witnesses in any civil case could be affected by media coverage if it delves so deeply into the circumstances of the case that witnesses' evidence given in advance of or at the trial could be coloured or their memories be contaminated by detail they read or see in reports.

When a jury is involved, particular care must be taken not to breach the strict liability rule, and material aired in court in the jury's absence should not be published while the jury remains involved in the case.

Case study

Mr Justice Poole, in the High Court sitting in Birmingham in 1999, reminded reporters that civil proceedings remained active until a case ended. A jury had decided in favour of a man claiming damages from West Midlands Police for malicious prosecution. Before the jury decided on the amount of damages, the *Birmingham Post* suggested he would get £30,000. The judge said the proceedings were therefore tainted. The claimant abandoned his case rather than go through a retrial (*Media Lawyer*, Issue 25, January/February 2000).

Sometimes when a journalist seeks a comment about a civil case, a lawyer involved →glossary will insist that little can be published because it is **sub judice** – a term indicating merely that the legal action has begun. But this is not the same as the case being active: a civil case becomes active at what may be a later stage, when a date is fixed for the trial or hearing – and even then, media coverage is not prohibited, provided the strict liability rule is obeyed.

Ch. 12, pp. 133–134 explains the contempt danger of reporting that a 'payment into court' has been made in a civil case.

Other contempts under the 1981 Act

Section 8 of the Act says it is a contempt to seek to discover or to publish how an individual juror voted in a verdict, or what was discussed by a jury to reach a verdict.

ch. 11 explains these sections

Section 9 of the Act says it is a contempt to use or take into court for use any audio recorder (except with the court's permission), and to broadcast any such recordings.

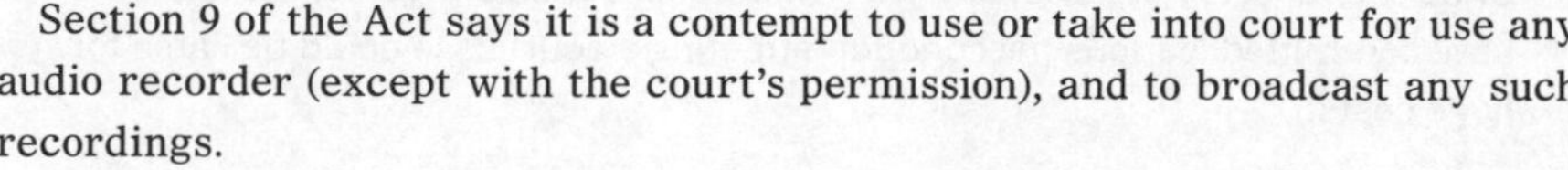

Section 11 of the Act gives courts powers, when they allow a name or other information to be withheld from the public, to prohibit publication of that name or material in connection with the proceedings. Breach of a section 11 order would be a contempt.

Contempt in reports of court hearings held in private

see ch. 11, pp. 120–123 on the 1960 Act

Section 12 of the Administration of Justice Act 1960 makes it a contempt for the media to publish an account of what was said or done at a court hearing held in private if the case falls within certain categories. The ban also covers quoting from court documents in such cases.

Recap of major points

- For the media, the greatest danger of committing contempt of court lies in publishing material which, under the Contempt of Court Act 1981, could be ruled to have created a substantial risk of serious prejudice to an 'active' case.
- Certain types of information are more likely than others to be regarded as creating such a risk – for example, details of the previous convictions of a defendant awaiting trial.
- Journalists should know when under the 1981 Act a criminal or a civil case becomes active, and when it ceases to be active – because the 'active period' determines what can be published.

- Juries are rarely used in civil cases, so the media have greater leeway about what can be published about active civil cases than they have in relation to active criminal cases.
- In prosecuting under the 1981 Act for strict liability contempt the Attorney General does not have to prove intent to cause prejudice.
- Under section 4(2) a court can order the media to postpone a report of a court case, or part of it, to avoid a substantial risk of prejudice.
- Section 5 provides a defence for a published discussion in good faith of public affairs where the risk of prejudice is merely incidental to the discussion.
- When during a trial there are legal discussions or rulings which occur when the jury is not in the courtroom, the media should not report such matter until all verdicts are reached.
- Under the Courts Act 2003, any party, including a media organisation, held to have committed 'serious misconduct' affecting a court case could be liable for huge costs.

((•)) Useful Websites

www.judiciary.gov.uk/publications-and-reports/guidance/2011crown-court-reporting-restrictions-guidance-2009/

Guidance on reporting restrictions, published by the Judicial College (formerly the Judicial Studies Board), the Newspaper Society, the Society of Editors and Times Newspapers Ltd

Part 3

Defamation and related law

19

Defamation – definitions and dangers

Chapter summary

This chapter explains what defamation is and why it is of such concern to journalists and publishers. It covers the risks of being sued for libel and losing, and so having to pay huge costs and damages, which could exceed £1 million. The chapter explains the definitions of what is defamatory. The following chapters explain who can sue for defamation, what the claimant must do to bring an action, and the defences. Defamation is one of the greatest legal dangers for anyone who earns a living with words and images – so handling a complaint or drafting an apology about something published is not a job for an inexperienced journalist.

Seeking legal advice

Defamation law is complex, so this book can provide nothing more than a rough guide. While media organisations can sometimes safely go further than many journalists suppose, they must also stop and reflect before taking what might be a dangerous course of action.

The golden rule for journalists is that if publication seems likely to bring a threat of libel, they should first take professional advice.

But the media's role in exposing wrongdoing is extremely important. As Lord Justice Lawton (then Mr Justice Lawton) said in a case in 1965:

> “It is one of the professional tasks of newspapers to unmask the fraudulent and the scandalous. It is in the public interest to do it. It is a job which newspapers have done time and time again in their long history.”

What is defamation?

The law protects an individual's personal and professional reputation from unjustified attack. In civil law a statement making such an attack may be found to be a tort – a civil wrong for which a court may award monetary damages.

Defamatory statements are those published or spoken which affect the reputation of a person, company, or organisation. A defamatory statement in written or in any other permanent form is a libel, for which damages can be awarded. But a statement may be protected by a defence.

A defamatory statement which is spoken is the tort of slander, which may also incur damages unless a defence applies. But there are exceptions – defamatory statements which are spoken in a broadcast on radio or television, by cable, or spoken in the public performance of a play are classed as libel, by the Broadcasting Act 1990 and Theatres Act 1968 respectively, if no defence applies. Libel and slander have different requirements about what a claimant must prove, as chapters 20 and 24 explain.

In the past, juries tried most defamation cases. But a judge may hear a case alone, if both sides want this, or he/she rules that a jury should not be used (for example, if the case is so complex that having to explain all the paperwork to a jury will make the trial considerably longer). Fewer cases are now heard by juries, and proposed reforms could make jury trial the exception rather than the rule.

In a case with a jury:

- the judge rules whether a statement complained of is capable of bearing a defamatory meaning;
- if the answer is yes, a jury must decide whether, in the circumstances in which the statement was made, it was in fact defamatory.

A key issue may be the meaning of words in the context of their use. If a jury decides the statement was defamatory, it decides how much in damages the publisher must pay the defamed party.

A judge taking a trial alone makes all these decisions.

See also ch. 12, pp. 136–137 on the historical reason why defamation cases can have juries.

Definitions of a defamatory statement

Judges explaining defamation to juries tell them that a statement about a person is defamatory if it *tends to*:

- expose the person to hatred, ridicule, or contempt; or
- cause the person to be shunned or avoided; or

- lower the person in the estimation of right-thinking members of society generally; or
- disparage the person in his/her business, trade, office, or profession.

The words 'tends to' are important. The claimant does not have to show that the words actually did expose him/her to hatred, etc.

Even lawyers sometimes find it difficult to decide whether a statement is defamatory, and judges sometimes disagree. A judge ruled that this story about the film stars Tom Cruise and Nicole Kidman, his then wife, was not capable of bearing a defamatory meaning and struck it out of the couple's claim. He said the allegation was 'unpleasant, maybe; defamatory, no'. The story appeared in the magazine section of the *Express on Sunday*, on October 5, 1997:

> 'Nicole bans brickies from eyeing her up' said the papers last year. Not much of a story, really: the Cruises had the builders in to do a little work on their LA mansion and Nicole ordered the hapless hodwielders to turn and face the wall as she passed. Quite natural, of course: you and I would do the same thing. They were brickies, after all, so they ought to be facing the wall.

The Court of Appeal restored the statement to the couple's claim, saying it was 'very much a matter for the jury to consider'. Their counsel had told the court that imputing arrogance was plainly capable of being defamatory.

Note the phrase 'right-thinking members of society generally' in the third definition. It is not enough for someone claiming libel to show that the words of which he/she complains have lowered him/her in the estimation of a limited class in the community who may not conform with that standard.

! Remember

It is almost always defamatory to say of a person that he/she is a liar, or a cheat, or a criminal, or is insolvent or in financial difficulties – whether the statement is a libel will depend on whether the publisher has a defence, for example it can be proved true.

Meaning of words

The legal test of what words mean is what a 'reasonable person' would think they mean – it is not necessarily the meaning intended by the author or publisher. Sir Anthony Clarke, Master of the Rolls, detailed the principles of deciding meaning in *Jeynes v News Magazines Ltd* ([2008] EWCA Civ 130), saying (at paragraph 14):

> They may be summarised in this way: (1) The governing principle is reasonableness. (2) The hypothetical reasonable reader is not naïve but he is not unduly suspicious. He can read between the lines. He can read in an implication more readily than a lawyer and may indulge in a certain amount of loose thinking but he must be treated as being a man who is not avid for scandal and someone who does not,

> and should not, select one bad meaning where other non-defamatory meanings are available. (3) Over-elaborate analysis is best avoided. (4) The intention of the publisher is irrelevant. (5) The article must be read as a whole, and any 'bane and antidote' taken together. (6) The hypothetical reader is taken to be representative of those who would read the publication in question. (7) In delimiting the range of permissible defamatory meanings, the court should rule out any meaning which, 'can only emerge as the produce of some strained, or forced, or utterly unreasonable interpretation...' (8) It follows that 'it is not enough to say that by some person or another the words might be understood in a defamatory sense'. ”

p. 241 explains 'bane and antidote'

see also ch. 20, p 252 on juxtaposition

The words must be read in full and in their context, because a statement which is innocuous when standing alone can acquire defamatory meaning when juxtaposed with other material. Juxtaposition is a constant danger for journalists, particularly for sub-editors and those dealing with production. Those editing footage must take care how pictures interact with each other, and with any commentary – and beware the meanings which are being created.

Inferences

Many statements may carry more than one meaning.

- **An inference is a statement with a secondary meaning which can be understood by someone without special knowledge who 'reads between the lines in the light of his general knowledge and experience of worldly affairs'.**

For example, an inference is created if someone says: 'I saw the editor leave the pub, and he was swaying and his speech was slurred'. The inference is that the editor was drunk, though the term 'drunk' is not used. But for some statements there may be dispute about whether a defamatory inference was created.

Innuendoes

- **An innuendo is a statement which may seem innocuous to some people but which will be seen as defamatory by people with special knowledge.**

For example, saying 'I saw our editor go into that house on the corner of Sleep Street' would not in itself be defamatory, unless the communication is to someone who knows that the house is a brothel.

The term innuendo comes from a Latin word meaning 'to nod to'.

The libel claimant who argues that he/she has been defamed by an innuendo must show not only that the special facts or circumstances giving rise to the innuendo exist, but also that they are known to people to whom the statement was published.

Case study

In 1986 Lord Gowrie, a former Cabinet Minister, received 'substantial' damages over a newspaper article which created the innuendo that he took drugs. He had recently resigned as Minister for the Arts and the *Daily Star* newspaper asked: 'What expensive habits can he not support on an income of £33,000? I'm sure Gowrie himself would snort at suggestions that he was born with a silver spoon round his neck.' His **counsel** said the reference to expensive habits, the suggestion that he could not support those habits on his ministerial salary, the use of the word 'snort' and the reference to a 'silver spoon around his neck' all bore the plain implication to all those familiar with the relevant terminology that Lord Gowrie took illegal drugs, particularly cocaine, and had resigned because his salary was not enough to finance the habit.

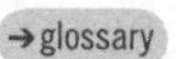

A journalist would clearly be mistaken to believe that using inference or innuendo is any safer in libel law than making a direct allegation.

Bane and antidote

Just as a defamatory meaning may be conveyed by a particular context, so it may be removed by the context. A judge said in 1835 that, if in one part of a publication something disreputable to the claimant was stated that was removed by the conclusion, 'the bane and the antidote must be taken together'.

The House of Lords applied this rule in 1995 (*Charleston v News Group Newspapers Ltd* [1995] 2 AC 65), when it dismissed a case in which Ann Charleston and Ian Smith, two actors from the television series *Neighbours*, sued the *News of the World* over headlines and photographs in which their faces were superimposed on models in pornographic poses.

The main headline read: 'Strewth! What's Harold up to with our Madge?' The text said:

> “What would the Neighbours say . . . strait-laced Harold Bishop starring in a bondage session with screen wife Madge. The famous faces from the television soap are the unwitting stars of a sordid computer game that is available to their child fans . . . The game superimposes stars' heads on near-naked bodies of real porn models. The stars knew nothing about it.”

The actors' counsel conceded that anyone who read the whole of the text would realise the photographs were mock-ups, but said many readers were unlikely to go beyond the photographs and headlines.

Lord Bridge said it was often a debatable question, which the jury must resolve, whether the antidote was effective to neutralise the bane. The answer depended not only on the nature of the libel a headline conveyed and the language of the text which was relied on to neutralise it, but also on the manner in which all the material was set out and balanced. In this case, no reader who read beyond the first paragraph could possibly have drawn a defamatory inference.

Lord Nicholls warned that words in the text would not always 'cure' a defamatory headline. 'It all depends on the context, one element in which is the layout of the article. Those who print defamatory headlines are playing with fire.'

Changing standards

Imputations which were defamatory a hundred years ago may not be defamatory today, and vice versa. During the First World War a UK court decided that it was a libel to write falsely of a man that he was a German.

Is it defamatory to call someone homosexual? It used to be, but now no 'right-thinking member of society' should think less of someone because they are gay. So to state wrongly that someone is gay would not in some circumstances be defamatory. But it could be defamatory if it implies the person lied about his/her sexual orientation.

Case study

Singer-songwriter Robbie Williams won 'substantial' damages from publisher Northern and Shell in 2005 after the magazines *Star* and *Hot Star* ran stories alleging that he had omitted from a forthcoming authorised biography details of an alleged sexual encounter with a man in a Manchester club's toilets, and that by disclosing details of his female conquests but not mentioning this episode he was concealing his true sexuality. The allegations were completely false – the publisher apologised, and paid damages and the singer's costs (*Robert Peter Williams v Northern and Shell Plc*, statement in High Court, December 6, 2005).

Why media organisations may be reluctant to fight defamation actions

Defamation law tries to strike a balance between the individual's right to a reputation and the right to freedom of speech, and so provides defences for the person who makes a defamatory statement about another for an acceptable reason – see subsequent chapters. But media organisations can be reluctant to fight defamation actions, for a variety of reasons.

Uncertainty of how a judge or jury will interpret meanings

The first is the uncertainty about how a judge or jury will decide the meaning of what was published. For example, a statement which seems innocuous to one person may, equally clearly, be defamatory to another.

It is difficult even for skilled defamation lawyers to forecast a jury's decision.

ch. 21 explains the truth defence

Difficulty of proving the truth

Even if a journalist and his/her editor are convinced of a story's truth, they may be unable to prove it in court. People needed as witnesses to an event may not want to get involved in a libel case; witnesses' memories may prove unreliable; they may forget detail by the time the trial begins; by the time the case gets to trial they may have moved address and cannot be traced.

Huge damages could be awarded if trial lost

Media organisations considering contesting a libel action also find it difficult to assess the damages which might be awarded should they lose, especially if they are to be decided by a jury.

Some juries have awarded huge sums.

Case study

In 2000 the magazine *LM* (formerly *Living Marxism*) shut down after a jury awarded a total of £375,000 damages to two television reporters and ITN over a story accusing them of having sensationalised the image of an emaciated Muslim pictured through barbed wire at a Serb-run detention camp in Bosnia (*The Guardian*, March 31, 2000).

The Court of Appeal has the power to substitute its own figure for a jury award it considers to be excessive or inadequate.

In 2002 libel judge Mr Justice Eady said that the ceiling for the most serious defamatory allegations was currently 'reckoned to be of the order of £200,000'. That was the figure he awarded in that year, when trying a case without a jury, to each of two nursery nurses wrongly accused of sexual abuse (*Christopher Lillie and Dawn Reed v Newcastle City Council, Richard Barker, Judith Jones, Jacqui Saradjian and Roy Wardell* [2002] EWHC 1600 (QB)).

But in October 2005 a jury awarded Southampton Football Club chairman Rupert Lowe £250,000 over an article which said he had behaved 'shabbily' in suspending the club's manager after child abuse allegations. It was the highest award for more than four years. Since then there have been fewer jury trials and more awards of damages, at much lower levels, by judges.

Huge costs

If damages are high, they are dwarfed by legal costs, which are generally paid by the loser.

In one case Mirror Group Newspapers paid £15,000 in settlement of a defamation action but was then presented with a costs bill of £382,000 – which was reduced on appeal.

In 1994 the BBC had to pay an estimated £1.5 million costs in a case heard by a judge who awarded £60,000 damages. The libel was in a *Panorama* programme, 'The Halcion nightmare', which reported that, long before the sleeping drug Halcion was banned in the UK, there was evidence that it might have had serious adverse side effects.

In June 2010 martial arts expert Matthew Fiddes, a former bodyguard to entertainer Michael Jackson, dropped, at the doors of the court, his defamation case against Channel 4 over a documentary about members of the Jackson family. By that time, Channel 4's costs exceeded £1.5 million. Mr Fiddes was operating on a no win, no fee **Conditional Fee Agreement (CFA)**.

→glossary

It may be better to settle

Unsurprisingly, faced with these kinds of figures for costs and damages should the case be lost in a trial, even ardent campaigning editors sometimes decide either not to carry a story or, having carried it, to avoid a trial by apologising and paying damages.

As the vast majority of libel cases settle out of court, with the amounts involved rarely being disclosed, the ongoing cost of libel actions to media organisations is often underestimated. Settlements usually involve paying some or all of the other side's costs.

'No win, no fee' legal representation

The introduction of CFAs, known as 'no win, no fee', for libel cases in 1998 had a serious chilling effect on the media, significantly restricting what the public was able to read and hear, most obviously when articles, books or programmes were changed because of legal considerations.

see Useful Websites, below, on 'no win, no fee'

Legal aid was never available for libel actions, so historically the libel courts were beyond the reach of people on modest incomes. But CFAs meant litigants without the means to sue could do so, represented by lawyers who received nothing if they lost a case but could claim up to a 100 per cent increase on fees if they won. In January 2010 the European Court of Human Rights held that a 100 per cent success fee claimed by Naomi Campbell's lawyers from Mirror Group Newspapers was a breach of the publisher's right to freedom of expression. In 2011 the coalition Government announced that it would implement reforms recommended by Lord Justice Jackson in his report on costs and stop success fees and premiums for insurance taken out by claimants to cover a winning defendant's costs from being reclaimed from a defendant who loses a case.

The media had argued that the CFA system meant it could be held to ransom by an impecunious claimant on a CFA. If the claimant lost, the media defendant was unlikely to recover its costs, while if the claimant won, the media defendant had to pay not only damages but also the lawyers' 'success fees', and the insurance premiums. There was also no incentive for a claimant on a CFA to exercise any control over what the solicitor was spending, as it would be paid by the defendant. The pressure to settle such cases rather than go to court is considerable.

Freedom of expression

Most journalists believe that defamation law, in attempting to 'strike a balance' between protecting reputation and allowing freedom of speech, has been tilted historically in favour of claimants.

But developments in recent years seem likely to tilt the balance, to a greater or lesser degree, in favour of freedom of expression.

ch. 1 explains the Convention generally

They are:

(1) The Human Rights Act, which took effect on October 2, 2000, requiring courts to pay regard to Article 10 of the European Convention on Human Rights, concerned with freedom of expression. The European Court of Human Rights has said that Article 10 does not involve a 'choice between two conflicting principles' but 'a freedom of expression that is subject to a number of exceptions which must be narrowly construed'.

(2) The decision of the House of Lords in *Reynolds v Times Newspapers* ([2001] 2 AC 127), which greatly extended the ambit of the defence of privilege, a decision which was further clarified in *Jameel v Wall Street Journal Europe Sprl* ([2006] UKHL 44, [2007] 1 AC 359).

ch. 22 explains the *Reynolds* defence

(3) Judges' increased willingness to strike out cases in which a claimant could not show that a substantial tort had been committed, for example because of limited publication of the material in question.

Further reforms are in the pipeline, although it is thought that these will not come into effect until 2013, possibly later. If they are introduced they should make English libel law less claimant-friendly and give greater weight to freedom of expression.

Errors and apologies

Sometimes publication of the words which cause a libel problem are the result of an innocent error. The arrival of a solicitor's letter from a potential claimant which could start the journey to the High Court is the moment to take legal advice. Libel law is not a matter for an inexperienced person, because of the dangers of aggravating a problem by mishandling it. A reporter who receives a complaint about something which has been published should refer the issue to the relevant executive or editor.

ch. 21, pp. 272–273 explains the danger of ill-considered apologies

Publishing an apology or an inadequate correction can itself, in certain circumstances, create a further libel problem.

But the correct legal steps, including, if necessary, publishing a prompt apology or correction can remove the heat from a libel threat, and save thousands of pounds even if the claim is settled.

! Remember

The most common cause of libel actions against media organisations is a journalist's failure to apply professional standards of accuracy and fairness. The best protection against becoming involved in an expensive action is to make every effort to get the story right.

Recap of major points

- A defamatory statement made in permanent form is generally libel; if in transient form it is generally slander.
- In a libel action, the test of what the words actually mean is the test of what a reasonable person would take them to mean.
- Words may carry an innuendo, a 'hidden' meaning clear to people with special knowledge, or create an inference, obvious to everybody.
- The financial implications of losing a libel action in terms of damages and costs are so punitive that journalists must always consider whether what they are writing or plan to broadcast will be defensible if a libel action results.
- The decision to publish an apology, and how any apology is worded, needs to be made by a person experienced in handling complaints.

Useful Websites

www.libelreform.org/
Libel Reform Campaign – says UK libel law is too repressive

www.justice.gov.uk/consultations/draft-defamation-bill.htm
Ministry of Justice proposals for libel reform

www.lawsociety.org.uk/choosingandusing/payingforservices/nowinnofee.law
Law Society explanation of 'no win, no fee' arrangements

20

The claimant and what must be proved

Chapter summary

This chapter details who can sue for libel, and explains that the law places a low burden of proof on people who do. A claimant has to prove that the material was published to a third party – a formality, in a case against the media, that it is capable of bearing the defamatory meaning complained of, and that he/she has been identified in it. But the claimant does not have the burden of proving the material is false. The publisher must prove the material true or be protected by another defence, as the next chapter explains. A claimant can sue anyone who 'publishes' the libel, including reporters and the publication's distributors.

Who might sue?

All citizens as individuals have the right to sue for libel – that is, to be a claimant.

The availability of 'no win, no fee' arrangements, described in chapter 19, has opened the libel courts to greater numbers of people. This reinforces the need for accuracy and to approach stories thus:

- Is what I am writing potentially defamatory?
- If so, do I have a defence?

Corporations

A corporation can sue for a publication which injures its trading reputation. The House of Lords ruled in 2006 that a corporation should not have to prove that it had suffered financial loss in order to collect damages (*Jameel v Wall Street Journal* [2006] UKHL 44). Lord Bingham gave some examples of injurious statements:

> that an arms company has routinely bribed officials of foreign governments to secure contracts; that an oil company has wilfully and unnecessarily damaged the environment; that an international humanitarian agency has wrongfully succumbed to government pressure; that a retailer has knowingly exploited child labour...

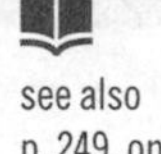

see also p. 249, on disparaging goods

Lord Bingham said a company's good name was a thing of value, as was an individual's. A damaging libel might lower its standing in the eyes of the public and even its own staff, make people less ready to deal with it, or less willing or less proud to work for it.

Local and central government

ch. 24 explains malicious falsehood

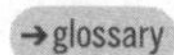

→glossary

The House of Lords ruled in *Derbyshire County Council v Times Newspapers* ([1993] AC 534) that institutions of local or central government cannot sue for defamation in respect of their 'governmental and administrative functions' as this would place an undesirable fetter on freedom of speech. But they can sue as institutions for libels affecting their property, and for malicious falsehood if they can show **malice**.

A council's individual members or officers *can* sue if what is published can be seen as referring to them personally. Lord Keith said in the *Derbyshire County Council* case:

> A publication attacking the activities of the authority will necessarily be an attack on the body of councillors which represents the controlling party, or on the executives who carry on the day-to-day management of its affairs. If the individual reputation of any of these is wrongly impaired by the publication any of these can himself bring proceedings for defamation.

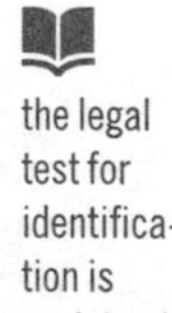

the legal test for identification is explained on p. 7

An individual can pursue a libel claim if what is published 'identifies' them, which can occur even if they are not named, as this chapter explains.

As a general rule, an association, such as a club, cannot sue unless it is an incorporated body, but words disparaging an association will almost invariably reflect on the reputations of one or more of the officials who, as individuals, can sue if 'identified'.

Trade unions

The practitioners' book *Duncan and Neill on Defamation*, 3rd edition points out at paragraph 10.11, p. 100, that the House of Lords apparently accepted in the *Derbyshire County Council* case cited above that trade unions can sue, even though they are not corporate bodies. A union's individual officers can also sue.

Members of Parliament

The Defamation Act 1996 allows Parliamentarians to waive their parliamentary privilege in defamation actions and sue.

Disparaging goods

The question of whether a publication can defame a person or a firm by disparaging goods is increasingly important as product testing becomes commonplace in newspapers, magazines and other media.

The answer is yes. But it is not enough that the statement should simply affect the person adversely in his/her business – it must also impute to him/her discreditable conduct in that business, or tend to show that he/she is ill-suited or ill-qualified to do it. (See *Griffiths v Benn* [1911] 927 TLR 26 CA, applied in *James Morford and Others v Nic Rigby and the East Anglian Daily Times Co Ltd*, Court of Appeal, February 17, 1998.)

For example, it is defamatory to write falsely of a businessman that he has been condemned by his trade association, or of a bricklayer that he/she does not know how to lay bricks properly.

Not all words criticising a person's goods are defamatory – for example, a motoring correspondent could criticise a car's performance without reflecting on the character of the manufacturer or dealer. But the statement might prompt an action for malicious falsehood.

The imputations which give most problems in this context are dishonesty, carelessness and incompetence.

In 1994 a jury awarded £1.485 million damages to the manufacturer of a yacht, Walker Wingsail Systems plc, over an article in *Yachting World* which contrasted the manufacturer's striking claims for the yacht's performance with its drastically poorer performance when tested by the journalist.

What the claimant must prove

A claimant suing for libel has to prove that:

- the publication is defamatory; and
- it may be reasonably understood to refer to him/her – that is, 'identification'; and
- it has been published to a third person.

This can be remembered as 'defamation, identification, publication'.

Defamation

Legal definitions of defamatory statements are given in chapter 19. Broadly speaking, any allegation which could affect someone's reputation among honest citizens is defamatory.

The claimant does *not* have to prove the statement is false. If a statement is defamatory, the court assumes it is false. If the statement is true and the journalist can prove it is true then there is a defence, as the next chapter explains.

ch. 21 explains 'offer of amends'

ch. 22 explains *Reynolds*

The claimant does not have to prove intention: it is no use the journalist saying 'I didn't mean to damage this person's reputation'. But intent is relevant in the 'offer of amends' defence.

The claimant does not have to prove that he or she has suffered actual damage, only that the statement *tends* to discredit – and may sue for libel even though the people to whom a statement was published knew it was untrue. The court presumes damage.

The *Reynolds* defence provides protection in some circumstances for publishing untrue statements in the public interest.

Identification

The claimant must prove that the published material identifies him/her.

Some journalists believe they can play safe by not naming an individual – but omitting the name may prove no defence.

- The test of whether the published statement identified the claimant is whether it would reasonably lead people acquainted with him/her to believe that he/she was the person referred to.

A judge said in 1826: 'It is not necessary that all the world should understand the libel; it is sufficient if those who know the claimant can make out that he is the person meant' (*Bourke v Warren* (1826) 2 C&P 307). That is still the law.

In the late 1980s and 1990s the Police Federation, representing junior police officers, brought many actions against newspapers on behalf of their members. During the 33 months to March 1996 it launched 95 libel actions, winning them all and recovering £1,567,000 in damages.

Many of the officers were not named in what was published, but it was claimed that acquaintances and/or colleagues would realise who they were. In one case, the *Burton Mail* paid £17,500 compensation plus legal costs to a woman constable who featured anonymously in a story following a complaint about an arrest. It was argued that the story's details identified her.

Derogatory comments about an institution can reflect upon the person who heads it – newspapers have had to pay damages to head teachers, who were not named in the paper, for reports which criticised schools.

Wrong photos or wrong caption

People are identified by what they look like, so using the wrong photo could identify someone in a defamatory context, even if they are not named.

Using file or 'stock' photographs or film to illustrate stories or features is fraught with libel risks. A photo of a social function, with people holding drinks, is perfectly acceptable – but if it is later used as a stock shot to illustrate the perils of drinking, those pictured may sue, particularly any who are teetotal.

Confusion about who is shown in a photograph can be costly. In 2007 the *Daily Mail* offered substantial damages to a former martial arts world champion whose photograph was mistakenly used in coverage of a robbery trial. The man had nothing to do with the trial, but shared a first name with a defendant who was also a martial arts champion (*Press Gazette*, July 26, 2007). In 2005 the *Sunday Mirror* paid out £100,000 plus costs to a man falsely identified in a photo as the rapist Iorworth Hoare (*Press Gazette*, June 3, 2005).

Importance of ages, addresses and occupations

It is dangerous to make a half-hearted effort at identification, particularly in court reports.

Case study

In *Newstead v London Express Newspapers Ltd* [1940] 1 KB 377, the *Daily Express* had reported that 'Harold Newstead, a 30-year-old Camberwell man', had been jailed for nine months for bigamy.

Another Harold Newstead, who worked in Camberwell, sued the newspaper, claiming that the account was understood to refer to him – and won. He argued that if the words were true of another person, which they were, it was the paper's duty to give a precise and detailed description of that person, but the paper had 'recklessly struck out' the convicted person's occupation and address.

! Remember

A defendant's age, address and occupation, if mentioned in court, or provided by the court, should be given with his/her name in reports of the case, unless the court directs otherwise. Chapter 14 explains that courts should give reporters such details.

Blurring identity increases risk

The problem with not fully identifying the subject of a story is not only that the person may argue in a libel case that he/she was the person referred to, but also that another may claim that the words were taken to refer to him/her. A newspaper quoted from a report by the district auditor to a local council, criticising the council's deputy housing manager. The paper did not name him. But a new deputy manager who had taken over sued, claiming he was thought to be the offending official.

Defamation of a group

If a defamatory statement refers to someone as being a member of a group, and includes no other identifying detail of that person, all members of the group, if it is sufficiently small, may be able to sue for defamation, although the publisher intended to refer to only one of them.

For example, saying: 'A detective at Blanktown police station is corrupt', without naming the allegedly corrupt individual, will allow all the detectives there to sue because the statement 'identifies' them to their acquaintances and colleagues.

Even if the publisher has evidence that one is corrupt, the rest will win damages. But if the group referred to is large, no one member will be able reasonably to claim to have been identified merely by a reference to the group. Case law does not set a clear figure for when a group is too large for those in it to claim that reference to the group identified them as individuals. But in one case, reference to a group of 35 police dog-handlers based in an area of London was ruled to be sufficient to identify them as individuals.

Case study

A case in 1986 concerned a reference published by a newspaper to an allegation that detectives at Banbury CID had raped a woman. The newspaper did not name those allegedly involved. It was successfully sued by members of the group, which comprised only 12 detectives (*Riches and others v News Group Newspapers Ltd* [1985] 2 All ER 845).

Referring to a group may also identify those with particular responsibility for it. Saying: 'The supermarket in Blanktown Road is run badly' refers to a small group of managers, each of whom could sue.

Juxtaposition

Placing a photograph incorrectly, or using the wrong picture, can cause expensive problems if it wrongly suggests by juxtaposition that someone shown is a person 'identified' in the accompanying story.

In 2002 motivational therapist and part-time nightclub doorman Shabazz Nelson won 'substantial' damages from *The Sun* after it used his picture with an article in which Oasis star Liam Gallagher alleged he and his girlfriend were assaulted by door attendants at the Met Bar in London. The piece was illustrated by a picture of Mr Nelson, who was working there that night as a doorman. Mr Nelson had not assaulted Mr Gallagher or his girlfriend but 'conducted himself in a perfectly proper and responsible manner', and was 'understandably concerned' that *Sun* readers who saw the article 'would have understood that he was the subject of Mr Gallagher's claims', Mr Justice Eady was told at the High Court.

The editing and 'voice-over' of footage can also cause trouble, if the commentary is 'juxtaposed' with an unconnected image.

Case study

In 1983 a Metropolitan Police detective constable won £20,000 damages from Granada TV after being shown during a *World in Action* programme on Operation Countryman, an anti-corruption investigation into the force, walking out of West End Central police station as the voice-over said: 'Since 1969 repeated investigations show that some CID officers take bribes'. The officer was not identified by name, and there was no suggestion that he was guilty of such behaviour – he was merely a figure in a background shot. But his recognisable, unexpected guest appearance earned him healthy damages because it wrongly 'identified' him as corrupt.

Publication

The claimant must prove that the statement was published. There is no defamation if the words complained of, however offensive or untrue, are addressed in speech or writing only to the person to whom they refer. To substantiate defamation, they must have been communicated to at least one other person. In the case of the news media, there is no difficulty – publication is widespread.

Internet publication

There is an exception to this rule about publication for claimants suing over items on the internet published by foreign parties. In 2005 the Court of Appeal ruled that it would be an abuse of process (resulting in the court rejecting the claim) for a claimant to sue for libel over material on the internet unless 'substantial publication' in England could be shown.

Case study

In *Dow Jones and Co Inc v Yousef Abdul Latif Jameel* ([2005] EWCA Civ 75) a Saudi Arabian businessman sued the Dow Jones company over an article on the *Wall Street Journal's* online internet subscriber service, which had a hyperlinked list of alleged donors to an organisation which was allegedly a front for Al Qaida. Mr Jameel claimed that the article was defamatory and meant that he was a financial supporter of Osama Bin Laden and Al Qaida. But the Court of Appeal said the list was downloaded by only five people in England – three, including his lawyers, were in Mr Jameel's 'camp', and the other two were unknown. There was no 'real or substantial' tort.

The court will not assume that internet publication is necessarily substantial publication (*Amoudi v Brisard* [2006] 3 All ER 294). A court in Canada ruled that hyperlinks to articles containing defamatory material did not amount in that particular case to substantial publication of defamatory statements by the publisher of the article containing the hyperlinks (*Crookes v Wikimedia Foundation Inc.* (2008) BCSC 1424).

Repeating statements of others

Every repetition of a libel is a fresh publication and creates a fresh cause of action. This is called the repetition rule. It is no defence to say that you, the publisher, are not liable because you are only repeating the words of others.

The person who originated the statement may be liable, but anyone who repeats the allegation, for example by quoting from a defamatory press release, may also be sued. One of the most common causes of libel actions is repeating statements made by interviewees without being able to prove the truth of the words. Also, a publisher who 'lifts' (copies and publishes) material published elsewhere is also liable.

In 1993 and 1994 papers paid damages to defendants in the Birmingham Six case, who were jailed for terrorism but later cleared on appeal. Former West Midlands police officers were accused of fabricating evidence in the case, but prosecution of the officers was abandoned. The *Sunday Telegraph* subsequently reported one of the three officers as referring to the Birmingham Six and saying: 'In our eyes, their guilt is beyond doubt.' *The Sun* published an article based upon the *Sunday Telegraph*'s interviews. It later carried an apology and reportedly paid £1 million in damages to the six.

Online archives and repetition

see www.mcnaes.com ch. 20 for details of this case

The repetition rule is particularly relevant to websites containing archive material. The rule dates from the 1849 case of the Duke of Brunswick, who sued a newspaper for defamation after sending his butler to buy a back copy. Nowadays the Duke would call up the archive version on the internet.

As chapter 21 explains, it is normally a defence to a libel action that it was not launched until more than a year after the publication. However, the law is that every time an article or footage or sound-recording in an archive is accessed by a reader or viewer or listener, this amounts to a new publication and can give rise to a new action. So, the limitation period does not apply to website material which the public can access. This makes it especially important to remove from an archive material which has been held to be libellous.

Case study

In 2001 the Court of Appeal confirmed that 'the rule in the Duke of Brunswick case' was still law and applied to the internet. *The Times* published articles alleging an international businessman had been involved in criminal activities, and he sued both for the stories in the paper and for those in its archive, available on the internet. The paper argued that the 'single publication' rule should apply to internet publication and that it should be the rule that an internet 'publication' took place only on the day the material was posted. But the appeal judges rejected this argument (*Loutchansky v Times Newspapers Ltd* [2001] EWCA Civ 1805; [2002] QB 783; [2002] 2 WLR 640; [2002] 1 All ER 652).

In 2006 a businessman, Jim Carr, won two libel damages payouts from the *Sunday Telegraph* over one story. In April that year he won £12,000 and an apology over an article published in November 2005. The newspaper later paid him a further £5,000 in damages over the same defamatory story, which, by an oversight, had remained available on its website.

Journalists must also be alert when handling the 'bygone days' column. A doctor received damages for statements published afresh in 1981 in the 'Looking

Back' column of the *Evening Star*, Ipswich. The statements, repeated from an article published 25 years previously, were unchallenged when first published.

Who are the 'publishers'?

A person who has been defamed may sue the reporter, the sub-editor, the editor, the publisher, the printer, the distributor, and the broadcaster. All have participated in publishing the defamatory statement and are regarded as 'publishers' at common law. However, some may be able to use the defence in section 1 of the Defamation Act 1996.

ch. 21 explains section 1

➡ Recap of major points

- A claimant suing for libel must prove three things: (1) it is defamatory, (2) it may be reasonably understood to refer to him, (3) it has been published to a third person.
- The test of 'identification' is whether the words would reasonably lead people who know the claimant to believe he/she was the person referred to.
- Publication is assumed in the case of traditional media. But this is not always the case with online publication.
- Every repetition is a fresh publication. The journalist is liable for repeating a defamatory statement made by an interviewee or source.
- As for internet publications, the law says every time an article is accessed, that amounts to a new publication.

21

Defences

Chapter summary

The law provides defences for media organisations sued for defamation – and without them many of the stories published and broadcast each day would be suppressed for fear of a libel action. This chapter explains the main defences, and gives practical advice on what a journalist must do when preparing a story to ensure it meets their requirements.

The main defences

Journalists need to know how libel defences work, as the steps they take in researching and writing a story will often determine whether a defence is available to avoid a costly libel action.

The main defences are:

- justification – truth;
- honest comment, previously called fair comment;
- absolute privilege;
- qualified privilege;
- accord and satisfaction;
- offer of amends.

Justification

It has been suggested that the justification defence should be re-named truth.

The requirements of justification

- The defence requires that the published material complained of can be proved in court to be substantially true.
- The standard of proof needed for a justification defence is that used in civil cases – the material must be proved true 'on the balance of probabilities'.

This is a lower requirement than 'beyond reasonable doubt', the standard of proof in criminal cases. But it means that a media organisation relying on justification must have enough evidence to persuade a jury, or the judge if there is no jury, that its version of the disputed event(s) is the correct one.

If this requirement is met, it gives complete protection against a libel action (a limited exception arises under the Rehabilitation of Offenders Act 1974.)

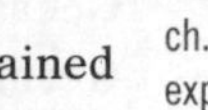

ch. 23 explains that Act

The justificaiton defence applies to statements of fact. If the words complained of are an expression of opinion they may be defended as honest comment.

Media organisations sued for libel often rely on both justification and honest comment as defences, applying each to different elements of what was published.

The 'sting' of the libel must be proved

Section 5 of the Defamation Act 1952 says that, in a defamation case involving publication of two or more 'charges' (allegations affecting the claimant's reputation) against the claimant, 'a defence of justification shall not fail by reason only that the truth of every charge is not proved if the words not proved to be true do not materially injure the [claimant's] reputation having regard to the truth of the remaining charges.'

This means that at trial the defendant does not have to prove the truth of every defamatory statement in what was published. But the most damaging or serious allegation (which lawyers call the 'sting') must be proved, and the damage to reputation it causes must dwarf any damage caused by unproved allegations. If a newspaper runs a story saying that a politician is cruel to his children and swears at his neighbours, the former allegation is the sting – the most damaging. But if in such a case a media organisation was unable to prove the minor allegations, it might find it harder to persuade a jury that the major allegation is true.

Examples of the justification defence

The *Daily Telegraph* succeeded with its justification defence when it was sued by tennis player Robert Dee after reporting that he was 'ranked as the worst professional tennis player in the world after 54 defeats in a row ...' The newspaper pleaded justification and fair comment. Mrs Justice Sharp held that the facts in the story were sufficient to justify any defamatory meaning the words were capable of bearing (*Robert Dee v Telegraph Media Group Ltd* ([2010] EWHC 924 (QB); [2010] EMLR 20).

The Sun newspaper succeeded with the justification defence in 1994 when it was sued by TV actress Gillian Taylforth and her fiancé Geoff Knights over a front-page splash headlined 'TV Kathy's "sex romp" on A1' saying the couple had indulged in oral sex in a parked car. (The *Independent*, January 13–26, 1994).

The Sun obtained confirmation from police that Knights had been cautioned for indecency because of the incident. When it was sued it 'joined' the police in the defence, with the result that the main defence witness was the officer who said he saw the incident. Two *Sun* reporters got into a car to show the jury, to a decent extent, that it was possible to achieve the positions in which the policeman said he saw Taylforth and Knights. It was estimated that losing the case cost the couple £500,000.

Cases in which the media plead justification can be extremely complex. In 1992 Scottish Television (STV) successfully defended a libel action brought by Antony Gecas, the former platoon commander of a Lithuanian police battalion under German occupation who settled in Edinburgh after the Second World War. It had accused him, in a 1987 programme called *Crimes of War*, of having been involved in murdering thousands of Jews. When sued, STV faced the difficult task of proving its account of events which happened nearly half a century before. The judge found for STV. The case cost an estimated £1.5 million.

Case study

In 1997 *The Guardian* newspaper and Granada TV risked paying huge libel damages and costs when they defended a case brought by former Conservative Cabinet Minister Jonathan Aitken over reports in the newspaper and the *World in Action* programme that he was involved in arms dealings with Saudi businessmen and that he allowed an Arab business associate to pay his bill at the Ritz hotel in Paris, in breach of ministerial guidelines. Aitken resigned from the Cabinet in order, he said, to pursue *The Guardian* and 'cut out the cancer of bent and twisted journalism in our country with the simple sword of truth and the trusty shield of British fair play'. *The Guardian* discovered vital evidence at a late stage in the trial and Aitken, who appeared to be winning, abandoned the case, facing a £2 million costs bill. He was later jailed for perjury (*The Guardian*, June 8, 1999).

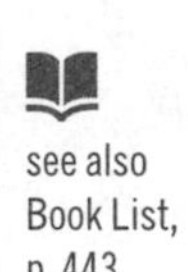

see also Book List, p. 443

Levels of meaning and reporting on police investigations

When considering reports linking a claimant with criminal or wrongful conduct, the courts recognise three levels of meaning:

- the report may mean the person is guilty of the criminal offence or misconduct (a level 1 meaning – if the court decides this meaning applies, then a publisher using the justification offence will have to prove that the offence or misconduct occurred); or

- the person is reasonably suspected of the offence or misconduct (level 2); or
- there are grounds for an investigation – for example, by the police (level 3).

These are known as *Chase* level 1, 2 and 3 meanings, having been detailed by Lord Justice Brooke in *Chase v News Group Newspapers* ([2002] EWCA Civ 1772; [2003] EMLR 2180).

Proving reasonable suspicion or that there were grounds for an investigation

It is defamatory to say someone is reasonably suspected of an offence, or there are grounds for an investigation into his/her conduct, because it implies there *was* conduct on the person's part which warrants the suspicion. So a successful plea of justification must prove conduct on the individual's part which gives rise to the suspicion or the grounds. It is no use saying other people told you about their suspicions (*Shah v Standard Chartered Bank* [1999] QB 241).

Case study

In *Chase v News Group Newspapers Ltd* (cited above) *The Sun* newspaper paid £100,000 damages to children's nurse Elaine Chase for a story headlined 'Nurse is probed over 18 deaths'. Police were investigating the deaths of a number of terminally ill children she had treated but concluded – after the newspaper's story appeared – that there were no grounds to suspect her of an offence. *The Sun* tried to show there were reasonable grounds for suspicion. But the Court of Appeal said it was relying almost entirely on the fact that a number of allegations against her had been made to the hospital trust and police. The only respect in which the newspaper focused upon the nurse's conduct concerned an allegation made after publication, which the court said could not be taken into consideration.

Avoid implying habitual conduct

The statement that someone 'is a thief' may be true – but if the basis for the statement is just one minor conviction, for example for stealing a packet of bacon from a shop, a defence of justification would almost certainly fail, as the individual would argue that the words meant he was a persistent thief, whereas he was essentially an honest man who had had a single lapse.

Inferences and innuendoes must be proved

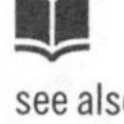

see also ch. 19 on meanings of words

Justification means proving not only the truth of each defamatory statement but also any reasonable interpretation of the words and any innuendoes lying behind them.

Persisting with the justification defence can be financially risky

Persisting in the justification defence has financial risks. If it fails the court will take a critical view of a defendant's persistence in sticking to a story which it decides is not true, and the judge or jury may award greater damages accordingly.

See also ch. 19, pp. 242–243 on why media organisations may be reluctant to fight defamation actions.

The investigative journalist – practical advice on procedure

www.mcnaes.com chapter 21 gives tips for journalists beginning to do investigations, to help them to prove the truth. For example, the journalist should persuade each witness to make a signed statement and date it, before the story is published. In some circumstance it may be best to persuade them to sign an

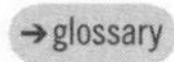
affidavit.

A media organisation's case is often weakened because a journalist has not kept notebooks or recordings in good order to prove what someone has said.

Honest comment

The defence of honest comment, as it is now called, protects published opinion, not any statement put forward as factual. The defence was formerly known as

fair comment, but its name was changed by a decision in the **Supreme Court** in December 2010. Media organisations using the honest comment defence will also be prepared to run another defence in tandem – it could be justification, absolute privilege or qualified privilege.

The requirements of honest comment

The main requirements of the honest comment defence are:

- the published comment must be the honestly held opinion of the person making it (though it may have been published by another party);
- it must be recognisable (that is, to the reader/viewer/listener) as comment rather than as a factual allegation;
- it must be based on provably true facts/privileged material;
- it must explicitly or implicitly indicate, at least in general terms, the facts on which it was based. But the facts might also be so widely known that this is not necessary; and
- the subject commented on must be a matter of public interest.

All these requirements must be met if the defence is to succeed. The third bullet point shows why the justification and privilege defences underpin it.

Only comment, not facts

A judge gave an example of an opinion protected by the honest comment defence, saying that if one accurately reported what some public man had done, then said 'Such conduct is disgraceful', that is merely an expression of one's opinion, a comment on the person's conduct. But if one asserted that the man was guilty of disgraceful conduct without saying what that conduct was, one was making an allegation of fact for which the only defences were justification or privilege.

This rule seemed to be relaxed by Mr Justice Eady's decision in *Lowe v Associated Newspapers* ([2006] EWHC 320) that a defendant was not confined to relying in support of the comment on facts actually stated or alluded to in the article itself, but might also rely on facts not to be discerned from the article, but known to the person commenting, either the journalist or the person whose opinion he or she was reporting, at the time he/she made the comment. But the defendant could not rely on facts which the person making the comment learned after publication.

Mr Justice Eady said the article did not need to state so much of the facts that readers could decide whether they agreed with the comment; it was enough if the reader could tell that it was comment, not fact.

This view was reinforced when the Supreme Court held in *Spiller and another v Joseph and Others* ([2010] UKSC 53) that it was incorrect to require that the comment must identify the matters on which it was based with sufficient particularity to enable the reader to judge for himself whether it was well founded. Instead, it said, the comment 'must explicitly or implicitly indicate, at least in general terms, the facts on which it was based'.

Case study

Sub-editors must take special care if they introduce comment into headlines. In 2003 the *Daily Telegraph* published articles making allegations about left-wing MP George Galloway after a reporter found documents said to refer to him in a ruined government building in Baghdad soon after the invasion of Iraq. One story was headlined 'Telegraph reveals damning new evidence on Labour MP'. When sued, the paper did not claim the allegations were true but said the headline was an expression of opinion. But the judge said 'damning' had a plain meaning – 'that is to say, that the evidence goes beyond a *prima facie* case and points to guilt'. The MP won the libel case (*George Galloway MP v Telegraph Group Ltd* [2004] EWHC 2786 (QB)).

ch. 22, pp. 282–283 has for a fuller account of this case

The exception to the rule that comment must be based on true facts is when the comment is based on privileged material, such as a report of judicial proceedings or proceedings in Parliament. A media organisation can safely make scathing comment about a defendant convicted of a crime, if based on privileged reports of the trial's evidence. The honest comment defence will succeed in relation to what was published at the time of the conviction even if the defendant is later acquitted on appeal. The defence can also protect publication of criticism of judges and magistrates, based on privileged reports of their actions in court.

Opinion must be 'honestly held', not 'fair'

The law does not require the 'truth' of the comment itself to be proved; by its nature it cannot be. Comment may be responsible or irresponsible, informed or misinformed – but cannot be true or false. Defendants pleading honest comment do not need to persuade either the judge or the jury to share their views – but they do need to satisfy the jury that the comment on established facts represents a view that a person could hold. Mr Justice Diplock told the jury in his summing up in *Silkin v Beaverbrook Newspapers* ([1958] 1 WLR 743 (QB)): 'The basis of our public life is that the crank and the enthusiast can say what he honestly believes just as much as a reasonable man or woman. It would be a sad day for freedom of speech in this country if a jury were to apply the test of whether it agrees with a comment, instead of applying the true test of whether this opinion, however exaggerated, obstinate, or prejudiced, was honestly held.'

Proof of malice can defeat the honest comment defence

In *Tse Wai Chun Paul v Albert Cheng* (Court of Final Appeal, Hong Kong [2001] EMLR 777) Lord Nicholls explained that when comment was being considered as a defence, the term 'malice' covered a situation where a defendant 'put forward as his view something which, in truth, was not his view. It was a pretence. The law does not protect such statements'.

While the defence was not defeated by the fact that the writer was actuated by spite, animosity, intent to injure, intent to arouse controversy, or other motivation, even if that was the dominant or sole motive, Lord Nicholls said, proof of such motivation might be evidence from which a jury could infer lack of an honestly held belief in the view expressed.

Imputing improper motives

The suggestion that someone has acted from improper motives has been hard to defend as honest comment.

But judges in the Court of Appeal took a more helpful view when entrepreneur Richard Branson sued his biographer Tom Bower for libel (*Branson v Bower* [2001] EWCA Civ 791; [2001] EMLR 800). Bower had written of Branson's attempt to run the national lottery: 'Sceptics will inevitably whisper that Branson's motive is self-glorification'. Bower said this was fair comment but Branson said it was a factual allegation (that he had a questionable intention in bidding for the national lottery) and was untrue.

Lord Justice Latham, giving the Court of Appeal's judgment, said comment was 'something which is or can reasonably be inferred to be a deduction, inference, conclusion, criticism, remark, observation', and that the judge in the lower court was fully entitled to conclude that Bower was expressing a series of opinions about Branson's motives.

Reviews

The honest comment defence protects the expressions of opinion contained in reviews of, among other things, performances, books, holidays and restaurants.

Humour, satire and irony

In 2008 Sir Elton John sued *The Guardian* for libel over a spoof article written by Marina Hyde under the headline 'A peek at the diary of... Sir Elton John' – a regular feature in the paper's Weekend section satirising the activities of celebrities and others. Sir Elton claimed the article meant his commitment to the Elton John Aids Foundation was insincere and that once the costs of his White Tie and Tiara fund-raising ball were met only a small proportion of the funds raised would go to good causes. *The Guardian*'s defence was that the words were clearly comment and could not have the meaning claimed by the claimant.

Mr Justice Tugendhat, striking out Sir Elton's claim, accepted *The Guardian*'s argument that the words were a form of teasing, and that had it actually unearthed a story about a charity ball's costs leaving nothing for good causes it would have treated it as a serious story and written it without any attempt at humour (*Sir Elton John v Guardian News and Media Ltd* [2008] EWHC 3066 (QB)).

Privilege

On some occasions the public interest demands that there should be complete freedom of speech without any risk of proceedings for defamation, even if the statements are defamatory and even if they turn out to be untrue. These occasions are referred to as privileged. Privilege exists under common law and statute.

Absolute privilege

The defence of absolute privilege, where applicable, is a complete answer and bar to any action for defamation. It does not matter whether the words are true or false, or whether they were spoken or written maliciously.

But while someone may be speaking on an occasion which is protected by absolute privilege it does not follow that a journalist's report of the comments is protected by absolute privilege. Members of Parliament may say whatever they wish in the House of Commons without fear of being sued for defamation.

The reports of parliamentary proceedings in *Hansard* are protected by absolute privilege; as are reports published by order of Parliament, such as White Papers. But media reports of the contents of parliamentary publications enjoy only qualified privilege, a defence which depends on there being a proper motive in publication.

The requirements of absolute privilege

ch. 17 explains tribunals

Journalists only enjoy absolute privilege when they are reporting court cases or the proceedings of certain types of tribunal.

In this context the requirements of absolute privilege are that what is published is:

- a fair and accurate report of judicial proceedings held in public within the United Kingdom, published contemporaneously.

The protection was extended, by the Defamation Act 1996, to reports of the European Court of Justice, or any court attached to that court, the European Court of Human Rights, and any international criminal tribunal (a war crimes tribunal) established by the Security Council of the United Nations or by an international agreement to which the UK is a party.

Privilege for court reports is vital for the media because what is said in court is often highly defamatory, and reporting it would be impossible without the protection of the privilege. The law recognises that the media help sustain open justice, a principle examined in chapter 14. Privilege does not apply if the court (or tribunal) hearing is held in private.

Reports must be fair

For absolute privilege to apply, a report of a court case must be 'fair and accurate'. This does not mean that the proceedings must be reported verbatim; a report will still be 'fair and accurate' if:

- it presents a summary of the cases put by both sides;
- it contains no substantial inaccuracies;
- it avoids giving disproportionate weight to one side or the other.

In a case in 2006 (*Bennett v Newsquest*, see *Media Lawyer*, No. 64), Mr Justice Eady pointed out that a newspaper report of a criminal case, which was the subject of a libel action, contained inaccuracies, then said:

> “The report must be fair overall and not give a misleading impression. Inaccuracies in themselves will not defeat privilege. Omissions will deprive a report of privilege if they create a false impression of what took place or if they result in the suppression of the case or part of the case of one side, while giving the other.”

A media organisation loses the protection of absolute privilege if its report is held to be unfair or inaccurate in any important respect. To be fair, a report of a trial must make clear that the defendant denies the charge(s) and, while it proceeds, that no verdict has been reached – for example, the report can conclude by stating: the case continues.

How much of a court case must be reported to be fair?

In 1993 the *Daily Sport* paid substantial damages to a police officer acquitted of indecent assault. It reported the opening of the case by the prosecution and the alleged victim's main evidence, but did not include her cross-examination by the defence, which began on the same day and undermined her allegation. Later the paper briefly reported the officer's acquittal. He still decided to sue but the case was settled, leaving the issue of how much of a day's proceedings in court must be covered for a report to be fair as something of a grey area.

A trial may last for weeks, or months, and the defendant may show that statements made by the prosecution in its early stages were wrong. Reports of proceedings may be published each day, but the safest practice is that a publication which has reported allegations that are later rebutted should also carry the rebuttals.

Reports must be accurate with quotes attributed

All allegations in court reports must be attributed because a report that presents an allegation as if it were a proved fact is inaccurate. Do not write 'Brown had a gun in his hand' but 'Smith said Brown had a gun in his hand'.

A media organisation which wrongly identifies as the defendant someone who is only a witness or unconnected with the case will have no protection. A report which gets the charge or charges a defendant faces wrong could prove expensive in libel damages.

Ch. 20, p. 251 explains the need for a report to fully identify a defendant.

Journalists must also avoid wrongly reporting that the defendant who was actually acquitted has been convicted. One paper paid damages when it reported a man's acquittal on drug charges – but in terms which gave the impression that he was guilty.

see also www.mcnaes.com ch 21: 'Case study on accuracy'

The courts do allow some leeway to publications compressing material in reports (*Elizabeth and Peter Crossley v Newsquest (Midlands South Ltd)* [2008] EWHC 3054 (QB)).

Reports must be contemporaneous

To have the protection of absolute privilege, court reports should be published contemporaneously with the proceedings. Contemporaneous means 'as soon as practicable' – for example, in the first issue of a newspaper following the day's hearing. For a broadcaster, it can be construed that the report should be aired on the same day of the hearing or early the next day. For a weekly paper, contemporaneous publication may mean publishing the following week.

Sometimes reports of court proceedings have to be postponed because a court order compels this. Section 14(2) of the Defamation Act 1996 says that in these

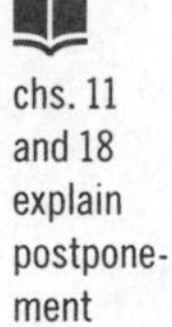

chs. 11 and 18 explain postponement orders

circumstances a story is treated as if it were published contemporaneously if it is published 'as soon as practicable after publication is permitted'.

Even if the report is not contemporaneous, it will still attract qualified privilege under statute and under common law, explained below.

Reports of earlier sections of a hearing published to put later reports in context should still be treated as having absolute privilege (*Elizabeth and Peter Crossley v Newsquest (Midlands South Ltd)* [2008] EWHC 3054 (QB)).

Privilege is only for reports of proceedings

Suppose a 'court report' in the media contains background matter or comment that did not originate from the court. In the *Bennett* case referred to above, the judge said this would not destroy the privilege of the report: 'Extraneous comments can be included or other factual material but it must be severable, in the sense that a reasonable reader could readily appreciate that the material did not purport to be a report of what was said in court.'

The additional material itself is not covered by privilege.

Outbursts from the public gallery

Privilege may not protect defamatory matter shouted out in court – from the public gallery, for example, by someone who is not part of the proceedings. But if the shouted comment is by someone who has given evidence as a witness in that case, privilege would protect its inclusion in a court report, provided all the defence's requirements were met. If the shouted comment is not defamatory, it can in libel law be reported safely, no matter who made it.

Qualified privilege

Qualified privilege is available as a defence where it is considered important that the facts should be freely known in the public interest.

Qualified privilege by statute

Schedule 1 of the Defamation Act 1996 lists 'statements' to which the statutory form of qualified privilege applies. For example, this defence applies to media reports of:

see also ch. 23 on past convictions

- debates held in public at any legislature in the world (including the UK Parliament) (Part 1 of the Schedule);
- court proceedings held in public anywhere in the world (so this protects non-contemporaneous reports of such proceedings, including reference to people's past convictions in the UK or elsewhere) (Part 1);
- public meetings (and press conferences) held in the European Union (Part 2);

- the meetings of councils, their committees and sub-committees held in public in the UK (Part 2);
- material – for example, official reports or *Hansard* – published by or on the authority of a government or legislature anywhere in the world (Part 1);
- statements issued for the public by government departments, councils, the police and other governmental agencies in the EU (Part 2).

The Schedule is set out in Appendix 3 of this book.

The requirements of qualified privilege

In all instances, the requirements of the defence must be met for it to succeed. These differ from those of absolute privilege. For absolute privilege, the publisher's motive is irrelevant. But a qualified privilege defence will fail if the claimant can show **malice** by the publisher or author.

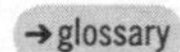

Fair and accurate, without malice and in the public interest

The basic requirements of the qualified privilege defence relating to those 'statements' listed in Schedule 1 are:

- the published report must be fair and accurate; and
- published without malice.

There is also a general requirement for qualified privilege that:

- the material published must be a matter of public concern, the publication of which is for the public benefit. This can be summed up as 'published in the public interest'.

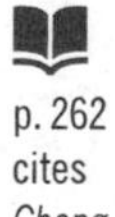

p. 262 cites *Cheng*

Malice in this context means ill-will or spite towards the claimant or any indirect or improper motive in the defendant's mind. Lord Nicholls explained in the *Cheng* case that the qualified privilege defence was intended to allow someone with a duty to perform, or an interest to protect, to provide information without the risk of being sued – and if a person's dominant motive was not to perform this duty or protect this interest, he/she could not use the defence.

A journalist or editor could be denied the protection of qualified privilege if, in a libel action, the court accepted that the motive for publication was not from a duty to inform the public but was spite – for example, publishing a defamatory allegation merely to settle a private score.

Statute only protects a report of the occasion or material specified

The protection of statutory qualified privilege applies only to reports of the actual proceedings, events or material listed in Schedule 1 of the 1996 Act.

For example, it protects a report of speeches by councillors in a council meeting held in public, but will not protect a report of defamatory allegations a councillor makes *after* the meeting when asked to expand on something said during it.

What the councillor says in the meeting – such as that a builder is corrupt – can be safely reported if the meeting was held in public. But if the comment is made afterwards, the publisher who airs it would have no privilege and so would need to rely on the justification defence, that is, would have to prove the builder was corrupt, which might be impossible.

Stories from documents open to public inspection

Paragraph 5 in Part 1 of the Schedule gives privilege for a fair and accurate copy of or extract from a document which the law requires to be open to public inspection. This means, for example, that the media have qualified privilege for material quoted fairly and accurately, etc., from publicly available records such as those at Companies House, the Land Registry or other public registries, even if the records themselves turn out to be inaccurate. The paragraph also gives qualified privilege to media reports of court documents officially made available to them. But it does not apply to reports of documents released under the Freedom of Information Act, though the *Reynolds* defence may apply to such reports.

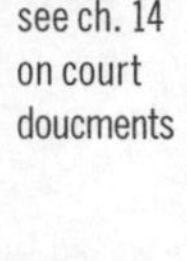

see ch. 14 on court doucments

ch. 22 explains *Reynolds*

Part 2 requirement to publish explanation or contradiction

Schedule 1 to the 1996 Act sets out in Part 1 a list of statements having qualified privilege 'without explanation or contradiction' and in Part 2 a list of statements thus privileged but 'subject to explanation or contradiction'.

This difference is important. A publisher relying on qualified privilege under Part 2 to protect a report must, to retain the protection, publish a 'reasonable letter or statement by way of explanation or contradiction' if required to do so by anyone defamed in the report.

This would apply, for example, if someone wanted a broadcaster or newspaper to air a letter or statement from them responding to a report of a council meeting which defamed them. Failure to publish such a letter or statement would destroy the defence of qualified privilege for what was published earlier. The Act says such a statement must be published 'in a suitable manner', which means 'in the same manner as the publication complained of or in a manner that is adequate and reasonable in the circumstances'.

! Remember

Get legal advice if any statement that the complainant wants published gives rise – because he/she makes counter-allegations – to any risk of libelling another person. Publication of a statement of 'explanation or contradiction' is not protected by privilege under the 1996 Act, so the statement must be 'reasonable' in this respect, though common law privilege may apply.

see also replies to attack, p. 271

A statement listed in Part 1 of Schedule 1 – for example, a report of what is said in public in a legislature such as the UK Parliament or in a public register open to inspection – is not subject to the requirement to publish such a letter/statement by anyone defamed by the report (though an editor may decide it is newsworthy or ethical to do this).

Part 1 is the means by which the 1996 Act greatly widened the categories of statements protected, by including reports of proceedings held in public in foreign legislatures, foreign courts and of all public inquiries appointed by government.

Reports of statements issued for the public by government agencies

Paragraph 9 in Part 2 of the Schedule gives qualified privilege, subject to explanation or contradiction, to 'a fair and accurate copy of or extract from' a notice or other matter issued for the public by authorities with governmental functions. This includes government departments, councils and police authorities, so it would cover, for example, fair and accurate reports of official police statements, and statements made on behalf of local authorities, for example press releases about consumer protection or environmental health matters.

These statements could be very defamatory – for example, a police press release which names a man and states that police want to trace him to question him about a murder. But the qualified privilege allows the media to report this without fear of being sued by the man, provided it publishes his 'reasonable letter or statement of explanation or contradiction', if he requests this.

There will be many occasions when a reporter wants to report a person's misdeeds but may be inhibited by fear of a libel action. The answer is often to obtain confirmation of the information in the form of an official statement by a police or local authority spokesman. This privilege then protects its publication.

! Remember

Statutory qualified privilege does not protect reports of information unofficially 'leaked' from such authorities, or of what was said by people who are not official spokesmen or women.

Not all authorities are covered

Paragraph 9 of the Schedule does not cover reports of all statements by people in authority – it does not cover, for example, reports of statements by spokespeople for British Telecom, a gas board, a water board, the rail companies, London Regional Transport, the British Airport Authority, or other bodies created by statute which are involved in providing day-to-day services to the public. But it seems likely that a fair and accurate account of the official statements of such a body would be held to be covered by privilege at common law.

Verbal comments by press officers

Suppose a reporter telephones a press officer at one of the bodies of the type specified under paragraph 9 of the Schedule. Is the report of the spokesperson's verbal

comments protected by qualified privilege under the Act? The general position seems to be, yes, unless the spokesperson was given no chance to make considered comments.

Case study

In *Blackshaw v Lord* [1984] QB 1, Lord Justice Stephenson, referring to the protection given to the media by paragraph 9, said: 'It may be right to include . . . the kind of answers to telephoned interrogatories which Mr Lord [a *Daily Telegraph* reporter], quite properly in the discharge of his duty to his newspaper, administered to Mr Smith [a government press officer]. To exclude them in every case might unduly restrict the freedom of the press . . . But information which is put out on the initiative of a government department falls more easily within the paragraph than information pulled out of the mouth of an unwilling officer of the department.'

Public meetings

Paragraph 12 of Schedule 1 says reports of public meetings enjoy qualified privilege and defines a 'public meeting' as:

> a lawful meeting held for the furtherance or discussion of a matter of public concern, whether admission to the meeting is general or restricted.

This definition is fairly wide, covering public meetings about a particular community or those held about national issues. The term 'restricted' may mean the definition can apply, for example, to a meeting called by residents of one village who exclude residents of the neighbouring village. Again, the privilege is subject to the 'explanation and contradiction' requirement.

A press conference is equivalent to a public meeting

The House of Lords ruled in the 2000 case of *McCartan Turkington Breen v Times Newspapers Ltd* ([2001] 2 AC 277) that a press conference is a public meeting, an important decision for journalists and the media.

Case study

Law firm McCartan Turkington Breen sued *The Times* over its report of a press conference, called by people campaigning for the release of a soldier convicted of murder, during which defamatory comments were made about the firm. It had represented the soldier. A jury awarded £145,000 damages to the firm, but on appeal Lord Bingham, the senior law lord, said: 'A meeting is public if those who organise it or arrange it open it to the public or, by issuing a general invitation to the press, manifest an intention or desire that the proceedings of the meeting should be communicated to a wider public.' Journalists could be regarded as 'the eyes and ears of the public'.

In *McCartan*, the House of Lords also ruled that a written press release, handed out at the meeting but not read aloud, and reported by the media, was in effect part of the press conference proceedings. This means that fair, accurate reports of documents handed out at a press conference have qualified privilege too, in the context of coverage of the press conference.

Disciplinary actions by private associations

Paragraph 14 in Part 2 of the Schedule bestows qualified privilege on media reports of the findings or decisions of a wide variety of bodies – for example, in the field of sport, business or learning – which have a constitution empowering them to make disciplinary decisions about members. So, for example, the media can safely report a decision by the Jockey Club to discipline a jockey, the Football Association to discipline a player, or a scientific association to censure an academic, if the association is of the type listed in paragraph 14. The protection does not apply to a report of *the proceedings* of such bodies, and is subject to the 'explanation and contradiction' requirement.

Reports about companies

The 1996 Act also greatly extended qualified privilege with respect to reporting company affairs. Earlier, qualified privilege only covered reports relating to proceedings at public companies' general meetings. The Act extended Part 2 privilege to documents circulated among shareholders of a UK public company with the authority of the board or the auditors or by any shareholder 'in pursuance of a right conferred by any statutory provision'.

Privilege at common law

There are some circumstances in which the media can benefit from privilege in common law. This will apply, within certain bounds, to publication of a person's response to an attack on his/her character or conduct. Also, privilege in common law applies to reports of court cases and parliamentary proceedings, if held in public, in addition to statutory privilege.

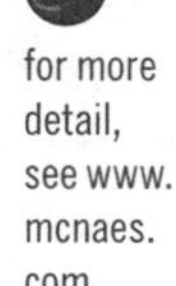

for more detail, see www.mcnaes.com ch. 21

Accord and satisfaction

A media organisation can use the defence of 'accord and satisfaction' to halt a libel case on the ground that the issue has already been disposed of – for example, by publishing a correction and apology which the claimant accepted at the time as settlement of the complaint. But negotiating an apology or correction is not a job for an inexperienced journalist.

'Without prejudice'

A solicitor who on behalf of a client demands a correction and apology will always avoid suggesting that this action by the media organisation will be enough in itself to settle the dispute and will make it clear that the request is made 'without prejudice' to any other action that might be thought necessary.

What does this mean? The principle is that parties attempting to settle their differences before going to law should be encouraged to speak frankly. So anything said or written in the course of negotiations to settle is described as 'without prejudice' (that is, off the record) and cannot subsequently be used against a party in court if negotiations fail. The rule applies whether or not the phrase 'without prejudice' is expressly used, but it is good practice for the media organisation to use it.

Journalists speaking with someone complaining about a story need to distinguish between:

- discussions over an offer to publish a follow-up story or a correction; and
- discussions over settling a claim.

In the former case, which often involves the journalist and the subject themselves, the discussion need not necessarily be 'without prejudice'; the journalist may well want to refer to this discussion in court, to show fairness or lack of malice, or to mitigate damages.

In the latter case, often involving solicitors and mention of money, the discussion should be 'without prejudice'. A leading lawyer has advised that as a general rule journalists should notify their insurers about potential claims at once and, if there are solicitors 'on the other side', the publisher should also involve its own lawyer.

Care needed in apologies and corrections

It is no defence for a media organisation to publish a correction and apology not agreed by the claimant.

Publishing such apology can make matters worse for the publisher, because:

- a court may find that it constitutes an admission that the material which prompted the complaint was defamatory; or
- a badly drafted apology or correction might also repeat the original defamatory statement, further angering the person who complained about it, or even unwittingly libel someone else.

For example: 'In our article yesterday we said Mr Red hit Mr Green. But we wish to point out that Mr Red says Mr Green struck him first'. If this is published Mr Green may sue over the wording of the apology.

On the other hand, if the jury finds for the claimant, the fact that the media organisation took prompt and adequate steps to correct the error, and to express regret, will reduce the damages.

Complainants might also be prepared to sign waivers – statements saying they waive their right to legal redress in exchange for the publication of a correction and apology – which will provide a complete defence of 'accord and satisfaction'.

see www.mcnaes.com ch. 21: 'Practical advice on waivers'

A practical danger for an editor who asks a complainant to sign a waiver is that the reader may not previously have realised that he or she has a claim for damages and, thus alerted, might consult a lawyer. The waiver is therefore most useful when the complainant has already threatened to consult a lawyer.

Inexperienced reporters will sometimes try to avoid the consequences of an error without referring it to the editor, by trying to shrug it off, or by incorporating a scarcely recognisable 'correction' (without apology) in a follow-up story – highly dangerous courses of action which may further aggravate the damage and annoy the person concerned, who might well take more formal steps to secure satisfaction. Reporters should always immediately tell the editor about a problem so it can be dealt with properly.

Offer of amends

The media can defame a person unintentionally. The classic example was the case of Artemus Jones, in which a journalist introduced a fictitious character into a descriptive account of a factual event in order to provide atmosphere – referring to what he thought of as his fictional character at the Dieppe motor festival 'with a woman who is not his wife'.

Unfortunately the name he chose was that of a real person, a barrister – and former journalist – from North Wales. Stung by the comments of his friends the real Artemus Jones sued and recovered substantial damages.

The Defamation Act 1996 provides for a defence known as 'offer to make amends'. To use it, a defendant who is alleged to have published a defamatory statement must make a written offer to make a suitable correction and apology, to publish the correction in a reasonable manner, and to pay the claimant suitable damages and legal costs.

If the offer of amends is rejected, and is not withdrawn, it will be a complete defence unless the claimant can show that the defendant 'knew or had reason to believe' that the published statement was false and was also defamatory of the claimant.

Editors planning to make an offer of amends must not delay. If the resulting compensation is to be assessed by a judge he/she will start by deciding what would be 'suitable damages' if the editor had made no offer of amends and will then award a 'discount' of perhaps 50 per cent as a 'reward' for making the offer. The *News of the World* received only a 40 per cent discount after it was slow to respond to a complaint and published an apology six months after the original story.

Once an offer is made it is binding.

Leave and licence

The 'leave and licence' defence is that the claimant suing for libel had previously agreed that the material could be published. If it is clear the material is defamatory, a publisher intending to rely on this defence needs to be sure he/she can prove there was such pre-publication agreement. The person who is going to be defamed by the material should be asked to sign a statement agreeing to its publication or be recorded agreeing. Otherwise it might be difficult to prove that consent was given if it was merely verbal.

Sometimes, even without an explicit agreement, the context will be that leave and licence *was* given – for example, by a pop star who chooses in an arranged interview to speak on-the-record about false allegations made against him, seeking to dispel them.

But in other circumstances – for example, a media investigation into wrongdoing – the leave and licence defence will not be secured merely by the journalist giving the target the opportunity to comment.

The section 1 defence and regulation 19

Newsagents and booksellers have a defence of innocent dissemination as they are merely the conduit for the passage of the words complained of, and are not responsible for them. But the defence was not available to others, such as distributors and broadcasters.

The Defamation Act 1996, in section 1, extended the defence. It now applies to anyone who was not the author, editor or publisher (as defined by the Act) of the statement complained of, who took reasonable care in relation to its publication, and who did not know and had no reason to believe that whatever part he/she had in the publication caused or contributed to the publication of a defamatory statement. These are the requirements, therefore, for the defence to succeed.

The Act also says that a court deciding whether a person took reasonable care, or had reason to believe that what he/she did caused or contributed to the publication of a defamatory statement, must have regard to:

- the extent of his/her responsibility for the content of the statement or the decision to publish it;
- the nature or circumstances of the publication; and
- the previous conduct or character of the author, editor or publisher.

Live broadcasts protected by section 1

The list of categories of people who are not authors, editors or publishers for the purposes of the defence includes broadcasters of live programmes who have no effective control over the maker of the statement complained of.

Case study

In 1999 research firm MORI and its head, Bob Worcester, sued the BBC over defamatory remarks made by politician Sir James Goldsmith during a live radio interview. The BBC said it had a defence under section 1 – but could it be said it had taken 'reasonable care'? It was argued that the BBC should have known Sir James was likely to say something defamatory and it should at least have used a 'delay button'. The case was settled before the jury reached a verdict (*Media Lawyer*, Issue No. 22, July 1999).

Broadcasters in 'live' situations need to react quickly to halt or cut off defamatory utterances to be sure of benefitting from section 1.

Internet service providers

The section 1 defence is also available for internet service providers (ISPs) which provide as 'host' a service to enable people and companies to publish their own content on websites. ISPs play a merely passive role in the process of transmission of any defamatory matter, and are therefore not publishers under section 1. But an ISP could be successfully sued for libel if it failed quickly to take down defamatory material on a site it hosts after receiving a complaint about it. In *Godfrey v Demon Internet Ltd* [2001] QB 201 the ISP was successfully sued for material on a newsgroup it hosted which it left online for about ten days after receiving a complaint. The claim was for damages for those ten days.

But there is an additional protection for those who 'host', 'cache' or are 'mere conduits' for internet publication – the Electronic Commerce (EC Directive) Regulations 2002/2013. In outline, they are protected from liability to pay damages or any other financial remedy unless and until they have notice of the defamatory publication. This is why many ISPs operate 'notice and take down' procedures.

Readers' comments posted on websites

Newspapers, magazines, TV channels and radio stations cannot use the section 1 defence in respect of content which staff place on their websites, as they are clearly publishers.

But section 1 may offer some protection in limited circumstances over comment posted there by readers. Also, a media organisation might have a defence under regulation 19 of the Electronic Commerce (EC Directive) Regulations 2002 over comments posted directly on to the sites by readers.

- Section 1 or regulation 19 is unlikely to apply if the media organisation's staff moderate – check – this material before it goes online, or if they subsequently check a comment which is clearly defamatory, or attracts complaint, but let it remain online.

- Also, neither defence will apply if the organisation has invited comment on a particular issue in a way likely to produce defamatory responses.
- In any of these circumstances the media organisation is likely to be shown to have been either editor or publisher of the comment, or both, or not to have taken reasonable care.
- The safest course is to remove a reader's comment from the website quickly if there is a complaint that it is defamatory. The material can be put back later if after consideration it is deemed safe.

In *Karim v Newsquest Media Group Ltd* (October 27, 2009) Mr Justice Eady held that the *Croydon Guardian* was not liable as the publisher for comments posted on its website by others. The newspaper was entitled to use the defence in regulation 19 because it had not had actual knowledge of any complaint of unlawful activity or information until it was pointed out by the claimant, and had removed the articles, and the related user comments, as soon as it became aware of the nature of the complaint. It was also clear, the judge said, that the recipient of the service was not acting under the authority or control of the service provider within the meaning of regulation 19.

Other defences

Defences which might be available are:

The claimant has died A libel action is a personal action. A dead person cannot be libelled. Similarly, an action begun by a claimant cannot be continued by his/her heirs and executors if he/she dies.

ch. 20, p. 235 explains 'the repetition rule'

Proceedings were not started within the limitation period That is, the person suing did not begin the action within 12 months of the material being published. This should be a complete defence, unless there is a new publication of offending material (as in a 'bygone days' column). The period, formerly three years, was reduced to one year by the Defamation Act 1996 – although the courts have the power to extend it if it is thought to be in the interests of justice to do so. Reporters should date their notebooks, recordings and research material and store them carefully in case this proof is needed if someone sues towards the end of the limitation period, or there is a possibility of using this material again after that. Journalists must remember that every repetition is a new publication.

Recap of major points

- The main defences against an action for libel are: justification, honest comment, absolute and qualified privilege.

- It is a complete defence (with one exception arising under the Rehabilitation of Offenders Act 1974) to prove that the words complained of are substantially true. This is the justification defence.
- A defendant can plead that an article expressing comment was an honestly held opinion on a matter of public interest. This is the honest comment defence.
- Absolute privilege applies to court reports, but reports must be fair, accurate and contemporaneous.
- Qualified privilege is available on many occasions under statute (for example, for a report of a public meeting). The defence is qualified because it is lost if the motive in publishing is malicious.
- Other defences include 'accord and satisfaction' and 'offer of amends'.

((•)) Useful Websites

www.mcnaes.com/
Chapter 21: test whether your story has a defence

22

The *Reynolds* defence

Chapter summary

The *Reynolds* defence was developed to allow journalists to fulfil their duty to report stories in the public interest, even if they included defamatory material, if the publication was the product of responsible journalism. Attempts to use the defence have led to the courts closely examining whether a story was truly in the public interest, and how it was researched and written. This chapter charts the development of the *Reynolds* defence and highlights the real difficulties in using it. Journalists should not consider using this defence without taking legal advice.

The birth of the defence

The *Reynolds* defence is intended to protect the publication of defamatory material which concerns a matter of public interest and is the product of responsible journalism, even if the material cannot be proved to be true.

It is named after the 1998 case in which former Irish premier Albert Reynolds sued the *Sunday Times* over an article he claimed meant he deliberately and dishonestly misled the Irish Parliament by suppressing information about the appointment of Ireland's Attorney General as President of its High Court. The paper's owner, Times Newspapers, argued in its defence that, in keeping with Article 10 of the European Convention on Human Rights, the public interest in media coverage of political issues and in scrutinising the conduct of elected politicians should be protected by a common law form of qualified privilege.

Ch. 1 explains the Convention's effect and ch. 21, pp. 266–271 explains qualified privilege.

Times Newspapers lost in the High Court. But in the Court of Appeal, the Lord Chief Justice, Lord Bingham, said: 'As it is the task of the news media to inform the public and engage in public discussion of matters of public interest, so is that to be recognised as its duty' (*Reynolds v Times Newspapers* [1998] 3 All ER 961).

Although the newspaper lost in the House of Lords in 1999, the Law Lords confirmed the principle that in some circumstances the media have a duty to publish material in the public interest, even if it cannot be proved to be true, and that therefore qualified privilege in common law should protect that publication. Thus the *Reynolds* defence was born (*Reynolds v Times Newspapers* [2000] 2 AC 127).

Lord Nicholls, in the leading judgment, set out a non-exhaustive list of factors a court should consider when examining whether a publication was the product of responsible journalism, and therefore whether it could be protected by the new defence. See below.

Lord Nicholls's list (*with summarised explanation added in italics*)

(1) The seriousness of the allegation. The more serious the charge, the more the public is misinformed and the individual harmed, if the allegation is not true – *therefore, the more serious the allegation, the greater should be the reporter's efforts to ensure that what is published is correct if the story is to be protected by the new defence.*

(2) The nature of the information, and the extent to which the subject matter is a matter of public concern – *the less the matter is of public concern, the weaker the defence. In some cases, if a judge decides the matter is not of public concern, the defence will fail. Judges often say that what interests the public and what is in the public interest are two different things.*

(3) The source of the information. Some informants have no direct knowledge of the events. Some have their own axes to grind, or are being paid for their stories – *it is important to note that courts are wary of unidentified informants, although a newspaper or broadcaster will not necessarily be penalised for refusing to identify a source.*

(4) The steps taken to verify the information – *it is always important to check, whenever possible, to ensure that what you have been told it true or correct. Making no or insufficient checks before publication will be regarded as irresponsible journalism and the defence will not apply.*

(5) The status of the information. The allegation may have already been the subject of an investigation which commands respect – *For example, if a reputable agency – such as the police – has already decided the relevant allegations are not true, then the media must have sufficient reason to air them, if the defence is to apply.*

(6) The urgency of the matter. News is often a perishable commodity – *that is, the courts, when deciding if the defence applies, must take into consideration that journalists need to work and publish quickly.*

(7) Whether comment was sought from the claimant, that is, the person who claims he/she was defamed. He/she may have information others do not possess or have not disclosed. An approach to the claimant will not always be necessary. *But generally, the person who is the subject of an allegation should be approached. It is also important to make it clear in a story that if the person*

about whom allegations have been made cannot be contacted, efforts have been made to reach him or her. Only rarely will an approach to the subject not be necessary.

(8) Whether the article contained the gist of the claimant's side of the story – *that is, the journalism must be fair to benefit from the defence. Leaving out the claimant's side is a recipe for disaster.*

(9) The tone of the article. A newspaper can raise queries or call for an investigation. It need not adopt allegations as statements of fact – *For example, the defence may not apply to material which brashly and unfairly suggests that unproven allegations are true. It is important to mind your phrasing. Make sure that what you write is what you mean – and that your meaning is clear to anyone who reads your copy, including the man on the Clapham omnibus. Sloppy writing will almost undoubtedly prove expensive.*

(10) The circumstances of the publication, including the timing – *That is, was it really so urgent that the story had to be published when it was? Could it have waited an hour or two or a day or so?*

Initially, judges dealing with cases in which media defendants pleaded the defence treated the 10 points listed above as hurdles which *all* had to be cleared if the defence was to succeed.

But in *Jameel v Wall Street Journal Europe* ([2006] UKHL 44) the House of Lords said this approach was too narrow. Lord Bingham said the material published had to be of public interest and the product of responsible journalism, adding: 'The publisher is protected if he has taken such steps as a responsible journalist would take to try and ensure that what is published is accurate and fit for publication.' He recalled that in *Reynolds* Lord Nicholls had 'listed certain matters which might be taken into account in deciding whether the test of responsible journalism was satisfied', and added that the rationale of the test was that 'there is no duty to publish, and the public has no interest to read, material which the publisher has not taken reasonable steps to verify'.

In the *Jameel* case the *Wall Street Journal* reported that, at the request of US authorities, Saudi Arabia's central bank was monitoring a number of accounts to stop them from being used, 'wittingly or unwittingly', to funnel funds to terrorist groups. Millionaire Saudi Arabian businessman Mohammed Jameel, who was named in the story, sued for defamation, and a jury found that the article defamed him and his companies.

The Court of Appeal upheld the trial judge's refusal to allow the newspaper to plead *Reynolds* privilege because it had refused to give Mr Jameel's spokesman 24 hours to produce a response.

But in the House of Lords Lord Bingham said denying *Reynolds* privilege just because the newspaper was not prepared to wait long enough for the claimants to comment was a very narrow ground – Mr Jameel could only have issued a denial, and Saudi Arabia's central bank would not have admitted to monitoring accounts.

See www.mcnaes.com ch. 22 for more detail on this case.

The public interest test

The *Reynolds* defence may be available to anyone who publishes material in the public interest, including in a book.

In *Charman v Orion Publishing Group Ltd and others* ([2007] EWCA Civ 972; [2008] 1 All ER 750) the Court of Appeal allowed the use of the defence to defeat a libel claim by a former police officer over Graeme McLagan's book, *Bent Coppers – The Inside Story of Scotland Yard's Battle Against Police Corruption*.

It seems from rulings so far that judges will consider material to be in the public interest if it is of 'real public concern' – but the test is not as strict as saying the public need to know. The concept is flexible, so the degree of public interest required will vary according to the publication and market. In the *GKR Karate* case in 2000, a judge found in favour of the *Leeds Weekly News*, which was sued over a front-page article warning readers about the activities of doorstep salesmen selling karate club membership, saying the fundamental question was one of public interest, and the people of Leeds clearly had an interest in receiving the information (*GKR Karate Ltd v Yorkshire Post Newspapers Ltd* [2001] 1 WLR 2571).

The responsible journalism test

The courts have examined the issue of 'responsible journalism' in a number of cases.

In the case which established the *Reynolds* defence the House of Lords held, by a majority, that the *Sunday Times* could not use it as it had failed to 'give the gist of the subject's response' (Lord Nicholls's point 8). Asked at the trial why his account contained no reference to Mr Reynolds' explanation, the reporter said: 'There was not a word of Mr Reynolds' defence because I had decided that his defence... there was no defence.' Mr Reynolds had addressed the Irish Parliament on the issue, but the paper did not report his statement.

In the *Loutchansky* case, *The Times* published articles alleging that international businessman Grigori Loutchansky controlled a major Russian criminal organisation involved in money-laundering and smuggling nuclear weapons.

The Court of Appeal, upholding the High Court's refusal to allow a *Reynolds* defence, said the articles dealt with matters of public concern (Lord Nicholls's point 2), but said that:

- Implicating Mr Loutchansky in misconduct of the utmost gravity would obviously be likely to be highly damaging to his reputation, so a proportionate degree of responsibility was required (Lord Nicholls's point 1). The newspaper had failed to show this – the allegations were vague, the sources unreliable, insufficient steps were taken to verify the information and no comment was obtained from Mr Loutchansky.
- The High Court judge was entitled to find that 'such steps as were taken' by the reporter in his unsuccessful attempts to contact Mr Loutchansky,

his company or its lawyers were far less diligent than the standards of responsible journalism required (Lord Nicholls's point 7).

The *Loutchansky* case also demonstrates the importance of journalists having good shorthand notes to support what they write. Asked in court to produce his note of a vital conversation he said he had had with his most important source, the reporter said he thought he must have made the note on a scrap of paper which he had subsequently thrown away (Lord Nicholls's point 4).

The Court of Appeal rejected the newspaper's appeal (*Loutchansky v Times Newspapers Ltd* [2001] EWCA Civ 1805).

The sources of information and the steps taken to verify it - Lord Nicholls's third and fourth points - are extremely important. In *Lord Ashcroft v Stephen Foley, Independent News and Media and Roger Alton* ([2011] EWCA 292 (QB)) the court accepted the claimant's argument that if sources provided no relevant information, or none that was relied upon, the fact that they were contacted was irrelevant. Journalists, said Mr Justice Eady, 'cannot collect "brownie points" for having rung round a number of people who had no relevant information to give'.

Seeking comment from the claimant

A key point is whether the publisher sought comment from the claimant (Lord Nicholls's point 7).

Journalists who intend to report damaging or defamatory allegations in the public interest should always put them to the subject before publication. As Lord Nicholls said: 'He [the subject] may have information others do not possess or have not disclosed'. This practice is an indication of responsible journalism. But point 7 also states: 'An approach to the claimant will not always be necessary' – the view the court took in the *Jameel* case because of its special circumstances.

The *Flood* case

The *Reynolds* defence suffered what journalists saw as a setback with the Court of Appeal decision in *Flood v Times Newspapers Ltd* ([2010] EMLR 26; [2010] EWCA Civ 804), about a report that a policeman was being investigated over corruption allegations.

The story had three main elements – the fact that an unnamed source made an allegation to the police, the fact that it was being investigated and material suggesting that there was some substance to the allegation.

At first instance ([2010] EMLR 8; [2009] EWHC 2375 (QB)), Mr Justice Tugendhat said the story in the printed edition and as it first appeared on the newspaper's website was protected by the *Reynolds* defence. But the defence ceased to protect the website publication from the date on which *The Times* learned that the police investigation had exonerated the officer of any wrongdoing because nothing was done to correct the website story – this failure was not responsible journalism.

Media wishing to use the *Reynolds* defence must keep a careful eye on their websites – material changes or developments in a story should be noted in the online archive version, for example by replacing the story with a new version, or by adding an explanatory note.

The Court of Appeal said the story was not protected by the *Reynolds* defence at all. Reporting that the officer was being investigated and the bare allegation against him were of public interest and protected by the privilege, but material adding credence to the allegation could only be protected if the journalists had verified it, which they had not – it was 'no more than unsubstantiated unchecked accusations, from an unknown source, coupled with speculation'.

The Times has appealed to the Supreme Court.

The case shows that journalists must be extremely careful when reporting investigations into an individual, and consider carefully whether to include anything more than an indication of the basic nature of the allegations involved.

Neutral reportage

Neutral reportage, a variant of the *Reynolds* defence, is a defence that a dispute or issue is being reported even-handedly – there are cases in which the fact that allegations are being made, or that something is a matter of controversy, is itself a matter of public interest.

In *Al-Fagih v HH Saudi Research & Marketing (UK) Ltd* ([2001] EWCA Civ 1634) the Court of Appeal said a newspaper could rely on the *Reynolds* defence for reporting, in an objective manner, an allegation about someone made by an opponent during a political dispute. The defence was not lost merely because the newspaper had not verified the allegation. The newspaper had argued that where two politicians made serious allegations against each other, it was a matter of public importance to report the dispute, provided it was done fairly and accurately and the parties were given the opportunity to explain or contradict.

The 'neutral reportage' defence can be used even when the journal and its staff are clearly not neutral. The test is not the journalists' stance, but how the matter is reported (*Christopher Roberts and Barry Roberts v Gerry Gable, Steve Silver and Searchlight Magazine Ltd* [2006] EWHC 1025 (QB)).

In contrast, in the *Galloway* case in 2004, the *Daily Telegraph* failed in its claim that its coverage of documents found in the ruins of the Foreign Ministry in Baghdad was 'neutral reportage'. A judge said the paper's allegations that left-wing MP George Galloway had received funds diverted from Iraq's oil-for-food programme conveyed a defamatory meaning which was not protected by *Reynolds* qualified privilege (*George Galloway MP v Telegraph Group Ltd* [2004] EWHC 2786 (QB)).

Mr Galloway won £150,000 damages.

 Ch. 21, p. 261, refers to this case when explaining the honest comment defence.

The newspaper had argued that the public had a right to know the contents of the documents, even if they were defamatory of Mr Galloway, and irrespective of whether the allegations were true.

The judge said *Reynolds* privilege protected the neutral reporting of attributed allegations rather than their adoption by a newspaper as if they were fact. The *Telegraph's* articles had not 'fairly and disinterestedly' reported the Baghdad documents, but went beyond by assuming them to be true.

Recap of major points

- The *Reynolds* defence protects publication of material if it can be shown to be a matter of public interest and responsibly reported.
- Lord Nicholls set down a list of pointers to publications indicating what the courts would look at to decide if the defence could be claimed.
- The courts emphasise the need to seek comment from the subject of the story in order to claim this defence.
- Courts will examine whether a defendant can claim to have been engaged in 'responsible journalism' and/or 'neutral reportage'.

Useful Websites

www.bbc.co.uk/journalism/law/reynolds-defence/
BBC College of Journalism's guidance on the *Reynolds* defence

www.publications.parliament.uk/pa/ld199899/ldjudgmt/jd991028/rey01.htm
House of Lords judgment in the *Reynolds* case

23

The Rehabilitation of Offenders Act 1974

Chapter summary

The Rehabilitation of Offenders Act 1974 allows people to live down previous criminal convictions after a specified period, which varies with the length of the sentence they receive. It limits the defences journalists have against libel claims over a published reference to a 'spent' conviction about which a claimant can prove malice. The Act presents no problem for journalists if revelation of someone's criminal record is in the public interest.

Rehabilitation periods

The Act created the concept of spent convictions. Convictions become 'spent' after a 'rehabilitation period', which varies according to the sentence imposed although some convictions, such as murder, which carry an automatic life sentence, are never spent.

The aim was to allow people convicted of less serious offences to live down previous convictions and have a fresh start. There is no legal obligation to declare a 'spent' conviction when applying for most jobs, whatever the application form says, although there is for some posts, such as working with children.

From the journalist's point of view, the Act also seeks to stop the media referring to someone's spent conviction for no good reason.

Rehabilitation depends on the length of sentence an offender is given. Serious crimes for which convictions never become spent are those for which an offender is given a jail sentence of more than two-and-a-half years, whether the sentence is immediate or suspended, or gets a term of more than two-and-a-half years of youth custody, or detention in a young offender institution, or of corrective training. Terms of preventive detention or an extended sentence for public protection, which are given for violent or sexual offences, never become spent.

Ch. 6, pp. 60–61, ch. 8, pp. 82–83 and ch. 9, p. 88 explain the various types of sentence.

The rehabilitation periods determining when less serious convictions become spent vary from ten years, for a prison sentence greater than six months, to six months, for an absolute discharge. But a further conviction during the rehabilitation period can extend it. Cautions become spent immediately. Rehabilitation periods for many convictions are halved for those under 18, and in some cases are even shorter for those aged 12–14. Suspended sentences are treated as if they were put into effect.

See www.mcnaes.com ch. 23 for a detailed breakdown, issued by the Nacro charity, of rehabilitation periods arising from particular sentences.

The Act's effect on the media

The Act limits the defences available for a media organisation sued for libel for publishing reference to a person's spent conviction.

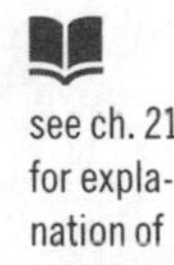

see ch. 21 for explanation of all these defences

(1) A defence of justification – that the report of the previous conviction was true – will fail if the claimant can prove that the conviction was spent and the publication was malicious. This breaches the principle that truth is a complete defence to a defamation action, because the Act aims to deter the media from referring to a spent conviction without good reason.

(2) The defences of absolute or qualified privilege are not available for reporting a spent conviction which is mentioned in court proceedings but is then ruled inadmissible by the court.

Example A man sues a newspaper for defamation after it publishes an accurate reference to his previous criminal conviction. The defences available are:

- ***Justification*** – because there was a conviction. Defamation law accepts that the conviction is proof that the person committed that crime. So a media organisation, once it proves the conviction – for example, from a court record – is not required to re-prove that the person suing committed the offence.

- ***Qualified privilege*** – protects non-contemporaneous reports of court cases if the defence's requirements are met. Mention of a conviction is, in effect, a report of the court case in which the conviction occurred when the defendant pleaded guilty or when magistrates or a jury announced the guilty verdict. The defence also protects quotations from the case, such as the judge calling the convicted defendant 'a scoundrel'.

- ***Honest comment*** – protects opinion expressed about the person based on the fact of the conviction, if the defence's requirements are met. If a council election candidate has a criminal conviction, an editorial comment column could safely publish the author's honestly held opinion that the conviction made the person unfit for public office. Similar comments from others could be published safely too, if these were their honestly held opinions. Even if no such comment is made explicitly, a media organisation publishing the conviction in this context creates an inference that it means the person could be regarded as unfit for public office. The honest comment defence should protect the media organisation over that inference.

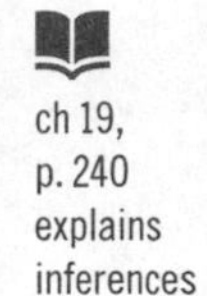
ch 19, p. 240 explains inferences

Even if the conviction referred to is 'spent', the above defences apply, unless the publication was malicious – for example, there was no public interest in referring to it. But a claimant would win if it was proved at a defamation trial that there was malice. There would be malice if a journalist or editor published a reference to a spent conviction merely to further some interest of his/her own or in spite. In such a case the Act means the justification defence cannot be used, even though the conviction is a fact. Proof of malice also destroys the defence of qualified privilege. The honest comment defence would also be undermined, as the published comment must be based on a matter of public interest – and a provably malicious reference to the conviction would be much harder to justify as being for the public good. A comment must also be based on a privileged statement or a fact defensible by justification.

! Remember

In most news stories the media can refer to and comment on spent convictions – for example, disclosing a council candidate's previous conviction or the criminal record of a dodgy businessperson – with no fear of libel consequences because the disclosures are in the public interest and no malice is involved.

Spent convictions revealed in court proceedings

A person giving evidence in any civil proceedings should not, generally, be asked questions about spent convictions.

The Act does not apply to later criminal proceedings. A rehabilitated person who appears before a criminal court again, after his or her conviction has become spent, can still be asked about it.

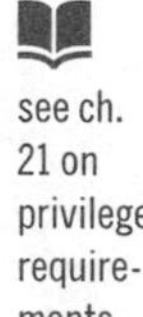
see ch. 21 on privilege requirements

Absolute or qualified privilege applies to media reports of a spent conviction mentioned in a court case unless the court ruled that the conviction was inadmissible.

Judges have been directed that spent convictions should never be referred to in criminal courts unless this is unavoidable, and that no one should refer in open court to a spent conviction without the judge's authority.

Criminal penalties

ch. 28 explains data protection

There is no criminal penalty for journalists who mention a spent conviction. But it may well be an offence for a public servant to disclose details of spent convictions other than in the course of official duties. It is a criminal offence to obtain information on spent convictions from official records by fraud, dishonesty or bribery.

In November 2011 the Government said it would reform the 1974 Act by tabling amendments to the Legal Aid, Sentencing and Punishment of Offenders Bill, after calls for rehabilitation periods to be reduced. Check www.mcnaes.com for updates.

Recap of major points

- Convictions become spent at the end of the rehabilitation period.
- A conviction which led to a jail term of more than two-and-a-half years is never spent.
- The rehabilitation period varies between ten years (in respect of a jail sentence exceeding six months) and six months (after an absolute discharge), though some offences are spent immediately.
- The Act restricts the libel defences available to journalists who refer with malice to spent convictions.

Useful Websites

www.nacro.org.uk/policy/change-the-record/what-is-the-rehabilitation-of-offenders-act-1974,1346,NAP.html

Nacro information on the Rehabilitation of Offenders Act

24

Slander, malicious falsehood and obscenity

Chapter summary

This chapter covers slander – defamation in its spoken form – which can present journalists with problems. It also examines malicious falsehood, which occurs with the publication of a statement which is not defamatory but is false and can be shown to be likely to have caused financial loss, and briefly examines obscenity.

Slander

The most obvious difference between the **torts** of libel and slander is, as chapter 19 explains, that libel is in some permanent form (for example, written words, a drawing, or a photograph), while slander is spoken or in some other transient form.

→glossary

The exceptions are that:

- defamatory statements broadcast on radio or television, or in a cable programme are treated as libel – Broadcasting Act 1990;
- as are defamatory statements in a public performance of a play – Theatres Act 1968.

In slander, as with libel, the statement must be published to a third person, and must refer to the claimant. Another difference between libel and slander is that while damage is presumed in a libel action, a claimant in a slander action must prove that damage has been suffered, except in these four cases:

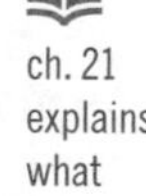

ch. 21 explains what a libel claimant must prove

- an imputation that an individual has committed a crime punishable by death or imprisonment;
- an imputation that an individual is suffering from certain contagious or objectionable diseases, such as venereal disease or leprosy: the test is whether the nature of the disease would cause the person to be shunned or avoided;

- any imputation of unchastity in a woman;
- any statement calculated to disparage an individual in his office, profession, calling, trade or business.

Risk of slander for journalists

Journalists are less likely to become involved personally in a slander action than in a libel action, but must be aware of the dangers.

Let us suppose that X has said that Y, a borough council member, used his position to secure building contracts. This is clearly actionable because it disparages Y in his office of councillor. The reporter checking the story will have to interview a number of people to reach the truth, and must be wary of being sued for slander as a result of the questions asked during those interviews in which the original slander might be repeated to a third party. There is also a risk that leaving messages on an answering machine could spark an action for slander if they are heard or re-played by someone other than the claimant. There is also a risk for broadcasters who, for example, shout allegations at people who have refused to be interviewed about them in front of a crowd: while the broadcast itself could spark a libel action, the fact that the question was shouted might tempt the subject into trying to sue for slander as well.

Malicious falsehoods

Publication of a false statement may still damage a person's reputation even though it does not cast aspersions on his/her character or fitness to hold a certain office or to follow a particular calling.

- For example, the false statement that a solicitor had retired from practice would doubtless cause loss as his/her clients would seek other solicitors to do their work. But it is clearly not defamatory to be considered retired.
- The wronged person cannot sue for libel or slander if a published statement is not defamatory – but might be able to bring an action for malicious falsehood.

What the claimant must prove

The three elements which the claimant must prove to show that the tort of malicious falsehood has occurred can be summarised as follows:

- The claimant must prove the statement is untrue (in contrast with libel, where the court assumes that a defamatory statement is false).
- The claimant in a malicious falsehood action must also prove that the statement was published maliciously.

- The statement must also have been likely to cause financial damage to his/her office, profession, calling, trade or business.

As with the defence of qualified privilege in libel, malice means a statement made by someone who knows it is false, or is reckless or uncaring as to its truth. A defendant who wrongly believes a statement is true but published it with the aim of injuring the claimant will also be viewed as motivated by malice (*Spring v Guardian Assurance plc* [1993] 2 All ER 273, CA). However, negligence – that is, wrongly believing a statement is true, and so failing to check it, when there was no aim to injure – is not malice.

The claimant in a malicious falsehood case does not have to prove that he/she has suffered actual damage if the words are in permanent form, such as printed words, and calculated to cause financial damage, or they are spoken or written and likely to cause him/her financial damage in his/her office, profession, calling, trade or business.

Case study

In 1990, the television actor Gorden Kaye was in hospital seriously ill. His representative sued the *Sunday Sport* and its editor for malicious falsehood after a journalist and a photographer got into the hospital and interviewed and photographed Kaye. The *Sunday Sport* planned to say in its article that Kaye agreed to be interviewed and photographed.

The Court of Appeal said the words were false as Kaye – who did not remember the 'interview' minutes afterwards – was in no state to be interviewed or give informed consent. As the reporter and photographer knew this, any publication suggesting he had agreed to the article would 'inevitably' be malicious (*Kaye v Robertson* [1991] FSR 62, (CA)). As to damage, Kaye had a potentially valuable right to sell the story of his accident to other newspapers for 'large sums of money' and the value of that right would be seriously lessened if the *Sunday Sport* were allowed to publish.

Limitation period

The limitation period for bringing a malicious falsehood action is one year, the same as for a defamation action – Defamation Act 1996.

Corrections

An editor may realise that the facts of a story are wrong, but they were not defamatory and it was an honest mistake. In such a case, he/she should act quickly to publish an adequate correction to avoid any suggestion of malice in a subsequent legal action.

Slander of goods and title

Two types of malicious falsehood are known as slander of goods (false and malicious statements disparaging the claimant's goods), and slander of title (false and malicious denial of the claimant's title to property).

The word slander is misleading in both cases. The damaging statement can be in permanent form or spoken.

Obscenity

The test of obscenity is whether the words or material would tend to deprave and corrupt those likely to read, see, or hear them.

The law used to be that no evidence could be brought to show the literary merits of any work which was the subject of proceedings. But the Obscene Publications Act 1959 largely replaced the common law offence of obscene libel, and introduced a defence that the publication was 'for the public good... in the interests of science, literature, art, or learning, or of other objects of public concern'. This led to the acquittal of the publishers of D H Lawrence's *Lady Chatterley's Lover* at a trial on an obscenity charge.

The law of obscenity once caught only those who published obscene works. But the Obscene Publications Act 1964 made it an offence to possess an obscene article for publication for gain.

Criminal libels

Until recently a number of common law offences made certain libels criminal offences rather than civil torts. The offences of criminal libel, sedition – words likely to disturb the peace and government of the country – and blasphemy, the use of language which tends to vilify the Christian religion or the Bible, have all been abolished.

Recap of major points

- Slander, a civil wrong (like libel), concerns defamatory words that (unlike libel) are spoken or are in some other transient form.
- In slander (unlike libel), actual damage may need to be proved.
- Malicious falsehoods are false statements that, though not defamatory, may still be damaging. The claimant must prove that the statement is untrue and malicious.

Part 4

Confidentiality, privacy and copyright

25

Breach of confidence

Chapter summary

The law of breach of confidence is based upon the principle that a person who has been given information in confidence should not take unfair advantage of it. This chapter explains the kind of information and relationships considered confidential. If a media organisation publishes this type of information, it needs a legal defence to avoid having to pay damages. Governments, businesses and individuals use this law to protect information they regard as officially or commercially secret, or private.

The main means of preventing a breach of confidence is an injunction banning publication of confidential information. This area of law is also the foundation of the law of privacy, which is the focus of the next chapter.

Development of the law

The law on breach of confidence is at its most straightforward in the protection of commercial secrets. An employee has a duty to protect commercially-sensitive information he/she creates or gains in the course of employment – for example, data on market research or development of new products. That duty arises from the employment relationship. If an employee disloyally passes that information to a commercial rival of his/her employer, that is a breach of confidence. In most instances the betrayed employer could, apart from sacking the employee, successfully sue him/her and the rival in the civil courts for damages to compensate for any financial loss suffered – because breach of confidence is a **tort**, a civil wrong. The duty to preserve confidentiality can automatically pass to anyone else who receives the material and realises its confidential nature. So, a media organisation to which a business's commercial secrets are leaked could also be successfully sued if it publishes these, unless it has a defence.

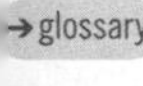

The law of breach of confidence can also protect material which is personally private. In some respects this is not new. Queen Victoria's husband Prince Albert used it in 1848 to prevent commercial publication of private family etchings which depicted their children and pets. Copies had been purloined from the printers to which they had been sent by the Royal household to be printed merely as a personal collection (*Prince Albert v Strange* (1848) 1 Mac & G 25).

However, the wide scope the law now has to protect personal privacy, and the use of the law of breach of confidence by successive governments to protect official secrets, are comparatively recent developments.

Development of privacy law

Until 2000, UK law recognised no general right to privacy. But people who believed their privacy was about to be infringed could try to use the law of breach of confidence to prevent intrusions. Their main difficulty lay in the different nature of the two kinds of right. An obligation of confidence, by definition, arises, first, from the circumstances in which the information is given – a relationship which gives rise to one party owing a duty of confidence to another.

By contrast, a right of privacy in respect of information would arise from the nature of the information itself; it would be based on the principle that certain kinds of information were private and for that reason alone should not be disclosed. Many cases involving invasions of privacy did not result from breaches of confidence.

pp. 299–300 explain *Spycatcher*

The law evolved as judges began to abandon their strict view on the circumstances in which an obligation of confidence could occur. In the *Spycatcher* case in the House of Lords in 1988 Lord Goff of Chieveley said (*A-G v Times Newspapers* (1992) 1 AC 191):

> “a duty of confidence arises when confidential information comes to the knowledge of a person (the confidant) in circumstances where he has notice, or is ruled to have agreed, that the information is confidential, with the effect that it would be just in all the circumstances that he should be precluded from disclosing the information to others.”

Lord Goff said he had expressed the duty in wide terms to include the situation where 'an obviously confidential document was wafted by an electric fan out of a window into a crowded street, or when an obviously confidential document such as a diary was dropped in a public place and then picked up by a passer-by.'

In this scenario the passer-by has no relationship with the person whose information he/she has picked up – but, because it is obviously confidential, in law the passer-by should not, for example, give or sell it to a media organisation for publication, unless there is a legal defence for this.

In 2000 the Human Rights Act 1998 came into force, and incorporated in UK law the European Convention on Human Rights, which guarantees the right to respect for privacy and family life, as chapter 1 explains. In cases involving alleged breach of personal privacy, the courts started abandoning the legal contrivance of implying a confidential relationship where none existed, and so a separate type of tort – misuse of private information – started to develop in case law. This is the focus of the next chapter, but the roots of that law are explained here.

In the *Douglas* case, which is explained below, Lord Justice Sedley said in the Court of Appeal: 'The law no longer needs to construct an artificial relationship of confidentiality between intruder and victim: it can recognise privacy itself as a legal principle drawn from the fundamental value of personal autonomy.'

Elements of a breach of confidence

There are three elements in a breach of confidence:

- the information must have 'the necessary quality of confidence';
- the information must have been imparted in circumstances imposing an obligation of confidence; and
- there must be an unauthorised use of that information to the detriment of the party communicating it (*Coco v AN Clark (Engineers) Ltd* [1969] RPC 41 at 47).

The phrase 'the party communicating it' means the person communicating the information originally, that is, the person to whom the confidence is owed. A patient who tells a doctor about an ailment, or allows him/her to take blood tests or conduct a pregnancy test, is communicating information. The doctor owes a duty of confidence to the patient in respect of that information.

But, again, it should be remembered that to enforce the law of confidentiality a court does not require there to be a direct relationship between the person who wishes to protect the information and the person who wishes to disclose it. The law operates on the conscience of the parties. The legal criterion is whether a reasonable person would understand from the nature and circumstances of a disclosure of information or material to him or her that he/she was receiving it in confidence. Under this law, a journalist who receives a leak of someone's medical records usually has a duty not to reveal it to others, just as the doctor has. The same principle applies to other types of information ruled to be confidential.

Case study

In 2000 the actors Michael Douglas and Catherine Zeta-Jones and the publishers of *OK!* magazine sued in the High Court for breach of confidence. Their lawsuit was against the rival *Hello!* magazine because it had published unauthorised photographs of the couple taken at their wedding reception in a New York hotel. The couple had struck an exclusive, £1 million deal for *OK!* to have pictures taken by their own photographer and for only those images they approved of to be published. But *Hello!* got unauthorised pictures from a paparazzi photographer who, in disguise, had infiltrated the hotel. *Hello!* rushed its next edition into print to spoil the impact of the *OK!* 'exclusive' pictures. Mr Justice Lindsay, ruling that *Hello!'s* publication of the unauthorised pictures had infringed the couple's privacy, ordered it to pay them £14,600 damages and also to pay £1 million damages to *OK!* magazine. *Hello!* appealed against the £1 million award, but in 2007 it was upheld by the House of Lords (*Michael Douglas, Catherine Zeta-Jones, Northern and Shell PLC v Hello! Ltd, Hola SA, Eduardo Sanchez Junco (4) Marquesa de Varela, Neneta Overseas Ltd and Philip Ramey* (first instance: [2003] 3 All ER 996; [2003] EMLR 31); Court of Appeal: [2005] EWCA Civ 595; [2005] 4 All ER 128; [2005] 3 WLR 881; House of Lords: [2007] UKHL 21; [2007] 2 WLR 920; [2007] 4 All ER 545).

In *Douglas* it was ruled that *Hello!* magazine, when it bought the unauthorised pictures, knew that the 'information' they contained – images of the couple – was regarded as private and confidential, and was also capable of commercial exploitation, and therefore *Hello!'s* conscience was touched – it was bound by the duty of confidentiality. It was noteworthy as regards the development of privacy law, and – for some in the media, controversial – that the decision in *Douglas* was that the couple's wedding was a private occasion. This was despite there being 350 guests and the couple's exploitation of it in the picture deal with *OK!* The ruling was that the security measures the couple took against intruders, and their insistence on approving which images were published, made it private.

The quality of confidence

The law of breach of confidence safeguards ideas and information imparted or obtained in confidential circumstances. Generally, information is not confidential if it is trivial – for example, a company's canteen menu – or is already in the public domain.

Obligation of confidence

An obligation of confidence can arise in a variety of ways, including:

Contractual relationship Employees may have signed agreements not to disclose an employer's secrets. This applies to a celebrity's chauffeur, who wants to sell to the media tales of what he saw and heard in his employment, just as it does to scientists employed in commercial research. Even if the written contract does not make this clear, there is an implied term in every employment situation that an employee will not do anything detrimental to an employer's interests.

Personal relationship In 1967 the Duchess of Argyll prevented the *People* newspaper, and her former husband, from publishing marital secrets (*Argyll v Argyll* [1967] Ch 302). By the 1980s the courts had extended the protection to prevent the publication of kiss-and-tell stories originating from less formal relationships. But these stories are now generally dealt with in privacy law.

see ch. 26, p. 311

Unethical behaviour It now seems to be established by case law that journalists who obtain confidential information by unethical means such as trespass, theft, listening devices or long-range cameras are usually in breach of an obligation of confidence owed to the targets of this activity – an obligation created and breached by the tactics used. If there is no obligation of confidence, then any such case would probably fall within the scope of privacy law.

Detriment

The detriment a party suffers from a breach of confidence could be financial loss from exposure of commercially sensitive information. But in the *Spycatcher* case in the Lords (*A-G v Times Newspapers* [1992] 1 AC 191), Lord Keith of Kinkel said it would be a sufficient detriment to an individual that information he/she gave in confidence was to be disclosed to people he/she would prefer not to know it. The detriment could be the adverse effect on someone's mental well-being or physical health caused by unauthorised publication of their confidential, personal information – for example, if it causes people to ridicule or shun them.

Breach of confidence and official secrets

In 1985 the UK Government used the law of breach of confidence when attempting to stop publication of information acquired by Peter Wright during his former job as senior officer of its internal security service, MI5. He planned to make money by selling his memoirs – a book called *Spycatcher*. Wright's book recounted his experiences in MI5, claiming, among other things, that MI5 officers plotted to destabilise the Government of Labour Prime Minister Harold Wilson in the mid-1970s, and that security services officers had plotted to assassinate Egypt's President Nasser. The UK's Attorney General, on behalf of the Government, began the proceedings against Wright in Australia, where he was in retirement.

The Attorney General sought an injunction to stop publication, arguing that former members of the security services had a lifelong duty not to reveal any details of their employment.

In June 1986 the *Observer* and *The Guardian* newspapers carried stories reporting the forthcoming hearing in Australia which included details of allegations Wright planned to publish. An English court then gave the Attorney General interim injunctions preventing both newspapers from disclosing any information Wright had obtained as a member of MI5. In 1988, after many legal actions involving the Government and newspapers, in the UK and abroad, and after *Spycatcher* was published in the United States (beyond the reach of UK law), the House of Lords ruled that the original articles in the *Observer* and *The Guardian* in 1986 were not published in breach of confidence; that the Government was not entitled to a permanent injunction preventing the two papers from further comment on the book and use of extracts from it; and that the Government was not entitled to a general injunction restraining the media from future publication of information derived from Wright.

((•)) See Useful Websites below for coverage of the Lords judgment.

Later the European Court of Human Rights ruled that the UK Government was right to obtain the initial injunctions against the *Observer* and *The Guardian* in 1986, but that the injunctions should not have been maintained once the book was published, because the information in it was no longer confidential.

The significance of the *Spycatcher* case is that it showed the Government prepared to use the civil law of breach of confidence, rather than rely on prosecutions under (controversial) official secrets law, whenever members or former members of the security services breached what it saw as their lifelong duty of confidence.

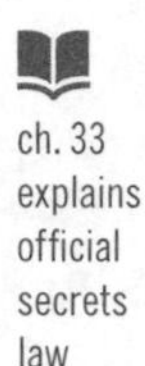

ch. 33 explains official secrets law

Also, the *Spycatcher* case established the principle that an injunction granted against one media organisation, to stop it publishing material, could cover all of them, as explained below.

Injunctions

If a person or an organisation discovers that confidential information is due to be published by the media without their consent, they can apply to the High Court for a temporary injunction to stop this.

On many occasions, temporary injunctions which appeared to be harsh and wide-ranging in their terms have been lifted when the media organisation's case was heard. This did not mean that the judge made a mistake, legally speaking, when imposing the temporary injunction. It is intended to 'hold the ring' until the case can be fully heard on whether a breach of confidence could occur. As a condition for the granting of an interim injunction the party that wants it has to give an undertaking to pay damages to the other side if, at the trial, it is ruled that the interim injunction should not have been granted.

But a media organisation, having been injuncted, may decide that the cost of fighting the injunction or the case in a full trial is not worth it.

Disobeying an injunction can result in an action for contempt of court which could lead to an unlimited fine.

Section 12 of the Human Rights Act 1998 is intended to provide some protection against injunctions in matters involving freedom of expression.

A claimant applying to a High Court judge for an injunction should only be given it if he/she can persuade the judge that he/she is 'likely' to establish at the trial that publication should not be allowed.

Before the 1998 Act was implemented, the application might be without notice, which meant that only one party – the claimant – was represented, and a media organisation, as the defendant, would only learn of the proceedings when it was told that an injunction had been granted. That can and still does happen. Section

12 says that if the defendant is not present when the application is made, the court must not grant an injunction unless it is satisfied either that the claimant seeking the injunction has taken all practicable steps to notify the defendant, or there are compelling reasons for not giving notice.

But these cases are generally conducted at speed, and it may not be possible to tell a defendant. Injunctions have sometimes been granted when a newspaper has been printed and ready to go on sale, or a programme was ready for broadcast, causing great inconvenience and expense.

The journalist's dilemma

The law of confidentiality regularly presents journalists with a dilemma. Suppose a reporter learns about some newsworthy misconduct from a source who received the information confidentially. The journalist should, as a matter of ethical conduct, and because of the law of libel, approach the person alleged to have misbehaved to get their side of the story and to check facts.

For example, the BBC Editorial Guidelines tells broadcasters:

> “When our output makes allegations of wrongdoing, iniquity or incompetence or lays out a strong and damaging critique of an individual or institution the presumption is that those criticised should be given a 'right of reply', that is, given a fair opportunity to respond to the allegations.”

((•)) See Useful Websites, below, for this part of the BBC Editorial Guidelines.

But if a journalist does make such an approach there is a risk that, as explained below, the subject will immediately obtain an injunction banning use of the information and thus kill the story before it can be published.

! Remember

You should certainly check a story if it might be defamatory – but if possible, phrase your questions so that you do not reveal that you have confidential material, to avoid laying yourself open to the risk of an injunction.

Injunction against one is against all

In 1987 the Court of Appeal ruled that when an interim injunction is in force preventing a media organisation from publishing confidential information, other media organisations in England and Wales that know of the injunction can be guilty of contempt of court if they publish that information, even if they are not named in the injunction.

In 1989 two papers were fined £50,000 each for publishing extracts from *Spycatcher* because at the time of publication they knew that interim injunctions were in force against the *Observer* and *The Guardian* preventing them from publishing this material.

The fines were later discharged, but the convictions were upheld and the ruling on the law was confirmed by the House of Lords in 1991.

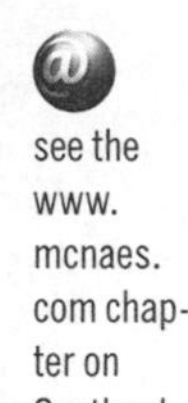

see the www.mcnaes.com chapter on Scotland

This legal device for silencing the media is all the more effective because the injunction is sometimes phrased in such a way that journalists are forbidden even to mention the existence of the proceedings – a so-called super-injunction.

An injunction obtained in an English court does not prevent publication in another country. In particular, it does not prevent publication in Scotland – though Scottish judges may be asked to impose their own injunction, known as an **interdict**.

Legal remedies for breach of confidence

A person or organisation who claims their confidential information has been unlawfully published can, as the claimant in legal action:

- ask a judge to impose an injunction to stop it being published again by that publisher or by others;
- seek a court order for the confidential material – for example, documents or pictures – to be 'delivered up' – that is, all copies to be given back to the claimant or destroyed;
- sue the publisher for damages, or for 'an account of profits';
- ask a judge to order the publisher to reveal the source of the information, if this is not known, so that legal action can be pursued against the source for damages and/or to stop more confidential information being disclosed.

Damages

These are likely to be higher in a case where the breach of confidence caused commercial loss – for example, the £1 million awarded to *OK!* magazine in the *Douglas* case – rather than loss of personal privacy.

Case study

The supermodel Naomi Campbell was only awarded £2,500 damages for distress and injury to her feelings in 2002 against Mirror Group Newspapers when she sued for breach of confidence and infringement of the Data Protection Act 1998. The *Daily Mirror* had published detail about her receiving therapy from Narcotics Anonymous for drug addiction. She was awarded an additional £1,000 for 'aggravated damages' as a result of an additional article published by the paper (*Campbell v Mirror Group Newspapers* [2004] UKHL 22).

However, in 2008 Max Mosley was awarded £60,000 against the *News of the World*, in an action alleging breach of confidence and unauthorised disclosure of personal information for its exposure of his participation in a sado-masochistic orgy with prostitutes.

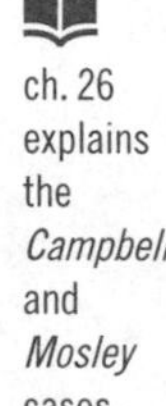

ch. 26 explains the *Campbell* and *Mosley* cases

Account of profits

A person misusing confidential information to make money may be asked to account for the profits to the person or organisation whose confidence was betrayed. A court may rule, after seeing this account, that the person who misused the information should pay some or all of these ill-gotten profits to the party betrayed. But for a media organisation, the order is more likely to be for damages, because of the difficulty for a judge to decide which news story led to what profit.

Order to reveal source

A court can order a journalist to reveal the name of the informant who provided the confidential information. If this source was promised anonymity by the journalist, the ethical position among journalists is that he/she must keep that promise – which means facing the consequences of disobeying the court. The defiance could be deemed a contempt of court which could lead to a fine or, conceivably, the journalist being jailed, though he/she may have some protection from Article 10 of the European Convention on Human Rights and the 'shield law' in section 10 of the Contempt of Court Act 1981.

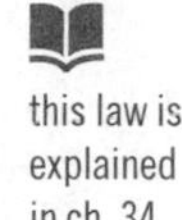

this law is explained in ch. 34

Case study

In 1989 an engineering company, Tetra Ltd, obtained injunctions against *The Engineer* magazine and its trainee reporter Bill Goodwin. The company, which was in financial difficulties, had prepared a business plan for the purpose of negotiating a substantial bank loan. A copy of the draft plan 'disappeared' from the company's offices and the next day an unidentified source telephoned Mr Goodwin and gave him information about the company, including the amount of the projected loan and the company's forecast results. Goodwin phoned the company and its bankers to check the information. The company obtained a without notice injunction restraining the magazine from publishing information derived from the draft plan and later obtained an order requiring Goodwin and *The Engineer* to hand over notes that would disclose the source of the information. Mr Goodwin refused to comply and was fined £5,000. In 1996 the European Court of Human Rights ruled that the court order and the fine violated his right to freedom of expression under Article 10. Goodwin was supported by the National Union of Journalists (*Goodwin v United Kingdom* (1996) 22 EHRR 123).

D Defences

A media organisation sued for an alleged breach of confidence in what it has published may have defences. These include:

- the information did not have 'the necessary quality of confidence' because
  - of its nature – for example, it was trivial and/or unlikely to cause much detriment,
  - or because it was already in the public domain;
- it was in the public interest to publish the information – for example, to expose wrongdoing, negligence or hypocrisy.

The same arguments can be used against an injunction being granted.

Information already in the public domain

If a media organisation publishes commercially sensitive information leaked from a business, or information leaked from a public institution, a court is unlikely to grant an injunction or to award damages for breach of confidence if it was already widely in the public domain – for example, already published by other media outlets or by members of the public on internet sites and other social media.

Judges, as some have said themselves, do not wish to make pointless orders like King Canute ordering the tide to recede.

But the scope for the public domain defence may be more limited if personal privacy has been infringed – for example, a judge might rule that embarrassing private footage improperly copied by a maid from a celebrity's computer should not – to spare the celebrity any further distress – be published by the mainstream media, even if thousands of copies are already visible on the internet.

Case study

In a 1982 case involving the *Watford Observer*, the Court of Appeal lifted an injunction which had stopped the newspaper covering developments at publisher Robert Maxwell's printing operation, Sun Printers. The paper wanted to publish that the company was considering making 180 workers redundant. It had been given a copy of a report, commissioned by the company, which suggested these job cuts were needed. The Court said this report could not be regarded as confidential because the company had widely circulated 120 copies to management and trade union officials, so they could discuss it. Therefore, whoever handed a copy to the *Watford Observer* had not breached any confidence. One judge, Lord Denning, said that publishing the information would also be in the public interest, because many people in the Watford area could be affected by the job losses (*Sun Printers v Westminster Press Ltd* [1982] IRLR 292).

Publication in the public interest

The Human Rights Act 1998, in section 12, says that when a court is considering imposing an injunction in a matter affecting freedom of expression, and where journalistic material is involved, it must have particular regard to the extent to which it is, or would be, in the public interest to publish the material.

But even before the Act was implemented, journalists have successfully argued that the disclosure of confidential information would be in the public interest.

Case study

The Court of Appeal ruled in 1984 that it was in the public interest for the *Daily Express* to publish information from an internal memo, leaked from a company making breathalyser equipment, which cast doubt on its accuracy at a time when police were using it to clampdown on drink-driving (*Lion Laboratories v Evans* [1985] QB 526).

The public interest argument failed in the case of *McKennitt v Ash* ([2006] EMLR 10) in which a well-known Canadian folk singer sued a former friend who had written and published a book, *Travels with Loreena McKennitt: My Life as a Friend*, which revealed a lot of information about the singer's private life. In the High Court, Mr Justice Eady ruled that several references in the book were intrusive and insensitive, and there was insufficient public interest in them being published. The Court of Appeal upheld this decision, though it said that the judge's statement that 'a very high degree of misconduct must be demonstrated' if behaviour was to trigger the public interest defence might well go too far, if treated as an 'entirely general statement, divorced from its context'. But the court said that the high test was appropriate on the facts of the *McKennitt* case.

Correcting 'a false public image'

In 2005 celebrities David Beckham and Victoria Beckham failed to get an injunction against the *News of the World* concerning information about the state of their marriage. The paper argued that that the Beckhams had portrayed a false image about their private life, and that therefore it was justified in the public interest for it to publish information from a former nanny they employed, saying she had witnessed blazing rows between the couple (*Media Lawyer*, April 25, 2005).

Relevance of ethical codes

Section 12 of the Human Rights Act also says that a court considering a matter affecting freedom of information must have particular regard to 'any relevant privacy code'. In cases involving alleged intrusion into privacy by the media, judges will consider, depending on the media sector involved, if the journalism has

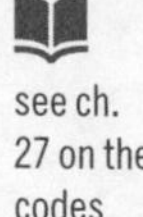
see ch. 27 on the codes

conformed to either the Editors' Code of Practice or the Ofcom Broadcasting Code. If it does conform, judges may be more likely to rule that any breach of confidence or privacy was justified by the public interest. The wording of the parts of each code which relate to public interest justifications are, anyway, influenced by case law.

➡ Recap of major points

- The law says that a person who has obtained information in confidence must not take unfair advantage of it.
- The person who believes his/her confidence is to be breached can get an injunction preventing this.
- An injunction preventing one publication from publishing confidential information prevents all the media from publishing it, if they know about it.
- Disobeying an injunction can result in an action for contempt of court.
- If confidential matter is published, the person whose confidences have been breached may be able to claim damages.

((•)) Useful Websites

http://news.bbc.co.uk/onthisday/hi/dates/stories/october/13/newsid_2532000/2532583.stm
BBC news archive story on the *Spycatcher* saga

www.bbc.co.uk/guidelines/editorialguidelines/page/guidelines-fairness-right-of-reply/
BBC Editorial Guidelines on right of reply

26

Privacy – the developing law

Chapter summary

The law of privacy developed from the action for breach of confidence, but has now taken on a life of its own, and has been used by a large number of people to prevent publication of information about their lives and activities. In 2008 it attracted widespread publicity with the case of Max Mosley, who won £60,000 in damages when he sued the *News of the World* over a story about his involvement in a sado-masochistic orgy with five prostitutes. Increasing numbers of sportsmen and celebrities sought injunctions to stop the media reporting on their activities. This chapter explains the development of privacy law, and warns that journalists who electronically snoop on people or hack into their phone messages may well be committing a crime.

Development of the law

The Human Rights Act 1998 came into force on October 2, 2000, incorporating into UK law the European Convention on Human Rights, Article 8 of which guarantees the right to respect for privacy and family life. The result was that the UK now had what it had previously lacked – a specific law of privacy.

As the legislation went through Parliament journalists and media organisations expressed concerns about the potential effect of the right to privacy on their freedom to publish true information of public interest. Section 12 of the Act requires courts considering granting an **injunction** banning publication of information to have 'particular regard' to the importance of freedom of expression, guaranteed by Article 10 of the Convention. The protection afforded by this provision has proved minimal. →glossary

In the *Douglas* case, outlined in chapter 25, Lord Justice Sedley rejected the view that section 12 gave greater weight to freedom of expression than to privacy rights, saying: 'Everything will ultimately depend on the proper balance between privacy and publicity in the situation facing the court'.

In 2004, in the *Campbell* case, the House of Lords established 'unjustified disclosure of private information' could be a cause of legal action. The Law Lords agreed that supermodel Ms Campbell was entitled to damages after the *Daily Mirror* reported that she was receiving therapy at Narcotics Anonymous. The paper was ruled to have infringed her privacy by giving some details of the therapy and her reaction to it, and by publishing surreptitiously taken photographs of her emerging from a therapy session (*Campbell v Mirror Group Newspapers* [2004] UKHL 22).

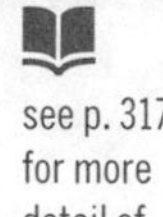

see p. 317 for more detail of this case

In 2004 the European Court of Human Rights held that Princess Caroline of Monaco's privacy was breached by the publication of photographs of scenes from her daily life, shopping or on holiday with her family, in public places. An important consideration in its decision was that she had suffered years of being stalked and photographed by paparazzi and this had interfered with her human right, protected by Article 8, to enjoy social interaction with people (*von Hannover v Germany*, Application no. 59320/00, June 24, 2004, ECtHR).

In the House of Lords, in *In Re S* (*FC*) (*a child*) (*Appellant*) ([2004] UKHL 47; [2005] 1 AC 593) Lord Steyn made it clear that neither Article 8, guaranteeing the right to respect for privacy and family life, nor the Article 10 right to freedom of expression 'has as such precedence over the other'.

This is also the view of the European Court of Human Rights in Strasbourg – meaning that section 12 of the Human Rights Act has little effect on the courts in relation to whether they will issue an injunction, as the Act also requires, in section 3, that the courts must act in a manner compatible with the Convention, while section 2 requires them to 'take account' of the decisions of the Strasbourg court. Judges have argued that criticism of the way in which they have applied and developed the law of privacy is misguided and unreasonable, because Parliament must have known what it was doing when it passed the Act.

It is now clear that, unless there is a strong public interest justification – the material in question must be held to contribute to a debate of general public importance – the courts will issue injunctions to prevent the publication of the sort of kiss-and-tell stories which were once the standard fare of tabloid journalism. The court does not need to find that the information is published in breach of confidence – but if it is, the argument for issuing an injunction is all the stronger.

ch. 25 explains breach of confidence

Remedies for breach of privacy

The remedies which courts will provide for a breach of privacy include damages and the granting of permanent injunctions to prevent material being published.

A person who considers his/her privacy to have been infringed can appeal to the European Court of Human Rights if he/she is dissatisfied by a decision in the UK courts system.

In 2008, Max Mosley, the president of the Fédération Internationale de l'Automobile (FIA), which runs Formula 1 grand prix racing, sued the *News of the World* over stories, photos and video footage about his participation in sado-masochistic activities with prostitutes. The case, which is examined in greater detail below, did not establish new principles of privacy but the level of damages awarded, at £60,000, was the highest yet, putting privacy on a par with other costly legal actions, such as libel.

Injunctions and super-injunctions

The issue of injunctions and so-called super-injunctions – orders which include a clause prohibiting the media or anyone from even publicising the fact that they have been made – attracted considerable media coverage in spring and early summer 2011, with detailed reporting on each new injunction which was issued and claims that freedom of expression was being irrevocably damaged. Footballers, actors and business people sought orders to give them anonymity and block publication of information about their private lives, while bloggers and users of the Twitter micro-blogging system sought to undermine the effects of the orders by naming those they claimed had obtained them. Liberal Democrat MP John Hemming used parliamentary privilege on May 23, 2011, to name, in the House of Commons, the sportsman who obtained an order banning publication of the fact that he had had an affair with a former TV reality show contestant.

The scope of Article 8

The right to privacy is guaranteed by Article 8 of the Convention on Human Rights, which says:

1. Everyone has the right to respect for his private and family life, his home and his correspondence.
2. There shall be no interference by a public authority with the exercise of this right except such as is in accordance with the law and is necessary in a democratic society
   - in the interests of national security, public safety or the economic well-being of the country,
   - for the prevention of disorder or crime,
   - for the protection of health or morals, or
   - for the protection of the rights and freedoms of others.

Article 8 gives protection for privacy against a 'public authority' and also against the media or other intrusions, such as internet blogging.

'Reasonable expectation of privacy'

Although founded in the law of breach of confidence, the law of privacy has now moved away from its roots and become established as a separate cause of action.

A claimant seeking an injunction to stop the media from publishing information about his/her private life and activities must first demonstrate that he/she has a 'reasonable expectation of privacy' in relation to the information. Only after that will the court move on to the second stage, balancing the right to privacy against the right to freedom of expression, and considering the proportionality of any interference with either right in a process called the parallel analysis, before conducting the 'ultimate balancing test' to reach a decision.

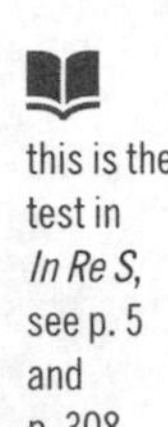

this is the test in *In Re S*, see p. 5 and p. 308

A court, when deciding if the expectation of privacy is reasonable, may take into account the location of the event(s) – because that expectation may not be reasonable, for example in respect of an act done in a public place. However, location may not be a key consideration. Someone who falls ill in a public street, or who is in an accident there, has a reasonable expectation that this vulnerability gives them a right of privacy – for example, to film them in their distress would infringe it.

Case study

In 2003 the European Court of Human Rights ruled that a British man's privacy was infringed by the media broadcasting footage of his suicide attempt in 1994 in the centre of Brentwood. The borough council had released the footage to show that its installation of CCTV cameras had helped save his life, because police had been alerted by the camera operators, and had taken a knife from him. But the man, who had been mentally ill at the time of the incident, was recognisable in images broadcast, despite the council's request that he should not be (*Peck v the United Kingdom*, Application no. 44647/98). His complaints about this were upheld in 1996 by the broadcast regulators but he took a case to the European Court, because the UK courts did not in 1996 recognise what they now do – a specific right of privacy.

The courts also recognise that people have a reasonable expectation that what they say and do intimately within a personal relationship is private – whether the relationship is a marriage, co-habitation, love affair or friendship. If after the relationship ends, one person wants (often, to earn money) the media to publish secrets from the relationship, the courts may injunct to protect the other person's Article 8 rights, or – if the information is already published – award damages for the infringement.

Ch. 27 gives examples of how the Press Complaints Commission has ruled on 'reasonable expectation'.

Privacy versus freedom of expression

A major consideration for the courts in a privacy case may be the question of whether the material which the media organisation seeks to publish contributes to a 'debate of general interest to society'. Decisions by the Strasbourg court indicate that it sees freedom of expression as being on various levels of value to society. In *The Law of Human Rights* (2nd edition, Oxford University Press) authors Richard Clayton and Hugh Tomlinson divide this into an eight-stage hierarchy, with political expression about the conduct of politicians in public office, and including statements made at elections, having the highest value. Second in rank are expressions about matters of public interest, including the private conduct of politicians, and the conduct of large corporations and other powerful bodies, third comes artistic expression – writing of all forms, painting, film and video, fourth are statements about the activities of civil servants, followed in fifth place by statements concerning the conduct of private individuals. Sixth come statements made for commercial purposes – including advertising and 'entertainment journalism' – while ranked seventh are pornography and expressions which undermine the rights of others, such as direct attack on religious sensibilities. In eighth and last place are expressions which promote or are intended to promote violence or attacks on the democratic order. The higher up the hierarchy, the greater the protection the courts should give freedom of expression, and vice versa, although each case will, as the Strasbourg and UK courts consistently stress, depend on its specific facts.

The privacy of sexual relationships

In the years immediately after the Human Rights Act came into force, courts took the view that not all sexual conduct was entitled to be viewed as confidential or, indeed, deserving of legal protection. In 2002 the Court of Appeal lifted an injunction banning publication of details of the extra-marital affairs of a professional footballer, Blackburn Rovers' captain Garry Flitcroft (*A v B (A Company)* [2002] EWCA Civ 337). It said there was a significant difference between the confidentiality that attached to what was intended to be a permanent relationship and that which attached to the category of relationships that Flitcroft was involved with in this case (*A v B (A Company)* [2002] EWCA Civ 337).

Since then, however, the tide has turned, in that – as the *Mosley* case demonstrates – the courts have been more willing to hold that adulterous or casual sexual affairs are matters in which one or both of the people involved have a reasonable expectation of privacy, and will issue gagging orders unless the defendant (the party from the relationship who wishes to reveal the intimate matters) or the media can persuade the judge that there is a strong public interest in publishing the information.

Case study

In 2008 the *News of the World* printed the story of Max Mosley's involvement in a sado-masochistic orgy with five prostitutes, claiming that it had a Nazi theme. The paper put secretly filmed footage of the orgy on its website. The newspaper's informant was one of the women who took part. The newspaper pointed out Mr Mosley was the son of the 1930s Fascist leader, Sir Oswald Mosley. But Max Mosley said the activities at the orgy were consensual, harmless and there were no Nazi overtones. Mr Justice Eady ruled that the woman who was the paper's informant owed a duty of confidence to Mr Mosley, the same kind of duty also held to apply in previous privacy cases involving transitory relationships. The judge said that if the activities had mocked the ways Jews were treated in concentration camps or parodied the Holocaust, there would have been a public interest in disclosing Mr Mosley's activities, at the very least to his employer. But the judge said there was no such behaviour and he could find no public interest to justify the intrusion, the filming or the publication. He said: 'It is not for journalists to undermine human rights, or for judges to refuse to enforce them, merely on grounds of taste or moral disapproval.' He added: 'It is perhaps worth adding that there is nothing "landmark" about this decision. It is simply the application to rather unusual facts of recently developed but established principles. Nor can it seriously be suggested that the case is likely to inhibit serious investigative journalism into crime or wrongdoing, where the public interest is more genuinely engaged.' But he refused to award exemplary damages (*Mosley v News Group Newspapers Ltd* [2008] EWHC 1777).

Mr Mosley later asked the European Court of Human Rights to rule that the UK was in breach of his rights to respect for privacy and family life because the media was under no legal obligation to give anyone about whom they planned to write a story advance notification so that the subject could, if necessary, obtain a privacy injunction to block the publication. The Court rejected his application.

In 2011 one footballer was known to have obtained two privacy injunctions banning the media from reporting on his sexual liaisons with two different prostitutes, with the court agreeing that the material was not in the public interest and that the player had a reasonable expectation that the information would remain private. However, the former England football captain John Terry obtained and then lost an interim injunction which had banned the media from reporting on his relationship with a former team-mate's ex-partner after the judge, Mr Justice Tugendhat, concluded that the aim of the order was to protect Terry's reputation, and sponsorship and commercial deals which might rely on it, rather than his privacy. This, the judge said, meant that the order was in reality a way of circumventing the rule in libel law from *Bonnard v Perryman* that a prior restraint injunction would not be granted to stop publication of an alleged libel if the defendant intended to plead that what was published was true (*LNS v Persons Unknown* [2010] EWHC 119 (QB)).

In another case in May 2011, Mr Justice Tugendhat held that a married footballer with children and his mistress were entitled to an injunction banning publication of details of their affair, and giving them anonymity, even though there had been publicity about the case through various electronic media, including Twitter. While this meant that once-secret private information was no longer secret, so to that extent one purpose of the injunction had been defeated, the extent of the publications and their tone demonstrated there was a pressing need for the injunction to prevent harassment and unjustified intrusion into the lives of the man, his family and his mistress (*TSE and ELP v News Group Newspapers* [2011] EWHC 1308 (QB)).

Chris Hutcheson, father-in-law and one-time business partner of celebrity chef Gordon Ramsay, failed in a bid to block publication of the fact that, although married, he had a grown-up 'second family' by his mistress, who had changed her surname to his. The Court of Appeal accepted Mr Justice Eady's view that even though the Article 8 right to respect for privacy could be 'engaged' in the sense that the information related to family life, it did not necessarily follow that there was a reasonable expectation of privacy. A very public row between Mr Hutcheson and Mr Ramsay, and allegations of misuse of company funds, meant that there was a public interest in allowing publication of his identity and the facts about the 'second family' (*Christopher Hutcheson (Formerly KGM) v News Group Newspapers Ltd and others* ([2011] EWCA Civ 808).

The permanent injunction

An interim injunction is held, under the *Spycatcher* principle, to bind all those on whom it is served or who are aware of it. But such an order, when made final, is thought to bind only those against whom it was obtained – meaning anyone else could then publish the information covered.

ch. 25 explains *Spycatcher*

The response of the courts in these circumstances has been to issue so-called *contra mundum* orders – orders of general effect which bind anyone who knows about them.

In 2000 Dame Elizabeth Butler-Sloss, the then President of the Family Division of the High Court, issued a ground-breaking injunction banning the media from revealing the new identities and whereabouts of Robert Thompson and Jon Venables, who murdered two-year-old James Bulger. The order was justified on the grounds that disclosure of the information would infringe their rights to privacy (Article 8 of the European Convention, Article 2 (right to life), and Article 3 (prohibition of torture)) following threats to their lives.

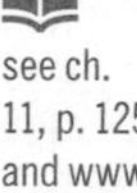

see ch. 11, p. 125 and www.mcnaes.com ch. 11 for details of these cases

This was followed by similar injunctions to prevent disclosure of information about child killer Mary Bell – on the grounds that her mental health would be put at risk by disclosure – and Maxine Carr, former girlfriend of Soham killer Ian Huntley, on the grounds of the need to protect her safety.

Case study

In April 2011 Mr Justice Eady went further, issuing a permanent *contra mundum* order to stop the media publishing 'intimate' pictures of a married television star with children – he was referred to as OPQ – and a woman. It was, said the judge, 'a straightforward blackmail case', with evidence that the first defendant, probably through her partner, had been negotiating with a newspaper group to sell pictures and other information obtained in circumstances which were 'clearly private' and in respect of which she owed OPQ a duty of confidence. Mr Justice Eady said the court's jurisdiction to grant an injunction *contra mundum* was 'widened, at first rather tentatively' immediately following the Human Rights Act 1998, but that there was now 'a new era'.

ch. 13 explains family law injuctions

He said: 'It is now acknowledged, therefore, that the court's power to grant an injunction *contra mundum* is not confined to the wardship jurisdiction; nor to children; nor to "individuals who cannot take care of themselves". The remedy is available, wherever necessary and proportionate, for the protection of Convention rights whether of children or adults.

'In the present case there is solid medical evidence as to the health, including the mental health, of the claimant and various family members. Their rights plainly need to be taken into account.

'It is clear that publicity relating to the subject-matter of the present dispute could have very serious consequences.

'The material was not in the public domain, there was no legitimate public interest in its disclosure, and it would not make any contribution to "a debate of general interest"' (*OPQ v BJM and CJM* [2011] EWHC 1059 (QB)).

The way in which the privacy or other rights of those linked to a claimant will also influence the outcome of an application for an injunction was illustrated in a decision by the Court of Appeal.

Case study

The Court of Appeal said a judge was wrong to refuse to grant an interim injunction to stop a newspaper publishing information about a married man in the entertainment industry who had had an affair with a woman with whom he was working. The man's wife found out about the relationship. The woman, who was also married, subsequently lost her job. The Court of Appeal held that a sexual relationship was essentially a private matter – the fact that the pair's work colleagues knew of it did not put the information into the public domain. But it said weight also had to be given not only to the man's right to respect for his privacy, but to the same rights in respect of his wife and children. Lord Justice Ward said of the children's position: 'They are bound to be harmed by immediate publicity, both because it would undermine the family as a whole and because the playground is a cruel place where the bullies feed on personal discomfort and embarrassment' (*ETK v News Group Newspapers Ltd* [2011] EWCA Civ 439; *The Times*, April 22, 2011).

The likelihood now is that anyone with a wife and children will seek to put their rights into the balance when applying for a privacy injunction banning publication of stories of extra-marital affairs or other questionable behaviour.

 See the www.mcnaes.com chapter on Scotland for a privacy case involving a married footballer.

Children

The media have to be careful over publicity about children, especially the children of celebrities and others in the public eye. Using paparazzi pictures taken of youngsters in the street could cause problems.

The Court of Appeal upheld the appeal by *Harry Potter* author J K Rowling and her husband against a judge's decision to strike out their claim against a photographic agency which photographed them with their son, who was in a pushchair, in a street in Edinburgh. The Court of Appeal said it was arguable that the child had a reasonable expectation of privacy. A child whose parents were not in the public eye could expect that the press would not use his photograph, and the same was true here – the photograph would not have been taken or published had he not been Ms Rowling's son. Even routine activities such as going to the shops might attract a reasonable expectation of privacy – it all depended on the circumstances. The law should protect children from intrusive media attention (*David Murray (By his litigation friends (1) Neil Murray (2) Joanne Murray) v Big Pictures (UK) Ltd* [2008] EWCA Civ 446; (2008) 3 WLR 1360).

see www.mcnae.com ch. 26 for more on injunctions

Information concerning health

Information concerning health is normally treated as being of the highest confidentiality – people can usually have 'a reasonable expectation' that information about their health is private. In 2002 the Court of Appeal banned the *Mail on Sunday* from naming a local health authority where a healthcare worker, referred to as H, had quit his job after being diagnosed HIV positive. The High Court had earlier said it could name the authority, but not the healthcare worker.

Lord Phillips, Master of the Rolls, said there was a public interest in preserving the confidentiality of healthcare workers who might otherwise be discouraged from reporting they were HIV positive. The *Mail on Sunday* believed H's patients were entitled to know they had been treated by someone who was HIV positive, but naming the authority would inevitably lead to the disclosure of H's identity, as only his patients would be offered HIV tests and counselling, he said. The paper could say the healthcare worker was a dentist.

But there are exceptions to the general rule. In 2006 Michael Stone, who was convicted of murdering Lin Russell and her 6-year-old daughter Megan, failed to ban the press and public from seeing an independent inquiry report into the treatment he had received from mental health, probation and social workers before the attack.

In his ruling the judge said:

> Publication of the report in full can, in my view, only assist the legitimate and ongoing public debate with regard to treatment of the mentally ill and of those with disturbed personalities in the community (*Michael Stone v South East SH* [2006] EWHC 1668).

Can information be private if it is in the public domain?

In 2005 a judge granted an injunction restraining a newspaper from publishing the addresses of buildings acquired for housing vulnerable adolescents, although the addresses would be known to neighbours and others who lived nearby and might also be available from the Land Registry (*Green Corns Ltd v Claverley Group Ltd* [2005] EMLR 31). Mr Justice Tugendhat said:

> There will be cases where personal information about a person (usually a celebrity) has been so widely published that a restraint upon repetition will serve no purpose, and an injunction will be refused on that account. It may be less likely that that will be so when the subject is not a celebrity. But in any event, it is not possible in a case about personal information simply to apply [the] test of whether the information is generally accessible, and to conclude that, if it is, then that is the end of the matter . . . I conclude that the information as to the addresses which is sought to be restrained is not in the public domain to the extent, or in the sense, that republication could have no significant effect, or that the information is not eligible for protection at all.

ch. 25 explains *Douglas*

What is the position with 'widely published' photographs? The Court of Appeal said in the *Douglas* case (paragraph 105):

> Once intimate personal information about a celebrity's private life has been widely published it may serve no useful purpose to prohibit further publication. The same will not necessarily be true of photographs. Insofar as a photograph does more than convey information and intrudes on privacy by enabling the viewer to focus on intimate personal detail, there will be a fresh intrusion of privacy when each additional viewer sees the photograph and even when one who has seen a previous publication of the photograph is confronted by a fresh publication of it.

Information obtained covertly

What if the information is obtained, for example, by bugging or long-lens photography?

In 2006 the Court of Appeal referred to cases where 'confidence' arose from information having been acquired by 'unlawful or surreptitious means'. The court regarded the taking of long-distance photographs as being 'an exercise generally considered to raise privacy issues' (*Niema Ash and Another v Loreena McKennitt and others* [2006] EWCA Civ 1714; [2007] 3 WLR 194).

In the *Douglas* case the wedding pictures were taken by an uninvited freelance photographer. Photographs of Naomi Campbell leaving a Narcotics Anonymous therapy session were also taken surreptitiously.

In 2007 former Prime Minister Tony Blair and his wife Cherie won damages – which they gave to charity – from Associated Newspapers over 'long-lens' pictures taken of them while they were on holiday at Cliff Richard's villa in Barbados. The pictures were taken in secluded and private places and the Blairs said while they accepted a certain level of scrutiny, here the photographers had overstepped the mark.

The public interest

Even before the Human Rights Act, journalists could plead that the disclosure of confidential information would be in the public interest. But judges, once possibly prepared to accept that a claimant's celebrity could generate a public interest in private conduct that would otherwise be protected, are now much less likely to do so.

In the *Naomi Campbell* case, publication of some information was held to be in the public interest, and some not. There were five distinct 'elements' of private information:

- the fact of Ms Campbell's drug addiction;
- the fact that she was receiving therapy for it;
- the fact that she was having therapy at Narcotics Anonymous (NA);
- details of the NA therapy and her reaction to it; and,
- surreptitiously obtained photographs of her emerging from an NA session.

Because the model had publicly denied using drugs previously, the first and second facts could be published in the public interest. But the rest could not, because of the intrusiveness of the disclosure and the likelihood that disclosure would interfere with or disrupt her treatment. Three of the judges – the majority – held that Article 10 considerations could not justify publication of the information.

Two of the judges considered that the third, fourth and fifth categories added little of significance to the disclosure of the first and second and that journalists should be given greater latitude – but as they were in the minority their views did not prevail. The difference of opinion between the judges illustrates the difficult decisions journalists might face when considering such stories.

data protection law is explained in ch. 28

The Data Protection Act

The *Naomi Campbell* case alerted the media to the implications for the law of privacy of the Data Protection Act (DPA) 1998. She sued the *Daily Mirror* for both breach of confidence and infringement of the DPA.

Electronic 'snooping', intercepting and hacking into communications

Journalists who use electronic equipment to spy on other people should be aware that, apart from the risk that this will lead to a lawsuit for breach of privacy, they could well be committing a crime.

The Wireless Telegraphy Act 2006

The Act prohibits the use without authority of wireless apparatus with intent to obtain information about the contents, sender or addressee of any message, and prohibits the disclosure of any such information.

The Regulation of Investigatory Powers Act 2000

The Regulation of Investigatory Powers Act (RIPA) prohibits interception of communications by post or phone or other telecommunication systems. It supersedes the Interception of Communications Act 1985 but, unlike that Act, applies to public and private systems.

RIPA says the sender or recipient of an intercepted message can sue, even if the person having the right to control the use of a private system permits interceptions, if the interception is 'without lawful authority'.

The Act sets the punishment for illegally hacking into mobile phones at a maximum of two years in jail, a fine, or both.

Journalist jailed

In 2006 Clive Goodman, royal editor of the *News of the World*, and private investigator Glenn Mulcaire admitted to conspiring to intercept mobile phone voicemail messages under the Criminal Law Act 1977, which covers conspiracy. Each was also charged with eight offences of intercepting communications by accessing telephone voicemail messages.

The case came to light when Prince William began to fear aides' mobile phone voicemail messages were being intercepted after a story about his knee injury appeared in the paper in November 2005, although few people were aware of it.

Section 2(7) of RIPA classifies messages stored for later retrieval as still being 'in the course of transmission', thus putting voicemail within the scope of 'interception'.

The scandal, set off by disclosures about the amount of phone-hacking allegedly done by the *News of the World*, and revelations that it had hacked into the voicemails on a murdered schoolgirl's phone, and had allegedly deleted some to allow more messages to be left, led to the newspaper being closed in June 2011. As this book went to press, the police were still investigating allegations of criminal phone-hacking at the newspaper.

See www.mcnaes.com ch. 2: 'The scandal of phone-hacking and payments to police'.

Journalists frequently record the calls they themselves make or receive. Under RIPA, interception occurs in the course of transmission, so recording telephone conversations by a device at either end of the communication is not interception and is lawful.

What media codes say

The Editors' Code of Practice, overseen by the Press Complaints Commission, has clauses which require newspapers, magazines and free-standing editorial websites to protect people's privacy. The general protection of privacy provided by these clauses is explained in the next chapter, which also explains rules and 'practices' in the Ofcom Broadcasting Code concerning privacy. That code governs standards for the broadcast media.

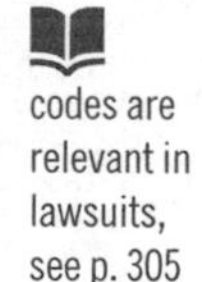
codes are relevant in lawsuits, see p. 305

Chapters 2 and 3 explains the parts of these codes which deal with undercover work by journalists, which has potential to breach privacy, and with journalists recording the phone calls they make. It should be noted that the Editors' Code specifically protects the privacy of 'digital communications' and bans the interception of private or mobile telephone calls, messages or emails.

Recap of major points

- The right to privacy is guaranteed by Article 8 of the European Convention on Human Rights.
- The law of privacy developed from the action for breach of confidence.
- The test in a privacy claim is whether the claimant has 'a reasonable expectation of privacy'.

- The right to privacy is not necessarily lost because the activity happened in public.
- Max Mosley won damages over a story about a sado-masochistic orgy, which the court held was not in the public interest to publish.
- There is a defence that publication was in the public interest.
- Other remedies for breach of privacy include: the Data Protection Act, the Wireless Telegraphy Act 2006 and the Regulation of Investigatory Powers Act 2000.

((•)) Useful Websites

www.bailii.org/uk/cases/UKHL/2004/22.html
The House of Lords judgment in the *Naomi Campbell* case

http://news.bbc.co.uk/1/shared/bsp/hi/pdfs/24_07_08mosleyvnewsgroup.pdf
The High Court judgment in the *Max Mosley* case

27

News-gathering – avoiding intrusion

Chapter summary

Journalists should avoid unnecessary intrusion into people's privacy, but also know when it can be justified. They should combine knowledge of the basics of relevant law with a good grasp of the Editors' Code of Practice or the Ofcom code, according to the media in which they work. PCC and Ofcom adjudications are based on these codes, and give guidance covering a far wider range of situations than is dealt with in privacy case law. Few people can afford to go to court if they feel their privacy is breached, but many complain to the PCC and Ofcom about journalists taking photos, filming and audio recording, and about what is published. Publishing 'user-generated' photographs or footage supplied by the public or material from social media sites can create particular ethical or legal problems. This chapter also explains that the codes seek to minimise intrusion into grief, and have particular rules for when children are interviewed by journalists.

Civil law on privacy – photography, filming and recording

Landmark cases in privacy law have concerned publication of intrusive photographs and video footage, as chapters 25 and 26 show. In these cases, judges weigh the individual's right to respect for privacy under Article 8 of the European Convention on Human Rights against the media's Article 10 rights to freedom of expression and to impart information, and the public's right to receive it. This checklist, compiled from court judgments, is a rough guide to when civil law may be breached if people are photographed or filmed or audio recorded without their consent (for convenience, references to filming include videoing).

ch. 1 explains

- Was the person filmed or photographed or recorded in a location where he/she had 'a reasonable expectation of privacy'? An individual could reasonably expect privacy at home, in a secluded garden or on a private beach, but would normally have less or no expectation of it in a public place.

see the *Princess Caroline* case in ch. 26

see the *Campbell* and *Peck* cases in ch. 26

- Has the person been persistently harassed by the media? If so, the court might decide that his/her privacy was violated even though he/she was pictured or filmed or recorded in a public place.
- Was the person in a condition, situation or event giving rise to a reasonable expectation of privacy, even though he/she was in or could be seen from a public place? For example, was the person mentally ill, or having medical treatment or therapy?
- Is there a 'public interest' factor in revelations in the journalism which overrides the person's right to privacy, whatever the location or situation?
- Is the photo or footage or recording already so widely published – for example, copied worldwide on hundreds of internet sites – that banning publication is pointless?

Courts also consider the degree of harm which publication might cause, or has caused, the person. They may also consider the detail or extent of images captured: was the photograph a long shot or close-up of a face, or was the film a brief clip or lengthy footage? Covert photography, filming or recording, such as using hidden cameras or microphones, is likely to be more intrusive as the target is unaware of it and may assume the situation is private, and act accordingly.

! Remember

Journalists also need to know the law on trespass, dealt with in ch. 36, pp. 418–419.

see also ch. 36 on the right to take photos, film and record

Law against harassment

There is no criminal law banning photography or filming or recording in the street or other public places.

But paparazzi who hound celebrities could be prosecuted under the Protection from Harassment Act 1997. The legislation created criminal offences and civil remedies primarily to deal with 'stalkers' – men or women who obsessively harass ex-partners or others – but has been used in civil law against paparazzi.

Case study

In 2008 actress Sienna Miller accepted a settlement of £53,000 in a claim for harassment and breach of privacy against Big Pictures UK Ltd. The agency agreed that its photographers would not pursue Ms Miller, and not take pictures of her leaving buildings where she had an expectation of privacy, which did not – she agreed – include bars, restaurants, nightclubs or when she attended a red carpet event (*Media Lawyer*, November 21, 2008).

The 1997 Act does not define harassment in detail but says it can include causing alarm and distress, and is 'a course of conduct' – that is, the conduct must have occurred more than once.

pp. 326–327 explain this

Harassment would also normally breach the Editors' Code of Practice and the Ofcom Broadcasting Code.

The Editors' Code of Practice and Ofcom Broadcasting Code

The Editors' Code of Practice, used by the Press Complaints Commission, and the Ofcom Broadcasting Code give guidance on when photography, filming or recording is unethical. Chapters 2 and 3 of this book explain the PCC's role in respect of newspapers and magazines (and their websites), and Ofcom's regulation of broadcasters. These codes have clauses or sections on covert photography, filming or recording, explained in those chapters. This chapter mainly deals with journalists openly using cameras or microphones, though it is possible even then that people – for example, in crowds or in the chaos after an accident – may be unaware that their images or voices are being captured.

See Appendix 2 for the full text of the Editors' Code. See Useful Websites, below, for the full text of the Ofcom code.

The codes' general protection of privacy

Breaching the codes is not necessarily to breach privacy law, but complying with the codes is ethical and helps reduce the likelihood of a privacy lawsuit.

The Editors' Code clause 3 (Privacy) states:

> “ i) Everyone is entitled to respect for his or her private and family life, home, health and correspondence, including digital communications.
>
> ii) Editors will be expected to justify intrusions into any individual's private life without consent. Account will be taken of the complainant's own public disclosures of information.
>
> iii) It is unacceptable to photograph individuals in private places without their consent.
>
> Note – Private places are public or private property where there is a reasonable expectation of privacy. ”

References to photography in the Editors' Code include filming. Neither the PCC nor Ofcom will normally adjudicate against the use of innocuous images of people in public places or in crowds. For example, Ofcom has said that as a general rule there is no obligation to get consent to film or show images of people shown incidentally as clearly random members of the public. But the PCC and Ofcom take account of situational factors as well as location, as do courts.

Case study

In 2008 the PCC criticised a newspaper's publication of an online image of a road accident victim, part of whose face was shown, receiving emergency medical treatment at the scene. It said: 'There is a clear need for newspapers to exercise caution when publishing images that relate to a person's health and medical treatment, even if they are taken in public places'. The public interest in reporting the accident, which was not a rare or large-scale event, was not sufficient to override clause 3 (Privacy) and justify use of the image. The PCC was particularly concerned that it was published shortly after the accident, and before the woman's condition was known, when her relatives might not have been told of the accident, or could have been in shock. But a photo published in the paper, showing the woman at the crash scene but with her face entirely obscured, was 'just on the right side of the line' (*Kirkland v Wiltshire Gazette & Herald*, adjudication issued April 23, 2008).

The Ofcom code tends to use the phrase 'legitimate expectation of privacy' rather than 'reasonable expectation of privacy'. But most principles in its rules for broadcasters are similar to those in the Editors' Code for newspapers and magazines. Use in the Ofcom code of the term 'warranted' refers to public interest exceptions, explained below.

Section 8 of the Ofcom code says, in rule 8.1: 'Any infringement of privacy in programmes, or in connection with obtaining material included in programmes, must be warranted'. It adds: 'Legitimate expectations of privacy will vary according to the place and nature of the information, activity or condition in question, the extent to which it is in the public domain (if at all) and whether the individual concerned is already in the public eye. There may be circumstances where people can reasonably expect privacy even in a public place. Some activities and conditions may be of such a private nature that filming or recording, even in a public place, could involve an infringement of privacy.'

Ofcom guidance is that property that is privately owned, as are, for example, railway stations and shops, can be a public place if readily accessible to the public.

The Ofcom code adds in practice 8.4: 'Broadcasters should ensure that words, images or actions filmed or recorded in, or broadcast from, a public place, are not so private that prior consent is required before broadcast from the individual or organisation concerned, unless broadcasting without their consent is warranted.'

Case study

In 2008 Ofcom ruled that the ITV documentary *The Truth About Binge Drinking* had not infringed the privacy of a man who was shown in two brief shots to be intoxicated in the street. One shot showed his face. Ofcom said that while his intoxication may have meant he was unaware of being filmed, the filming had not been surreptitious but in the open, on a public street, when his actions had been clearly visible to others around him, and his actions were not of a particularly sensitive or private nature (*Ofcom Broadcast Bulletin*, No. 112, June 23, 2008).

Ofcom's guidance to section 8 gives, as examples of when people can reasonably expect a *degree* of privacy even in a public place, someone with a disfiguring medical condition or CCTV footage of a suicide attempt.

Practice 8.16 of the Ofcom code says: 'Broadcasters should not take or broadcast footage or audio of people caught up in emergencies, victims of accidents or those suffering a personal tragedy, even in a public place, where that results in an infringement of privacy, unless it is warranted or the people concerned have given consent.'

! Remember

Both the PCC and Ofcom make some exception to their normal rules in respect of coverage of major incidents, see p. 330, and mcnaes.com chapter 27 which has case studies. Practice 8.2 of the Ofcom code says that information which discloses the location of a person's home or family should not be revealed without permission, unless it is warranted

Doorstepping

In section 8 of the Ofcom code the term 'doorstepping' means 'the filming or recording of an interview or attempted interview with someone, or announcing that a call is being filmed or recorded for broadcast purposes, without any prior warning.'

Doorstepping, then, is in this context an ambush technique which can be used against someone unlikely to agree to an interview – for example, a crook being investigated, or a politician in a scandal – when they open the door at their home or workplace.

Practice 8.11 of the code says: 'Doorstepping for factual programmes should not take place unless a request for an interview has been refused or it has not been possible to request an interview, or there is good reason to believe that an investigation will be frustrated if the subject is approached openly, and it is warranted to doorstep.'

But the practice adds that broadcasters may normally interview, film or record people in the news when in public places without prior warning.

Also, it makes clear that vox pops (sampling the views of random members of the public) are not considered 'doorstepping'.

The PCC has made clear, in adjudications based on the Editors' Code, that a photograph taken from a public highway of someone on their threshold or in their garden does not breach the code, even if public interest considerations do not apply, if there is no 'reasonable expectation of privacy' and the picture does not show anything private (for example, *Phyllis Goble v The People*, adjudication issued September 29, 2009, and *A Woman v Scottish Sun*, issued April 7, 2010).

Hospitals and institutions

Clause 8 of the Editors' Code says journalists must identify themselves and obtain permission from a responsible executive before entering non-public areas of hospitals or similar institutions to pursue inquiries.

The Ofcom code's practice 8.8 says: 'When filming or recording in institutions, organisations or other agencies, permission should be obtained from the relevant authority or management, unless it is warranted to film or record without permission. Individual consent of employees or others whose appearance is incidental or where they are essentially anonymous members of the general public will not normally be required. However, in potentially sensitive places such as ambulances, hospitals, schools, prisons or police stations, separate consent should normally be obtained before filming or recording and for broadcast from those in sensitive situations (unless not obtaining consent is warranted). If the individual will not be identifiable in the programme then separate consent for broadcast will not be required.'

By 'separate consent', the code means there needs to be a two-stage consent – that is, consent must normally be obtained before filming/recording begins, and then further consent must be obtained for the broadcasting of the footage or audio. Broadcasters may need to ask the people filmed or recorded to sign consent forms to ensure that, should there be a complaint, there is proof of consent.

The codes' protection against harassment

p. 330 explains public interest expections

Under the Editors' and Ofcom codes, a journalist should normally respect a person's refusal to answer questions or their request to stop photographing, filming or recording of them.

Clause 4 (Harassment) of the Editors' Code says:

> i) Journalists must not engage in intimidation, harassment or persistent pursuit.
>
> ii) They must not persist in questioning, telephoning, pursuing or photographing individuals once asked to desist; nor remain on their property when asked to leave and must not follow them. If requested, they must identify themselves and whom they represent.

iii) Editors must ensure these principles are observed by those working for them and take care not to use non-compliant material from other sources. ”

The Ofcom code's practice 8.7 says: 'If an individual or organisation's privacy is being infringed, and they ask that the filming, recording or live broadcast be stopped, the broadcaster should do so, unless it is warranted to continue.'

Case study

In 2007 the *Daily Mirror* apologised after Prince William's then girlfriend Kate Middleton complained to the PCC. The paper had published a photo, taken by a freelance photographer, of her walking down a street holding a cup of coffee. Her lawyers said it was taken in circumstances amounting to harassment (*Middleton v Daily Mirror*: Report 75).

Prohibitions on intrusion into grief and shock

Clause 5 (Intrusion into grief or shock) of the Editors' Code says (in part):

> “ In cases involving personal grief or shock, inquiries and approaches must be made with sympathy and discretion and publication handled sensitively. This should not restrict the right to report legal proceedings, such as inquests. ”

The PCC has made clear in various adjudications that articles breaking news of violent or accidental deaths should not contain graphic detail likely to add to the distress of relatives as this breaches clause 5.

see ch. 3

Broadcast journalists should be aware that images or descriptions of such material could breach the Ofcom code's prohibitions on harm and offence, depending on context.

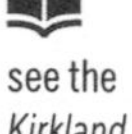
see the *Kirkland* case on p. 324

The PCC has said journalists should not break news of a death to the deceased's family or close friends, either personally or by what they publish, This would be a breach of clause 5 (adjudication in *Oliver v Manchester Evening News*, Report 43). The PCC censured a newspaper for publishing online a photo showing, identifiably, an accident victim at a crash scene, when family members might not have been informed or would have been in a state of shock.

see also p. 331, below, on journalistic use of social media material aggravating grief

Practice 8.18 of the Ofcom code says broadcasters should take care not to reveal the identity of a person who has died or of victims of accidents or violent crimes, unless and until it is clear that the next of kin have been informed or unless it is warranted.

The PCC has censured newspapers for publishing photographs of funerals taken without bereaved families' consent (*Smillie v Sunday Mail*: Report 50, 2000 and *Mrs Hazel Cattermole v Bristol Evening Post*: Report 80, 2009). But the code does not ban this outright.

Case study

The PCC upheld a complaint by Paul McCartney against *Hello!* magazine's publication in 1998 of a photo of him and two of his children lighting a candle in a Paris cathedral for his wife Linda, who had died a month earlier. The PCC deplored publication of the photo as breaching clauses 3 (Privacy) and 5 (Intrusion into Grief and Shock) of the Editors' Code, saying the cathedral was 'a clear example of a place where there is a reasonable expectation of privacy' (*McCartney v Hello!*: Report 43, 1998).

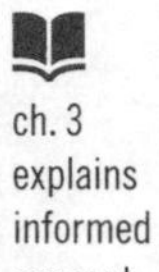
ch. 3 explains informed consent

The Ofcom code warns broadcasters that a bereaved person may need special consideration as a 'vulnerable person' who may not be able to give informed consent to be featured in a programme. Ofcom guidance is that at funerals, programme-makers should respect requests to withdraw.

Practice 8.19 of the Ofcom code says broadcasters should try to reduce the potential distress to victims and relatives when making or broadcasting programmes intended to examine past events that involve trauma to individuals (including crime) unless it is warranted to do otherwise. It adds that so far as reasonably practicable, surviving victims and the immediate families of those whose experience is to feature in a programme should be told of the plans for the programme and its intended broadcast, even if the events or material to be broadcast are already in the public domain.

Protecting children's privacy and welfare

The Editors' Code, clause 6 (Children) says:

> “ i) Young people should be free to complete their time at school without unnecessary intrusion.
>
> ii) A child under 16 must not be interviewed or photographed on issues involving their own or another child's welfare unless a custodial parent or similarly responsible adult consents.
>
> iii) Pupils must not be approached or photographed at school without the permission of the school authorities.
>
> iv) Minors must not be paid for material involving children's welfare, nor parents or guardians for material about their children or wards, unless it is clearly in the child's interest.
>
> v) Editors must not use the fame, notoriety or position of a parent or guardian as sole justification for publishing details of a child's private life. ”

The code does not seek to place a general inhibition on interviewing, photographing or filming children. But the PCC has made clear that publishing photographs in which children are identifiable and which could cause embarrassment or show them in distress – for example, after an accident – concerns their welfare and therefore should not normally be done without a parent or legal guardian's consent. Obscuring the child's identity could avoid an adverse adjudication, as long as the way in which the picture was obtained did not breach the code.

see Useful Websites, below, for relevant PCC adjudications

The PCC has also said parental consent for publishing a child's image can in some instances be implied because of the context – for example, if a parent has allowed the child to be a spectator at a televised sports event – and that 'innocuous' pictures of children in crowds or public places will not normally breach the code (*Quigley v Zoo*, adjudication issued June 23, 2006).

see also www.mcnaes.com ch. 27: 'Images of youngsters committing crime'

Case study

In 2007 the PCC criticised a newspaper for publishing on its website mobile phone footage shot by a child showing disruptive behaviour by some of her classmates. The PCC accepted it was in the public interest to show the behaviour, which the girl said contributed to her poor exam results, but criticised the paper for failing to conceal the children's identities (*Gaddis v Hamilton Advertiser*, adjudication issued July 30, 2007).

The Ofcom code says in practice 8.20: 'Broadcasters should pay particular attention to the privacy of people under sixteen. They do not lose their rights to privacy because, for example, of the fame or notoriety of their parents or because of events in their schools.'

ch. 3 explains the code's general protection for under-18s

Practice 8.21 adds:

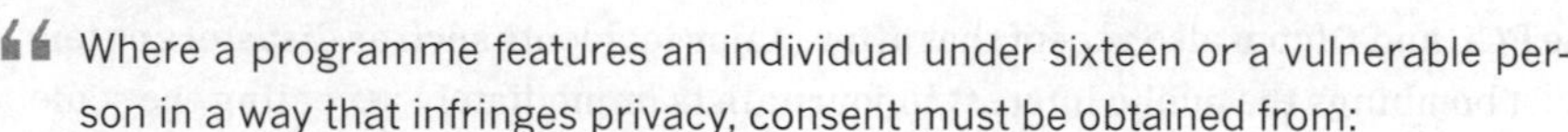

> Where a programme features an individual under sixteen or a vulnerable person in a way that infringes privacy, consent must be obtained from:
>
> - a parent, guardian or other person of eighteen or over in loco parentis; and
> - wherever possible, the individual concerned;
> - unless the subject matter is trivial or uncontroversial and the participation minor, or it is warranted to proceed without consent.

The code says a vulnerable person may include those with learning difficulties, mental health problems, the bereaved, the traumatised and the sick.

The Ofcom code, like the Editors' Code, states that normally broadcasters must get a school's permission before filming pupils – see practice 8.8, cited above.

! Remember

Paranoia about paedophiles may prompt irrational objections by officials or the public to journalists filming or photographing children in innocuous situations. Media photographers should, before photographing youngsters taking part in organised events such as sports, liaise with organisers and carry a press card or similar identification. See Useful Websites below for Football Association guidelines.

Public interest exceptions in the codes

The Editors' Code and Ofcom code allow that some rules may be breached if the journalist is covered by 'public interest' exceptions. The exceptions cover types of valuable journalistic activity, as outlined in chapters 2 and 3, and include exposing crime or negligence imperilling people's safety, and exposing deception of the public by an organisation or a hypocritical politician. If the public interest factor is sufficient, and any intrusion into privacy proportionate, the PCC and Ofcom will say that a photographer's persistent pursuit of a criminal to take his picture, or surveillance or undercover filming by journalists was justified.

Case study

In 2008 Ofcom rejected complaints by several parents whose children were filmed by the BBC during an undercover investigation into standards at a nursery as part of an inquiry into how nurseries were regulated. Ofcom said the filming was justified by the strong public interest and that the broadcast of the programme, *Whistleblower: Childcare*, in which the children's faces were blurred to obscure their identity, had not infringed their privacy. The nursery's poor standards included broken glass in the garden, power tools left unattended near children and failure to check the false qualifications and references of a new member of staff (in fact, the undercover reporter) (*Ofcom Broadcast Bulletin*, No. 116, September 1, 2008).

see also chs. 2 and 3 on subterfuge and deception by journalists

see www.mcnaes.com ch. 27: 'Coverage of major incidents'

The PCC and Ofcom also accept that after major incidents such as disasters or terrorist bombings the public interest in journalists immediately revealing the scale or effect is so strong that breaching privacy to show victims needing or receiving medical treatment may be justified, even though they have not consented to being pictured. But some parts of each code have no public interest exceptions – for example, the first part of clause 5 (Intrusion into grief or shock) of the Editors' Code.

User-generated content

Pictures and footage supplied by readers and viewers – for example, mobile phone footage – frequently feature in media coverage. This is particularly the case in major events such as the aftermath of the terrorist bombings in London on July 7, 2005. Journalists handling this 'user-generated content' (UGC) – whatever the nature of the coverage – should realise it might breach the privacy of those depicted.

See also p. 329 on mobile phone footage of unruly children at a school which was UGC.

Case study

In 2007 the PCC condemned *FHM* magazine for publishing a topless picture of a girl aged 14 in a 'gallery' of mobile phone pictures sent in by readers. Her parents had complained there was no consent to publication and that the appearance of the photo in the magazine had had a significant effect on her emotionally and at school. The magazine said it thought she was older and had consented to the picture being published. The PCC said the magazine had not taken adequate care to check the picture's provenance (*Complaint by a married couple against FHM magazine*, August 15, 2007).

Some UGC pictures published have turned out to be faked, or supplied in breach of someone else's copyright.

ch. 29 explains copyright

Material from social media sites

Journalists routinely search social media sites, including Facebook, Flikr, and Twitter for pictures or footage of people in the news, or to find news. Again, publishing this material may breach copyright.

It might also be an intrusion into privacy if the person was portrayed in a private situation, and was unaware that he/she was being pictured or that the material was being posted on the social media site. The Editors' Codebook, produced by the committee of editors who oversee the Editors' Code, suggests these questions can be asked when considering when such a photo should be used in news coverage: How personal is it?; What is the public interest in its publication?; Was access restricted? (for example, were privacy settings used?); Did the subject upload it personally?

see Useful Websites for the Codebook

Even if the person shown is the one who placed his/her own image in the public domain by originally uploading the material onto the site journalists must consider if it is ethical to use the image in the context of a news story projected to a different, and probably much bigger, audience. For example, the grieving family of a teenager who has died may be even more distressed if media reports include a social website picture showing the youngster apparently drunk or behaving wildly on a social occasion.

The PCC guidance 'Privacy in the age of social networking' warns editors that they could breach clause 5 (Intrusion into grief or shock) of the Editors' Code by publishing such a picture in a way which is insensitive to the feelings of close friends and family.

see Useful Websites for this guidance

But the PCC ruled in 2005 that publication of an innocuous image, obtained from a public resource such as the internet, of someone who died in a shocking event – in that instance, the 2005 tsunami disaster – was not insensitive (*The family of Alice Claypoole v Daily Mirror*: Report 71).

It has also ruled that news media can publish statements people make on social media sites, even when access is restricted to 'friends', though generally only if in the public interest to do so. In 2009 it rejected a complaint made on behalf of a police officer that his privacy was breached when a newspaper published an apparently flippant message he posted on Facebook about the death of a member of the public, Ian Tomlinson, during the G20 protest in London. Two years after the incident, in 2011 another officer was charged with Mr Tomlinson's manslaughter.

The PCC ruled in 2011 that a newspaper which published remarks a civil servant 'tweeted' about her job in her Twitter account, which had 700 followers, did not breach her privacy because this was publicly accessible information and not of an intimate nature (*Sarah Baskerville v Independent on Sunday*, adjudication issued February 2, 2011).

Recap of major points

- The civil courts use the criterion of 'a reasonable expectation of privacy' when deciding if the media have breached a person's human rights by photographing or filming him or her. Intrusion into privacy can be lawful if there is a 'public interest' justification.
- Law against harassment can be used to stop paparazzi stalking celebrities.
- People who object to being filmed or photographed or recorded by the media may complain to the Press Complaints Commission or Ofcom.
- Their codes require journalists to have parental consent for interviewing, photographing, filming or recording a child if his/her welfare or privacy is involved.
- Journalists must take care when deciding whether to publish pictures or footage supplied by the public or copied from social media sites, as publication may breach privacy or copyright.
- Journalists should not intrude into grief, for example when filming or photographing funerals or publishing photos from social media sites.

Useful Websites

http://stakeholders.ofcom.org.uk/broadcasting/broadcast-codes/broadcast-code/
The Ofcom Broadcasting Code

http://stakeholders.ofcom.org.uk/broadcasting/guidance/programme-guidance/bguidance/
Ofcom's guidance on the code

www.editorscode.org.uk/the_code_book.html
Editors' Codebook – advice on PCC adjudications

www.pcc.org.uk/news/index.html?article=NjMwNg==/
PCC adjudication against *Leicester Mercury* concerning a child's welfare

www.pcc.org.uk/news/index.html?article=MjA0NQ==/
PCC adjudication against *OK!* magazine concerning JK Rowling's daughter's welfare

www.pcc.org.uk/newdirectory/newsletter/december/privacyandsocialnetworking.html
PCC guidance on media attention following a death

www.pcc.org.uk/assets/482/Media_attention_following_a_death_web_version.pdf
PCC guidance: 'Privacy in the age of social networking'

www.bbc.co.uk/editorialguidelines/page/guidelines-privacy-privacy-consent/
BBC Editorial Guidelines of filming in public places, sensitive places, private property, and use of social media material

www.bbc.co.uk/editorialguidelines/page/guidance-social-media-pictures/
BBC editorial guidance on use of pictures from social media sites

www.bbc.co.uk/editorialguidelines/page/guidelines-fairness-contributors-access-agreements/
BBC Editorial Guidelines on access agreements

www.bbc.co.uk/editorialguidelines/page/guidelines-children-introduction/
BBC Editorial Guidelines on children and young people as contributors

www.thefa.com/TheFA/WhatWeDo/FootballSafe/~/media/Files/PDF/TheFA/PhotographyGuidelines.ashx/PhotographyGuidelines.pdf/
Football Association guidelines on photography of children

28

Data protection

Chapter summary

The privacy of personal information kept on computers and in filing systems is safeguarded by data protection law. This covers data we give about ourselves to government departments, councils, banks, telephone companies and other commercial and public institutions, and data they generate about us. The law affects journalists in three ways. Firstly, a journalist who uses underhand methods to gain access to people's personal data may be prosecuted, unless he/she has a 'public interest' or other defence. Secondly, institutions – including police forces and schools – sometimes misunderstand data protection law when claiming it stops them releasing information to the media. Thirdly, because journalists generate and store data about people – in research, news stories, recordings, pictures and footage – media organisations and freelance journalists must be lawful in how they process and publish sensitive data, to avoid paying damages for breaching privacy.

Protection for stored data

ch. 26 explains general law on privacy

In 2000 the Human Rights Act created a specific right of privacy. But even before then, the law recognised rights of privacy as regards the vast amount of information held on computer and in manual records. It has been estimated that public and commercial institutions hold in total around 700 databases on each working adult. For personal data held on computer, these privacy rights were provided in the Data Protection Act 1984. The Data Protection Act 1998 strengthened them and extended them to information about people contained in 'structured manual files'.

This law requires personal data to be kept securely. Many news stories have highlighted lax observance by employees of public bodies or companies– for example, when huge amounts of official or commercial data about individuals, including lists of clients or customers, their dates of birth, addresses and bank account details, are found in laptops or on memory sticks left in pubs or taxis.

However, in recent years parliamentary debate has focused on what is seen as widespread breach of data protection law by some journalists – mainly those of national newspapers – when seeking information.

Data protection principles

Under the 1998 Act a 'data controller' is someone or an organisation who determines the purposes for which and the manner in which any personal data are processed. Data controllers include local authorities, health trusts, government departments, commercial organisations, magistrates courts and the police – in fact, any organisation or individual keeping personal data about others in a computer or in structured filing systems.

A 'data subject' is a person about whom the information is held.

The 1998 Act says people handling personal data must comply with data protection principles. Data must, for example, be:

- fairly and lawfully processed;
- processed for limited purposes – for example, for the purpose for which a person (the data subject) provided it to the data controller; for instance, to open a bank account, claim benefits, get a mobile phone account, etc.;
- processed in accordance with the data subject's rights;
- secure.

Crimes of procuring, gaining or disclosing personal data

Anyone who, without a lawful purpose, obtains or procures personal data from a data controller, or anyone who unlawfully discloses it (for example, by publishing it) commits an offence under section 55 of the 1998 Act. A conviction is punishable by a fine of up to £5,000 in a magistrates court or an unlimited amount on conviction in the Crown court.

Section 55 says:

> A person must not knowingly or recklessly, without the consent of the data controller
>
> (a) obtain or disclose personal data or the information contained in personal data, or
>
> (b) procure the disclosure to another person of the information contained in personal data.

'Blagging' by a journalist to gain someone else's personal data could be an offence under this section – for example, the journalist posing as someone else when phoning a bank to get information from that person's account. It might also be an offence if a journalist persuaded or paid someone to leak personal data from a data controller's records.

Defences are available to those who act in the reasonable belief they would have obtained permission from the data controller for their actions, and to anyone who shows that obtaining, disclosing or procuring the information was 'justified in the public interest'. However, the public interest is not defined. Section 55 also contains a defence that obtaining, disclosing or procuring the information was necessary for the purpose of preventing or detecting crime, which might aid investigative journalists.

Although data protection law has been in force for nearly three decades, most journalists know little about it, probably because threats of prosecution against journalists have been rare. But this may change.

Increasing concern about data breaches

see Useful Websites below for these reports

In 2006 the Information Commissioner urged Parliament to make the section 55 offence punishable by up to two years' imprisonment. In reports entitled 'What Price Privacy?' and 'What Price Privacy Now?' he said that his office and the police had uncovered evidence of a widespread and organised undercover market in confidential personal information, procured and sold by dishonest private detectives.

Some of the information they had 'blagged', and some was obtained corruptly from dishonest individuals – including police officers – whose jobs within institutions and companies gave them routine access to personal data.

Among the 'buyers' for this information were many journalists wanting details to trace people or inquire about them.

Case study

The Information Commissioner reported in 2006 that a criminal investigation into one private detective's agency had revealed it had committed thousands of section 55 offences. The detective's records showed he had sold information to 305 named journalists working for a range of newspapers. The data he supplied included records of people's criminal convictions, the number plates of people's cars, driving licence details, ex-directory phone numbers, mobile phone numbers and details of people's 'family and friends' phone contacts. The Commissioner said that some of those whose confidential information was violated were celebrities or public figures, but others were people who had simply 'strayed by chance into the limelight' because they had some connection with people in the news. He said that some of the disclosures of information to journalists 'may have been in the public interest', but noted that the public interest defence was not used by the private detective and three other men (not journalists) who were convicted in the case ('What Price Privacy?' and 'What Price Privacy Now?').

It should be remembered that no journalists were prosecuted in this investigation, and that journalists who dealt with this agency may in many instances have had a public interest justification for seeking out such information, or for accepting it when offered.

However, following publication of the Commissioner's reports, Parliament legislated to introduce jail terms of up to two years for breach of section 55. The measure is in section 77 of the Criminal Justice and Immigration Act 2008. But the new power has not been brought into effect.

Media lobbying led to the inclusion in the 2008 Act of a new defence for someone charged under section 55 – but it has not yet been brought into force. If it does come into force, it will give someone who has obtained, disclosed or procured data 'with a view to the publication by any person of any journalistic, literary or artistic material' a defence if they did so with 'the reasonable belief that in the particular circumstances' their actions were 'justified as being in the public interest'.

! Remember

The focus on how journalists gain information is due to be intensified by the official inquiry headed by Lord Justice Leveson which, as chapter 2 explains, began work in 2011 to investigate 'the culture, practices, and ethics of the press'. That chapter also notes that the Editors' Code of Practice used by the Press Complaints Commission normally bans the accessing of digitally-held private information without consent.

When journalists' lawful inquiries are thwarted

When journalists ask for information, the 1998 Act is sometimes cited by organisations to justify their refusal to give it. But Act covers personal data, not all data, and even personal data can be lawfully released in some circumstances – for example, if the 'data subject' agrees.

Data is only personal if it can lead to an individual being identified.

Getting information from police

Police officers who claim they are prevented by the Act from releasing information may have misunderstood the law. People involved in road accidents and the victims of crime may request the police not to release their details to the media. Guidelines issued by the Association of Chief Police Officers say that these requests should be honoured unless police feel on a case-by-case basis that there is an exceptional reason why the details must be given, for example to help solve a crime. But victims, witnesses or next of kin are not entitled to ask police to give no information about an incident. Police, when asking for their consent to release information, should use the question format in the ACPO guidelines: 'We often

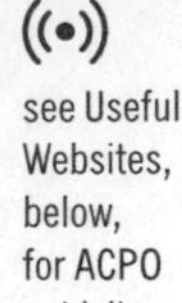

see Useful Websites, below, for ACPO guidelines

find it helpful in our enquiries to pass on someone's details to the media. Do you object if we do that in your case?'

The Act does not apply to dead people. Victims who have died may therefore be named once they are positively identified and immediate relatives have been told.

Getting information from courts

see also ch. 14 'Open justice and access to court information'

Journalists sometimes have difficulty obtaining information from courts.

Guidance for court staff prepared by HM Courts Service published in November 2010 states, on page 11: 'The Data Protection Act must not be used as a blanket excuse for withholding information.' It also makes clear that a defendant's address may be supplied to reporters even if it has not been read out in court.

Getting information from schools

Schools have cited the Act as a reason for refusing to allow photographs of sports and activities, or – if photography has been been allowed – refusing to name the children in the pictures.

Department for Education guidance is that schools and local authorities are free to decide their own policies about when photos can be taken, and on the release of associated information for publicity, but that it will require the consent of pupils' parents or legal guardians.

((•)) see Useful Websites below for the Dept and ICO guidance

The Information Commissioner has issued this guidance about photographs being taken by a local newspaper of a school awards ceremony: 'As long as the school has agreed to this, and the children and/or their guardians are aware that photographs of those attending the ceremony may appear in the newspaper, this will not breach the Act.'

The Commissioner's guidance is also that schools do not breach the Act by releasing exam results to the local media for publication, and that in general, because a school has a legitimate interest in publishing results, pupils or parents or guardians do not need to give their consent to publication.

Media and journalists as 'data processors'

Media organisations and freelance journalists are data controllers because they process - by computer or in structured manual files – personal data about individuals. The Information Commissioner keeps a public register of data controllers. The registration requirement mainly affects media managements principally, but freelancers should also register.

A privacy case brought against a media organisation or journalist may include an element claiming breach of data protection law.

Case study

In 2002 supermodel Naomi Campbell was awarded £3,500 damages for breach of confidence and infringement of data protection rights over the *Daily Mirror's* publication of details about her therapy at Narcotics Anonymous (NA), an award upheld by the House of Lords (*Campbell v Mirror Group Newspapers Ltd* [2004] UKHL 22). But the judgment did not treat the data protection element as a separate issue from the breach of confidence, and the court ruled that both elements concerned the same misuse of private information acquired (and therefore processed) by the newspaper – a photo of her leaving the therapy and some detail of it.

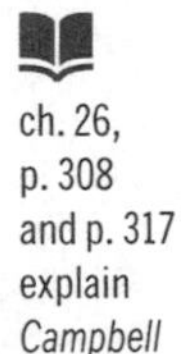

ch. 26, p. 308 and p. 317 explain *Campbell*

In 2003 damages for infringement of rights under the 1998 Act were awarded to the film stars Michael Douglas and Catherine Zeta-Jones, after *Hello!* magazine published pictures covertly taken of their wedding. But they were awarded only £50 each for the infringement. Most of the damages were for breach of confidence/privacy – see chapter 25 for other detail on this case.

These cases show that a media organisation which breaches someone's privacy is likely, in the processing of information gained, to have also breached their data protection rights, but that the courts will examine the total effect on the claimant, and not differentiate between the wrong caused by each breach.

Sensitive personal data

The Act provides particular privacy protection for 'sensitive personal data', which means information about:

- the data subject's racial or ethnic origin;
- political opinions;
- religious beliefs or other beliefs of a similar nature;
- membership of a trade union;
- physical or mental health or condition;
- sexual life;
- criminal offences and any proceedings for an offence alleged to have been committed.

The judge in the *Naomi Campbell* case held that the information about the nature of and details of the therapy that Miss Campbell was seeking was 'sensitive personal data' in respect of her physical or mental health.

Under the law as originally enacted, sensitive personal data can usually only be processed lawfully if two conditions are met, for example the person gave 'explicit' consent or deliberately made the information public; or the use to which the information was to be put was necessary for the administration of justice.

However, as a result of media representations, the Government introduced a statutory instrument that widened the grounds for any third party's lawful release of information to the media for publication, by adding another 'gateway' for the lawful processing of sensitive personal data. This is the Data Protection (Processing of Sensitive Personal Data) Order 2000 (SI 2000/417).

See mcnaes.com ch. 28 for detail of how this Order and other exemptions in the Act protect media activity which is in the public interest, and whether a 'subject access request' could threaten a journalist's protection of the identity of a confidential source.

➡ Recap of major points

- Journalists seeking information should realise that it is a criminal offence to procure the disclosure of personal data, unless there is a legal defence.
- Sometimes the Act is mistakenly used as a reason to deny journalists information.
- The Act has exemptions protecting journalism which is in the public interest.

((•)) Useful Websites

www.ico.gov.uk/
Information Commissioner's website

www.ico.gov.uk/news/current_topics/what_price_privcy_now.aspx
The Information Commissioner's reports 'What Price Privacy?' and 'What Price Privacy Now?'

www.acpo.presscentre.com/content/default.aspx?NewsAreaID=19
Association of Chief Police Officers (ACPO) Communication Advisory Group – Guidance 2010

www.education.gov.uk/popularquestions/schools/healthandsafety/a005632/does-the-department-have-a-policy-for-schools-on-the-use-of-photographs-in-newspapers-and-magazines
Department of Education guidance for schools about use of photographs in newspapers and magazines

www.ico.gov.uk/for_the_public/topic_specific_guides/schools/photos.aspx
Information Commissioner's guidance for schools about photos

www.ico.gov.uk/for_the_public/topic_specific_guides/schools/exam_results.aspx
Information Commissioner's guidance for schools about exam results

29

Copyright

Chapter summary

Copyright is a property right in law, to control who can copy work created by artistic and other intellectual endeavour. This is referred to by judges as 'skill, labour and judgement'. Copyright protects journalism articles, website content, books, photographs, films, TV and radio broadcasts and sound recordings including of music. This chapter explains how copyright law, by deterring and punishing plagiarism, protects the ability of journalists and media employers to earn profit from their output. Copyright lasts for decades – for example, for literary work for the author's lifetime, and then another 70 years to benefit his/her heirs. Copyright also protects work created by others which journalists may wish to copy, for example by quoting from or showing. Journalists need to know how much they can copy without infringing someone's copyright, and the legal consequences of infringement.

What material does copyright protect?

The source of most UK law on copyright is the Copyright, Designs and Patents Act 1988, as amended by subsequent law.

Section 1 says copyright subsists in:

- 'original literary, dramatic, musical or artistic works' – this includes all kinds of text whether handwritten, printed or online, such as journalistic and scientific articles, poems, lyrics, books, plays, scripts, shorthand or longhand records of speeches and interviews; music manuscripts; photographs; design documents, websites and bureaucratic forms; graphic works, maps, plans, sketches, paintings, sculptures; databases and computer programs;
- 'sound recordings, films or broadcasts', including journalism in these media; files and CDs of music; home and cinema movies; TV and radio output;
- 'the typographical arrangement of published editions'.

Unauthorised copying of the whole or 'any substantial part' of any work in these categories is a criminal offence and a civil **tort**, unless justified by a defence or exception.

→glossary

Case study

In 2009 the *Mail On Sunday* paid substantial damages to pop star Madonna after infringing copyright by publishing ten pictures of her wedding to Guy Ritchie. The paper was sold pictures which were copied from her private wedding album without her knowledge (*Media Lawyer*, October 6, 2009).

More than one type of copyright, with different owners, may exist in a single product. For example, a film will have copyrights in the script, footage and music.

Who owns copyright under the 1988 Act?

The 'first owner' of copyright in a literary, dramatic, musical or artistic work is the author as creator. This definition includes the journalist as an article's writer, the photographer as creator of a photo, the artist who makes painting or sculpture, etc. If authorship is joint, each author is a 'first owner' and permission is needed from each to copy the work.

The 'first owner' has the copyright unless he/she agrees, for example for payment, to assign to another party that right to control who makes copies – see below. Assign means to transfer ownership of the copyright, while license means to permit a use of the copyright work.

Who is the first owner?

Sound recording	The producer is the first owner. The Act says a producer is the person or organisation who undertook 'the arrangements necessary' for the work's creation.
Film made on or after July 1, 1994 (whether made for journalism or entertainment)	The producer and principal director are jointly the first owner. The producer owns the copyright in films made earlier which are covered by the Act.
Broadcast	The first owner is the person or organisation 'making the broadcast' – that is, transmitting it if responsible for content, or providing that content and arranging transmission. This is usually a broadcast company.
'Typographical arrangement of a published edition' (e.g. a book)	The publisher is the first owner.
Computer-generated work – a category which the Act limits to circumstances of 'no human author'	The person or organisation undertaking 'the arrangements necessary' for the work's creation.

However, the Act says an employer owns the copyright in a literary, dramatic, musical or artistic work – including a journalistic article or photo – which is created by an employee in the course of his/her employment. This is usually stated in the employment contract. A staff journalist only has the copyright in an article or photo if the employer has specifically agreed to this, for example in the contract of employment (1988 Act, section 11). Self-employed journalists, including freelance and commercial photographers, are the 'first owners' of copyright in their works.

p. 347 explains custom and practice

The terms, including of payment, under which freelancers assign or license copyright in their work to media publishers may be specific to each deal, or governed by custom and practice.

Commissioner's copyright

Section 4 of the Copyright Act 1956 governs who owns copyright in literary, dramatic and artistic work created before August 1, 1989 – that is, before the 1988 Act came into force. Copyright in such a work, including a journalism article, which was created in the course of staff employment is owned by the employer unless the employer agreed to assign it to someone else. So for such work, the two Acts are alike.

But if a work was created by a freelance paid or commissioned to do it, the 1956 Act says that, in the absence of any other agreement, the copyright is owned by the commissioner (for example, a newspaper or magazine), not by the freelance.

This difference between the two Acts decides who, as copyright holder, can successfully object to the use of an archived photo or demand payment for the use.

Copyright in a commissioned photograph taken before August 1, 1989 is owned by the commissioner, even though the freelance or commercial photographer who took the photo may own the negatives or have digital copies of it. The photographer or his/her employer owns the copyright in a photo taken before August 1, 1989 which was not commissioned. (This summary assumes that copyright in the photograph has not been assigned to someone else.)

A family wedding photo taken by a commercial photographer before August 1, 1989 will almost certainly have been commissioned by someone in the family, so that family member will probably own the copyright. Under the 1988 Act, the copyright in a photograph taken on or after August l, 1989 is owned by the photographer's employer, or by the photographer if he or she is self-employed, *unless* there is an agreement to the contrary.

A celebrity who hires (commissions) a photographer to take pictures of a family occasion may well insist on being assigned all copyright in them, to control their use.

Private and domestic photographs and films

The 1988 Act gives a 'moral right', in essence a privacy right, to a person who commissions the taking of photographs or making of films for private and domestic purposes. This 'moral right' is that no copy of the photograph or film should be published, issued to or exhibited to the public without the commissioner's agreement.

The commissioner has this moral right even if he/she does not own the copyright and can sue for damages anyone who publishes a commissioned photo or film of a private and domestic occasion without his/her permission.

A publisher who uses the photo or film in breach of copyright could also be sued, for example by a photographer who holds the copyright.

Consider this hypothetical case: a woman is hurt in a train crash. A journalist traces a relative, who emails the journalist a copy of a picture of the woman, taken some years previously at her wedding. If the relative took the picture himself, and agrees for it to be published, there is no infringement of copyright. If the wedding picture was taken by a commercial photographer commissioned by the bridegroom (that is, the injured woman's husband) the photographer will probably own the copyright, and may be glad to accept a fee for media publication of the picture. But the husband may not want it published. He may sue for breach of his moral right, and win, even if he is not in the photo.

ch. 26 explains general privacy rights

This 'moral right', defined in sections 85–88 of the Act, can be waived. But otherwise it lasts as long as the copyright, see below.

! Remember

When a big story breaks, the media tend to rush to get 'pick-up' pictures or family-held footage of those involved, or copy material from social media sites and adopt a 'publish first, worry later' approach. Most families know little about copyright or moral rights, so financial consequences for media organisations are rare – but they could occur.

See p. 354 for an explanation of moral rights held by creators.

Copying from the internet, including social networking sites

Publishing material such as a photo or an extract of 'original' text copied from the internet infringes any copyright in the work, unless the copyright owner consents or a defence or exception applies. Downloading can itself be an infringement.

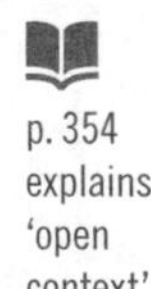
p. 354 explains 'open context' licences

! Remember

Publishing photos copied from a social networking site may infringe the copyright in the site, and/or the person who created the picture, who might not even be aware that someone else has uploaded a copy on to the site.

 **Case study**

In 2010 a photographer who put his pictures of the Haitian earthquake disaster on to Twitter sued the AFP news agency for using them, claiming damages of up to 150,000 dollars (*Media Lawyer*, May 5, 2010).

The PCC has warned against insensitive use of social networking material after a death, see ch. 27, pp. 331–332.

Photos of TV images, and photos shown on TV

Publishing a photo (for example, a 'screengrab') of the whole or a substantial part of a television or film image without permission can infringe copyright under section 17 of the 1988 Act. Showing a photo on a TV programme without the copyright owner's permission is also an infringement, unless a defence applies.

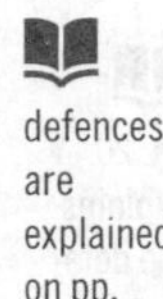

defences are explained on pp. 350–354

The scope of copyright protection

Copyright is automatically in force as soon as a work is created in any permanent form. In the UK, copyright does not have to be registered.

What is 'original'?

Copyright protects an 'original literary, dramatic, musical or artistic work'. 'Literary' in this context includes any work, written or spoken, which exists in some form, but has no reference to a work's literary or artistic merits. The legal definition of 'original' simply requires that the work was originated by the creator(s) using some element of 'skill, labour and judgement' (see, for example, *Express Newspapers plc v News (UK) Ltd* [1990] 3 All ER 376).

The elements of skill, labour, judgement, time or expense need not be great. Judges have cited the rough guideline that 'anything worth copying is usually worth protecting'.

- Skill, labour and judgement spent in creating a bus or rail timetable, or tide table, or sports fixture list, or a database, means that such works are protected by copyright, vested in the 'first owner' as creator or, if employed, his/her employer.
- Copyright could also subsist in even a fairly basic form of map, diagram, drawing or sketch, so journalists should beware, too, of reproducing these without permission.

But a commonplace expression such as 'Love is Blind', if used in a book title, is not protected by copyright because of lack of originality.

No copyright in news or in unrecorded ideas

Copyright does not protect ideas – it controls the right to copy the form or manner in which ideas are expressed or executed. The law of breach of confidence, explained in chapter 25, would apply in some circumstances if a considered 'idea' with commercial value was exploited in breach of 'confidential' discussions about it.

There is also no copyright in facts, news or information. Copyright exists in the form – for example, sentences, a photo, footage – in which these things are expressed, and in the selection and arrangement of the material for publication.

'Lifting' stories

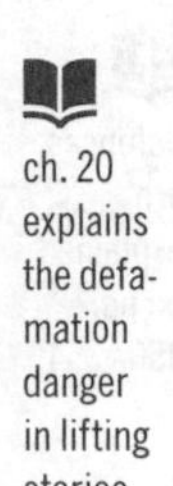
ch. 20 explains the defamation danger in lifting stories

News organisations often include in their own coverage facts in stories 'broken' by rivals, such as political initiatives or a famous person's death. This is known as 'lifting' a story. There is no copyright infringement in reporting in a *re-written* version the facts uncovered or published by others (*Springfield v Thame* (1903) 89 LT 242). But there may be infringements in 'lifting' verbatim phrases and quotes from the original report, depending on the extent. See below: 'What is 'substantial'?' and 'Copyright in speeches and interviews'.

High Court judge Sir Nicolas Browne-Wilkinson said in 1990 (*Express Newspapers plc v News (UK) Ltd* [1990] 3 All ER 376):

> " For myself, I would hesitate a long time before deciding that there is copyright in a news story which would be infringed by another newspaper picking up that story and reproducing the same story in different words... If it were the law that such practice constituted breach of copyright, the consequences, as it seems to me, would be that a paper that obtained a scoop from a confidential source would obtain a monopoly on that piece of news. That would not be in the public interest... "

p. 354 explains 'acquiescence'

He also observed that because the practice among UK national newspapers of copying quotes from each other was so widespread, and rarely led to copyright disputes, it could be argued that the newspapers gave each other implied licence for the practice by 'acquiescence'.

Changing the odd word or two when writing a news report by 'lifting' facts from a rival report will not be enough to avoid copyright infringement. But the 1988 Act's defence of 'fair dealing' for reporting current events can allow a media organisation to copy some quotes and other sentences from a rival's report, and to broadcast short extracts of film or sound footage already broadcast by a rival. See below.

Assignment and licensing of copyright

Copyright holders can 'assign' copyright, wholly or in part, to another person or organisation, either temporarily or for the copyright's duration. This transfers control to exploit the work. Or the owner can, while retaining the copyright, 'license' another party to exploit the work in a particular deal or territory. Section 90 of the 1988 Act says an assignment of copyright is not effective unless it is in writing and is signed by or on behalf of the person assigning it – for example, the 'first owner'.

A licence need not be in writing. In journalism, licences are often agreed verbally, or implied by what has become custom and practice. For example, freelance journalists who regularly send articles or photos to newspapers know their fee rates, and whether they also want the right to use the work in magazine supplements and on websites, or possibly in overseas editions and for syndication. Any doubts on either side about licence terms should be discussed and agreed in writing before the work is published.

Material from non-journalist contributors

A reader sending a letter for publication has by implication licensed the media organisation to publish it once, but retains the copyright. If the organisation subsequently wants to publish a compilation of readers' letters as a book, it will need to contact each letter-writer to seek a further licence to re-publish the letters.

Results and listings

A sporting or trade association may make material such as weekly tables of results of local matches, or tide tables available to media organisations for publication free of charge. But it still holds the copyright, and can withdraw the stated or implied licence for publishing the material, or charge for doing so.

TV and radio listings

Section 176 of the Broadcasting Act 1990 says those who provide a broadcast service, and own the copyright in the programme listings, must make the listing information available, through a copyright licensing scheme, to any organisation wishing to publish it, but can charge.

Copyright in speeches and interviews, and in notes or recordings of them

Copyright exists in spoken words such as public speech as soon as the speaker's words are recorded in some form, with or without permission. The copyright arises even if the speech is not delivered from a script, but is, for example, uttered in an improvised comedy show, or in an interview with a journalist. The speaker, as the author of a 'literary work' – that is, his/her words as recorded – owns the copyright in that work, unless he/she is speaking in the course of his/her employment, in which case the employer owns the copyright, or is reciting words in which someone else holds copyright (for example, from a play script).

As copyright protects the 'original' product of 'skill, labour and judgement', there is no copyright in casual conversational or trite remarks, short jokes already in circulation or in commonplace or ill-judged sayings.

Section 58 of the 1988 Act – a specific defence for journalism – says it is not infringement of copyright to use a record of all or part of a speaker's words for reporting current events, as long as:

(1) The record of the words – that is, as recorded on tape or digitally, or in shorthand or longhand – is a direct record of their utterance, and is not taken from a previous record or broadcast.

(2) The speaker did not forbid any note or recording being made of his/her words, and making the record of them did not infringe any pre-existing copyright.

(3) The use made of the record of the words, or extracts from it, is not of a kind prohibited by the speaker (or anyone else who owns copyright in words used by the speaker) before the record was made.

(4) The record is used with the authority of the person who is lawfully in possession of it.

The first and fourth conditions reflect the fact that, apart from the speaker's copyright in the recorded words, a separate copyright exists in the actual record – the audio-recording, shorthand or longhand note – because of the skill, labour and judgement involved in making it (*Walter v Lane* [1900] AC 539). The journalist who made the record will, if a freelance, be 'first owner' of that copyright. If the record was made in the course of his/her employment, the employer owns it.

Journalists should not be over-concerned about infringing copyright when reporting verbatim speech from a note or recording they make, as usually a speaker who knows they are journalists has consented, expressly or by implication, to publication. Even if a speaker withholds consent, one or both of the fair dealing defences can apply, see below.

Parliament and the courts

There is no copyright infringement in reporting what is said in proceedings of the UK and Scottish Parliaments, the Northern Ireland and Welsh Assemblies, or the public proceedings of statutory public inquiries. There is no copyright infringement in reporting what is said in court cases.

How long does copyright last?

Durations of copyright, set out in section 12–15 of the 1988 Act, can be summarised as:

- Copyright in a literary, dramatic, musical or artistic work – including a journalism article or a photo – lasts for the author's (that is, creator's) lifetime and then for another 70 years from the end of the calendar year in which he/she dies. So, copyright owned by an author can be bequeathed to his/her heirs. The duration is the same even if the copyright is owned by an employer or has been assigned to a company.

- Copyright in a sound recording and in a work of computer-generated music or graphics lasts for 50 years from the end of the year in which it was made. For a sound recording published or communicated to the public, it lasts 50 years from the end of the year in which that first happened. The performer's copyright in musical recordings is due to be extended to 70 years following a European Union decision in September 2011.
- Copyright in a broadcast lasts 50 years from the end of the year in which it was made.

There are different (but still lengthy) periods of copyright for various other works, such as films, works of unknown authorship and for some particular circumstances.

Crown copyright

Work produced by civil servants in the course of their employment is protected by Crown copyright, which can last for up to 125 years.

Legal remedies for infringement of copyright

Civil law

- A copyright holder who discovers that someone plans to infringe it can get a High Court or county court **injunction** to stop this. 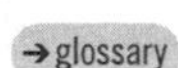

- If the infringement has happened, an injunction can ban any repetition. The copyright owner can also sue the infringer for damages or 'an account of profits', to claim all or some of any profit made.
- The court can also order all infringing copies of the work to be handed to the copyright owner or destroyed.
- The damages awarded by a court may reflect its view that there has been a flagrant breach of copyright.

Criminal law

The 1988 Act makes infringing copyright a criminal offence, though prosecutions tend to be confined to cases of large-scale piracy. Fines can be as high as £50,000. In 2009 two men from Essex who ran a big operation to make and sell pirated DVDs of blockbuster films were jailed for six years for various offences, including conspiracy to contravene copyright (*Media Lawyer*, July 28, 2009).

Defences to alleged infringement of copyright

What is 'substantial'?

see the *Ashdown* case, pp. 352–353

Section 16 of the 1988 Act says there is an infringement of copyright if the whole or 'any substantial part' of a work is copied. 'Substantial' refers to 'the quality of originality', including the importance of the copied material in relation to the rest of the original work, rather than merely to how much was copied (*Newspaper Licensing Agency Ltd v Meltwater Holding BV* [2010] EWHC 3009 (Ch)). For example, a face may be a small part of a photograph but is probably more important, as regards its commercial value, than the rest of the picture. A court dealing with a 'literary work' would consider to what degree unauthorised, verbatim publication of part of it might devalue the work's copyright. The issue of what is a 'substantial part' is not always relevant for the news media, as documents can be paraphrased or summarised to avoid quoting verbatim. Also, editors can aim to rely on a fair dealing defence, because then the issue of how much can be copied/quoted must be assessed in terms of 'fairness' rather than substantiality, see below.

The *Meltwater* case shows the impact of a recent development in European law on what can be considered a 'substantial part'.

Case study

A High Court judge ruled in 2010 that subscribers to *Meltwater News*, a commercial monitoring service, had infringed the copyright of UK national newspapers. In response to search terms chosen by its subscribers, Meltwater would electronically 'scrape' headlines, the opening words and short extracts from newspapers' online articles, making copies of the 'scraped' material available to subscribers, hyperlinked to each relevant article so they could read it in full if they chose to. This service meant Meltwater's subscribers also made computer copies of the headlines and text extracts. Meltwater agreed to pay the newspapers for a licence to copy the 'scraped' material. But the cost of this licence was also dependent on whether each of Meltwater's subscribers needed one. Mrs Justice Proudman's ruling meant they did. She said some headlines would, in their own right, be protected by copyright, and so would many of the extracts. She drew on a 2009 ruling by the European Court of Justice (ECJ) that a single extract of 11 consecutive words from a newspaper article could be protected by copyright if the extract had sufficient originality. She said 'the ECJ makes it clear that originality rather than substantiality is the test to be applied to the part extracted. As a matter of principle this is the only real test.'

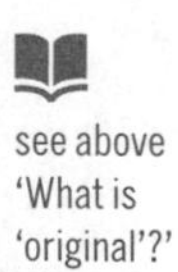

see above 'What is 'original'?'

The Court of Appeal upheld her ruling in June 2011. Meltwater said it would appeal to the Supreme Court (check www.mcnaes.com for updates).

Fair dealing defences

The two 'fair dealing' defences in sections 30 and 178 of the 1988 Act recognise the public interest in media coverage being free of some copyright restraints.

Defence of fair dealing for the purpose of reporting current events

Section 30 of the Act allows publication of work protected by copyright 'for the purpose of reporting current events', even if there is no consent from the copyright owner. Case law is that the term 'current events' should be interpreted liberally.

However, there must be 'fair dealing' by those publishing the work for this purpose, and an accompanying 'sufficient acknowledgement' of the work copied.

- 'Fair dealing' means fair practice – for example, the publisher should not take unfair commercial advantage of the copyright owner by excessive publication of the copied work.
- 'Sufficient acknowledgement' means that a report, in a newspaper, magazine, website or other textual medium, must
  - cite the work's title, or include some identifying description of it, and
  - name its author/creator, unless it was published anonymously.

Photographs are specifically excluded from the fair dealing defence of 'reporting current events', because otherwise no news photographers could earn their living by selling their pictures.

Case law suggests that a court will be less likely to uphold the defence if the work copied has been 'leaked' to the media organisation. But the defence would probably not be undermined if the leak, for example, of an internal company memo, revealed wrongdoing or a threat to public safety. In such a case, the defence may protect verbatim publication of an entire document. But if the copyright in a text or document has a legitimate, commercial value, judges will expect the media to make only limited use of verbatim extracts, so that the copyright owner's ability to exploit that value is not compromised unfairly. See the *Ashdown* case, below.

Although the fair dealing defence does not cover using still photographs, it does cover media use – that is, if 'fair' – of copied film footage and sound recordings, including in digital forms.

Case study

In 1991, the High Court dismissed a copyright action by the BBC against British Satellite Broadcasting over the satellite company's sports programme's use of highlights from BBC coverage of the World Cup football finals, to which the corporation had bought exclusive rights. The court said BSB's use of short clips showing goals scored, varying from 14 to 37 seconds, broadcast up to four times in 24 hours, with a BBC credit line included as acknowledgement, was protected by the defence of fair dealing for reporting current events (*BBC v British Satellite Broadcasting* [1991] 3 All ER 833, Ch D).

Rival broadcast organisations sometimes agree protocols for limited copying of each other's output.

The Act says sound recording, film or broadcast reports of current events do not need to acknowledge the copied work's title, or other description of it, or the identity of its author/creator 'where this would be impossible for reasons of practicality or otherwise.' This reflects the difficulty of including all such detail in a broadcast of a short piece of copied footage. But acknowledgements help prove fairness.

Defence of fair dealing for the purpose of criticism or review

- Section 30 of the Act allows publication of copies of a work, even without the copyright owner's consent, 'for the purpose of criticism or review'.
- But the work must already have been 'made available to the public' *with* the copyright owner's consent – for example, published or exhibited. The defence does not protect use of leaked material.
- There must also be 'fair dealing' by those publishing it for criticism or review, and an accompanying 'sufficient acknowledgement' of the work copied.

See above for explanation of 'fair dealing' and 'sufficient acknowledgement'. These requirements are in essence the same as those required for the defence of fair dealing in reporting current events.

Authors or creators who have released works to the public may well be happy for extracts from them to be published in criticisms or reviews, as they will receive wider publicity. But the defence applies irrespective of whether they object. The defence would, for example, cover publication of a whole photo from an exhibition or book of artistic photos.

The requirement of fairness means that in a dispute about the extent of the use of copied material a court would consider if the media organisation genuinely sought to criticise the copied work(s), or had the baser motive of taking commercial advantage.

Case study

Paddy Ashdown, when leader of the Liberal Democrats, kept a private diary. After stepping down as leader he decided to publish it. But before he did, the *Sunday Telegraph* published, from a leaked copy, verbatim quotes from a confidential minute he made of a discussion in 1997 with Labour Prime Minister Tony Blair and two other senior politicians on the idea of a coalition Cabinet. Lord Ashdown sued for breach of copyright. The *Sunday Telegraph*, which had quoted verbatim or nearly verbatim some 20 per cent of the five-page minute, attempted to use both fair dealing defences. The Court of Appeal rejected both defences, ruling that there was no criticism or review of the minute as a literary work – the criticism was of the actions of Blair and Ashdown. It also ruled that arguably the 1997 meeting could be regarded in 1999 as a current event, but that 'one or two short extracts' of verbatim quotes from the minute would have sufficed to make the paper's account authoritative. But the newspaper had substantially and extensively 'filleted' the minute to add flavour to its coverage, in furtherance of its commercial interests, which competed with Ashdown's plan to sell his memoirs. The fact that the minute was leaked in breach of confidence was also material (*Ashdown v Telegraph Group Ltd* [2001] All ER (D) 233 (Jul)).

ch. 25 explains breach of confidence

see www.mcnaes.com ch. 29 for more case studies of copyright disputes

Public interest defence

A public interest defence is likely to protect a media organisation's publication of copyrighted work if the purpose is to expose it as an immoral work, or one damaging to public life, health, safety or the administration of justice, or as a work which incites immoral behaviour, and in some other circumstances.

Case study

In 2010 the *Reading Post* succeeded with the public interest defence in the small claims court after being sued by the owner of copyright in several photos which it had copied from a website. Police had directed the *Post* to the site, which showed the apparent exploits of 'urban explorers' inside abandoned buildings. The *Post* said it published the pictures to highlight police concerns that these activities involved criminal damage, including graffiti, and to help identify those involved. The judge said he felt the pictures were posted on the website to encourage the activities, which could cause an accident, and the public to suffer, and were a serious social problem (*Newspaper Society* website, January 28, 2010).

Incidental infringement and publicly displayed artworks

Section 31 of the Act says that copyright in a work is not infringed by its incidental inclusion in a photo, sound recording, film or a broadcast. So there is no infringement if a TV news report incidentally shows, in the background, a work of art, or its sound track of coverage of a wider event incidentally includes a band playing, although deliberately including music would need to be covered by another defence or exception, for example fair dealing.

Innocent infringement

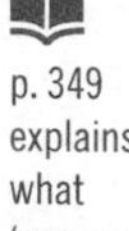

p. 349 explains what 'account of profits' means

If an infringer did not know and had no reason to believe the copied work was subject to copyright, for example he/she genuinely believed the copyright had run out, the copyright owner would be entitled to an account of profits but not to damages.

Acquiescence

A copyright holder who encourages or allows another to make use of his/her work without complaining may destroy any claim for infringement.

'Open content' licences

see Useful Websites below for creative commons site

Some creators – including some who post photographs on social media sites such as Flickr – give a general, 'open content' licence for people to copy and distribute their work free of charge, provided that attribution to the creator is included and specified conditions are honoured. The licence may be in the Creative Commons format. One condition may be that the use of the work is not commercial, which would exclude use in journalism which consumers pay for. A different licence would have to be agreed with the copyright owner to permit such journalistic use, unless a defence applies.

Moral rights for creators

The 1988 Act, to comply with an international convention, gives 'moral rights' to authors (creators) of some categories of copyright work, including literary and artistic work – for example, a photo – and to the director of a film. He/she can assert the right to be identified when his/her work is published, and has the right not to have it subjected to 'derogatory' (for example, distortive) treatment. A person has a moral right not to have a work falsely attributed to him/her. This law is in sections 77–84 of the Act. The rights to be identified and not to have the work subject to derogatory treatment do not apply to work created in the course of employment, or for reporting current events, or to other types of content in a newspaper, magazine or periodical. But a freelance with sufficient clout because his/her work is in demand can insist, as a term of the copyright licence, on being identified by a media publisher as the work's author.

'Passing off' and trade marks

Other civil law provides remedies against someone who, to gain profit, falsely 'passes off' their products or services as being produced or retailed by a more prestigious organisation. A celebrity could use this law to stop his/her name or image being falsely used to endorse a product. The system of registration of trade marks gives similar protection in the retail of goods and services.

➡ Recap of major points

- Copyright law controls who can commercially exploit literary, musical, dramatic and artistic works, including journalism articles and photos, as well as the exploitation of sound recordings, film, broadcast and typographical arrangements.
- There is no copyright in news itself, only in the form in which it is expressed.
- Defences of fair dealing are available for publication of copyrighted work, if the copying is not excessive and if the publisher honours requirement for attribution to the creator(s).
- But photographs are excluded from the fair dealing defence which covers reporting news and current events.
- A copyright owner whose rights are infringed can seek an injunction and/or damages.

((•)) Useful Websites

www.ipo.gov.uk/types.htm
Intellectual Property Office, a Government agency – see its guides to copyright and trade marks

www.londonfreelance.org/advice.html
London freelance branch of the National Union of Journalists – advice on copyright

www.ipkitten.blogspot.com/
IPKat blog on copyright and other rights

www.creativecommons.org/licenses/
Guide to creative commons copyright licences

Part 5

Information and expression

30

Freedom of Information Act 2000

Chapter summary

The Freedom of Information (FoI) Act 2000, which came into effect in 2005, created the UK's first general right of access to information held by government departments and public authorities. Use of the Act has produced many exclusive stories, some about the highest reaches of Government. But the Act is bedevilled by bureaucratic delay and wide-ranging exemptions, and a requester must be prepared to argue that the 'public interest' justifies disclosure of information. This chapter deals with FoI law as it applies in England, Wales and Northern Ireland, and information access rights in the Environmental Information Regulations.

Introduction to the Act

The Freedom of Information Act came into force in January 2005, giving people the right to require 'public authorities' to disclose information they would not otherwise publish. Authorities must supply information without charging for finding and collating it, subject to cost limits.

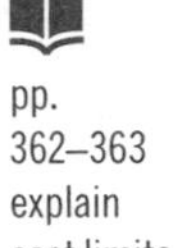

pp. 362–363 explain cost limits

The parliamentary expenses scandal in spring 2009 highlighted the Act's shortcomings. FoI requests by campaigner and journalist Heather Brooke forced House of Commons officials to disclose details of what some MPs were claiming in expenses for their second homes. But official disclosures were anodyne in comparison with the truth, which emerged when virtually every detail about MPs' expenses was leaked to the Telegraph Media Group – and showed that MPs 'flipped' their main and second homes to maximise expenses, claimed for items such as moat-clearing and duck houses, could make claims without producing receipts and had reclaimed the cost of things ranging from dog biscuits to bath plugs. None of that material emerged in the official disclosures.

In July 2010 Information Commissioner Christopher Graham, who oversees the Act's workings, said it was 'completely unacceptable' that House of Commons authorities had delayed releasing embarrassing details about MPs' unpaid bar and restaurant bills until after the general election. The authorities took more than seven months to disclose these bills of 74 MPs. Most ran to hundreds of pounds – some were for thousands. All were more than three months overdue. The debts should have been disclosed within 20 working days of the Press Association's request in September 2009. Instead, despite repeated deadlines for disclosure from the Commissioner, they were kept secret until May 19, 2010, after the election, by which time many of the MPs had quit politics or lost their seats.

Difficulties with FoI obligations

Although some public bodies are helpful when responding to FoI requests, many delay answering requests and are extremely slow when considering the 'public interest test' (see below on this test). In October 2010, the Information Commissioner put more than 30 public bodies, including the Cabinet Office, Home Office, Ministry of Defence, Metropolitan Police, Department for Work and Pensions, Transport for London and Scotland Office on a list of organisations to be monitored for three months as they appeared to be flouting the rules by taking too long to respond to FoI requests. In April 2011 he said the Cabinet Office – the Government department in charge of openness – was among the worst offenders for delays in meeting FoI requests, and, with the Ministry of Defence and Birmingham City Council, had failed to improve its response after three months of monitoring.

Government departments and other public bodies often seek to use the Act's exemptions to thwart requests for information, and numerous requesters win appeals to the Information Commissioner and what is now called the First-tier Tribunal (Information Rights) – formerly the Information Tribunal. Journalists using the Act need to be systematic and persistent. Despite the drawbacks it is a worthwhile tool for investigative journalism.

What is a 'public authority' under the Act?

The Act covers about 100,000 major and minor bodies in the public sector, including:

- national government departments and ministries such as the Home Office, Foreign Office and Prime Minister's Office;
- the House of Commons, the House of Lords, the national assemblies of Northern Ireland and Wales;
- the armed forces;
- local government – metropolitan, city, county, district, and parish councils, transport executives, waste disposal agencies, police forces, fire services;
- national park authorities;

- universities, colleges and schools in the state sector;
- the National Health Service, including primary care trusts, hospital trusts, health authorities, doctors' and dentists' practices;
- various advisory councils, and regulatory bodies with statutory powers such as Ofcom and the General Medical Council.

It does not define 'public authority', but lists, in Schedule 1, the bodies and organisations it covers. More have been added by statutory instruments.

Institutions and agencies not covered by the Act

The security and intelligence agencies – MI5, MI6 and GCHQ – are exempt, and therefore not required to respond to FoI requests. Courts and tribunals are not covered, though some information gathered or created in their functions will be available if a request is made to the government department holding it, such as the Ministry of Justice.

The following are not public authorities under the Act: housing associations; charities; private prisons; harbour authorities; and MPs and peers, as individuals.

The Royal Family never came under the Act. But an amendment introduced in section 46(1) and Schedule 7 of the Constitutional Reform and Governance Act 2010, which came into force in January 2011, gives the three senior royals – the Queen, the Prince of Wales and Prince William – absolute exemption from any application for information. This ends the situation under which FoI campaigners, requesters and the press could ask the Government and other public bodies to release details about them on the grounds that there was a legitimate public interest in disclosure. Other members of the Royal Family, such as the Duke of Edinburgh and Prince Harry, remain subject to a qualified exemption – public bodies holding information relating to them should release it if there is a public interest in disclosure.

The coalition Government announced at the start of 2011 that it intended to make many more bodies, including the Association of Chief Police Officers (ACPO), and companies entirely owned by local authorities, subject to the Act, and would consult many more on bringing them within its remit.

See this book's Late News section on ACPO and check www.mcnaes.com ch. 30 for FoI law updates.

How the Act works

A public authority should respond to a request for information within 20 working days, either supplying the information or explaining that it cannot do so because:

- it does not hold it – in most circumstances this must be made clear;
- it would exceed the cost limits for free provision – see below;
- it is exempt from disclosure.

In the case of some exempt categories, for example information held in confidence or concerning national security, an authority does not have to say what it holds if denying or confirming the information's existence would undermine the purpose of the exemption

pp. 364–366 explain exempt categories

Journalists should check an authority's website, if it has one, for information before making an FoI request, as it might already publish the material there. The Act says each authority must have a 'publication scheme'. If the information sought is not listed there, the journalist should ask the official who coordinates the authority's FoI matters about the types of information it holds. Authorities must, under section 16 of the Act, offer 'advice and assistance', including on how to frame requests to stay within the cost limits for free information, although sometimes this is not done, as this chapter explains.

A requester's reason for wanting information plays no part in an authority's decision on providing it (unless a request is 'vexatious', for example from someone who repeatedly seeks the same or similar information).

An authority which has to apply the 'public interest test' (see below on this test) to consider if information is exempt may take more than 20 working days to give its final response. It must consider, even if some information specified in a request is deemed exempt from disclosure, if the request can be met in part by releasing non-exempt information.

What is information?

Section 84 of the Act defines information as 'information recorded in any form'. An authority is not required to gather information it does not already have. The right under the Act is for *information* to be communicated to the requester, not necessarily in the form of particular documents, though requests often refer to particular documents, which are supplied. Mr Justice Calvert-Smith decided in *Dominic Kennedy v Information Commissioner and Charity Commission* ([2010] EWHC 475 (Admin); [2010] 1 WLR 1489) that 'document' includes electronic documents.

Cost limits

A government department required to disclose requested information must do so free if it costs no more than £600. All other public authorities covered by the Act must provide such information free if it costs no more than £450. Cost is estimated by assessing the staff time reasonably needed to determine whether a body holds the information, to find and retrieve it, and, if necessary, extract it from a document. Staff time is rated at £25 an hour. If the cost limit is, after a bona fide estimating process, exceeded, the authority is not obliged to supply any information requested, but may choose to supply it without charge, or at a price which reflects the cost of providing it if the requester is willing to pay. An authority which can comply with part, but not all, of a request within the cost limits has a duty under section 16 to offer a requester advice to see if he/she wishes to redefine or limit the request. If the information is to be provided on paper, the requester can be charged a reasonable price for photocopying. Information can often be sent by email.

Journalists should make requests as specific as possible. A requester may get round a cost limit by breaking a 'large' request into several smaller ones, sent serially. But authorities may 'aggregate' the cost of two or more requests made within 60 days by the same person for the same or similar types of information – that is, treat them as being part of a single request, and refuse them, if in total they breach the cost limit for one request. Authorities should not use aggregation powers to frustrate a sequence of requests each of which, on the basis of information sent previously, digs further into a topic by asking for further, different information.

Advice and assistance

Section 16 requires a public body to give prospective or actual requesters 'advice and assistance, so far as it would be reasonable to expect the authority to do so'.

- It should, if asked, tell a requester *before* he makes a request what information of the type sought might be available, and help frame a request.
- It should give guidance to avoid a request breaching the cost limit for providing information free.

Some staff in public bodies, particularly national government departments, are not always helpful. But the Information Tribunal has made clear that it expects the Information Commissioner, when adjudicating an appeal against a refusal to supply information, to consider the extent to which a body met its obligations under section 16, so a requester should if necessary remind the body, in writing, of these obligations. The Act says an authority which, in relation to the duty to advise and assist, conforms to the Code of Practice issued by the Ministry of Justice is to be taken as complying with that duty.

see Useful Websites, below for this code

Paragraph 8 of the code says that authorities should, 'so far as is reasonably practicable', assist an applicant to describe more clearly the information requested. The Information Tribunal has said: 'There is nothing to prevent an authority volunteering advice and assistance: an applicant does not have to ask for it. Moreover, nothing on the face of the section [16] restricts the duty to advise and assist only to those cases when some form of request has been made. In the Tribunal's view, the duty must include at least one to advise and assist an applicant with regard to the formulation of an appropriate request' (Appeal no. EA/2006/0046).

Section 1(3) allows a body which 'reasonably requires' further detail to identify and locate information to clarify this with the requester, and, if such further detail is not provided, not to comply with the request. The Information Commissioner has made it clear that if a public authority tells a requester that the information is already in the public domain it should, to comply with section 16, indicate where it can be found.

Exemptions

((•)) see Useful Websites, below for ICO guidance

Bodies may refuse to supply information on various grounds – exemptions. The Information Commissioner's Office website has guidance on these.

Absolute exemptions

Some exemptions are 'absolute' – the authority does not have to give a reason for refusing disclosure beyond stating that the exemption applies because of the nature of the information. Absolute exemptions include:

Section 21 – information reasonably accessible by other means.

Section 23 – information supplied to the public authority by or relating to bodies dealing with security matters, *for example supplied by* MI5, MI6 and GCHQ.

Section 32 – court records This exemption covers documents held by a public authority because it is a litigant or an interested party in a court case – for example, copies of material filed with a court for the purposes of proceedings.

Section 40 – personal information The Act does not override data protection law. A public body may decide that an FoI request encompasses exempt 'personal data'. But it should consider whether deleting references which could identify an individual could allow disclosure of non-exempt information.

ch. 28 explains data protection law

The Commissioner has made clear that when considering personal data issues, authorities should distinguish between 'professional personal information' such as staff job descriptions and details of their responsibilities and 'private personal information' such as sickness records.

Section 41 – information provided to the authority in confidence by another party This does not cover information which the public body has generated itself, so does not cover any contract the authority has entered into.

But the Information Tribunal, as it was, has said that the section 40 or 41 exemptions are not as absolute as they first appear, because a body should apply a public interest test under data protection law and/or the law of confidence when deciding on disclosure.

Section 44 – information the disclosure of which is forbidden by other law For example, the Information Tribunal upheld a ruling that the Independent Police Complaints Commission could not, because of a provision in the Police Act 1996, disclose under the Act copies of files relating to complaints against the police.

Qualified exemptions

((•)) see Useful Websites below for this ICO guide

The other exemptions are 'qualified' – if a public body decides against supplying information in these categories it must give reasons, showing how it has applied the public interest test. The Act says information may be withheld only if the public interest in withholding it is greater than the public interest in disclosure.

It does not define 'the public interest'. But in an Awareness Guide in July 2009, the Information Commissioner gave these examples of public interest arguments that could weigh in favour of disclosure (here given in summary):

- that disclosure would promote transparency, accountability and participation;
- that disclosure might enhance the quality of discussions and decision making generally;
- that the information requested involved a large amount of public money;
- that, in the case of information created some time ago, the passage of time has reduced the strength of argument against disclosure;
- that, in respect of information relating to an investigation, the request is made at a time when the strength of argument against disclosure has reduced. This would depend on the stage the investigation had reached and how much information was in the public domain;
- that the impact of disclosure would be beneficial to individuals and/or the wider public.

The Campaign for Freedom of Information has stressed the importance of applicants pursuing requests all the way to the First-tier Tribunal (Information Rights) if necessary, and not accepting a public authority's initial refusal. Requesters should not assume that the Information Commissioner will automatically recognise the public interest case for disclosing information, and should raise in appeal correspondence. But appeals take time, even when authorities have clearly misapplied absolute or qualified exemptions, as the Information Commissioner's office is overworked and under-resourced.

Qualified exemption include:

Section 24 – information which if disclosed is likely to prejudice national security This concerns information other than that already absolutely exempt under section 23, see p. 364.

Section 27 – information which if disclosed is likely to prejudice international relations.

Section 31 – information held by an authority for law enforcement functions This is exempt if its disclosure would, or would be likely to, prejudice the prevention or detection of crime, the apprehension and prosecution of offenders or the administration of justice. So details of when a speed camera at a particular site is active do not have to be disclosed as this would compromise the camera's effect. But more general information, such as how many drivers a particular camera caught speeding on a particular day could be published without such adverse effect.

Section 35 – information relating to formulation or development of Government policy The Information Tribunal – now First-tier Tribunal (Information Rights) – has been robust in disapproving of some attempts to use this exemption, noting that there is a public interest in involuntary disclosure of information under the Act as it acts as a check on information disclosed voluntarily. The older the information, the less sensitive it is as an indication of an authority's policy options.

Section 36 – information the disclosure of which is likely to prejudice effective conduct of public affairs This exemption is controversial as it is so vague. Parliament intended it to cover material which did not fall into other categories but which, if disclosed, would damage a public body's ability to carry out its duties. Heather Brooke says a public authority relying on it 'is desperate and grasping at straws'.

Section 43 – commercial interests This covers trade secrets and information which, if disclosed, 'would, or would be likely to, prejudice the commercial interest of any person (including the public authority holding it)'.

Case study

In *John Connor Press Associates v Information Commissioner* (EA/2005/0005), the Information Tribunal held that the National Maritime Museum should have disclosed financial information concerning its purchase of a set of artworks. The museum had argued that when it received the freelance news agency's FoI request it was negotiating with another artist about another project and its ability to ensure value for public money would have been prejudiced had financial details about the previous deal been released. The Tribunal held that no real and significant risk of such prejudice existed, partly because the deal under negotiation – which included payment for 'performance art' – differed in scope from the museum's previous deal for artworks.

Delays in the public interest test

The Act does not set public authorities a deadline for completing the 'public interest test'. When applying it to an FOI request they are not required to make a decision in the 20-day period, and may take months. But a public body must tell a requester within the 20-day limit that a qualified exemption might apply.

If the information is not supplied

If an authority takes no decision on supplying the information within the 20-day limit, or refuses to supply it because of the cost limit or an exemption, a requester can ask for an 'internal review' of the decision, which should be conducted by an official other than the one involved in the refusal. There is no timescale for completing this review. The Information Commissioner's Office has said 20 working days (from the time a request for a review is received) is a reasonable time for a review, and that in no case should the time exceed 40 working days. A requester dissatisfied with the result of a review can appeal to the Information Commissioner.

The Information Commissioner and the First-tier Tribunal (Information Rights)

The Freedom of Information Act is enforced by the Information Commissioner, who also oversees the Data Protection Act 1998. The current Commissioner is Christopher Graham.

The Commissioner can order a body to release information if he disagrees with a refusal to disclose it. He can question an authority's claim not to hold requested information and its estimate that disclosure would exceed the cost limit for free provision.

If a requester claims an authority has not responded within the 20-day limit, the Commissioner can, under section 52, serve it with an enforcement notice requiring compliance with the Act. As an ultimate sanction, he can ask the High Court to punish an authority's failure to comply with the notice as contempt of court. Section 48 gives him the power to issue a 'good practice recommendation' specifying the steps an authority should take to improve compliance. FoI campaigners have criticised the Commissioner for not using his powers frequently enough.

Requesters and public authorities dissatisfied with the Information Commissioner's decision can appeal to the First-tier Tribunal (Information Rights). Appeals should be made within 28 days of receipt of the Commissioner's decision. The Tribunal, part of the First-tier Tribunal in the administrative justice system – see chapter 17 – publishes its decisions online.

see Useful Websites, below for the Tribunal's site

Ministers' power of veto

Cabinet Ministers can veto notices issued by the Commissioner requiring government departments to disclose requested information. The then Justice Secretary, Jack Straw, first used this power in 2009 to block an enforcement notice from the Commissioner (upheld by the Information Tribunal) requiring release of the Cabinet minutes of the decision to go to war with Iraq.

The FoI Act's coverage of media organisations

The BBC, Channel 4 and S4C – public service broadcasters – were made subject to the Act, but in a limited way as disclosure provisions only apply to information they hold 'for purposes other than those of journalism, art or literature'. It does not require these broadcasters to comply with:

(1) requests attempting to reveal journalists' confidential sources;

(2) requests by rival news organisations, or by the subjects of journalistic investigations (that is, 'data subjects'), aimed at securing, before or after broadcast, material gathered in a journalistic investigation, including any footage/audio not broadcast.

But the distinction between material held for journalism purposes and management or governance purposes is not straightforward, and is due to be considered by the Supreme Court in the latest stage of the BBC's battle over the Balen Report, an internal document which reviewed, and made recommendations about its coverage of the Middle East, including best practice on matters such as impartiality.

chs. 2 and 3 explain the roles of the PCC and Ofcom

The Court of Appeal held in 2010 that if information was held for journalistic purposes, it was exempt from disclosure even if it was also held for other purposes.

Ofcom is subject to the Act, but the Press Complaints Commission, which is not a public authority, is not.

Environmental information

The Environmental Information Regulations (EIR), the latest version of which came into force in 2005 (SI 2004/3391), require public authorities to provide information about environmental matters. They implement a European Union directive and give, in the environmental field, the public – and journalists – more powerful rights of access to information than those in the FoI Act. A public authority receiving a request for information within the scope of the EIR should automatically deal with it under the EIR rather than under the Act (ideally the request should refer to the EIR). For guidance on using the EIR, see Useful Websites below.

ch. 1 explains EU directives

Environmental information covers air, water, land, natural sites, and living organisms – including GM crops – and discharges as well as noise and radiation. The EIR cover more bodies than the FoI Act, with fewer exemptions. For example, information about emissions cannot be withheld because of commercial confidentiality.

All bodies subject to the FoI Act are also subject to the EIR and the same 20-day deadline applies to requests for information. Privatised water and sewerage companies in England and Wales are not subject to either the Act or the EIR, although they are in Scotland.

The EIR require that public authorities must assist those requesting information.

EIR requests can be turned down on grounds of national security. But all refusals are subject to a public interest test and requests can be refused only if the public interest in non-disclosure far outweighs the public interest in disclosure. A 'reasonable' fee can be charged for EIR requests.

The EIR, which are enforced by the Information Commissioner, can be used, for example, to obtain reports of hygiene inspections at factories and restaurants as they cover information on 'the state of human health and safety, including the contamination of the food chain'.

Case study

The Times used the Scottish EIR to by-pass the exemption in the FoI Act to force local authorities north of the border to disclose details of lobbying by the Prince of Wales. The Scottish Information Commissioner held (Decision 039/2011: *Mr Dominic Kennedy of The Times and the Scottish Ministers*) that the newspaper had more right to the information than the Prince had to keep it quiet. The newspaper pointed out that the EIR, which were imposed by Brussels, had no opt-outs or exemptions for royalty.

D Legal issues in using FoI disclosures in stories

Publication of material disclosed under the FoI Act or the EIR brings no special protection against an action for defamation. The FoI Act and EIR do not confer statutory qualified **privilege** on such reports. Such reports may be protected by other defences, such as justification.

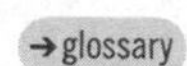

Material disclosed under either the Act or the EIR will be protected by copyright, which must be respected. If you have any doubts about copyright, consult the public authority about the status of information. In some cases copyright may be waived or information licensed for re-use.

Chs. 21 and 22 explain libel defences.

Copyright protects photographs, maps and diagrams, but does not protect facts as such, only the way in which they are recorded. Thus, a journalist using information from material supplied under FoI and putting it into a news story does not have to fear that factual revelations will raise copyright issues. Also, the **fair dealing** defence applies to citing some text verbatim.

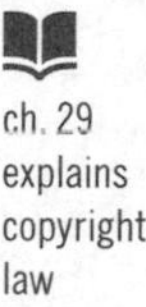

ch. 29 explains copyright law

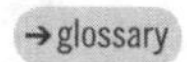

Recap of major points

- The Freedom of Information Act gives a general right of access to information held by public authorities including government departments and local authorities.
- But there are wide-ranging exemptions, and plenty of potential for delays in responding.
- The Act obliges public authorities to offer requesters advice to enable them to word their requests in such a way that they are more likely to succeed.
- The Information Commissioner hears appeals against a body's refusal to supply information. The First-tier Tribunal (Information Rights) can hear appeals against the Commissioner's decisions.
- The Environmental Information Regulations provide powerful rights of access to information in fields they cover.

((•)) Useful Websites

www.legislation.gov.uk/ukpga/2000/36/contents
The Freedom of Information Act

www.informationcommissioner.gov.uk/
Information Commissioner

http://www.ico.gov.uk/upload/documents/library/freedom_of_information/detailed_specialist_guides/22_06_09_FoI_advice_and_assistance_v2.pdf
Information Commissioner's Guidance on advice and assistance for requesters

www.ico.gov.uk/for_the_public/official_information/how_access.aspx
Information Commissioner's guidance on accessing official information

www.ico.gov.uk/Global/faqs/environmental_information_regulations.aspx
Information Commissioner's guidance on Environmental Information Regulations

www.cFoI.org.uk/
Campaign for Freedom of Information

http://foia.blogspot.com/
The Campaign's UK Freedom of Information blog

www.ico.gov.uk/upload/documents/library/freedom_of_information/detailed_specialist_guides/fep038_public_interest_test_v3.pdf
Information Commissioner's guidance on the FOI public interest test

www.heatherbrooke.org/
Heather Brooke's website

www.guardian.co.uk/politics/freedomofinformation/
The Guardian newspaper guidance on FoI and Environmental Information Regulations

www.holdthefrontpage.co.uk/category/news/foi
Holdthefrontpage stories on journalists using the FoI Act

www.direct.gov.uk/en/Governmentcitizensandrights/Yourrightsandresponsibilities/Freedomofinformationanddataprotection/DG_4003239
Government advice on making an FOI request

www.justice.gov.uk/downloads/guidance/freedom-and-rights/foi-section45-code-of-practice.pdf
Code of Practice for public authorities on FoI requests – useful for advice and assistance issues

http://FoIman.com
Blog written by an FOI practitioner, and with a useful guide on making FOI requests

http://foiwiki.com/foiwiki/index.php/Main_Page
FoI Wiki site

http://davidhiggerson.wordpress.com/
Journalist's FoI and journalism blog

31

Other information rights and access to meetings

Chapter summary

The public and journalists have rights to information under various laws, most notably as regards the workings of local government. These rights can be used to get policy documents from public bodies, and ensure journalists can report on important meetings. For some types of material the laws are better than the Freedom of Information Act (see previous chapter), as they offer quicker rights to obtain or inspect copies of documents.

Local government

Local government is a major source of stories and should be subjected to rigorous scrutiny by journalists.

Authorities fall into two categories. Principal authorities include county councils, district councils, London boroughs, the London Assembly, and combined police and fire authorities. The others – parish councils and community councils – are not principal authorities.

Access to information from principal authorities was governed by the Public Bodies (Admission to Meetings) Act 1960, the Local Government Act 1972, and the Local Government (Access to Information) Act 1985. But the Local Government Act 2000 has reformed the way authorities are run. It was intended to be a modernising reform, making local government more transparent, but introduced new restrictions on the rights of the public and press to attend meetings or obtain documents. There is some overlap between the access provisions of the 2000 Act and the 1985 Act. The 2000 Act introduced new models of 'cabinet style' government, of which two survive – a leader (elected by council members) and cabinet, and a directly elected Mayor and cabinet. It also introduced 'political advisers' and the power to exclude the press and public from meetings if such an adviser's advice was likely to be disclosed. It also allows executive decisions to be taken at meetings which can be held in private except when 'key decisions' are to be made – although even they may be made in private.

The Local Government Act 2000

Regulations covering access to information under the LGA 2000 are contained in various statutory instruments, which apply to unitary authorities, London borough councils, county councils, and district councils in England and Wales which operate executive arrangements under the 2000 Act.

see also www.mcnaes.com ch. 31 for details of these regulations

The full texts of these regulations – should any journalist need to cite part of them to unhelpful officials – are available at www.legislation.gov.uk/uksi.

When cabinets must meet in public

A cabinet must meet in public when a key decision is to be made. A key decision is one which is likely:

- to result in the authority incurring spending or making savings which are significant having regard to its budget for the relevant service or function; or
- to be significant in terms of its effects on communities living or working in an area comprising two or more wards or electoral divisions.

The full council must agree limits above which items are 'significant', which must be published.

! Remember

In 2011 a Government Minister urged councils to allow blogging, filming and 'tweeting' by journalists covering council meetings – see Useful Websites, below.

Documents that must be made available

A written statement must be produced 'as soon as reasonably practicable' after a public or private cabinet meeting at which an executive decision is made. It must include:

(1) a record of the decision;
(2) a record of the reasons for the decision;
(3) details of any alternative options considered and rejected;
(4) a record of any conflict of interest and, in that case, a note of any dispensation granted by the authority's standards committee.

An executive decision made by an individual or a key decision made by an officer must be similarly recorded.

The record must be made available at the council office for inspection by the public as soon as 'reasonably practicable'. With it must be any report considered at the meeting or by the individual member or officer making the decision.

A media organisation which requests copies of any of the documents available for public inspection must be supplied to them on payment of postage, copying, 'or other necessary charge for transmission'.

A report which an executive member or officer intends to take into consideration when making a key decision must be available for public inspection for at least five clear days before the decision is made.

Agendas and reports

A copy of the agenda and every report for a public meeting must be available for public inspection when made available to cabinet members. The regulations say an item of business shall be considered at a public meeting only:

(1) when a copy of the agenda or part of the agenda, including the item, has been available for public inspection for at least five clear days before the meeting; or

(2) when the meeting is convened at short notice, a copy of the agenda including the item has been available for public inspection from the time the meeting was convened.

If a meeting is convened at short notice a copy of the agenda and associated reports must be available for inspection at that time.

When an item which would be available for public inspection is added to the agenda, a copy of the revised agenda and of any report relating to the item must be available for public inspection when it is added.

A local authority must supply a media organisation which asks with:

(1) a copy of the agenda for a public meeting and a copy of each report for consideration at the meeting;

(2) such further statements or particulars, if any, as are necessary to indicate the nature of the items contained in the agenda; and

(3) if 'the proper officer' thinks fit in the case of any item, a copy of any other document supplied to members of the executive in connection with the item.

Forward plans

Each month every authority must publish a 'forward plan' detailing key decisions to be taken in the following four months. These plans must be available, free, for inspection 'at all reasonable hours'. Authorities must also give the dates in each month in the following 12 months on which each forward plan will be published.

A forward plan must include:

- the matter to be decided, the identity of the decision-maker or makers;
- the identity of the principal groups or organisations to be consulted on the decision;
- the means of consultation;
- the way people may make representations; and
- a list of the documents to be considered.

Powers to exclude the press

Even if key decisions are discussed, a cabinet can exclude the press and public when:

(1) it is likely that if the public were present, confidential information would be disclosed; or

(2) the cabinet has passed a resolution excluding the public because it is likely exempt information would be disclosed; or

(3) the cabinet has passed a resolution excluding the public because it is likely the advice of a political adviser or assistant would be disclosed.

Confidential information

'Confidential information' is information provided to the local authority by a government department upon terms (however expressed) forbidding its disclosure to the public, or information the disclosure of which to the public is prohibited by or under any enactment or by the order of a court.

Exempt information

A resolution to exclude on the grounds of exempt information must identify the proceedings or part of them to which the exclusion applies and the category of exempt information involved.

Principal authorities in England must also perform the public interest test – consider whether the public interest in disclosure outweighs the public interest in secrecy – when deciding whether to exclude the press and public.

A part of an agenda, report or other document which contains exempt information does not have to be made available for inspection.

Exempt information in England is information relating to:

(1) an employee, job applicant, or office holder of the council, or an employee, applicant, or official of the magistrates courts or probationary committee;

(2) a particular council tenant or applicant for council services or grants;

(3) the care, adoption, or fostering of a child;

(4) a particular person's financial or business affairs;

(5) the supply of goods or services to or the acquisition of property by the council, if disclosing the information would place a particular person in a more favourable bargaining position or otherwise prejudice negotiations;
(6) labour relations matters between the council and its employees, if and so long as disclosing it would prejudice negotiations or discussions;
(7) instructions to and advice from counsel;
(8) the investigation and prosecution of offenders, if disclosing the information would enable the wrongdoer to evade notice being served on him.

The public can be excluded only for the part of the meeting during which the matter is being discussed.

Exempt information in Wales is similar, but less wide-ranging.

The categories of exempt information are wider than the categories of information which an authority is not obliged to disclose under the Freedom of Information Act – so exempt material might be obtained through an FoI request.

ch. 30 explains the FoI Act

Backbench and scrutiny committees

Meetings of backbench 'scrutiny committees' should be open to the press and public, with advance agendas and papers available beforehand.

Register of interests

The Government in 2010 announced plans to abolish the national Standards Board regime, and use the Localism Bill to replace it with alternative measures. But it also said the requirement for councillors to register certain personal interests on a publicly available register would stay, with failure to register and disclose interests being a criminal offence.

see www.mcnaes.com ch. 31 for updates

Obstruction is an offence

A person who has custody of a document which must be available for public inspection who intentionally obstructs any person exercising a right to inspect or make a copy of it, or refuses to supply a copy of it, commits an offence punishable by a fine of up to £200 under section 100H(4) of the Local Government Act 1972, as added by the Local Government (Access to Information) Act 1985, section 11.

The Local Government (Access to Information) Act 1985

The Local Government (Access to Information) Act 1985 predates the introduction of cabinet-style councils.

When meetings must be in public

The 1985 Act says all meetings of principal authorities, their committees and sub-committees must be open to the public unless dealing with confidential or exempt information.

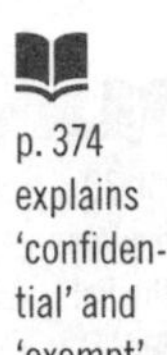

p. 374 explains 'confidential' and 'exempt'

The position regarding working parties and advisory or study groups, which may in effect act as sub-committees without the name, is unclear.

This Act says principal authorities, their committees and sub-committees must exclude the public when confidential information is likely to be disclosed.

A local authority may, by passing a resolution, exclude the public when it is likely that exempt information will be disclosed. The resolution must state the part of the meeting to which the exclusion applies and describe the category of exempt information.

While the meeting is open to the public, 'duly accredited representatives' of newspapers or news agencies must, under section 5(6)(c) of the 1985 Act, be afforded reasonable facilities for taking their report.

Documents that must be made available

The 1985 Act says a newspaper or news agency must on request (and on payment of postage or other transmission charge) be supplied with (a) agendas, (b) further particulars necessary to indicate the nature of the items on the agenda, and (c) if the 'proper officer' thinks fit, copies of any other documents supplied to council members, although he/she may exclude from what he/she sends out any report, or part of a report, relating to items not likely to be discussed in public.

Late items, reports, and supplementary information can be admitted at the meeting only if the chairperson regards the matter as urgent and specifies the reason for the urgency.

Copies of agendas and of any report for a meeting of a council must be open to public inspection at least five clear working days before the meeting (except for items not likely to be discussed in public). Where a meeting is called at shorter notice they must be open to inspection from the time the meeting is convened.

Copies of minutes and reports and summaries of business discussed in private – except confidential or exempt information – must be open to public inspection for six years.

A list of background papers must be included in each officer's report considered at a meeting, and a copy of each background paper must be open to public inspection for four years. Background papers are those unpublished papers on which a report for a meeting is based and which, in the officer's opinion, have been relied upon to a material extent in preparing the report.

See www.mcnaes.com ch. 31 for other rights to inspect council records – for example, planning applications.

Police and fire authorities

The 1985 Act also applies to combined police or fire authorities, meetings of joint consultative committees of health and local authorities, and to some joint boards.

Parish and community councils

The 1985 Act does not apply to parish town and community councils, which are covered by the Public Bodies (Admission to Meetings) Act 1960. This Act says these bodies must admit the public to their meetings and to meetings of committees which consist of all members of the body. It also allows for the public to be excluded for all or part of a meeting 'whenever publicity would be prejudicial to the public interest because of the confidential nature of the business to be transacted or for other special reasons stated in the resolution and arising from the nature of that business or of the proceedings.'

Public notice of the time and place of a meeting must be given by posting it at the offices at least three days before the meeting, or if the meeting is convened at shorter notice, when it is convened.

On request and on payment of postage, if required, the body must supply to any media organisation a copy of the agenda as supplied to its members, but excluding, if thought fit, items to be discussed when the meeting is not likely to be open to the public.

The 1960 Act says that, so far as is practicable, reporters shall be afforded reasonable facilities for taking their report.

Minutes of the proceedings of a parish or community council must, under the Local Government Act 1972, as amended by the 1985 Act, be open to inspection.

Parish meetings and other public bodies

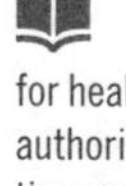

for health authorities and NHS Trusts, see p. 380

Rights to admission and to reporting facilities, agendas, and telephones, see above, under the terms of the 1960 Act also apply to:

(1) parish meetings of rural parishes where there are fewer than 200 electors;
(2) bodies set up under the Water Act 1989 – regional and local flood defence committees, regional rivers advisory committees, salmon and freshwater fisheries advisory committees, and customer service committees.

Defamation and council meetings

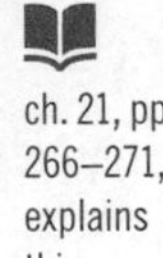

ch. 21, pp. 266–271, explains this privilege

If a local authority holds a meeting in private under any of the Acts referred to above, a defamatory media report of the discussion in such meetings, and of documents considered in them, if leaked unofficially to the media, would not be protected by qualified privilege under Schedule 1 of the Defamation Act 1996.

Media coverage of an official statement issued to journalists about a meeting held in private will be privileged under the 1996 Act if the defence's requirements are met.

Media coverage of the public proceedings of local authorities, whether in full council, committees or sub-committees, and of minutes, agendas, reports or other documents officially made available to journalists or the public, will also be privileged.

Getting access to financial accounts

Journalists often miss golden opportunities to dig out local authority stories provided by the provisions of the Audit Commission Act (ACA) 1998 and the Accounts and Audit Regulations 2003 (SI 2003/533). 'Local authorities' includes police and fire and civil defence authorities.

Section 15 of the Act says 'any persons interested' may inspect a local authority's accounts and 'all books, deeds, contracts, bills, vouchers and receipts related thereto', and make copies. Each authority in England and Wales and Northern Ireland must make the accounts and documents available for public inspection for 20 full working days before a date appointed by the auditor, or 15 days in Scotland. A public notice about this right, giving contact details for the officer responsible and the name and address of the external auditor, and the date from which he/she may be contacted by any local taxpayer or elector, must be published in at least one newspaper 14 days before the date on which the accounts and documents become available.

Lawyers differ about whether the phrase 'any persons interested' includes reporters, but if the reporter is also a local elector there is no problem. A journalist's employer which is a ratepayer is an interested party. A party's motive for wishing to see the material is irrelevant – see *R (on the application of HTV) v Bristol City Council* [2004] EWHC 1219 (Admin); [2004] 1 WLR 2717. The coalition Government has announced its intention to abolish the Audit Commission.

Section 8 says auditors must consider whether, in the public interest, they should report on any matter which came to their attention during the audit, which they do by issuing public interest reports covering the mundane to major stories such as how local authorities lost local taxpayers' money when Icelandic banks collapsed in 2008. Under the Local Government Finance (Publicity for Auditors' Reports) Act 1991 a council must make available immediately any report on a matter of particular concern produced by the auditors.

Case study

In *Veolia ES Nottinghamshire Ltd v Nottinghamshire County Council, and (1) Shlomo Dowen and (2) The Audit Commission for Local Authorities and the National Health Service for England* ([2010] EWCA Civ 1214), an elector Shlomo Dowen sought to examine contracts and other documents relating to Veolia's waste disposal contracts. The company went to court to stop the council allowing him to see and copy what it claimed was confidential information. The Court of Appeal held that the phrase 'accounts to be audited' had to be given a wide meaning. But it also held that councils and police authorities could withhold information in documents and financial records covering: legitimate trade secrets and commercial confidential information which was recognised as such in domestic and European law; personal data about third parties (such as children in care, wards of court, persons in residential care, etc.) which must be treated as confidential information under Article 8 of the Convention – but the council/police authority must check with the external auditor that the information should be withheld, and could not withhold it without the auditor's agreement; payments made to any employee or ex-employee, including pension details, which appear on the documents as a direct (but not an indirect) result of them working or having worked for the council or police authority.

Councils and police authorities cannot use the Data Protection Act to deny access to the accounts or the documents, and cannot blank out other details on Data Protection Act grounds – sections 34 and 35 of that Act make it clear that it does not trump local electors' and taxpayers' statutory rights to view and copy the accounts.

Journalists should deal directly with the officer identified in the public notice (see above), who is legally responsible for dealing with requests to view and copy the accounts.

Some journalists ask the council or police authority (via the press office) to send them photocopies or electronic copies of 'spending on such and such an issue'. This takes them outside the Audit Commission Act system, giving the authority the chance to delay responding until the journalist runs out of time to examine the material himself, or to treat the request as an FoI request and deny access on grounds which do not apply under the Audit Commission Act.

The Act makes it a criminal offence for any officer or councillor to obstruct local taxpayers or electors exercising their rights to view and copy the (non-exempt) material. Council press officers who try to involve themselves in the actual inspection should be warned off.

Personal expenses of councillors

There is no right to examine documents relating to personal expenses incurred by a council's officers. However, the Local Government (Allowances) Regulations 1986 (SI 1986/724) enable electors at any time of the year to demand to see a breakdown of allowances and expenses paid to councillors.

County, district and London borough councils must, under regulation 9 of the Local Authorities (Members' Allowances) (England) Regulations 2001, send information about amounts paid to councillors in the previous financial year to the local media, and, under regulation 6, publicise reports on recommendations about the levels of allowances in the local media.

Health authorities and NHS Trusts

Admission to meetings of local health authorities and NHS Trusts, and rights to their agendas, are subject to the Public Bodies (Admission to Meetings) Act 1960.

Department of Health guidance to these bodies in 1998 (Health Service Circular 1998/207) said the Government was 'committed to ending what it sees as excessive secrecy in decision making in public bodies' and that although authorities and trusts could exclude press and public in the public interest under the terms of the 1960 Act, they were expected to conduct their business in public in as open a manner as possible.

pp. 376–377 explain the 1985 Act

The 1960 Act gives the same rights of admission to any committee of a health authority consisting of all members of the authority.

The Health and Social Care Act 2001 gave new powers to overview and scrutiny committees of those local authorities with social services responsibilities (county councils, London borough councils, unitary authorities), and these are subject to similar access to information provisions as other committees covered by the 1985 Act. Extended exemptions do apply however – see Schedule 1 to the Health and Social Care Act 2001. These go further than the exemptions in the 1985 Act by also exempting information on: (1) a person providing or applying to provide NHS services, (2) an employee of such person, or (3) information relating to a person's health. Minutes, agendas and reports are open to public inspection for only three years and background papers for only two years.

Police authorities' plans

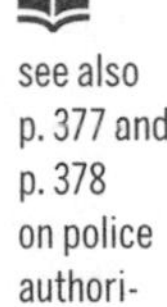

see also p. 377 and p. 378 on police authorities' obligations

The Police and Magistrates' Courts Act 1994 says police authorities must draw up local policing plans. They must also issue and arrange publication of an annual report, which must include an assessment of the extent to which the local policing plan has been carried out, as soon as possible after the end of the financial year.

Magistrates courts committees

The public must be admitted to a meeting of the magistrates courts committee at least once a year. The minutes of every meeting must be open to public inspection at the committee's office. Confidential information can be excluded, but the committee must explain why. Copies must be made available, for a fee.

➡ Recap of major points

- People have rights to other information from local authorities, such as annual budget figures and agendas, as well as rights to attend meetings.
- In certain circumstances authorities have the right to withhold documents or to deny public access to meetings.
- Laws giving rights to examine accounts can be a very good source of stories.
- There are rights to attend the meetings of health authorities and these bodies are required to publish each year their performance in key areas of health provision.

((•)) Useful Websites

www.communities.gov.uk/
For guidance on the Local Government Act 2000 and exemptions from rights to access meetings

www.openlylocal.com/
A project to develop a unified way of accessing local government information

www.orchardnews.com/accounts.htm
Website run by journalist Richard Orange of Orchard News Bureau, who specialises in local government

www.communities.gov.uk/documents/localgovernment/pdf/1850773.pdf
Letter from Government Minister urging councils to allow blogging, filming, and tweeting in council meetings

32

Reporting elections and referendums

Chapter summary

The Representation of the People Act 1983 makes it a criminal offence to make or publish false statements about election candidates. There are restrictions on publishing 'exit polls'. Broadcast journalists must maintain impartiality in coverage of elections and referendums.

False statements about candidates

Section 106(1) of the Representation of the People Act 1983 makes it a criminal offence to make or publish a false statement of fact about the personal character or conduct of an election candidate, if the purpose of publishing the false statement is to affect how many votes he/she will get.

The falsity must be expressed as a fact, rather than a statement which is clearly merely comment or an opinion about the candidate. It is a defence for someone accused of publishing such a statement to show that he/she had reasonable grounds for believing when it was published that it was true, and believed it was true (even if it turns out to be untrue).

Section 106(5) makes it an offence to publish a false claim that a candidate has withdrawn from the election, if the publisher knows it to be false and published it to promote or procure the election of another candidate.

Breaching section 106 is punishable by a fine of up to £5,000. If the publisher is a company, its directors can be convicted. The law aims to deter 'dirty tricks' by election candidates and their supporters, and is not aimed specifically at the media.

Case study

It was this law which in 2010 led to former Labour Government Minister Phil Woolas losing the Oldham East and Saddleworth seat which he had held at that year's general election with a majority of 103. He was banned from standing for Parliament for three years after being convicted of knowingly publishing two false statements about the Liberal Democrat candidate, Robert Watkins, in election leaflets. The statements falsely suggested that Watkins was wooing the extremist Muslim vote and had refused to condemn extremists who advocated the use of violence (*The Guardian*, November 5, 2010).

In 2007 Miranda Grell, a Labour candidate in a council election in London was convicted of making a false statement that her Liberal Democrat rival was a paedophile (*BBC News* website, September 21, 2007).

The ban on such false statements applies from the time formal notice is given that an election is to take place until the end of the election. For national parliamentary elections this period starts with the date of the dissolution of Parliament, or any earlier time at which Her Majesty's intention to dissolve Parliament is announced.

If a false statement is defamatory, the publisher may also face a libel action. But the criminal sanction in the 1983 Act enables quicker remedial action, as a candidate who can prove a **prima facie** case that he/she has been traduced by a false statement can obtain an **injunction** preventing its repetition, whereas the rule against '**prior restraint**' makes it almost impossible to get an injunction in a libel action, which could take months or more to settle or resolve at trial.

→glossary
→glossary
→glossary

False statements banned by the Act may not be defamatory. A journalist who in 1997 published false allegations on the internet that an election candidate was a homosexual was fined £250 under the Act. An inaccurate statement that someone is homosexual may not be defamatory but it could cost a candidate votes if, for example, voters with religious beliefs decided, on the basis of that statement, not to support the candidate.

Defamation dangers during elections

Election candidates and their supporters may make defamatory allegations about rivals, using terms such as 'racist', 'fascist', and 'liar'. A media organisation which publishes them may be sued for libel and have no defence. There is no statutory privilege for the media to re-publish election material produced by candidates, or what they say. But qualified privilege protects fair and accurate reports of public meetings and of press conferences.

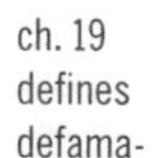

ch. 19 defines defamatory statements and ch. 21 explains privilege

! Remember

Reports of candidates' speeches are subject to the laws, examined in the www.mcnaes.com chapter on 'Incitement of Hate', against stirring up hatred, including on racial and religious grounds.

Election advertisements

Only an election candidate or his/her agent may incur any expenses relating to their campaign, including for publishing advertisements. It is an offence for anyone else to pay for such an advertisement unless he/she is authorised in writing by the election agent. This stops well-wishers putting advertisements in a newspaper on a candidate's behalf without his/her express authority.

Broadcasters' duty to be impartial

Section 6 of the Ofcom Broadcasting Code has detailed rules on how broadcast output must be impartial in election and referendum periods. Ofcom has fined several radio stations after presenters or others made partial declarations of support for political candidates or parties. The BBC is not subject to this section but has similar provision in its Editorial Guidelines.

 See also ch. 3 on impartiality, and Useful Websites, below for the Ofcom code.

Case study

In 2008 Ofcom fined *Talksport* radio £20,000 for breach of the impartiality requirement after presenter James Whale directly encouraged listeners to vote for Conservative candidate Boris Johnson in the London mayoral elections and criticised Labour candidate Ken Livingstone (*Ofcom Broadcast Bulletin*, No. 123, December 8, 2008).

Among the rules in section 6 of the Ofcom code are that:

- **due weight must be given to the coverage of major parties during the election period, and broadcasters must also consider giving appropriate coverage to other parties and independent candidates with significant views and perspectives (rule 6.2);**
- **if a candidate takes part in an item about his/her particular constituency, or electoral area, then candidates of each of the major parties must be offered the opportunity to take part (rule 6.9);**
- **broadcasters must offer the opportunity to take part in constituency or electoral area reports and discussions, to all candidates within the constituency or electoral area representing parties with previous significant electoral support or where there is evidence of significant current support, including any such independent candidate (rule 6.10); and**
- **any constituency or electoral area report or discussion after the close of nominations must include a list of all candidates standing, giving first**

names, surnames and the name of the party they represent or, if they are standing independently, the fact that they are an independent candidate. This must be conveyed in sound and/or vision. Where a constituency report on a radio service is repeated on several occasions in the same day, the full list need only be broadcast on one occasion, but the audience should be directed to where the list can be seen – for example, a website (rule 6.11).

Exit polls

An 'exit poll' is a survey in which people who have voted are asked as they leave the polling station which candidate and/or party they voted for. This can produce information which accurately predicts an election result hours ahead of official declarations. Some nations, including the UK, have restrictions on publishing such information and predictions, reasoning that publication when some people have yet to vote could skew the result, as it might persuade them to switch their choice to another candidate to have a better chance of winning, or not to vote. These possible effects are seen as potential contamination of the democratic process, in that: (a) the later group of voters would make choices on information not available to those who voted earlier and (b) the information, and any prediction apparently based on it, might be inaccurate or even falsified to influence voting.

Section 66A of the Representation of the People Act 1983 makes it a criminal offence:

- to publish, before a poll is closed, any statement about how people have voted in that election, where this statement is, or might reasonably be taken to be, based on information they gave after voting;
- to publish, before a poll is closed, any forecast – including any estimate – of the election result if the forecast is based on exit poll information from voters, or which might reasonably be taken to be based on it.

So, for example, it would be illegal to broadcast, or put on a website, before polling stations closed, the statement: 'Fifty-five per cent of the people we questioned say they voted Labour'. The law applies to Parliamentary, Welsh Assembly, council and by-elections, and in respect of exit polls conducted which focus on an individual constituency or ward, or on voting nationally. The penalty for publishing matter which breaches section 66A is a fine of up to £5,000 or a jail term of up to six months. Publishing exit polls during polling for European Parliamentary elections is also prohibited.

It is legal to publish, at any time, opinion poll information on voting intentions which was gathered before voting begins, as such information is not based on how people say they have actually voted. It is also legal to report the results of exit polls, and any forecast based on them, as soon as polling stations have closed. But it is not always accurate to talk of 'election day' – experiments to encourage more people to vote may mean that in some places voting takes place over several days. It is an offence to publish an exit poll, or forecast apparently based on it, during any of the polling days, until the polls close on the final day.

Case study

During European Parliamentary elections in June 2004, *The Times* published an opinion poll which asked people how they voted in areas using all-postal ballots. The Electoral Commission, the independent elections watchdog, said this amounted to an exit poll, and referred the matter to the Crown Prosecution Service, but later reported that the CPS, after discussions with *The Times*, had concluded that it would not be appropriate to take any further action (Electoral Commission report on European Parliamentary elections, December 21, 2004).

Regulatory codes for broadcast journalists place similar controls on publishing exit polls, and indeed go further. Rule 6.5 of the Ofcom Broadcasting Code states: 'Broadcasters may not publish the results of any opinion poll [that is, not just an exit poll] on polling day itself until the election or referendum poll closes. (For European Parliamentary elections, this applies until all polls throughout the European Union have closed.)' Rule 6.4 bans discussion and analysis of election and referendum issues during polling, a period which begins when polling stations open. This rule does not apply to any poll conducted entirely by post.

Attendance at election counts

see Useful Websites below for Commission site

Journalists, including photographers and TV crews, attend election counts so declarations of the result can be quickly aired. There is no statutory right to attend a count – admission is at the discretion of the Returning Officer, who has legal responsibility for security and procedures at the count. The Electoral Commission's media handbook for the 2010 General Election said members of the media wishing to attend a count had to apply to the Returning Officer, and should abide by any direction he gave. Returning Officers' decisions were final, it said, adding: 'They do not have to allow any member of the press into the count (unless they are also a candidate, candidate's agent, counting agent or an accredited observer etc).'

Case study

In the 2010 General Election, the media were initially banned from the count at Staffordshire Moorlands, and told by council officials running it that they had to stay in a separate room, apparently because of fears that their presence in the counting hall would be disruptive. The ban was lifted after lawyers for the *Staffordshire Sentinel, Leek Post and Times* and the BBC wrote to the acting Returning Officer protesting that it was undemocratic and a breach of the right to freedom of expression under Article 10 of the European Convention on Human Rights. The *Sentinel* also planned to get round the ban by having three staff members accredited as 'observers' at the count (*Media Lawyer*, May 6, 2010).

Registering as an observer takes ten days, and it seems observers cannot be barred from a count – see Useful Websites below.

The Returning Officer at the high-profile by-election at Oldham East and Saddleworth in January 2011, which followed Phil Woolas's removal as MP, see pp. 382–383, refused to allow journalists into the count, despite protests from the BBC and Press Association, saying there would be too many of them to accommodate comfortably. Journalists had to stay on a balcony overlooking the hall, with any communication with candidates, agents and others being 'facilitated' by Oldham Council press officers (*Media Lawyer*, January 13, 2011).

Recap of major points

- Once an election has been called it is a criminal offence to publish a false statement about the personal character or conduct of a candidate for the purpose of affecting the number of votes he/she gets.
- It is an offence to publish before the end of polling any data obtained in exit polls on how people have voted, or any prediction of the election result based on such data.
- The Ofcom Broadcasting Code and the BBC Editorial Guidelines require broadcasters to follow certain practices to ensure impartiality in coverage of elections and referendums, and restrict use of opinion (including exit) polls.

Useful Websites

http://stakeholders.ofcom.org.uk/broadcasting/broadcast-codes/broadcast-code/elections/
Section 6 of the Ofcom Broadcasting Code, on elections and referendums

http://stakeholders.ofcom.org.uk/binaries/broadcast/guidance/831193/section6.pdf
Ofcom's guidance on section 6 of the code

www.bbc.co.uk/guidelines/editorialguidelines/page/guidelines-politics-practices-elections/
Section 10 of BBC Editorial Guidelines on 'Politics, Public Policy and Polls'

www.bbc.co.uk/guidelines/editorialguidelines/page/guidance-polls-surveys-full
BBC Editorial Guidance on opinion polls, surveys, questionnaires, votes and straw polls

www.electoralcommission.org.uk/
Electoral Commission

www.electoralcommission.org.uk/elections/electoral_observers
Electoral Commission guidance on observers

33

Official secrets

Chapter summary

Official secrets legislation protects national security. It has not been used in recent years to prosecute journalists, but has been used to jail civil servants and others who have given journalists sensitive information. Successive governments have also used injunctions to stop leaked material being published. Police could search the home and newsroom of a journalist who is thought to have breached this law, seize their records, and make sustained efforts to discover the source's identity. There is no public interest defence for anyone facing prosecution.

Introduction

The Official Secrets Acts of 1911 and 1989 protect national security and can be used to enforce the duty of confidentiality owed to the UK state by Crown servants or employees of companies doing military and other sensitive work. Crown servants include civil servants, members of the armed services, the police and civilians working for them. The Act imposes a similar duty on members of the security and intelligence services.

Part of the legislation was designed to punish spies working for foreign powers.

Case study

In 2008 Daniel James, aged 45 of Brighton, a British army corporal who worked as an interpreter in Afghanistan for a NATO general, was jailed for ten years for spying for Iran. A psychiatrist found he had a narcissistic personality and believed he had a 'special purpose' to work as a peace-maker. James sent emails to the military attaché at the Iranian embassy in Kabul (*Daily Telegraph*, November 28, 2008).

Official secrets legislation can also punish the leaking of sensitive information to a journalist or a member of the public. Publishing such material makes it available to hostile powers, terrorists and criminals, and can embarrass the UK's allies, for example by disclosing diplomatic correspondence.

Using the law to punish leaks is controversial. Attorney Generals have approved prosecutions of Crown servants and others who, on grounds of conscience, leaked information to the media to throw light on controversial Government policies. In such cases media and others have questioned whether the prosecution was intended to protect vital state secrets or stifle debate about matters which embarrassed the Government. A journalist seen as being an accomplice to a leak could be prosecuted. Journalists and their editors could also be prosecuted for circulating or publishing such information. As the law is complex, www.mcnaes.com chapter 33 provides a longer version of this chapter.

ch. 1, p. 7 explains the Attorney General's role

The law's consequences for journalists

ch. 34 'The journalist's sources' explains police powers

As this book went to press no journalist had been successfully prosecuted, let alone jailed, under official secrets legislation for many years. The reasons for officialdom's reluctance to prosecute journalists are discussed below. But journalists must be aware of the Acts and be ready to protect the identities of their confidential sources of information. The journalist might not be jailed for his/her story, but the source might be. Police seeking to identify the source of leaked information could raid a journalist's newsroom, office or home, and the journalist might be arrested and threatened with prosecution.

Examples of journalists investigated or warned

In 2003 armed police raided the home of Liam Clarke, the Northern Ireland editor of the *Sunday Times*, and arrested him and his wife, Kathryn Johnston, following publication of an updated version of their book *From Guns to Government*. This contained transcripts of tape-recordings taken from a joint police/MI5 surveillance operation, which detailed bugged telephone conversations acutely embarrassing to the UK Government. The couple were detained at their home for five hours. Later the police admitted the raid was unlawful because, although a search warrant was issued under the Police and Criminal Evidence Act 1984, it was authorised by a magistrate, not a judge, as the law required. In 2006 the two journalists reportedly received a 'five-figure' sum from police in settlement of a claim for false imprisonment.

pp. 401–403 explain the 1984 Act

In 2005 the Attorney General, Lord Goldsmith, warned newspapers after the *Daily Mirror* published a story headlined 'PM halted Bush plan to bomb Arab TV channel off the air'. The story began: 'George Bush's plot to bomb an Arab TV station in friendly Qatar was crushed by Tony Blair, who feared it would spark horrific revenge.'

The paper said the story was based on a leaked memo about a conversation in which the Prime Minister and the President discussed the Arabic broadcaster Al-Jazeera, which had angered the American and British Governments by broadcasting footage of soldiers and others killed in the Iraq war. The Attorney General warned that the media would be contravening official secrets law by publishing the memo's contents.

The fate of sources

Sources are generally dealt with more severely than journalists.

Case study

In the *Al-Jazeera* case, a former civil servant, David Keogh, and Leo O'Connor, who had worked as an MP's researcher, were jailed in 2007 for six months and three months respectively for leaking the memo received by the *Mirror* (*Daily Mirror*, May 11, 2007).

The media may be excluded from secrets trials

Section 8 of the Official Secrets Act 1920 says the public (and therefore the media) can be excluded from secrets trials when publication of evidence would be 'prejudicial to the national safety'.

Reluctance to prosecute journalists

These cases raise the question of why the source was so often prosecuted but the journalist was not. This is partly an effect of the legislation. The Official Secrets Act 1989 contains defences which journalists can use, but sources cannot. For example, a journalist has a defence that disclosure of the information was not 'damaging' to state interests.

John Wadham, former director of the civil rights organisation Liberty, has said of the lack of recent prosecutions of journalists:

> "It is partly because governments don't like to be seen to be trying to put journalists in prison and partly because juries are less sympathetic to civil servants – who are employed to keep their mouths shut, who are aware of the rules but break them, and who breach the trust with employers and colleagues – compared with journalists, who are paid to find things out and publish them."

The use of injunctions

From the 1980s onwards Governments have used injunctions to stop publication of leaked material, allowing them to silence the media without a criminal prosecution and the accompanying danger of serious political embarrassment if a jury decided

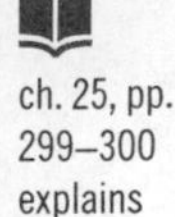

ch. 25, pp. 299–300 explains the *Spycatcher* case

the publication was lawful. Injunctions are granted by judges sitting alone. It is an offence of contempt of court to disobey an injunction. Several sets of injunctions were issued to stop the media publishing extracts from the book *Spycatcher*, the memoirs of the intelligence officer Peter Wright, which was published abroad.

The 1911 Act

Section 1 of the 1911 Act is concerned with spying, but journalists need to know about it. Section 1 makes it an arrestable offence, carrying a penalty of up to 14 years' imprisonment, to do any of the following 'for any purpose prejudicial to the safety or interests of the state':

(a) approach, inspect, pass over, be in the neighbourhood of or enter any prohibited place (see below);

(b) make any sketch, plan, model or note that might be or is intended to be useful to an enemy;

(c) obtain, collect, record or communicate to any person any information that might be or is intended to be useful to an enemy.

Offences under (c) are most relevant for journalists. Section 3 of the 1911 Act gives a lengthy and wide-ranging definition of a 'prohibited place' as including 'any work or defence, arsenal, naval or air force establishment or station, factory, dockyard, mine, minefield, camp, ship, or aircraft' as well as 'any telegraph, telephone, wireless or signal station, or office' when any such property is used by the state. Statutory instruments added British Nuclear Fuels plc and Atomic Energy Authority sites to the list of prohibited places. The Energy Act 2008 added any site where there is equipment or software for the enrichment of uranium or information about the process – additions reflecting fears that terrorist groups might wish to build a nuclear bomb or a 'dirty', radio-active one.

The media must remember that taking photos or gathering information outside or near prohibited places, even for routine news coverage of events such as peace protests, could be held to be a breach of the Act, for example if material gathered and published jeopardises security at a defence base.

The 1989 Act: the journalist's position

The 1989 Act defines offences of disclosure by reference to various classes of information. These include information about security and intelligence; defence; international relations; official investigations into crime, for example by the police or other agencies; official phone-tapping and the official interception of letters or other communications; prison and custody facilities; and matters entrusted in confidence to other states or international organisations.

Section 5 of the Act says a person – for our purposes, a journalist – commits an offence if he/she discloses without lawful authority information protected by the Act, knowing or having reasonable cause to believe that it is thus protected against disclosure, if he/she received it from a Crown servant or Government contractor either without lawful authority or in confidence, or received it from someone else who received it in confidence from such a person.

See www.mcnaes.com ch. 33 for more detail of what must be proved.

Damage test but no public interest defence

Though the 1989 Act can catch journalists and members of the public, it is directed particularly at security services members, other Crown servants and government contractors. The degree of damage (by disclosure) to state interests necessary for conviction under the Act varies according to the class of information and the category of person accused. The damage alleged to have occurred could be, for example, to the capacity of the armed forces to carry out certain duties, or to British relations with another state.

There is no public interest defence in official secrets cases – and information can be classed as secret even if it has been published previously.

Breaching the 1989 Act is punishable by a jail term of up to two years and/or a fine.

Defence Advisory Notices

The Defence Press and Broadcasting Advisory Committee, a joint government/media body, gives the media guidance on national security and defence issues through Defence Advisory Notices (DA-Notices, formerly known as D-Notices) and other correspondence.

((•)) see Useful Websites below

The five DA-Notices in force cover:

(1) military operations, plans and capabilities;
(2) nuclear and non-nuclear weapons and operational equipment;
(3) cyphers and secure communications;
(4) identification of specific installations and home addresses;
(5) UK security and intelligence services, and special forces.

The system is, in effect, voluntary self-censorship by the media. Editors who consult the DA-Notice secretary sometimes decide to limit what is published, and sometimes publish information that they might otherwise have left out. The committee has no statutory enforcement powers.

www.mcnaes.com ch. 31 has further details including on wikileaks disclosures.

Recap of major points

- Official secrets law is frequently controversial. Because it is complex, there is a longer version of this chapter on www.mcnaes.com.
- This law protects national security and the safety of citizens, and can be used against foreign spies, terrorists or other criminals.
- But journalists say it is sometimes used to punish those who leak information which is politically embarrassing for the Government, and to deter the media from revealing such information.
- The law has wide definitions of what is secret. There is no public interest defence for anyone prosecuted for breaching it.
- The DA-Notice system is a means by which the media can check if material they are considering publishing could be regarded as a breach of national security.

Useful Websites

www.dnotice.org.uk/
The Defence Press and Broadcasting Advisory Committee website

www.parliament.uk/commons/lib/research/briefings/snpc-02023.pdf
House of Commons Library, Note on Official Secrecy

www.sis.gov.uk
Secret Intelligence Service website (MI6)

www.cpbf.org.uk/
Campaign for Press and Broadcasting Freedom

34

The journalist's sources and neutrality

Chapter summary

It is an ethical principle that journalists do not disclose sources of confidential information. Journalists often have to rely on information from people whose safety or careers would be at risk if they were known as the sources. If disclosing such sources became commonplace, the journalist's job would be much harder as fewer people would be willing to speak to them, and many important stories would not be revealed. Various bodies have legal powers to demand that journalists reveal where they got a story. This chapter explains what those powers are, how journalists can protect confidential sources, and warns that investigative journalists suspected of receiving leaks of sensitive, official information may be placed under secret surveillance. On some occasions, when journalists refuse voluntarily to hand over material or give evidence, their object is not to protect an individual source but to maintain a reputation for neutrality.

Protecting your source: the ethical imperative

Clause 14 of the Editors' Code of Practice, overseen by the Press Complaints Commission, says simply: 'Journalists have a moral obligation to protect confidential sources of information.' This clause is not subject to the code's 'public interest' exceptions, and so the code does not give any circumstance which justifies breaching it. The PCC system is explained in chapter 2.

see Useful Websites below for NUJ Code

The National Union of Journalists Code of Conduct has a similar clause. It too has no exception to this principle.

Journalists' codes in nations all round the world state the same principle. If confidential sources were not sure that journalists would not betray their identities, many stories of great public interest would never see the light of day.

If a court order is made that a journalist should disclose a source's identity, the journalist or his/her editor may well decide it is ethical to defy the court. But they must be prepared to face the legal consequences. This could be a substantial fine, or conceivably a jail sentence for contempt of court, though in the last four decades no UK journalist has been sent to prison for this.

The Ofcom Broadcasting Code, explained in chapter 3, says in practice 7.7: 'Guarantees given to contributors, for example relating to the content of a programme, confidentiality or anonymity, should normally be honoured.'

This chapter examines cases in which journalists have needed to protect the identities of their sources from companies or public agencies which resorted to court action when attempting to flush out who had leaked information. But it should be remembered that, even in routine stories, failure to protect a source's identity can have life-changing consequences for that person.

Case study

In 2007 the Press Complaints Commission ruled that a newspaper had breached clause 14 of the Editors' Code of Practice in an article about the possible closure of Burnley mortuary. A man who spoke to the paper on condition he was not identified was referred to in the article as 'a worker at Burnley's mortuary'. Because he was one of only two people who worked there – the other being his boss – his employers identified him as the paper's source, and he was sacked on grounds of gross misconduct. The paper said the reporter had not known, and had no reason to know, that the man was one of only two employees. But the PCC said the paper should have established with the man how he should be described (*A Man v Lancashire Telegraph*, adjudication issued October 31, 2007).

Who might ask you to divulge your source?

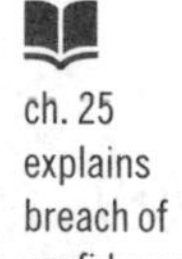

ch. 25 explains breach of confidence

In common law judges have the power to order disclosure of the identity of wrongdoers (*Norwich Pharmacal Co v Customs and Excise Comrs* [1974] AC 133).

In law, a 'wrongdoer' may include a person who breaches a duty of confidence – for example, owed by an employee to a government department or company – by leaking to the media sensitive information gained in that employment.

Judges

Until fairly recently, UK judges – for example, in the *Goodwin* case, explained below – tended not to place much weight on the idea that there is a general public interest in journalists protecting sources who want to remain anonymous. But judgments in the European Court of Human Rights and the adoption by the UK of the European Convention on Human Rights, explained in chapter 1, have made the legal climate more favourable. Journalists can point to their, and the public's, rights under the Convention's Article 10, guaranteeing freedom of expression and the right to impart and receive information.

Case study

In 1989 a High Court judge ordered Bill Goodwin, a trainee reporter on *The Engineer* magazine, to disclose the source of information he used in a story about an engineering company's financial difficulties. He refused, and was fined £5,000 for contempt of court (*X Ltd v Morgan-Grampian (Publishers) Ltd* [1991] 1 AC 1).

The Court of Appeal and House of Lords upheld the High Court's decision, saying that disclosure was 'necessary in the interests of justice' because the company had a right to know who was leaking information about it. Mr Goodwin took the case to the European Court of Human Rights which in 1996 agreed that the UK courts had breached his Article 10 rights (*Goodwin v United Kingdom* (1996) EHRR 123). It said protection of journalistic sources was a basic condition for press freedom, and that a court order compelling a journalist to disclose a source could not be compatible with Article 10 unless justified by an overriding requirement in the public interest.

see ch. 25, p. 303 for more detail on the *Goodwin* case

In some circumstances a journalist may need to rely on another Convention right – Article 2, the right to life.

Case study

In 2009 Suzanne Breen, the then Northern Editor of Ireland's *Sunday Tribune* newspaper, won the right to withhold from the police notes and records of a mobile phone call she received from a spokesperson for the Real IRA. In the call, this group claimed that it was responsible for the murder of two soldiers at a barracks gate. A judge ruled that her life would be at 'real and immediate' risk from the Real IRA if she was forced to give this information to the police, and that therefore her refusal was protected by her right to life under Article 2 of the European Convention. The police had wanted her made subject to a 'production order', under the Terrorism Act 2000, which law is explained below (*In the matter of an application by D/Inspector Justyn Galloway, PSNI, under paragraph 5 Schedule 5 of the Terrorism Act 2000 and Suzanne Breen* [2009] NICty 4). She has interviewed terrorists from both 'sides' of Northern Ireland's sectarian divide and condemned violence.

ch. 15, pp. 175–176 explains such risk

Recent European Court cases

The European Court of Human Rights Grand Chamber ruled in September 2010 that Dutch police and prosecutors who forced a magazine to hand over a CD containing photographs taken at an illegal road race, so that they could investigate a ram raid, had breached journalists' rights to protect confidential sources – their actions were not prescribed by law, as required by Article 10, as there were no effective safeguards for the source protection rights of the journalists and the magazine involved (*Sanoma Uitgevers BV v Netherlands*, Application no. 38224/03).

In November 2007, the European Court ruled that the Netherlands breached the rights of journalist Koen Voskuil of *Spl!ts* newspaper when it jailed him for refusing to disclose the source of a story about alleged arms-traffickers. The European Court said that ordering a journalist to disclose a confidential source of information should be done only when there was an overriding requirement in the public interest. It also criticised the far-reaching measures the Netherlands took to learn the source's identity, saying they could only discourage people with true and accurate information relating to wrongdoing from contacting the press in future cases.

Tribunals of inquiry

In 1963 two journalists appearing before a UK tribunal of inquiry were jailed for refusing to identify sources of information in stories about John Vassall (*Attorney General v Clough* [1963] 1 QB 773). He had been convicted of spying for the Soviet Union. The tribunal was established under the Tribunals of Inquiry (Evidence) Act 1921 to find out if his activities should have been detected sooner than they were. The Act gave tribunals wide powers to send for and examine witnesses.

Lord Saville, chairman of the inquiry set up in 1998 under the same Act to investigate the 1972 Bloody Sunday killings in Northern Ireland, threatened three journalists with actions for contempt of court after they refused to name the sources of stories about the killings. In 2000 one of them, Tony Harnden, of the *Daily Telegraph*, was 'placed in contempt' of the inquiry and told the matter was being referred to the High Court. But in 2004 the contempt proceedings were dropped.

Requests by police

Journalists, like other citizens, have no general obligation to give police information.

If police want journalistic material to assist investigations – into journalists or others – they normally have to apply to a judge first. They also generally need a judge's consent before searching a journalist's premises for such material. See this chapter's explanation of the Police and Criminal Evidence Act 1984 and other statutes.

Be ready for a long battle

A journalist protecting a source's identity must be ready for a lengthy and tortuous legal battle. In 2000 Ashworth High Security Hospital obtained an order that the

Daily Mirror should disclose the source of a story on Moors murderer Ian Brady, concerning his treatment at the hospital, starting a legal case which lasted six years. The Court of Appeal upheld the order, as did the House of Lords, saying in 2002 that while disclosing sources had a 'chilling effect' on freedom of the press it was 'necessary and proportionate and justified' in this case (*Ashworth Security Hospital v MGN Ltd* [2002] UKHL 29; [2002] 4 All ER 193). Freelance journalist Robin Ackroyd then said he was the source of the *Mirror* story – but refused to identify his own source. He was then ordered to do so by the High Court. But in May 2003 the Court of Appeal upheld his appeal against the order and ruled there should be a full trial of the issue, saying he had an arguable defence. The court now knew, as the earlier court had not, that the person who gave Mr Ackroyd the information for his story was not paid for it. If that individual had a public interest defence to any breach of confidence or contract claim by the hospital, a claim could not succeed against Mr Ackroyd. The Court of Appeal also said it did not automatically follow that the public interest in non-disclosure of medical records should override the public interest in maintaining the confidentiality of his source (*Mersey Care NHS Trust v Robin Ackroyd* [2003] EWCA Civ 663). At the High Court trial, in February 2006, Mr Justice Tugendhat rejected Ashworth Hospital's argument that the need to protect the confidentiality of medical records overrode the public interest in protecting a journalist's sources. Requiring disclosure, he said 'would not be proportionate to the pursuit of the hospital's legitimate aim to seek redress against the source, given the vital public interest in the protection of a journalist's source' (*Mersey Care NHS Trust v Robin Ackroyd* [2006] EWHC 107 (QB)). The NHS Trust appealed but the Court of Appeal found for Mr Ackroyd in February 2007 (*Mersey Care NHS Trust v Robin Ackroyd* [2007] EWCA Civ 101). The House of Lords rejected the Trust's petition to appeal against that decision.

The 'shield law' has not always shielded

In section 10 of the Contempt of Court Act 1981 Parliament created what is sometimes referred to as a 'shield law' to protect journalistic activity, though some UK journalists would argue that other democracies have better shield laws.

- Section 10 says: 'No court may require a person to disclose, nor is any person guilty of contempt of court for refusing to disclose, the source of information contained in a publication for which he is responsible, unless it is established to the satisfaction of the court that disclosure is necessary in the interests of justice or national security, or for the prevention of disorder or crime.'

Journalists hoped the section would lead judges to create a high threshold of 'necessity' in cases involving corporate or official attempts to flush out the identities of a journalist's source. But three cases show that the protection the section gives journalists has not proved to be as great as many had hoped.

The first concerned the scope of the phrase 'national security'. In 1983 *The Guardian* was ordered to return to the Government a leaked photocopy of a

Ministry of Defence document revealing the strategy for handling the controversial arrival of US Cruise nuclear missiles, due to be based in the UK. *The Guardian* did not know the informant's identity, but, realising that it might be revealed by official examination of the document, claimed that section 10 meant it did not have to hand it over. The House of Lords said the interests of national security required disclosure of the informant's identity – publishing this document posed no threat to national security, but the person who leaked it might leak another. *The Guardian* handed over the document, and consequently the informant, Foreign Office clerk Sarah Tisdall, was convicted under the Official Secrets Act and jailed for six months (*Secretary of State for Defence v Guardian Newspapers Ltd* [1985] AC 339).

! Remember

Had *The Guardian* destroyed the document after using it to prepare the article and before being ordered to hand it over, Ms Tisdall's identity might have remained secret.

The second case, involving City journalist Jeremy Warner, showed what the courts understood by the word 'necessary' and the phrase 'prevention of crime'.

Inspectors investigating 'insider dealings' in shares sought a court order that Warner, then on *The Independent*, should reveal his sources for a business story he wrote in 1988. Lord Grififths said in the House of Lords that 'necessary' in section 10 of the Contempt of Court Act 1981 had a meaning which lay somewhere between 'indispensable' on the one hand and 'useful' or 'expedient' on the other. The House of Lords ruled against Warner's appeal, but he continued to refuse to reveal who his source was, and was fined £20,000 (*In Re An Inquiry under the Company Securities (Insider Dealing) Act 1985* [1988] AC 660, and *The Times* January 27, 1988).

In 1990, in the *Goodwin* case, the House of Lords considered the phrase 'interests of justice'. Lord Bridge said it could simply refer to an employer's wish to discipline a disloyal employee 'notwithstanding that no legal proceedings might be necessary to achieve this end'.

However, the jurisprudence of the European Court of Justice, outlined above, and Article 10 of the European Convention have, since these cases about the scope of section 10 of the 1981 Act, improved the legal climate for journalists' protection of sources.

Statutory powers of investigators

Various statutes have provision for the police and other official investigators, when investigating crime, to get a court order requiring a person to surrender material, or in some circumstances to search premises without warning to seize it. In the case of a journalist, this could be notes of interviews, computers or phones, etc. which could reveal the identity of a source of published stories about the crime being investigated.

The Police and Criminal Evidence Act 1984 (PACE)

Police, if they wish someone to be compelled to surrender documents or other material, need a court order in most circumstances. PACE is the legislation they use most when applying for these orders.

Special procedure material

In PACE, special protection is given to 'journalistic material', defined as 'material acquired or created for the purposes of journalism'. When seeking to compel journalists or media organisations to surrender such material, police investigating a crime must use PACE's 'special procedure', which means they must apply to a High Court judge, a recorder, or a circuit judge. If the application succeeds the judge makes a 'production order' – that is, an order requiring the person or organisation holding the material to produce it to the police.

The application must normally be 'on notice', so the holder of the material has the chance to attend the hearing to argue against the order being granted.

Before making the order a judge must be satisfied that there are reasonable grounds for believing that a serious offence has been committed; that the material the police want would be admissible evidence at a trial for that offence and of substantial value to the investigation; that other methods of obtaining it have been tried without success, or have not been tried because it appears they would be bound to fail; and that production of the material to the police would be in the public interest, having regard to:

(1) the benefit likely to accrue to the investigation if the material is obtained; and

(2) the circumstances under which the person in possession of the material holds it.

The Act's 'special procedure' appears to give journalistic material useful protection. But judges have interpreted it in a way which makes the protection less valuable than was hoped.

In several cases, applications by the police for production orders have concerned photographs or film taken during rioting and other public disturbances. Although such material does not reveal the identity of any sources promised anonymity, there is another principle involved for the media, that of maintaining neutrality. Most editors and journalists take the view that they should hand over such material only after careful consideration, and generally only after a court order, arguing that if it becomes routine for police to obtain unpublished photographs or film, journalists, photographers and camera operators will be seen as arms of the state. This could increase the danger that they will be attacked when covering such events. For example, untransmitted footage of the riots in London

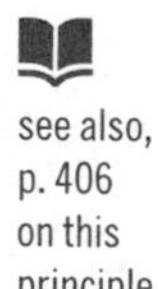

see also, p. 406 on this principle

in August 2011 was handed to the police by BBC, ITN and Sky News only after police obtained production orders.

A judge may reject the application for a production order if, among other things, he/she does not consider it in the public interest to grant it. Media lawyers have argued that it is not in the public interest to prevent the media doing their job. But in nearly every case judges have found that the police's need for evidence outweighed that argument.

Case study

In 1990, 25 newspapers and television companies were ordered to hand over unpublished photographs and untransmitted film of a Trafalgar Square riot against the poll tax. Two weeks later the police obtained similar orders against four other news organisations. At the second hearing the news organisations' counsel said the applications were premature because the police had not yet examined all the material handed over by the other 25 organisations. But the judge said that until the police had seen the material they could not say if it was relevant or not.

A more liberal view of PACE was taken in the *Martin Bright* case in 2000, when police used the Act in an attempt to obtain an email David Shayler sent reporter Martin Bright. Lord Justice Judge said a judge could consider the importance of open discussion in the media of important issues when deciding whether to make a production order for journalistic material. This case is cited below.

Excluded material

Under PACE, 'excluded material' is exempt from compulsory surrender. It includes journalistic material which a person holds in confidence – for example, from a source promised confidentiality by a journalist.

But material which was already liable to search and seizure under the previous law is not protected. For example, a stolen document acquired by a journalist, even from a confidential source, would not be 'excluded material' because it would already be liable to seizure under a warrant issued under the Theft Act 1968.

Expect your premises to be searched

Increasingly authorities with powers to demand information also have powers to search the premises of the person they believe has it. But freedom from an oppressive search is an important civil liberty, safeguarded as early as 1765 in a case concerning a clerk called Entick whose house was entered and papers seized by 'the king's messengers' on the authority of a warrant from the Secretary of State (*Entick v Carrington* (1765) 19 State Tr 1029). In that case, a court condemned the action as unlawful.

That ruling was referred to and endorsed in the High Court in 2000 when the court rejected a police application for an order that *The Guardian* and *Observer* should hand over all files, documents and records they had relating to a letter in *The Guardian* from former MI5 officer David Shayler and an article in the *Observer* by reporter Martin Bright repeating allegations that MI6 officers were involved in a failed attempt to assassinate the Libyan leader, Colonel Gaddafi. The police particularly wanted an email letter sent by Shayler so they could discover his email address (*R v Central Criminal Court, ex p Martin Bright* [2001] 2 All ER 244).

Lord Justice Judge said that the principle that an Englishman's home was his castle was linked to freedom of speech and continued: 'Premises are not to be entered by the forces of authority or the state to deter or diminish, inhibit or stifle the exercise of an individual's right to free speech or the press of its freedom to investigate and inform, and orders should not be made which might have that effect unless a circuit judge is personally satisfied that the statutory preconditions to the making of an order are established, and, as the final safeguard of basic freedoms, that in the particular circumstances it is indeed appropriate for an order to be made.'

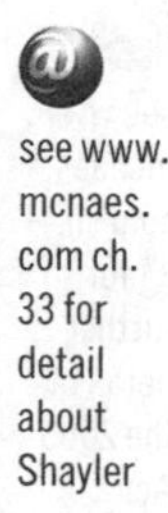
see www.mcnaes.com ch. 33 for detail about Shayler

Search warrants under PACE

Instead of asking for an order for a journalist or media organisation to produce (surrender) material, police can apply to a circuit judge for a search warrant under PACE to obtain either non-confidential or confidential material. The person or media organisation does not have to be told of the application, and has no right to be heard by the judge.

Before granting a warrant, a judge must be satisfied that the criteria for ordering the production of the material are satisfied, and that one of the following circumstances applies:

- it is not practicable to communicate with anyone entitled to grant entry to the premises;
- it is not practicable to communicate with anyone entitled to grant access to the material;
- the material contains information which is subject to an obligation of secrecy or a restriction on disclosure imposed by statute (for example, material subject to the Official Secrets Act) and is likely to be disclosed in breach of that obligation if a warrant is not issued; or
- giving notice of an application for an order may seriously prejudice the investigation.

ch. 33 explains official secrets law, and see p. 404

Once inside a journalist's property or a media organisation's building, police lawfully executing their search warrant have powers under PACE to remove additional journalistic material without getting a new production order or warrant.

The Serious Organised Crime and Police Act 2005

The Serious Organised Crime and Police Act 2005 allows police, subject to the PACE procedure for search warrants for journalistic material (above), to obtain a warrant to search all property occupied or controlled by the person named in the warrant and not merely specific premises.

But before issuing an all-premises warrant a judge must be satisfied that:

see www.mcnaes.com ch. 34 for further detail of the 2005 Act

(1) there are reasonable grounds for believing that it is necessary to search premises occupied or controlled by the person in question which are not specified in the application, as well as those which are, in order to find the material in question; and

(2) it is not reasonably practicable to specify all the premises which he/she occupies or controls which might need to be searched.

Official Secrets Acts

The Official Secrets Act 1920 operates where a chief officer of police is satisfied that there is reasonable ground for suspecting that an offence under section 1, covering espionage, has been committed and for believing that any person is able to furnish information about the offence.

The officer may ask the Home Secretary for permission to authorise a senior police officer to require the person to divulge that information. Failing to comply is an offence.

A chief officer of police who has reasonable grounds to believe that the case is an emergency and that immediate action is necessary in the interests of the state may demand the information without the Home Secretary's consent.

Section 9 of the Official Secrets Act 1911 gives police powers to make searches, subject to PACE as regards journalistic material.

Counter-terrorism legislation

Counter-terrorism legislation includes a number of offences which could relate to journalists' sources, and gives police powers to seize a journalist's research material.

The Terrorism Act 2000 enables a court to issue a warrant for police investigating a terrorist offence to search premises. See also chapter 35 on counter-terrorism law, which details cases in which journalists have faced court action over sources.

see www.mcnaes.com ch. 34 for further detail

Other statutes

Various other statutes could affect journalists by placing them under a legal obligation to disclosure information, for example to an official investigation into fraud or share-dealings.

You may be put under surveillance

Journalists in touch with secret sources yielding information on crime or what the state considers should be secret should realise that various statutes give police and other agencies the right to carry out surveillance of them personally, their correspondence including emails, and phone calls.

Case study

In 2008, *Milton Keynes Citizen* reporter Sally Murrer and Mark Kearney, a former detective accused of leaking information to her, walked free after a court ruled that prosecution evidence gathered by police bugging Mr Kearney's car was inadmissible. Mr Kearney faced charges of misconduct in a public office and Ms Murrer was charged with aiding and abetting misconduct in a public office. Judge Richard Southwell said gathering evidence by using the listening device was an unjustifiable violation of the freedom of expression rights of both, and of Ms Murrer's rights to protect her sources. The information in question was not sensitive, let alone 'highly sensitive' and the police action could not be justified. Ms Murrer's counsel, Gavin Millar, QC, told the court: 'One of the protections of the Strasbourg [European Court] law is a practical one ... It is the right to be brought before a court and have a court decide whether you are required to disclose your source. What they did here was a no-no in Strasbourg terms – and a pretty big no-no' (*R v Kearney and Murrer* (2008)).

The Police Act 1997

The Police Act 1997 allows police to authorise themselves to break into premises and place bugs if they believe doing so will help them investigate serious crime. Under sections 93 and 94, entering or interfering with property or 'wireless telegraphy' is lawful when a chief constable or, in urgent cases, an assistant chief constable, 'thinks it necessary ... for the purpose of preventing or detecting serious crime'.

Under the Act, the Government appoints a small number of Commissioners, current or former High Court judges. Police must obtain a Commissioner's prior approval for bugging homes, offices and hotel bedrooms, and in respect of doctors, lawyers and 'confidential journalistic material'. Prior approval is not necessary in urgent cases, but the chief officer must apply for approval as soon as reasonably practicable and say why he/she could not do so before.

The Regulation of Investigatory Powers Act 2000

Journalists remain concerned about many aspects of this Act, fearing in particular that the ability of the police to gain information about phone calls and access to their emails could stop them assuring contacts that their confidentiality would be protected. Had the Act been in force when police were attempting to access the email David Shayler sent *The Guardian* (see above), there would have been no need for the authorities to ask a judge for an order; they could simply have obtained a warrant from the Home Secretary. The Act also gives official agencies extensive powers of surveillance. A journalist who needs to protect, from such agencies, the identity of a source should be aware that these powers may be deployed and so avoid using emails if necessary, as well as using only untraceable pay-as-you-go mobile phones.

See www.mcnaes.com ch. 34. for details of how police and other official agencies can use RIPA.

Maintaining a reputation for neutrality

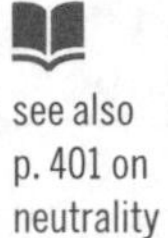
see also p. 401 on neutrality

Reporters who cover events which lead to prosecutions of those involved, or to civil lawsuits, may be asked – for example, by prosecution or defence – to give evidence of what they themselves have seen. Most journalists in this situation will wish to retain their reputation for neutrality and will agree to be a witness only after receiving a subpoena (in civil cases) or witness summons (in criminal cases).

Recap of major points

- It is a matter of professional principle that a reporter does not reveal his/her source of confidential information.
- The European Court of Human Rights has said that an order to disclose the source of information cannot be compatible with Article 10 of the European Convention on Human Rights (freedom of expression) unless it is justified by an overriding requirement in the public interest.
- Section 10 of the Contempt of Court Act 1981 says that a disclosure order must not be made 'unless it is established to the satisfaction of the court that disclosure is necessary in the interests of justice or national security, or for the prevention of disorder or crime.'
- There are various laws which enable the authorities to put journalists and others under surveillance.

Useful Websites

www.nuj.org.uk/innerPagenuj.html?docid=2226
National Union of Journalists code of conduct

35

Terrorism and the effect of counter-terrorism law

Chapter summary

The heightened threat of terrorism in recent years has led to more counter-terrorism laws in the UK, some controversial because of their actual or potential interference with journalists' work. These laws ban the gathering of certain information, and restrict what can be published. As this chapter shows, the wide scope of counter-terrorism law has the potential to deter journalistic investigation of the causes and control of terrorism.

Definition of terrorism, and of its 'glorification'

The definition of a terrorist is a value-loaded one. As has often been said, a terrorist group – for example, within a separatist movement – may be celebrated as freedom fighters by its supporters, though despised by the population being terrorised.

The UK's legal definition of terrorism, as expressed in section 1 of the Terrorism Act 2000, as amended by the Terrorism Act 2006 and the Counter-Terrorism Act 2008, can be summarised as:

- the use or threat of action where the use or threat is designed to influence the government [of any country], or an international government organisation, or to intimidate the public [in any country] or a section of the public, and the use or threat is made for the purpose of advancing a political, religious, racial or ideological cause.

To meet this definition the 'action' must involve serious violence against a person or serious damage to property, or endanger a person's life (other than the

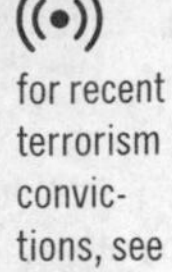

for recent terrorism convictions, see Useful websites, below

→glossary

perpetrator's); or create a serious risk to the health and safety of the public; or be designed seriously to interfere with an electronic system.

Section 3 of the Act makes it illegal – punishable by a maximum jail term of ten years – to be a member or to profess to be a member of a 'proscribed group' – that is, one deemed to be engaged in or promoting terrorism. Schedule 2 of the 2000 Act is the latest law to proscribe groups, in a list which can be updated by **statutory instruments**. In early 2012 it proscribed more than 50 groups from around the world, including Al Qaeda and Basque group ETA, and paramilitary groups with roots in Northern Ireland – for example, the IRA and UDA – which have been proscribed for decades. The legal definition of terrorism is not confined to proscribed groups' activities – it could apply, for example, to violence by 'animal liberation' groups.

Section 1 of the Terrorism Act 2006 specifically prohibits encouragement of terrorism, including indirect encouragement through 'glorification'. A person commits an offence if he/she publishes, or causes to be published, a statement which:

- glorifies the commission or preparation (whether in the past, in the future or generally) of acts of terrorism; and which
- is a statement from which 'members of the public could reasonably be expected to infer that what is being glorified is being glorified as conduct that should be emulated by them in existing circumstances.'

For this offence to occur, the statement must be likely to be understood by at least some members of the public (anywhere in the world) as an encouragement to them to commit, prepare for or instigate acts of terrorism. The person accused of such glorification must have intended some people to be thus affected, or have been 'reckless' as to the statement's effect, though it is irrelevant whether anybody was in fact led to perpetrate terrorism. Encouragement of terrorism, including through glorification, can be punished by a prison sentence of up to seven years or by a fine or both. This law was created primarily as a response to extremist, Islamic 'preachers of hate'. But, according to some experts, the glorification offence could catch any praise of any group using political violence anywhere in the world. Case law is that support for terrorism directed against a repressive government, for example that which was headed by Colonel Gaddafi in Libya, is illegal, but has drawn some distinction between indiscriminate acts of violence and directed military action in a civil war (*R v F* [2007] EWCA Crim 253, *DD (Afghanistan) v Secretary of State for the Home Department* [2010] EWCA Civ 1407). Some journalists remain uneasy about the potentially wide scope of the 'glorification' offence.

It is a defence under section 1 of the 2006 Act – if it has not been proved that the defendant intended the statement to encourage, etc., acts of terrorism – for him/her to show that the statement published neither expressed his/her views, nor had his/her endorsement and that it was clear in all the circumstances of the publication that this was the case. This defence should protect journalists, and their publishers, when their journalism includes interviews with people glorifying terrorism, if the journalism reports such words in a neutral (or condemnatory) fashion and neither the journalists nor their publishers associate themselves with the glorification.

The section 1 defence would also protect the publisher of a website forum if a member of the public posts such glorification on it. But section 3 of the Act means that the defence would not apply if the police gave a website publisher notice that a statement encouraging terrorism was being published on the site and the publisher then failed to remove it, without reasonable excuse, after more than two working days.

Failure to disclose information to police

Section 38B of the Terrorism Act 2000 makes it a crime for a person to fail to disclose to police, as soon as reasonably practical, information that he/she knows or believes might be of material assistance in preventing the commission by another person of an act of terrorism anywhere in the world, or in securing the apprehension, prosecution, or conviction of another person in the UK for a terrorist offence. The maximum penalty is up to five years in prison, or a fine, or both. A person accused of such failure has a defence if he/she can prove he/she had a 'reasonable excuse'. A reporter who discovers information about terrorism by, for example, interviewing a terrorist leader but fails to disclose it quickly to police, may be at risk of prosecution. Section 19 of the 2000 Act imposes similar disclosure obligations relating to information gained which leads to a belief or suspicion that a financial transaction is linked to funding terrorism. Section 39 of the 2000 Act makes it a crime to disclose information which 'tips off' someone who is being or is due to be investigated by police for terrorist activity.

Collecting and eliciting information

Section 58 of the 2000 Act makes it an offence to collect or make a record of 'information of a kind likely to be useful to a person committing or preparing an act of terrorism' or to possess 'a document or record containing information of that kind'. There is a defence if the person accused of breaching section 58 can prove that he/she has a reasonable excuse. But there is no specific exemption for journalists as regards their research. A journalist researching terrorist manuals available on the internet could conceivably be prosecuted under this section.

Case study

In 2008 the University and College Union condemned the arrest of Rizwaan Sabir, a Nottingham University post-graduate student whose research was into terrorism. He had downloaded a declassified open-source document called the *Al-Qaeda Training Manual*, available on a US government website. He was held for six days, then released without charge. He accepted £20,000 in settlement from Nottinghamshire police after a claim for wrongful arrest (*The Guardian*, August 26, 2009, September 19, 2011; *BBC News* website, September 14, 2011).

The Counter-Terrorism Act 2008, by inserting a section 58A into the 2000 Act, makes it an offence to 'elicit or attempt to elicit' information about an individual who is or has been a member of Her Majesty's forces, of the UK intelligence services or a police officer, if the information 'is of a kind likely to be useful to a person committing or preparing an act of terrorism'. It is also an offence to publish or communicate such elicited information. Both offences have a maximum penalty of a ten-year jail term or a fine or both. Anyone prosecuted will have a defence if he/she can prove there is a 'reasonable excuse' for his/her actions.

Santha Rasaiah, head of the Newspaper Society's political and regulatory affairs department, has expressed concern that such an 'eliciting' offence is wide enough to potentially catch journalists in a huge number of everyday situations in newsgathering.

Police powers to seize journalists' material

Schedule 5 to the Terrorism Act 2000 provides the police with a battery of powers to investigate terrorism, including procedure to seize material held by journalists. These powers are re-enactments or successors of parts of the Prevention of Terrorism (Temporary Provisions) Act 1989.

Case study

It was under the 1989 Act that in 1992 Channel 4 and the independent production company Box Productions were fined £75,000 for contempt of court after refusing to comply with a court order requiring them to disclose to police the identity of a source used in a television programme *The Committee*, part of the 'Dispatches' series, which investigated killings in Northern Ireland (*Director of Public Prosecutions v Channel Four Television Company Limited and another* [1993] 2 All ER 517).

ch. 34, pp. 401–402 explains the terms 'excluded' and 'special procedure'

Schedule 5 empowers a circuit judge (or in Northern Ireland a Crown court judge) or (when paragraph 9 of Schedule 4 of the Courts Act 2003 comes into force) a district judge to issue a 'production order' for journalistic material – that is, an order for material held by a journalist to be surrendered to the police. The 2000 Act permits such an order to compel disclosure of 'excluded' material as well as 'special procedure' material, and therefore, in the investigation of terrorism, gives police greater power to demand access to journalists' research and contacts material than exists in the Police and Criminal Evidence Act.

The order will be granted if the judge is satisfied there are reasonable grounds for believing the material will be of substantial value to that investigation and for believing it is in the public interest that police should have access to it. This threshold of justification for compelling disclosure is lower in several respects than in PACE for special procedure material, and – unlike in PACE – there is no requirement under the 2000 Act for a journalist to be given notice of police intention to apply for a production order. But it was held in *Ex p Salinger* ([1993] QB 564) that the police must provide a media organisation with a written application and evidence as early as possible, and that the police must explain their case *on oath* at the hearing.

Case study

In 1999 a judge made an order under the 1989 Act that Ed Moloney, northern editor of the *Sunday Tribune*, should hand over to police notes of an interview with a Loyalist later charged with murder. But the order was quashed by the Lord Chief Justice of Northern Ireland, Sir Robert Carswell, who said: 'Police have to show something more than a possibility that the material will be of some use. They must establish that there are reasonable grounds for believing that the material is likely to be of substantial value to the investigation' (*Re Moloney's Application* [2000] NIJB).

Under the 2000 Act, someone made subject to a production order would normally be given seven days in which to disclose the material to the police. It is contempt of court, punishable by up to two years in jail, to disobey the order. If it is disobeyed, a judge can issue a search warrant for the material's seizure by police. A police superintendent can issue such a warrant if he/she has reasonable grounds for believing the case is one of great emergency and that immediate seizure is necessary. The police can also apply to a judge for an order requiring any person to provide an explanation of any material seized, produced or made available.

Case study

In 2008 freelance journalist Shiv Malik was required, by a production order granted under the Terrorism Act 2000 by a judge, to hand over to Greater Manchester police all drafts of and source material for a book he had researched and which was due to be published. It had the title *Leaving Al-Qaeda: Inside the Mind of a British Jihadist*. It was about Hassan Butt, who – when cooperating with Malik for the book – had claimed to have been in some way involved, before renouncing terrorism, with an attack in Pakistan which killed 11 people and with recruiting people to a 'proscribed' group. The production order required all Malik's notes, audio and video recordings associated with the book. The High Court was asked by Malik to consider in **judicial review** if the order was lawful. He argued that it required him to disclose confidential sources, in breach of his rights under Article 10 of the European Convention on Human Rights, and that this would affect how sources trusted him, and possibly put

see ch. 34 on Article 10

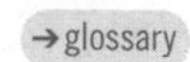

him in danger. The High Court judges ruled that the granting of the production order was valid. However, they limited its scope to include only material disclosed to Malik by Butt, not material from other sources, and ruled that Malik did not have to surrender his contact lists (*Malik v Manchester Crown Court and the Chief Constable of Greater Manchester Police* [2008] EWHC 1362). They ordered Malik, who complied with the amended order, to pay the police costs for the High Court case, as well as his own. *The Guardian* reported that in total these costs were more than £100,000, but that they were to be funded jointly by the National Union of Journalists and Times Newspapers Ltd, in support of Malik.

see www.mcnaes.com ch. 35 for a fuller account of the *Malik* case

See also ch. 36, pp. 417–418 for concern about anti-terrorism law being cited by police officers seeking to justify interference with routine photography and filming by the media.

Anonymity for terrorism suspects

In 2011 the Government, as part of a review of counter-terrorism law, announced it would abolish the system of 'control orders' whereby, under the Prevention of Terrorism Act 2005, people suspected of involvement in terrorism, but who have not been prosecuted, could be restricted from – for example – travelling abroad or using phones or the internet. People subject to control order proceedings could apply to a judge for anonymity in media reports of the case. The system which replaces it is the control order regime in the Terrorism Prevention and Investigation Measures Act 2011, which has provision for rules of court to include the making of anonymity orders.

Recap of major points

- Terrorism is given a wide definition in UK law.
- It is an offence to publish a statement which 'glorifies' the commission or preparation of acts of terrorism.
- It is an offence to fail to disclose to police information gained about suspected terrorist offences.
- It is an offence to collect or make a record of information 'of a kind likely to be useful to a person committing or preparing an act of terrorism'.
- It is an offence to 'elicit' or publish information about someone who is or has been a member of Her Majesty's forces, of the UK intelligence services or a police officer, if the information 'is of a kind likely to be useful to a person committing or preparing an act of terrorism'.

- There are some limited defences to the offences listed above.
- Police powers to compel a journalist to surrender research material are stronger under counter-terrorism law than under law covering other police inquiries.

Useful Websites

www.homeoffice.gov.uk/counter-terrorism/
Home Office counter-terrorism webpages

www.cps.gov.uk/your_cps/our_organisation/ctd.html
Crown Prosecution Service Counter-Terrorism Division webpages

www.cps.gov.uk/publications/prosecution/ctd_2010.html
Crown Prosecution Service list of recent terrorism cases

www.liberty-human-rights.org.uk/human-rights/terrorism/overview-of-terrorism-legislation/index.php
Criticism by civil rights campaign group Liberty of some counter-terrorism laws

36

The right to take photographs, film and record

Chapter summary

Journalists should know their rights when gathering visual images or making recordings in the streets or countryside. There is no criminal law restricting photography or filming or recording in public places. As this chapter explains, concern has grown in the media that over-zealous police officers, security guards and members of the public raise invalid objections to journalists using cameras. Photographers have been wrongly arrested. This chapter covers laws which are sometimes officiously cited or used against journalists, and the civil law of trespass.

Introduction

Many police officers and members of the public offer help to the media. But some do not, and become officious or hostile to journalists going about their lawful business to gather material. In tense situations, journalists may find laws being invalidly used or cited against them. They need good legal knowledge to make decisions on how to handle events.

Trouble with the police in public places

A reporter using a notebook and phone to cover incidents in a public place, including a demonstration, protest or riot, can choose when to blend into the background. But a photographer, radio reporter, video-journalist, or film crew cannot – they must get in close for their pictures and/or sound. They may be attacked by disorderly people and – even during a small-scale event – be improperly arrested by police as tension rises.

Case study

In 2010 the Metropolitan Police paid photojournalists Marc Vallée and Jason Parkinson £3,500 each in damages after armed officers stopped them from taking video footage and photos at a protest outside the Greek Embassy. Diplomatic Protection Group officers, claiming the pair were not allowed to film them, pulled Marc's camera away from his face and covered the lens of Jason's camera (*Media Lawyer*, June 28, 2010).

False imprisonment

A journalist who is subject to unlawful physical restraint – such as being locked in the cells, or physically restrained by a police officer – might be able to sue for false imprisonment. Movement must be completely restricted; barring a photographer from going in one particular direction – for example, towards the scene of a crash — is not false imprisonment.

Case study

Wiltshire police paid compensation to photojournalist Robert Naylor after an incident in 2009 when he went to a canal to report on a death in a boat fire. A police sergeant told him he could not take photos because of 'respect for deceased'. Soon afterwards, as he started back to this car, he was dragged to the ground, arrested and handcuffed for allegedly 'breaching the peace'. Wiltshire police later accepted he was unlawfully detained, and apologised (*Media Lawyer*, March 30, 2011).

Even during festive or carnival occasions, police, police community support officers or private security guards may obstruct journalists, in apparent ignorance of the fact that there is no criminal law against them or any citizen taking photos or filming or recording in the street.

In 2008, the Labour MP Austin Mitchell secured widespread support amongst MPs for a House of Commons 'early day motion' expressing concern that police and other officials were infringing citizens' rights to take photos in public places.

Police guidelines on media photography and filming

In 2010 the Association of Chief Police Officers (ACPO) issued updated guidelines for the police on how to deal with the media.

The guidelines remind police that the media have a duty to report from accident and crime scenes, that police should not prevent filming or photography in public places, and say that if police cordon off a scene it is best practice to give the media a good vantage point.

ch. 27, covers instrusion into grief and shock

see Useful Websites below for ACPO guidelines

The guidelines also say that if a distressed or bereaved person asks the police to stop the media taking pictures or filming, officers can pass on the request directly or through the Press Complaints Commission, but have no power to prevent or restrict such activity.

The ACPO guidelines also point out: 'Once an image has been recorded, police can only seize the film or camera at the scene on the strictly limited grounds that it is suspected to contain evidence of a crime. Once the photographer has left the scene, police can only seize images with a court order. In the case of the media, the usual practice is to apply for a court order under the Police and Criminal Evidence Act for production of the photograph or film footage.'

! Remember

If police want to view or seize journalistic material, they must normally first get a court order under the Police and Criminal Evidence Act, explained in chapter 34. Police at the scene of an incident have no power to insist that a journalist deletes images.

Public order offences

Police officers sometimes warn media photographers or video-journalists that they may be arrested. The arrest would probably be under common law for breach of the peace, or under section 5 of the Public Order Act 1986. Arrest for breach of the peace is only justified if harm has been done or is likely to be done to a person or their property in their presence, or when a person is in fear of being harmed. Section 5 allows arrest if anyone's behaviour is disorderly and likely to cause 'harassment, alarm or distress' to another person. Though the journalist is not intending to cause distress, etc., in some situations the mere fact that he/she is taking pictures or shooting footage, perhaps of someone or a group who object to this, may prompt an arrest.

See Useful Websites, below, for further guidance on public order offences. Ch. 4 explains the general power of arrest which police have.

Ch. 27, covers privacy issues in photography, filming and recording, and explains that paparazzi who stalk celebrities could be sued or prosecuted for harassment.

Obstructing the highway

Section 137 of the Highways Act 1980 makes it an offence for someone 'without lawful authority or excuse' to wilfully obstruct free passage along a highway in any way. This power allows police to arrest journalists in a public place who fail to move on when asked to do so.

Obstructing the police

Section 89 of the Police Act 1996 says that a person commits an offence if he/she 'resists or wilfully obstructs a constable in the execution of his duty, or a person assisting a constable in the execution of his duty'. The obstruction does not have to be a physical act – it may occur, for example, if someone makes it more difficult for the constable to perform his/her duty. A journalist who persists in taking photographs or shooting footage, and engages in argument with a police officer, therefore runs the risk of arrest.

Case study

A freelance photographer was arrested in 2007 as he tried to take pictures of a man threatening to jump from the Tyne Bridge in Newcastle. He was later charged with obstructing the police. A district judge at the city's magistrates court acquitted the photographer, saying he had acted 'professionally' (*Media Lawyer*, 15 October 2007).

'Stop and search' under the Terrorism Act 2000

Photographers have for some years complained of excessive use by police of 'stop and search' powers under the Terrorism Act 2000 – for example, if a photographer is taking pictures of buildings. Police use of these powers can stop or delay a photographer doing his/her job. Once an area has been designated by a police force as being at risk of terrorist attack, sections 44 and 45 of the Act allowed police officers to 'stop and search' even if they did not have reasonable suspicions that the individual concerned was a potential terrorist. A designated area could be very large – all of Greater London. In 2010 the European Court of Human Rights ruled that these sections were incompatible with the European Convention on Human Rights. This ruling upheld an appeal by student Kevin Gillan and journalist Pennie Quinton (Application No. 4158/05, *Gillan and Quinton v United Kingdom* (2010) 28 BHRC 420). In response, in 2011 the Government replaced sections 44 and 45 with 'a more tightly defined power enabling stop and search only in response to specific intelligence or information about a suspected terrorist attack'. This revised power was created temporarily by means of a 'remedial order' (SI 2011/631) creating new sections (47A–47C and Schedule 6B) in the 2000 Act. The Government said the revised power would be made permanent by inclusion in the Protection of Freedoms Bill which, if approved by Parliament, is due to become law in 2012. Check www.mcnaes.com for updates. This change in the law is primarily concerned with the criteria police can use to designate areas as being at risk of terrorist attack. In the revised power, police in these designated

areas are still permitted to stop and search an individual without 'reasonable suspicion'.

A revised code of practice issued to police in 2011 makes clear that they have no power under the 2000 Act to stop filming or photography of incidents or of police officers, and that it is not an offence to film/photograph a public building or in public places. Police retain power under section 43 of the Act to stop and search, and to seize equipment, if they reasonably suspect someone is a terrorist.

((•)) See Useful Websites, below, for this code of practice in full.

Ch. 35 explains other counter-terrorism laws which could affect journalists.

Trespass

Property and land owners who object to photography or filming or recording on their sites may decide to enforce objections by using the civil law of trespass, which forbids unlawful entry to land or buildings. Because trespass is a tort, the remedy is an action in the civil courts which could result in an injunction to prevent further trespass, and/or damages. Also, the occupier of property or land may use reasonable force to eject the trespasser. Police may lawfully assist, though they have no duty to do so.

→glossary

Some 'public places' such as shopping malls are private property, and security staff may intervene unless journalists get permission to take pictures, film or record there.

There is no trespass if a journalist photographs, films or records an event on adjoining private land from a site where he/she has permission or a right to be – for example, on a public highway. But such media activity might lead to a subject suing for intrusion into privacy or complaining to the PCC or Ofcom.

ch. 27, explains relevant parts of their codes

Trespass can also include 'trespass to the person' – for example, compelling a person to be filmed by stopping him/her from entering home or a workplace. Trespass to goods means, for instance, picking up a document without permission and photographing it.

Trespass is not usually a criminal offence, and so a police officer threatening an arrest for civil trespass is wrong in law. However, there are trespass offences for certain sites, for example Ministry of Defence (MoD) land and railway property, and there is a specific offence of aggravated trespass. Also, bye-laws ban photography in MoD establishments.

Ch. 33 explains official secrets law on 'prohibited places'.

Aggravated trespass

Section 68 of the Criminal Justice and Public Order Act 1994 created the offence of aggravated trespass. It has been used against protesters – for example, those who, demonstrating against alleged tax avoidance by the rich, occupied the Fortnum and Mason store in London in 2011. A journalist covering such an event could be accused of the offence. A person commits aggravated trespass if he/she trespasses and, in relation to any lawful activity which other persons are engaged in on that or adjoining property, does anything intended to have the effect of:

- intimidating any of them so as to deter them from engaging in that activity; or
- obstructing that activity; or
- disrupting that activity.

((•)) see Useful Websites, below, for Crown Prosecution Service guidelines on this offence

The penalty for aggravated trespass is up to three months' imprisonment or a fine.

Section 69 of the Act says a senior police officer present at the scene has power to order any person believed to be involved in aggravated trespass to leave the property. Failure to leave, or returning within three months, is an offence. A journalist who fails to leave may have a defence under the Act that he/she had 'a reasonable excuse' to stay.

➡ Recap of major points

- There is no law against photography, filming or recording in public places.
- But journalists need to be familiar with the law on trespass, and powers police have to arrest those 'obstructing' them or the highway.
- Police have been issued with guidelines that they should help the media take photos and gain footage, but individual officers may need reminding of these.
- The guidelines also cover controversial 'stop and search' powers.

((•)) Useful Websites

www.acpo.presscentre.com/content/default.aspx?NewsAreaID=19
Association of Chief Police Officers (ACPO) Communication Advisory Group – Guidance 2010

www.met.police.uk/about/photography.htm
Metropolitan Police 'Photography Advice'

www.cps.gov.uk/legal/p_to_r/public_order_offences/index.html#Section_5
Crown Prosecution Service guidance on public order offences

www.homeoffice.gov.uk/publications/counter-terrorism/terrorism-act-remedial-order/code-of-practice?view=Binary
Code of practice for police 'stop and search' powers under Terrorism Act 2000

www.cps.gov.uk/legal/s_to_u/trespass_and_nuisance_on_land/
Crown Prosecution Service guidance on trespass offences

www.epuk.org/
Editorial Photographers website which has guides to relevant law

media.gn.apc.org/photo/index.html
National Union of Journalists London Freelance branch advice for photographers

37

Northern Ireland

Chapter summary

Media law in Northern Ireland is, with some minor exceptions, the same as that in England and Wales. In the few important cases involving the media that have come before the High Court in Northern Ireland, cases in England have been freely cited. The Supreme Court in London is the final court of appeal for both criminal and civil cases in Northern Ireland. Restrictions on reports of preliminary hearings before magistrates, prior to committal to Crown court, follow Northern Ireland law but restrictions on reports of criminal proceedings involving juveniles are along the lines of those on the mainland. Victims of sexual offences must remain anonymous. It is an offence to disclose the identity of a juror who is serving or has served on a trial in Northern Ireland, or of a person who is on the jury list there.

The law is broadly the same as in England and Wales

The law in Northern Ireland, including the courts structure, is broadly the same as that in England and Wales. Scotland has its own system.

see www.mcnaes.com chapter on Scotland

Many of the laws applicable in England and Wales extend to Northern Ireland by means of Orders made by the Secretary of State.

The Lord Chief Justice of Northern Ireland is assisted by seven High Court judges and 15 circuit judges who try cases in the Crown court. The Crown court also hears appeals from magistrates courts. High Court judges sitting in the Northern Ireland High Court also hear civil cases, as do circuit judges sitting in the county court. Three Lords Justices of Appeal, sometimes sitting with other High Court judges, hear appeals from the Crown court, county court or High Court in the Court of Appeal in Belfast.

Most cases in magistrates courts are heard before district judges (magistrates courts), who are legally qualified and full time.

The UK **Supreme Court** is the final court of appeal for both criminal and civil cases in Northern Ireland.

Defamation

chs. 19–24 explain defamation law

The Defamation Act (Northern Ireland) 1955 is identical to the Defamation Act 1952, which covers the rest of the United Kingdom. Sections 5 and 6 of the 1955 Act (failure to prove every allegation of fact in the defences of justification and honest comment) are still in force. The Defamation Act 1996 is, however, the main factor in most instances.

Contempt of court

The Contempt of Court Act 1981 is effective in Northern Ireland and the many contempt decisions by the High Court in London are equally applicable there.

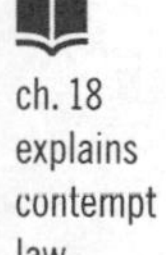

ch. 18 explains contempt law

Special courts (the 'Diplock courts'), introduced in Northern Ireland for the trial by judge alone of terrorists charged with scheduled offences, now sit only rarely. It has been contended that the risk of contempt through creating a substantial risk of serious prejudice to these proceedings is much less in the absence of a jury. The danger remains, however, of witnesses being affected in that their evidence might be coloured by accounts given by others.

Reporting restrictions

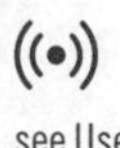

see Useful Websites, below, for this guidance

Guidelines on reporting restrictions issued in 2008 by the Judicial Studies Board for Northern Ireland, under the chairmanship of Lord Justice Higgins, say courts are encouraged to exercise their discretion to hear media representations when considering discretionary reporting restrictions.

Preliminary hearings

Committal proceedings must be in open court except where it appears to the court that the ends of justice would not be served by reports of the whole or part of the hearing. The Magistrates' Courts (Northern Ireland) Order 1981 (SI 1981/1675) prohibits publication of a report of any opening statement made by the prosecution. There is no automatic ban on reporting evidence, but the Act allows a court to prohibit publication of any evidence if it is satisfied that publication would prejudice the defendant's trial. The court may impose additional restrictions where objection is taken to the admissibility of evidence. The court may, if satisfied that the objection is made in good faith, order that such evidence and any discussion on it shall not be published.

Crown courts

Restrictions under the Criminal Justice Act 2003 on reporting prosecution appeals against the termination of a trial by a judge, or against an acquittal, were extended to Ulster under the Criminal Justice (Northern Ireland) Order 2004 (SI 2004/1500).

ch. 8 explains these appeals

The Court of Appeal in Belfast held in 1995 that hearing plea bargaining submissions in open court could inhibit rather than secure the achievement of justice.

Juveniles in court

A child under 10 cannot be charged with a criminal offence in Northern Ireland. Youth courts deal with offences committed by those below the age of 18. The Criminal Justice (Children) (Northern Ireland) Order 1998 (SI 1998/1504), as amended, makes it an offence in reporting the proceedings to publish the name, address or school, or any particulars likely to lead to the identification of anyone under 18 involved in youth court proceedings, or in an appeal from a youth court, as defendant or witness. It is also an offence to publish a picture of or including anyone under 18 so involved. A youth court may lift or relax the restrictions on a convicted young offender in the public interest but must first afford parties to the proceedings an opportunity to make representations.

ch. 9 explains the comparable section 39 orders used in England and Wales

Ch. 9 explains similar law in youth courts in England and Wales.

Under article 22 of the 1998 Order, an adult court may make an order that nothing should be published which would identify those under 18 involved in the proceedings as a defendant, witness or party. An order is not effective if the person has reached 18.

ch. 14. p. 154 explains section 37

The 1998 Order empowers a court in any criminal proceedings to exclude everyone not concerned in the case, where it considers the evidence of a child is likely to involve matter of an indecent or immoral nature. There is no specific provision for the press to remain, unlike the position in England and Wales under section 37 of the Children and Young Persons Act 1933.

Domestic proceedings

see also ch. 13 and www.mcnaes.com ch. 13 on family cases

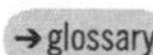

Representatives of newspapers and news agencies may attend domestic proceedings but reports must be confined to four points, as is the case for family and domestic proceedings in England and Wales. The court may, under the Children (Northern Ireland) Order 1995 (SI 1995/755), direct that any report of non-criminal proceedings must not lead to the identification of any person under 18 as being involved where any power is being exercised under that order, except to the extent which the court may allow. The court has power to sit **in private** when exercising any power under the 1995 Order.

Sexual offences

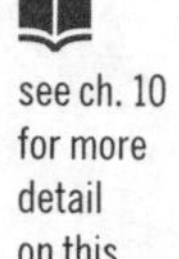

see ch. 10 for more detail on this anonymity in England and Wales

The Sexual Offences Act 2003 and the Youth Justice and Criminal Evidence Act 1999 amended the Sexual Offences (Amendment) Act 1992 and the Criminal Justice (Northern Ireland) Order 1994 (SI 2004/2795) in relation to media reports of sexual offences in Northern Ireland. This law, which provides anonymity in media reports for victims/alleged victims of sexual offences, is essentially the same as in England and Wales.

Identifying defendants in sexual offence cases

There is nothing in the 1994 Order giving a court discretionary powers, in addition to the automatic restrictions protecting victims/alleged victims, to impose further restrictions such as prohibiting identification of the defendant.

A number of Crown courts and magistrates courts have attempted to make orders banning the naming of a defendant, citing the 1994 Order, on the grounds that publishing his/her name would either lead to the identification of the complainant or be detrimental to the complainant's well-being. Such purported orders would seem to be ultra vires. The Order's article 19 prohibits publication of particulars which would lead to the identification of the complainant, but there is no provision in the article for a court to determine which particulars they might be.

See also ch. 15, p.173, for the judgment in *R v Newtownabbey Magistrates' Court, ex p Belfast Telegraph Newspapers Ltd* (1997) and p. 188.

In 1999 at Newtownabbey magistrates court in the case of a police officer accused of indecently assaulting a child, the prosecution and defence made a joint application for the press to be excluded. Mr Phillip Mateer, a deputy resident magistrate, refused the application, referring to *R v Newtownabbey Magistrates' Court*.

Identifying jurors

It is an offence to identify someone as being or having been a juror in Northern Ireland, or as being listed as a juror or selected for inclusion on the jury list. The offence is contained in the Juries (Northern Ireland) Order 1996 (SI 1996/1141), as amended, which provides a defence that there was reasonable belief that disclosure of the juror's identity was lawful.

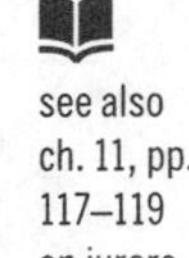

see also ch. 11, pp. 117–119 on jurors

Photography, filming and recording at court

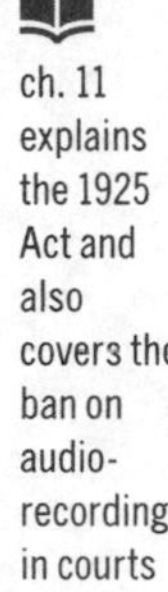

ch. 11 explains the 1925 Act and also covers the ban on audio-recording in courts

The Criminal Justice (Northern Ireland) Act 1945, operating in a similar way to the mainland Criminal Justice Act 1925, prohibits photography, filming or sketching in a court or its precincts. Guidelines from the Judicial Studies Board say the court can issue guidance, by way of a map, on the extent of the precincts.

! Remember

www.mcnaes.com has a chapter outlining Scottish media law.

Recap of major points

- The law in Northern Ireland, including the courts structure, is broadly the same as in England and Wales, with minor variations.
- Reporting restrictions in Northern Ireland broadly follow those in England and Wales but many of them are contained in Orders made by the Secretary of State rather than in Acts of Parliament.
- When a child is giving evidence involving indecent or immoral matters the court may exclude everyone not concerned in the proceedings.
- It is an offence to identify a juror, a former juror or a person selected for jury service.

((•)) Useful Websites

www.jsbni.com/Publications/reporting-restrictions/Pages/default.aspx
Judicial Studies Board for Northern Ireland guide to reporting restrictions

www.courtsni.gov.uk
Northern Ireland Courts Service

Appendix 1 Extracts from the European Convention for the Protection of Human Rights and Fundamental Freedoms (known as the European Convention on Human Rights)

Article 2: Right to life

1) Everyone's right to life shall be protected by law. No one shall be deprived of his life intentionally save in the execution of a sentence of a court following his conviction of a crime for which this penalty is provided by law. [*see also * below*]
2) Deprivation of life shall not be regarded as inflicted in contravention of this Article when it results from the use of force which is no more than absolutely necessary:
   (a) in defence of any person from unlawful violence;
   (b) in order to effect a lawful arrest or to prevent the escape of a person lawfully detained;
   (c) in action lawfully taken for the purpose of quelling a riot or insurrection.

Article 3: Prohibition of torture

No one shall be subjected to torture or to inhuman or degrading treatment or punishment.

Article 6: Right to a fair trial [the Article is quoted in part]

1) In the determination of his civil rights and obligations or of any criminal charge against him, everyone is entitled to a fair and public hearing within a reasonable time by an independent and impartial tribunal established by law. Judgment shall be pronounced publicly but the press and public may be excluded from all or part of the trial in the interest of morals, public order or national security in a democratic society, where the interests of juveniles or the protection of the private life of the parties so require, or to the extent

strictly necessary in the opinion of the court in special circumstances where publicity would prejudice the interests of justice.

2) Everyone charged with a criminal offence shall be presumed innocent until proved guilty according to law.

Article 8: Right to respect for private and family life

1) Everyone has the right to respect for his private and family life, his home and his correspondence.

2) There shall be no interference by a public authority with the exercise of this right except such as is in accordance with the law and is necessary in a democratic society in the interests of national security, public safety or the economic well-being of the country, for the prevention of disorder or crime, for the protection of health or morals, or for the protection of the rights and freedoms of others.

Article 10: Freedom of expression

1) Everyone has the right to freedom of expression. This right shall include freedom to hold opinions and to receive and impart information and ideas without interference by public authority and regardless of frontiers.

   This Article shall not prevent States from requiring the licensing of broadcasting, television or cinema enterprises.

2) The exercise of these freedoms, since it carries with it duties and responsibilities, may be subject to such formalities, conditions, restrictions or penalties as are prescribed by law and are necessary in a democratic society, in the interests of national security, territorial integrity or public safety, for the prevention of disorder or crime, for the protection of health or morals, for the protection of the reputation or rights of others, for preventing the disclosure of information received in confidence, or for maintaining the authority and impartiality of the judiciary.

* Article 1 of the Thirteenth Protocol of the Convention, which was adopted into UK law in 2004, stated: 'The death penalty shall be abolished'. It had already been abolished in the UK.

For the Convention's full text see the 'Basic Texts' link at www.echr.coe.int/echr/

Appendix 2
The Editors' Code of Practice

The Press Complaints Commission is charged with enforcing the following Code of Practice which was framed by the newspaper and periodical industry and was ratified by the PCC in December 2011. Clauses marked * are covered by exceptions relating to the public interest.

THE CODE

All members of the press have a duty to maintain the highest professional standards. The Code, which includes this preamble and the public interest exceptions below, sets the benchmark for those ethical standards, protecting both the rights of the individual and the public's right to know. It is the cornerstone of the system of self-regulation to which the industry has made a binding commitment.

It is essential that an agreed code be honoured not only to the letter but in the full spirit. It should not be interpreted so narrowly as to compromise its commitment to respect the rights of the individual, nor so broadly that it constitutes an unnecessary interference with freedom of expression or prevents publication in the public interest.

It is the responsibility of editors and publishers to apply the Code to editorial material in both printed and online versions of publications. They should take care to ensure it is observed rigorously by all editorial staff and external contributors, including non-journalists.

Editors should co-operate swiftly with the Press Complaints Commission in the resolution of complaints. Any publication judged to have breached the Code must publish the adjudication in full and with due prominence agreed by the Commission's Director, including headline reference to the PCC.

1 **Accuracy**

i) The Press must take care not to publish inaccurate, misleading or distorted information, including pictures.

ii) A significant inaccuracy, misleading statement or distortion once recognised must be corrected, promptly and with due prominence, and – where appropriate – an apology published. In cases involving the Commission, prominence should be agreed with the PCC in advance.

iii) The Press, whilst free to be partisan, must distinguish clearly between comment, conjecture and fact.

iv) A publication must report fairly and accurately the outcome of an action for defamation to which it has been a party, unless an agreed settlement states otherwise, or an agreed statement is published.

2 Opportunity to reply

A fair opportunity for reply to inaccuracies must be given when reasonably called for.

3 *Privacy

i) Everyone is entitled to respect for his or her private and family life, home, health and correspondence, including digital communications.

ii) Editors will be expected to justify intrusions into any individual's private life without consent. Account will be taken of the complainant's own public disclosures of information.

iii) It is unacceptable to photograph individuals in private places without their context.

Note – Private places are public or private property where there is a reasonable expectation of privacy.

4 *Harassment

i) Journalists must not engage in intimidation, harassment or persistent pursuit.

ii) They must not persist in questioning, telephoning, pursuing or photographing individuals once asked to desist; nor remain on their property when asked to leave and must not follow them. If requested, they must identify themselves and whom they represent.

iii) Editors must ensure these principles are observed by those working for them and take care not to use non-compliant material from other sources.

5 Intrusion into grief or shock

i) In cases involving personal grief or shock, enquiries and approaches must be made with sympathy and discretion and publication handled sensitively. This should not restrict the right to report legal proceedings, such as inquests.

*ii) When reporting suicide, care should be taken to avoid excessive detail about the method used.

6 *Children

i) Young people should be free to complete their time at school without unnecessary intrusion.

ii) A child under 16 must not be interviewed or photographed on issues involving their own or another child's welfare unless a custodial parent or similarly responsible adult consents.

iii) Pupils must not be approached or photographed at school without the permission of the school authorities.

iv) Minors must not be paid for material involving children's welfare, nor parents or guardians for material about their children or wards, unless it is clearly in the child's interest.

v) Editors must not use the fame, notoriety or position of a parent or guardian as sole justification for publishing details of a child's private life.

7 *Children in sex cases

1. The press must not, even if legally free to do so, identify children under 16 who are victims or witnesses in cases involving sex offences.
2. In any press report of a case involving a sexual offence against a child –
   i) The child must not be identified.
   ii) The adult may be identified.
   iii) The word 'incest' must not be used where a child victim might be identified.
   iv) Care must be taken that nothing in the report implies the relationship between the accused and the child.

8 *Hospitals

i) Journalists must identify themselves and obtain permission from a responsible executive before entering non-public areas of hospitals or similar institutions to pursue enquiries.

ii) The restrictions on intruding into privacy are particularly relevant to enquiries about individuals in hospitals or similar institutions.

9 *Reporting of Crime

(i) Relatives or friends of persons convicted or accused of crime should not generally be identified without their consent, unless they are genuinely relevant to the story.

(ii) Particular regard should be paid to the potentially vulnerable position of children who witness, or are victims of, crime. This should not restrict the right to report legal proceedings.

10 *Clandestine devices and subterfuge

i) The press must not seek to obtain or publish material acquired by using hidden cameras or clandestine listening devices; or by intercepting private or mobile telephone calls, messages or emails; or by the unauthorised removal of documents or photographs; or by accessing digitally-held private information without consent.

ii) Engaging in misrepresentation or subterfuge, including by agents or intermediaries, can generally be justified only in the public interest and then only when the material cannot be obtained by other means.

11 Victims of sexual assault

The press must not identify victims of sexual assault or publish material likely to contribute to such identification unless there is adequate justification and they are legally free to do so.

12 Discrimination

i) The press must avoid prejudicial or pejorative reference to an individual's race, colour, religion, gender, sexual orientation or to any physical or mental illness or disability.

ii) Details of an individual's race, colour, religion, sexual orientation, physical or mental illness or disability must be avoided unless genuinely relevant to the story.

13 **Financial journalism**

i) Even where the law does not prohibit it, journalists must not use for their own profit financial information they receive in advance of its general publication, nor should they pass such information to others.

ii) They must not write about shares or securities in whose performance they know that they or their close families have a significant financial interest without disclosing the interest to the editor or financial editor.

iii) They must not buy or sell, either directly or through nominees or agents, shares or securities about which they have written recently or about which they intend to write in the near future.

14 **Confidential sources**

Journalists have a moral obligation to protect confidential sources of information.

15 **Witness payments in criminal trials**

i) No payment or offer of payment to a witness – or any person who may reasonably be expected to be called as a witness – should be made in any case once proceedings are active as defined by the Contempt of Court Act 1981.

This prohibition lasts until the suspect has been freed unconditionally by police without charge or bail or the proceedings are otherwise discontinued; or has entered a guilty plea to the court; or, in the event of a not guilty plea, the court has announced its verdict.

*ii) Where proceedings are not yet active but are likely and foreseeable, editors must not make or offer payment to any person who may reasonably be expected to be called as a witness, unless the information concerned ought demonstrably to be published in the public interest and there is an over-riding need to make or promise payment for this to be done; and all reasonable steps have been taken to ensure no financial dealings influence the evidence those witnesses give. In no circumstances should such payment be conditional on the outcome of a trial.

*iii) Any payment or offer of payment made to a person later cited to give evidence in proceedings must be disclosed to the prosecution and defence. The witness must be advised of this requirement.

16 ***Payment to criminals**

i) Payment or offers of payment for stories, pictures or information, which seek to exploit a particular crime or to glorify or glamorise crime in general, must not be made directly or via agents to convicted or confessed criminals or to their associates – who may include family, friends and colleagues.

ii) Editors invoking the public interest to justify payment or offers would need to demonstrate that there was good reason to believe the public interest would be served. If, despite payment, no public interest emerged, then the material should not be published.

The public interest

There may be exceptions to the clauses marked * where they can be demonstrated to be in the public interest.

1. The public interest includes, but is not confined to:
   i) Detecting or exposing crime or serious impropriety.
   ii) Protecting public health and safety.
   iii) Preventing the public from being misled by an action or statement of an individual or organisation.
2. There is a public interest in freedom of expression itself.
3. Whenever the public interest is invoked, the PCC will require editors to demonstrate fully that they reasonably believed that publication, or journalistic activity undertaken with a view to publication, would be in the public interest and how, and with whom, that was established at the time.
4. The PCC will consider the extent to which material is already in the public domain, or will become so.
5. In cases involving children under 16, editors must demonstrate an exceptional public interest to over-ride the normally paramount interest of the child.

Appendix 3
Schedule 1 to the Defamation Act 1996

Statements having qualified privilege (see chapter 21, pp. 266–270)

This is the text of Parts 1 and 2 of Schedule 1 to the 1996 Act, paras 1–15.

Part 1: Statements privileged without explanation or contradiction

1. A fair and accurate report of proceedings in public of a legislature anywhere in the world.
2. A fair and accurate report of proceedings in public before a court anywhere in the world [*para. 17 makes clear that this includes the European Court of Justice, the European Court of Human Rights, and any international criminal tribunal established by the United Nations or by an international agreement to which the UK is a party*]
3. A fair and accurate report of proceedings in public of a person appointed to hold a public inquiry by a government or legislature anywhere in the world.
4. A fair and accurate report of proceedings in public anywhere in the world of an international organisation or an international conference. [*para. 17 limits these definitions to a conference attended by representatives of two or more governments or an organisation of which two or more governments are members, including any committee or other subordinate body of such an organisation*]
5. A fair and accurate copy of or extract from any register or other document required by law to be open to public inspection.
6. A notice or advertisement published by or on the authority of a court, or of a judge or officer of a court, anywhere in the world.
7. A fair and accurate copy of or extract from matter published by or on the authority of a government or legislature anywhere in the world.
8. A fair and accurate copy of or extract from matter published anywhere in the world by an international organisation or an international conference. [*same definitions as for para. 4*]

Part 2: Statements privileged subject to explanation or contradiction

9. (1) A fair and accurate copy of or extract from a notice or other matter issued for the information of the public by or on behalf of
   (a) a legislature in any member state [*of the European Union*] or the European Parliament;
   (b) the government of any member state, or any authority performing governmental functions in any member state or part of a member state, or the European Commission;
   (c) an international organisation or international conference.

   (2) In this paragraph 'governmental functions' includes police functions.

10. A fair and accurate copy of or extract from a document made available by a court in any member state or the European Court of Justice (or any court attached to that court), or by a judge or officer of any such court.

11. (1) A fair and accurate report of proceedings at any public meeting or sitting in the United Kingdom of –
   (a) a local authority or local authority committee;
   (aa) in the case of a local authority which are operating executive arrangements, the executive of that authority or a committee of that executive
   (b) a justice or justices of the peace acting otherwise than as a court exercising judicial authority;
   (c) a commission, tribunal, committee or person appointed for the purposes of any inquiry by any statutory provision, by Her Majesty or by a Minister of the Crown, a member of the Scottish Executive, the Welsh Ministers or the Counsel General to the Welsh Assembly Government, or a Northern Ireland Department;
   (d) a person appointed by a local authority to hold a local inquiry in pursuance of any statutory provision;
   (e) any other tribunal, board, committee or body constituted by or under, and exercising functions under, any statutory provision.

   (1A) In the case of a local authority which are operating executive arrangements, a fair and accurate record of any decision made by any member of the executive where that record is required to be made and available for public inspection by virtue of section 22 of the Local Government Act 2000 or of any provision in regulations made under that section.

   (2) In sub-paragraphs (1)(a), (1)(aa) and (1A)
   'local authority' means—
   (a) in relation to England and Wales, a principal council within the meaning of the Local Government Act 1972, any body falling within any

paragraph of section 100J(1) of that Act or an authority or body to which the Public Bodies (Admission to Meetings) Act 1960 applies,

(b) in relation to Scotland, a council constituted under section 2 of the Local Government etc (Scotland) Act 1994 or an authority or body to which the Public Bodies (Admission to Meetings) Act 1960 applies,

(c) in relation to Northern Ireland, any authority or body to which sections 23 to 27 of the Local Government Act (Northern Ireland) 1972 apply; and

'local authority committee' means any committee of a local authority or of local authorities, and includes –

(a) any committee or sub-committee in relation to which sections 100A to 100D of the Local Government Act 1972 apply by virtue of section 100E of that Act (whether or not also by virtue of section 100J of that Act), and

(b) any committee or sub-committee in relation to which sections 50A to 50D of the Local Government (Scotland) Act 1973 apply by virtue of section 50E of that Act.

(2A) In sub-paragraphs (1) and (1A) 'executive' and 'executive arrangements' have the same meaning as in Part II of the Local Government Act 2000.

(3) A fair and accurate report of any corresponding proceedings in any of the Channel Islands or the Isle of Man or in another member state.

12. (1) A fair and accurate report of proceedings at any public meeting held in a member state.

(2) In this paragraph a 'public meeting' means a meeting bona fide and lawfully held for a lawful purpose and for the furtherance or discussion of a matter of public concern, whether admission to the meeting is general or restricted.

13. (1) A fair and accurate report of proceedings at a general meeting of a UK public company.

(2) A fair and accurate copy of or extract from any document circulated to members of a UK public company –

(a) by or with the authority of the board of directors of the company,

(b) by the auditors of the company, or

(c) by any member of the company in pursuance of a right conferred by any statutory provision.

(3) A fair and accurate copy of or extract from any document circulated to members of a UK public company which relates to the appointment, resignation, retirement or dismissal of directors of the company.

(4) In this paragraph 'UK public company' means –

(a) a public company within the meaning of section 4(2) of the Companies Act 2006 or

(b) a body corporate incorporated by or registered under any other statutory provision, or by Royal Charter, or formed in pursuance of letters patent.

(5) A fair and accurate report of proceedings at any corresponding meeting of, or copy of or extract from any corresponding document circulated to members of, a public company formed under the law of any of the Channel Islands or the Isle of Man or of another member state.

14. A fair and accurate report of any finding or decision of any of the following descriptions of association, formed in the United Kingdom or another member state, or of any committee or governing body of such an association –

(a) an association formed for the purpose of promoting or encouraging the exercise of or interest in any art, science, religion or learning, and empowered by its constitution to exercise control over or adjudicate on matters of interest or concern to the association, or the actions or conduct of any persons subject to such control or adjudication;

(b) an association formed for the purpose of promoting or safeguarding the interests of any trade, business, industry or profession, or of the persons carrying on or engaged in any trade, business, industry or profession, and empowered by its constitution to exercise control over or adjudicate upon matters connected with the trade, business, industry or profession, or the actions or conduct of those persons;

(c) an association formed for the purpose of promoting or safeguarding the interests of a game, sport or pastime to the playing or exercise of which members of the public are invited or admitted, and empowered by its constitution to exercise control over or adjudicate upon persons connected with or taking part in the game, sport or pastime;

(d) an association formed for the purpose of promoting charitable objects or other objects beneficial to the community and empowered by its constitution to exercise control over or to adjudicate on matters of interest or concern to the association, or the actions or conduct of any person subject to such control or adjudication.

15. (1) A fair and accurate report of, or copy of or extract from, any adjudication, report, statement or notice issued by a body, officer or other person designated for the purposes of this paragraph –

(a) for England and Wales, by order of the Lord Chancellor

(b) for Scotland, by order of the Secretary of State, and

(c) for Northern Ireland, by order of the Department of Justice in Northern Ireland.

[sub-paras 2 and 3 specify the procedure by which such orders shall be made]

Glossary

Absolute discharge A decision by a court after conviction that the defendant should not be punished for the offence.

Affidavit A statement given on oath to be used in court proceedings.

Alibi The defence case of an accused who asserts that he/she was not at the scene of a crime when it occurred and that he/she is therefore innocent.

Arraignment The procedure at Crown courts in which charges are put to defendants for them to plead guilty or not guilty.

Automatic, automatically Terms used for reporting restrictions which ban publication of certain information if no court order is needed to put it into effect in respect of a particular case or individual. Statute specifies the circumstances when it operates.

Bail The system by which a person awaiting trial, or appeal, may be freed by a court pending the next hearing. *See also* Police bail, *below*.

Bailiff A court official who enforces its orders.

Case law The system by which reports of previous cases and the judges' interpretations of the common law are used as precedents where the legally material facts are similar.

Circuit judge Judge who has been appointed to sit at Crown court or county court within a circuit – one of the regions of England and Wales into which court administration is divided. Unlike High Court judges, circuit judges do not go on circuit, that is travel to various large centres dispensing justice.

Claim form *Previously known as* writ or default summons. A document that begins many forms of civil action.

Claimant *Previously known as* plaintiff. The person who takes an action to enforce a claim in the civil court.

Committal hearing A hearing in a magistrates court at which magistrates sitting as examining justices decide if there is sufficient evidence to commit a defendant facing an indictable or either-way charge to Crown court for trial. Usually these are now no more than formalities.

Committal for trial What happens when examining justices at a magistrates court in a Committal hearing, *see above*, decide that there is sufficient evidence for a defendant's case to go to Crown court for trial. The defendant may subsequently plead guilty at Crown court, meaning there will be no trial. The term is also used of the procedure under which a youth court transfers the case of a juvenile accused of a grave offence to a Crown court.

Committal for sentence, committed for sentence When a defendant at magistrates court who has admitted an offence or been convicted in a trial is then sent to Crown court to be sentenced because the magistrates decide their powers of punishment are insufficient. (There are no reporting restrictions on committals for sentence.)

Common law Law based on the custom of the realm and the decisions of judges through the centuries rather than on an Act of Parliament.

Community punishment An order that an offender must carry out unpaid work in the community under a probation officer's supervision.

Concurrent sentences Two or more sentences of imprisonment imposed for different offences; the longest one is the sentence actually served.

Conditional discharge a decision by a court that a convicted defendant should not be punished unless he/she reoffends: that is, a condition is imposed that if he/she commits another crime within a specified period, e.g. a year, he/she can be punished for the original offence as well as for the reoffending.

Conditional fee agreements (CFAs) No win, no fee agreements – their use was extended to defamation cases in 1998 under the Conditional Fee Agreements Order 1998 (SI 1998/1860).

Counsel Barrister (singular or plural), not solicitor.

Discharge When magistrates decide at a committal hearing (*see above*) that the evidence against a defendant is insufficient for the case to go to Crown court. This ends that prosecution for that charge. Not to be confused with an absolute discharge (*see above*).

Disclosure and inspection *Previously known as* discovery. The process whereby each side in a court action serves relevant documents on the other, which has the right to inspect them.

Discovery *See* Disclosure.

District judge An official of the county court who also adjudicates in smaller cases, presides at public examinations in bankruptcy, and deals with cases under the informal arbitration procedure.

District judge (magistrates courts) The title given to full-time, legally qualified magistrates, *formerly known as* Stipendiary magistrates.

Editors' Code of Practice Code of ethics used by the Press Complaints Commission to adjudicate on complaints against newspapers, magazines and website-only publications.

Either-way offence One triable either summarily at magistrates court or before a jury at Crown court. In an either-way case a defendant who has indicated a plea of not guilty has the right to opt for jury trial at Crown court. But if he/she chooses to be tried by the magistrates court, it may overrule him by deciding the Crown court should deal with his case – *see* Mode of trial hearing, *below*.

Ex parte *See* Without notice.

Excluded material Such material is exempt from compulsory disclosure under the Police and Criminal Evidence Act 1984 (PACE). It includes journalistic material (*see below*) that a person holds in confidence and that consists of documents or records.

Fair dealing A defence to breach of copyright for use of extracts of a copyrighted work, properly attributed to its author.

Hearsay Evidence of what a witness was told, rather than what they actually saw or heard for themselves.

Honest comment A defence to a libel action, *formerly known as* fair comment; the defendant does not have to show the words were fair, but must show they were an honestly held opinion.

In camera Proceedings in a courtroom which are heard in secret, with the media and public excluded (for example in Official Secrets Act cases).

In chambers Used to describe the hearing of an application which takes place in the judge's room. If there is no legal reason for such a hearing to be held in private (*see below*), journalists who want to report it should be admitted if 'practicable' (*see* ch. 12).

In private A term used of a court hearing in camera (*see above*), or one in chambers (*see above*) which the press and public are not entitled to attend.

Indictable offence A charge which may be tried by a jury at Crown court, which will therefore be either an indictable-only offence (*see below*) or an either-way offence (*see above*).

Indictable-only offence One that can only be tried by a jury at Crown court.

Indictment A written statement of the charges which is put to the defendant at the arraignment (*see above*) at Crown court.

Information A written statement alleging an offence, that is laid before a magistrate who is then asked to issue a summons or warrant for arrest.

Inherent jurisdiction The powers of a court which derive from common law rather than statute. The inherent jurisdiction of lower courts, for example magistrates courts, is more limited than that of the higher courts, for example the High Court.

Injunction A court order requiring someone, or an organisation, to do something specified by the court, or forbidding a specific activity or act.

Interdict In Scottish law, an injunction (*see above*).

Journalistic material Material acquired and created for the purposes of journalism. Special protection is given to journalistic material in the sections of the Police and Criminal Evidence Act 1984 that lay down the procedure whereby the police may search premises for evidence of serious arrestable offences.

Judicial review A review by the Queen's Bench Divisional Court, part of the High Court, of decisions taken by a lower court, tribunal, public body or public official.

Justification The defence in libel actions that the words complained of were true. The word is misleading, because there is no requirement that the words were published justly or with good reason.

Legal aid Public money provided to pay for legal advice and legal representation in court for a party in a civil case or a defendant in a criminal case, if their income is low enough to qualify for such aid.

Malice In law not only spite or ill-will but also dishonest or improper motive. Proof of malice can be used by a claimant (*see above*) in a libel action to deprive the defendant of the defences of fair comment or qualified privilege.

Mitigation A plea for leniency in the sentence due to be imposed, citing extenuating circumstances, which is made in court or on behalf of a convicted defendant.

Mode of trial hearing The hearing at a magistrates court which determines whether an either-way case (*see above*) is dealt with by that court or proceeds to a committal hearing (*see above*) from which it may be committed to Crown court.

Moral rights The rights of an author of a work, in addition to copyright, to be correctly identified as the author and the right to object to derogatory treatment of that work.

Narrative verdict/narrative determination The system of allowing a coroner or inquest jury to make a short statement of the circumstances of a person's death, rather than the traditional 'short-form' verdicts.

Newton hearing A hearing in which, after a defendant is convicted, the court hears evidence to help it decide on sentence because the prosecution version of the circumstances of the offence differs substantially from the defence version. Newton was the defendant's name in the relevant, precedent case.

Ofcom Broadcasting Code Code of ethics used by Ofcom to adjudicate on complaints against broadcasters.

Police bail The system administered by police whereby a person under ongoing investigation can be released from arrest on conditions, including that they return to a police station on a later date, at which time they may be questioned again, charged or be told there will be no charge. They can be arrested if they breach the conditions. After being charged, they can be bailed by police to attend court, or may be taken there in custody.

Preliminary hearing A hearing at magistrates or Crown court before any trial.

Prima facie Literally, 'at first sight'. In criminal law a 'prima facie case' is one in which a preliminary examination by a court has established that there is sufficient prosecution evidence for it to proceed to trial. In journalism ethics, the term prima facie grounds means that preliminary inquiries have established there is sufficient evidence or sufficient ground of suspicion to justify use of undercover tactics in an investigation.

Prior restraint The power which courts have to stop material being published. The UK's tradition of a free media means there is a general rule against prior restraint in defamation law, making judges very reluctant to ban publication of material which the media argue can be successfully defended in any future libel trial. However, in privacy cases judges are more likely to grant injunctions.

Privilege A defence, absolute or qualified, against an action for libel which attaches to reports produced from certain events, documents or statements.

Public interest The phrase 'in the public interest' is used by judges to define when an individual's rights, for example to privacy, can legally be infringed if this produces a sufficiently major benefit to society, for example from investigative journalism. But judges may also decide that a general 'public interest', for example in the confidentiality of medical records, needs to be upheld against media activity. Codes of ethics use the phrase too, to indicate when journalists may be justified in infringing people's rights.

Recorder An assistant judge at Crown court who is usually appointed to sit part time (for example for spells of a fortnight). Solicitors and barristers are both eligible for appointment as a recorder.

Remand An individual awaiting trial can be remanded on bail, or in custody.

***Reynolds* defence** A form of privilege available to journalism that fulfils tests laid down by the courts in the case of *Reynolds v Sunday Times* and subsequent cases.

Robbery Theft (*see below*) by force, or threat of force. The word is often used, wrongly, to describe simple theft.

Sending for trial The fast-track procedure by which an indictable-only offence (*see above*) is sent from the magistrates court to a Crown court without any consideration of the strength of evidence against the defendant.

Spent conviction A conviction that is no longer recognised after the time (varying according to sentence) specified in the Rehabilitation of Offenders Act 1974. After this time, a newspaper referring to the conviction may not have available some of the normal defences in the law of libel.

Statements of case Documents including the claim form (*see above*) particulars of claim, defence, counterclaims, reply to the defence and 'further information documents' in a civil action – reports of which are now protected by privilege (*see above*).

Statute An Act of Parliament – that is, primary legislation created by Parliament.

Statutory instrument Secondary legislation which can be enacted without parliamentary debate by a Minister to make detailed law (for example, rules and regulations) or amendment to the law, under powers given earlier by a statute (an Act of Parliament, the primary legislation). Statutory instruments are also used to phase in gradually, for administrative convenience, legal changes brought about by Acts.

Strict liability A strict liability offence does not require the prosecution to show intent on the part of the accused. Statutory contempt of court is a strict liability offence.

Sub judice Literally 'under law'. Often applied to the risk which may arise in reporting forthcoming legal proceedings. Frequently used by authority as a reason for not disclosing information. This is not the test for strict liability under the Contempt of Court Act 1981.

Subpoena A court order compelling a person to attend court to give evidence.

Summary offence A comparatively minor offence which can usually only be dealt with by magistrates.

Summary proceedings Cases dealt with by magistrates. At the end of a summary trial of an either-way offence (*see above*), however, magistrates can, if they consider their powers of sentence insufficient, commit for sentence (*see above*).

Summary trial A trial at a magistrates court.

Supreme Court The name originally given to the Court of Appeal, the High Court, and the Crown court as a combined system. However, from October 2009 the House of Lords appellate committee (the court commonly referred to merely as 'the House of Lords') became the UK Supreme Court.

Surety A person, usually a friend or relative of the defendant, to whom a court entrusts the responsibility to ensure that the defendant, having been given bail (*see above*), returns to court on the due date. The surety may pledge a sum of money as guarantee that the defendant will answer bail, and risks losing it if the defendant fails to do so.

Theft Dishonest appropriation of another's property with the intention of permanently depriving the other of it.

Tort A civil wrong for which monetary damages may be awarded if the person affected sues in civil law, for example defamation, medical negligence.

Warranted Term used in the Ofcom Broadcasting Code (*see above*) to indicate that an ethical norm can be breached if there is a public interest justification, or some other exceptional justification.

Without notice *Previously known as* ex parte, of the one part. An injunction without notice is one granted after a court has heard only one side of the case.

Book list

Chapter 1, Introduction

Free Speech, E M Barendt (Oxford University Press, 2nd edition, 2007)

Chapter 2, The Editors' Code of Practice

A Press Free and Responsible: Self Regulation and the Press Complaints Commission, 1991–2001, Richard Shannon (John Murray, 2001)

Chapter 14, Open justice and access to court information

Media Law, Geoffrey Robertson and Andrew Nicol (Penguin, 5th edition, 2008)

Chapter 18, Contempt of court

Arlidge, Eady and Smith on Contempt, Sir David Eady and Professor A T H Smith (Sweet & Maxwell, 4th edition, 2011)

Contempt of Court, C J Miller (Oxford University Press, 3rd edition, 2000)

Chapter 19, Defamation – definitions and dangers

Carter-Ruck on Libel and Privacy, Alastair Mullisan and Cameron Dole (eds) (LexisNexis Butterworths, 6th edition, 2010)

Defamation and Freedom of Speech, Dario Milo (Oxford University Press, 2008)

Defamation: Law, Procedure and Practice, David Price, Nicola Cain and Korieh Duodu (Sweet & Maxwell, 4th edition, 2009)

Gatley on Libel and Slander, Patrick Milmo QC, Prof W V H Rogers, Richard Parkes QC, Godwin Busuttil and Professor Clive Walker (eds) (Sweet & Maxwell, 11th edition, 2010)

Chapter 21, Defences

The Liar: The Fall of Jonathan Aitkin, Luke Harding, David Leigh and David Pallister (Penguin, 1997)

Chapter 25, Breach of confidence

Confidentiality, Charles Phipps and Roger Toulson (Sweet & Maxwell, 2nd edition, 2006)

The Law of Confidentiality: A Restatement, Paul Stanley (Hart Publishing, 2008)

Chapter 26, Privacy – the developing law

The Law of Privacy and the Media, Mark Warby QC, Nicole Moreham and Iain Christie (eds) (Oxford University Press, 2nd edition, 2011)

Privacy and Freedom of Expression, Richard Clayton QC and Hugh Tomlinson QC (Oxford University Press, 2nd edition, 2010)

Chapter 28, Data protection

Data Protection: A Guide to UK and EU Law, Peter Carey (Oxford University Press, 3rd edition, 2009)

Data Protection Law and Practice, Rosemary Jay (Sweet & Maxwell, 3rd edition, 2007)

Chapter 29, Copyright

Intellectual Property: Patents, Copyrights, Trademarks and Allied Rights, Professor William Cornish (Sweet & Maxwell, 7th edition, 2010)

Chapter 30, Freedom of Information Act 2000

Your Right to Know, Heather Brooke (Pluto Press, 2nd edition, 2006)

Chapter 33, Official secrets

Media Law, Geoffrey Robertson and Andrew Nicol (Penguin, 5th edition, 2008)

National Security and the D-Notice System, Pauline Sadler (Dartmouth Publishing Co Ltd, 2001)

Official Secrets: The Use and Abuse of the Act, David Hooper (Coronet Books, 1988)

Secrecy and the Media: The official history of the D-notice System, Nicholas John Wilkinson (Routledge, 2009)

Chapter 35, Terrorism and the effect of counter-terrorism law

Media Freedom under the Human Rights Act, Helen Fenwick and Gavin Phillipson (Oxford University Press, 2006)

Table of Cases

Table of Legislation

The European Convention on Human Rights is tabled under Sch 1 of the Human Rights Act 1998

Table of Statutory Instruments

Index

A

D

E

K

L

M

N

P

Q

R

U

V

W

Y

Z